I0752631

THE DANGER MARK

ROBERT W. CHAMBERS

The Danger Mark

Robert W. Chambers

PO Box 2211
Fairfield, IA 52556
www.1stworldlibrary.com
First Edition

LCCN: 2006935359

Softcover ISBN: 1-4218-2504-X
Hardcover ISBN: 1-4218-2404-3
eBook ISBN: 1-4218-2604-6

1st World Library Literary Society

Giving Back to the World

"If you want to work on the core problem, it's early school literacy."

- James Barksdale, former CEO of Netscape

"No skill is more crucial to the future of a child, or to a democratic and prosperous society, than literacy."

- Los Angeles Times

Literacy... means far more than learning how to read and write... The aim is to transmit... knowledge and promote social participation."

- UNESCO

"Literacy is not a luxury, it is a right and a responsibility. If our world is to meet the challenges of the twenty-first century we must harness the energy and creativity of all our citizens."

- President Bill Clinton

"Parents should be encouraged to read to their children, and teachers should be equipped with all available techniques for teaching literacy, so the varying needs and capacities of individual kids can be taken into account."

- Hugh Mackay

TO

MY FRIEND

JOHN CARRINGTON YATES

CONTENTS

CHAPTER I

THE SEAGRAVES

All day Sunday they had raised the devil from attic to cellar; Mrs. Farren was in tears, Howker desperate. Not one out of the fifteen servants considered necessary to embellish the Seagrave establishment could do anything with them after Kathleen Severn's sudden departure the week before.

When the telegram announcing her mother's sudden illness summoned young Mrs. Severn to Staten Island, every servant in the household understood that serious trouble was impending for them.

Day by day the children became more unruly; Sunday they were demons; and Mrs. Farren shuddered to think what Monday might bring forth.

The day began ominously at breakfast with general target practice, ammunition consisting of projectiles pinched from the interior of hot muffins. Later, when Mrs. Farren ventured into the schoolroom, she found Scott Seagrave drawing injurious pictures of Howker on the black-board, and Geraldine sorting lumps of sugar from the bowl on the breakfast-tray, which had not yet been removed.

“Dearies,” she began, “it is after nine o'clock and -”

“No school to-day, Mrs. Farren,” interrupted Scott cheerfully;

"we haven't anything to do till Kathleen comes back, and you know it perfectly well!"

"Yes, you have, dearie; Mrs. Severn has just sent you this list of lessons." She held out a black-edged envelope.

Geraldine, who had been leisurely occupied in dropping cologne on a lump of sugar, thrust the lump into her pink mouth and turned sharply on Mrs. Farren.

"What list?" she demanded. "Give that letter to me.... Oh, Scott! Did you ever hear of anything half so mean? Kathleen's written out about a thousand questions in geography for us!"

"I can't stand that sort of interference!" shouted Scott, dropping his chalk and aiming a kick at the big papier-mache globe. "I'm sorry Kathleen's mother is probably going to die, but I've had enough geography, too."

"Mrs. Severn's mother died on Friday," said the housekeeper solemnly.

The children paused, serious for a moment in the presence of the incomprehensible.

"We're sorry," said Geraldine slowly.... "When is Kathleen coming back?"

"Perhaps to-night, dearie -"

Scott impatiently detached the schoolroom globe from its brass axis: "I'm sorry, too," he said; "but I'm tired of lessons. Now, Mrs. Farren, watch me! I'm going to kick a goal from the field. Here, you hold it, Geraldine; Mrs. Farren, you had better try to block it and cheer for Yale!"

Geraldine seized the globe, threw herself flat on the floor, and, head on one side, wriggled, carefully considering the angle.

Then, tipping the globe, she adjusted it daintily for her brother to kick.

"A little higher, please; look out there, Mrs. Farren!" said Scott calmly; "Harvard is going to score this time. Now, Geraldine!"

Thump! came the kick, but Mrs. Farren had fled, and the big globe struck the nursery door and bounced back minus half of South America.

For ten minutes the upper floors echoed with the racket. Geraldine fiercely disputed her brother's right to kick every time; then, as usual, when she got what she wanted, gave up to Scott and let him monopolise the kicking until, satiated, he went back to the black-board, having obliterated several continents from the face of the globe.

"You might at least be polite enough to hold it for me to kick," said his sister. "What a pig you are, Scott."

"Don't bother me; I'm drawing Howker. You can't kick straight, anyway -"

"Yes, I can!"

Scott, intent on his drawing, muttered:

"I wish there was another boy in this house; I might have a little fun to-day if there was anybody to play with."

There ensued a silence; then he heard his sister's light little feet flying along the hallway toward their bedrooms, but went on calmly with his drawing, using some effective coloured crayon on Howker's nose. Presently he became conscious that Geraldine had re-entered the room.

"What are you going to do to-day?" he asked, preoccupied.

Geraldine, dressed in her brother's clothes, was kneeling on one knee and hastily strapping on a single roller-skate.

"I'll show you," she said, rising and shaking the dark curls out of her eyes. "Come on, Scott, I'm going to misbehave all day. Look at me! I've brought you the boy you wanted to play with."

Her brother turned, considered her with patronising toleration, then shrugged his shoulders.

"You look like one, but you're no good," he said.

"I can be just as bad as any boy!" she insisted. "I'll do whatever you do; I'll do worse, I tell you. Dare me to do something!"

"You don't dare skate backward into the red drawing-room! There's too much bric-a-brac."

She turned like a flash and was off, hopping and clattering down-stairs on her single skate, and a moment later she whirled into the red drawing-room backward and upset a Sang-de-boeuf jar, reducing the maid to horrified tears and the jar to powder.

Howker strove in vain to defend his dining-room when Scott appeared on one skate; but the breakfast-room and pantry were forcibly turned into rinks; the twins swept through the halls, met and defeated their nurses, Margaret and Betty, tumbled down into the lower regions, from there descended to the basement, and whizzed cheerily through the kitchen, waving two skateless legs.

There Mrs. Bramton attempted to buy them off with tribute in the shape of cup-cakes.

"Sure, darlints, they do be starvin' yez," purred Mrs. Bramton. "Don't I know the likes o' them? Now roon away quietlike an' ladylike -"

"Like a hen," retorted Scott. "I want some preserves."

"That's all very well," said Geraldine with her mouth full, "but we expected to skate about the kitchen and watch you make pastry. Kindly begin, Mrs. Bramton."

"I'd like to see what's inside of that chicken over there," said Scott. "And I want you to give me some raisins, Mrs. Bramton -"

"I'm dying for a glass of milk," added Geraldine. "Get me some dough, somebody; I'm going to bake something."

Scott, who, devoured by curiosity, had been sniffing around the spice cupboard, sneezed violently; a Swedish kitchen-maid threw her apron over her head, weak with laughter.

"If you're laughing at me, I'll fix you, Olga!" shouted Scott in a rage; and the air was suddenly filled with balls of dough. Mrs. Bramton fled before the storm; a well-directed volley drove the maids to cover and stampeded the two cats.

"Take whatever is good to eat, Geraldine. Hurrah! The town surrenders! Loot it! No quarter!" shouted Scott. However, when Howker arrived they retired hastily with pockets full of cinnamon sticks, olives, prunes, and dried currants, climbing triumphantly to the library above, where they curled up on a leather divan, under the portrait of their mother, to divide the spoils.

"Am I bad enough to suit you?" inquired Geraldine with pardonable pride.

"Pooh! That's nothing. If I had another boy here I'd - I'd -"

"Well, what?" demanded Geraldine, flushing. "I tell you I can misbehave as well as any boy. Dare me to do anything and you'll see! I dare you to dare me!"

Scott began: "Oh, it's all very easy for a girl to talk -"

"I *don't* talk; I *do* it! And you know perfectly well I do!"

"You're a girl, after all, even if you have got on my clothes -"

"Didn't I throw as much dough at Olga and Mrs. Bramton as you did?"

"You didn't hit anybody."

"I did! I saw a soft, horrid lump stick to Olga!"

"Pooh! *You* can't throw straight -"

"That's a lie!" said Geraldine excitedly.

Scott bristled:

"If you say that again -"

"All right; go and get the boxing-gloves. You *did* tell a lie, Scott, because I did hit Olga!"

Scott hastily unstrapped his lone skate, cast it clattering from him, and sped up-stairs. When he returned he hurled a pair of boxing-gloves at Geraldine, who put them on, laced them, trembling with wrath, and flew at her brother as soon as his own gloves were fastened.

They went about their business like lightning, swinging, blocking, countering. Twice she gave him inviting openings and then punished him savagely before he could get away; then he attempted in-fighting, but her legs were too nimble. And after a while he lost his head and came at her using sheer weight, which set her beside herself with fury.

Teeth clenched, crimson-cheeked, she side-stepped, feinted, and whipped in an upper-cut. Then, darting in, she drove home her left with all her might; and Scott went down with an unmistakable thud.

"One - two - three - four," she counted, "and you *did* tell a lie, didn't you? Five - six - Oh, Scott! I've made your nose bleed horridly! Does it hurt, dear? Seven - eight -"

The boy, still confused, rose and instinctively assumed the classic attitude of self-defence; but his sister threw down her gloves and offered him her handkerchief, saying: "You've just got to be fair to me now, Scott. Tell me that I throw straight and that I did hit Olga!"

He hesitated; wiped his nose:

"I take it back. You can throw straight. Ginger! What a crack you just gave me!"

She was all compunction and honey now, hovering around him where he stood stanching honourable wounds. After a while he laughed. "Thunder!" he exclaimed ruefully; "my nose seems to be growing for fair. You're all right, Geraldine."

"Here's my last cup-cake, if you like," said his sister, radiant.

Embarrassed a little by defeat, but nursing no bitterness, he sat down on the leather divan again and permitted his sister to feed him and tell him that his disaster was only an accident. He tried to think so, too, but serious doubts persisted in his mind. There had been a clean-cut finish to that swing and jab which disturbed his boy's conceit.

"We'll try it again," he began. "I'm all right now, if you like -"

"Oh, Scott, I don't want to!"

"Well, we ought to know which of us really can lick the other -"

"Why, of course, you can lick me every time. Besides, I wouldn't want to be able to lick you - except when I'm very, very angry. And I ought not to become angry the way I do. Kathleen tries so hard to make me stop and reflect before I do things, but I can't seem to learn.... Does your nose hurt?"

"Not in the least," said her brother, reddening and changing the subject. "I say, it looks as though it were going to stop raining."

He went to the window; the big Seagrave house with its mansard roof, set in the centre of an entire city block, bounded by Madison and Fifth Avenues and by Ninety-fifth and Ninety-sixth Streets, looked out from its four red brick facades onto strips of lawn and shrubbery, now all green and golden with new grass and early buds.

It was topsy-turvy, March-hare weather, which perhaps accounted for the early April dementia that possessed the children at recurring intervals, and which nothing ever checked except the ultimate slumber of infantile exhaustion.

If anybody in the house possessed authority to punish them, nobody exercised it. Servants grown gray in the Seagrave service endured much, partly for the children's sakes, partly in memory of the past; but the newer and younger domestics had less interest in the past glories and traditions of an old New York family which, except for two little children, ten years old, had perished utterly from the face of the land.

The entire domestic regime was a makeshift - had been almost from the beginning. Mrs. Farren, the housekeeper, understood it; Howker, the butler, knew it; Lacy knew it - he who had served forty years as coachman in the Seagrave family.

For in all the world there remained not one living soul who through ties of kinship was authorised to properly control these children. Nor could they themselves even remember parental authority; and only a shadowy recollection of their grandfather's lax discipline survived, becoming gradually, as time passed, nothing more personal to them than a pleasant legend kept alive and nourished in the carefully guarded stories told them by Kathleen Severn and by Anthony Seagrave's old servants.

Yet, in the land, and in his own city of Manhattan, their grandfather had been a very grand man, with his large fortune, now doubled and still increasing; he had been a very distinguished man in the world of fashion with his cultivated taste in art and wine and letters and horses; he had been a very important man, too, in the civic, social, and political construction of New York town, in the quaint days when the sexton of Old Trinity furnished fashionable hostesses with data concerning the availability of social aspirants. He had been a courtly and fascinating man, too. He had died a drunkard.

Now his grandchildren were fast forgetting him. The town had long since forgotten him. Only an old friend or two and his old servants remembered what he had been, his virtues, his magnificence, his kindness, and his weakness.

But if the Seagrave twins possessed neither father nor mother to exercise tender temporal and spiritual suzerainty in the nursery, and if no memory of their grandfather's adoring authority remained, the last will and testament of Anthony Seagrave had provided a marvellous, man-created substitute for the dead: a vast, shadowy thing which ruled their lives with passionless precision; which ordered their waking hours even to the minutest particulars; which assumed machine-like charge of their persons, their personal expenses, their bringing-up, their schooling, the items of their daily routine.

This colossal automaton, almost terrifyingly impersonal, loomed always above them, throwing its powerful and gigantic shadow across their lives. As they grew old enough to understand, it became to them the embodiment of occult and unpleasant authority which controlled their coming and going; which chose for them their personal but not their legal guardian, Kathleen Severn; which fixed upon the number of servants necessary for the house that Anthony Seagrave directed should be maintained for his grandchildren; which decided what kind of expenses, what sort of clothing, what recreations, what accomplishments, what studies, what religion they should be provided with.

And the name of this enormous man-contrived machine which took the place of father and mother was the Half Moon Trust Company, acting as trustee, guardian, and executor for two little children, who neither understood why they were sometimes very unruly or that they would one day be very, very rich.

As for their outbreaks, an intense sense of loneliness for which they were unable to account was always followed by a period of restlessness sure to culminate in violent misbehaviour.

Such an outbreak had been long impending. So when a telegram called away their personal guardian, Kathleen Severn, the children broke loose with the delicate fury of the April tempest outside, which all the morning had been blotting the western windows with gusts of fragrant rain.

The storm was passing now; light volleys of rain still arrived at intervals, slackening as the spring sun broke out, gilding naked branches and bare brown earth, touching swelling buds and the frail points of tulips which pricked the soaked loam in close-set thickets.

From the library bay windows where they stood, the children noticed dandelions in the grass and snowdrops under the trees and recognised the green signals of daffodil and narcissus.

Already crocuses, mauve, white, and yellow, glimmered along a dripping privet hedge which crowned the brick and granite wall bounding the domain of Seagrave. East, through the trees, they could see the roofs of electric cars speeding up and down Madison Avenue, and the houses facing that avenue. North and south were quiet streets; westward Fifth Avenue ran, a sheet of wet, golden asphalt glittering under the spring sun, and beyond it, above the high retaining wall, budding trees stood out against the sky, and the waters of the Park reservoirs sparkled behind.

"I am glad it's spring, anyway," said Geraldine listlessly.

"What's the good of it?" asked Scott. "We'll have to take all our exercise with Kathleen just the same, and watch other children having good times. What's the use of spring?"

"Spring *is* tiresome," admitted Geraldine thoughtfully.

"So is winter. I think either would be all right if they'd only let me have a few friends. There are plenty of boys I'd like to have some fun with if they'd let me."

"I wonder," mused Geraldine, "if there is anything the matter with us, Scott?"

"Why?"

"Oh - I don't know. People stare at us so - nurses always watch us and begin to whisper as soon as we come along. Do you know what a boy said to me once when I skated very far ahead of Kathleen?"

"What did he say?" inquired Scott, flattening his nose against the window-pane to see whether it still hurt him.

"He asked me if I were too rich and proud to play with other children. I was so surprised; and I said that we were not rich at all, and that I never had had any money, and that I was not a bit proud, and would love to stay and play with him if Kathleen permitted me."

"Did Kathleen let you? Of course she didn't."

"I told her what the boy said and I showed her the boy, but she wouldn't let me stay and play."

"Kathleen's a pig."

"No, she isn't, poor dear. They make her act that way - Mr. Tappan makes her. Our grandfather didn't want us to have friends."

"I'll tell you what," said Scott impatiently, "when I'm old enough, I'll have other boys to play with whether Kathleen and - and that Thing - likes it or not."

The Thing was the Half Moon Trust Company.

Geraldine glanced back at the portrait over the divan:

"Do you know," she ventured, "that I believe mother would have let us have fun."

"I'll bet father would, too," said Scott. "Sometimes I feel like kicking over everything in the house."

"So do I and I generally do it," observed Geraldine, lifting a slim, graceful leg and sending a sofa-cushion flying.

When they had kicked all the cushions from the sofas and divans, Scott suggested that they go out and help Schmitt, the gardener, who, at that moment, came into view on the lawn, followed by Olsen wheeling a barrowful of seedlings in wooden trays.

So the children descended to the main hall and marched through it, defying Lang, the second man, refusing hats and overshoes; and presently were digging blissfully in a flower-bed under the delighted directions of Schmitt.

"What are these things, anyway?" demanded Scott, ramming down the moist earth around a fragile rootlet from which trailed a green leaf or two.

"Dot vas a verpena, sir," explained the old gardener. "Now you shall vatch him grow."

The boy remained squatting for several minutes, staring hard at the seedling.

"I can't see it grow," he said to his sister, "and I'm not going to sit here all day waiting. Come on!" And he gave her a fraternal slap.

Geraldine wiped her hands on her knickerbockers and started after him; and away they raced around the house, past the fountains, under trees by the coach-house, across paths and lawns and flower-beds, tearing about like a pair of demented kittens. They frisked, climbed trees, chased each other, wrestled, clutched, tumbled, got mad, made up, and finally, removing shoes and stockings, began a game of leapfrog.

Horror-stricken nurses arrived bearing dry towels and footgear, and were received with fury and a volley of last year's horse-chestnuts. And when the enemy had been handsomely repulsed, the children started on a tour of exploration, picking their way with tender, naked feet to the northern hedge.

Here Geraldine mounted on Scott's shoulders and drew herself up to the iron railing which ran along the top of the granite-capped wall between hedge and street; and Scott followed her, both pockets stuffed with chestnuts which he had prudently gathered in the shrubbery.

In the street below there were few passers-by. Each individual wayfarer, however, received careful attention, Scott having divided the chestnuts, and the aim of both children being excellent.

They had been awaiting a new victim for some time, when suddenly Geraldine pinched her brother with eager satisfaction:

"Oh, Scott! there comes that boy I told you about!"

"What boy?"

"The one who asked me if I was too rich and proud to play with him. And that must be his sister; they look alike."

"All right," said Scott; "we'll give them a volley. You take the nurse and I'll fix the boy.... Ready.... Fire!"

The ambuscade was perfectly successful; the nurse halted and looked up, expressing herself definitely upon the manners and customs of the twins; the boy, who appeared to be amazingly agile, seized a swinging wistaria vine, clambered up the wall, and, clinging to the outside of the iron railing, informed Scott that he would punch his head when a pleasing opportunity presented itself.

"All right," retorted Scott; "come in and do it now."

"That's all very well for you to say when you know I can't climb over this railing!"

"I'll tell you what I'll do," said Scott, thrilled at the chance of another boy on the grounds even if he had to fight him; "I'll tell you what!" sinking his voice to an eager whisper; "You run away from your nurse as soon as you get into the Park and I'll be at the front door and I'll let you in. Will you?"

"Oh, *please*!" whispered Geraldine; "and bring your sister, too!"

The boy stared at her knickerbockers. "Do *you* want to fight my sister?" he asked.

"I? Oh, no, no, no. You can fight Scott if you like, and your sister and I will have such fun watching you. Will you?"

His nurse was calling him to descend, in tones agitated and peremptory; the boy hesitated, scowled at Scott, looked uncertainly at Geraldine, then shot a hasty and hostile glance at the interior of the mysterious Seagrave estate. Curiosity overcame him; also, perhaps, a natural desire for battle.

"Yes," he said to Scott, "I'll come back and punch your head for you."

And very deftly, clinging like a squirrel to the pendant wistaria, he let himself down into the street again.

The Seagrave twins, intensely excited, watched them as far as Fifth Avenue, then rapidly drawing on their shoes and stockings, scrambled down to the shrubbery and raced for the house. Through it they passed like a double whirlwind; feeble and perfunctory resistance was offered by their nurses.

"Get out of my way!" said Geraldine fiercely; "do you think I'm going to miss the first chance for some fun that I've ever had in all my life?"

At the same moment, through the glass-sheeted grill Scott discovered two small figures dashing up the drive to the porte-cochere. And he turned on Lang like a wild cat.

Lang, the man at the door, was disposed to defend his post; Scott prepared to fly at him, but his sister intervened:

"Oh, Lang," she pleaded, jumping up and down in an agony of apprehension, "please, *please*, let them in! We've never had any friends." She caught his arm piteously; he looked fearfully embarrassed, for the Seagrave livery was still new to him; nor, during his brief service, had he fully digested the significance of the policy which so rigidly guarded these little children lest rumour from without apprise them of their financial future and the contaminating realisation undermine their simplicity.

As he stood, undecided, Geraldine suddenly jerked his hand from the bronze knob and Scott flung open the door.

"Come on! Quick!" he cried; and the next moment four small pairs of feet were flying through the hall, echoing lightly across the terrace, then skimming the lawn to the sheltering shrubbery beyond.

"The thing to do," panted Scott, "is to keep out of sight." He seized his guests by the arms and drew them behind the rhododendrons. "Now," he said, "what's your name? You, I mean!"

"Duane Mallett," replied the boy, breathless. "That's my sister, Naida. Let's wait a moment before we begin to fight; Naida and I had to run like fury to get away from our nurse."

Naida was examining Geraldine with an interest almost respectful.

"I wish they'd let *me* dress like a boy," she said. "It's fun, isn't it?"

"Yes. They don't *let* me do it; I just did it," replied Geraldine. "I'll get you a suit of Scott's clothes, if you like. I can get the boxing-gloves at the same time. Shall I, Scott?"

"Go ahead," said Scott; "we can pretend there are four boys here." And, to Duane, as Geraldine sped cautiously away on her errand: "That's a thing I never did before."

"What thing?"

"Play with three boys all by myself. Kathleen - who is Mrs. Severn, our guardian - is always with us when we are permitted to speak to other boys and girls."

"That's babyish," remarked Duane in frank disgust. "You are a mollycoddle."

The deep red of mortification spread over Scott's face; he looked shyly at Naida, doubly distressed that a girl should hear the degrading term applied to him. The small girl returned his gaze without a particle of expression in her face.

"Mollycoddles," continued Duane cruelly, "do the sort of things you do. You're one."

"I - don't *want* to be one," stammered Scott. "How can I help it?"

Duane ignored the appeal. "Playing with three boys isn't anything," he said. "I play with forty every day."

"W-where?" asked Scott, overwhelmed.

"In school, of course - at recess - and before nine, and after one. We have fine times. School's all right. Don't you even go to school?"

Scott shook his head, too ashamed to speak. Naida, with a flirt of her kilted skirts, had abruptly turned her back on him; yet he was miserably certain she was listening to her brother's merciless catechism.

"I suppose you don't even know how to play hockey," commented Duane contemptuously.

There was no answer.

"What do you do? Play with dolls? Oh, what a molly!"

Scott raised his head; he had grown quite white. Naida, turning, saw the look on the boy's face.

"Duane doesn't mean that," she said; "he's only teasing."

Geraldine came hurrying back with the boxing-gloves and a suit of Scott's very best clothes, halting when she perceived the situation, for Scott had walked up to Duane, and the boys stood glaring at one another, hands doubling up into fists.

"You think I'm a molly?" asked Scott in a curiously still voice.

"Yes, I do."

"Oh, Scott!" cried Geraldine, pushing in between them, "you'll have to hammer him well for that -"

Naida turned and shoved her brother aside:

"I don't want you to fight him," she said. "I like him."

"Oh, but they must fight, you know," explained Geraldine earnestly. "If we didn't fight, we'd really be what you call us. Put on Scott's clothes, Naida, and while our brothers are fighting, you and I will wrestle to prove that I'm not a mollycoddle -"

"I don't want to," said Naida tremulously. "I like you, too -"

"Well, *you're* one if you don't!" retorted Geraldine. "You can like anybody and have fun fighting them, too."

"Put on those clothes, Naida," said Duane sternly. "Are you going to take a dare?"

So she retired very unwillingly into the hedge to costume herself while the two boys invested their fists with the soft chamois gloves of combat.

"We won't bother to shake hands," observed Scott. "Are you ready?"

"Yes, you will, too," insisted Geraldine; "shake hands before you begin to fight!"

"I won't," retorted Scott sullenly; "shake hands with anybody who calls me - what he did."

"Very well then; if you don't, I'll put on those gloves and fight you myself."

Duane's eyes flew wide open and he gazed upon Geraldine with newly mixed emotions. She walked over to her brother and said:

"Remember what Howker told us that father used to say - that squabbling is disgraceful but a good fight is all right. Duane called you a silly name. Instead of disputing about it and calling each other names, you ought to settle it with a fight and be friends afterward.... Isn't that so, Duane?"

Duane seemed doubtful.

"Isn't it so?" she repeated fiercely, stepping so swiftly in front of him that he jumped back.

"Yes, I guess so," he admitted; and the sudden smile which Geraldine flashed on him completed his subjection.

Naida, in her boy's clothes, came out, her hands in her pockets, strutting a little and occasionally bending far over to catch a view of herself as best she might.

"All ready!" cried Geraldine; "begin! Look out, Naida; I'm going to throw you."

Behind her the two boys touched gloves, then Scott rushed his man.

At the same moment Geraldine seized Naida.

"We are not to pull hair," she said; "remember! Now, dear, look out for yourself!"

Of that classic tournament between the clans of Mallett and Seagrave the chronicles are lacking. Doubtless their ancestors before them joined joyously in battle, confident that all details of their prowess would be carefully recorded by the family minstrel.

But the battle of that Saturday noon hour was witnessed only by the sparrows, who were too busy lugging bits of straw and twine to half-completed nests in the cornices of the House of Seagrave, to pay much attention to the combat of the Seagrave children, who had gone quite mad with the happiness of companionship and were expressing it with all their might.

Naida's dark curls mingled with the grass several times before Geraldine comprehended that her new companion was absurdly at her mercy; and then she seized her with all the desperation of first possession and kissed her hard.

"It's ended," breathed Geraldine tremulously, "and nobody gained the victory and - you *will* love me, won't you?"

"I don't know - I'm all dirt." She looked at Geraldine, bewildered by the passion of the lonely child's caresses. "Yes - I do love you, Geraldine. Oh, *look* at those boys! How perfectly disgraceful! They *must* stop - make them stop, Geraldine!"

Hair on end, grass-stained, dishevelled, and unspeakably dirty, the boys were now sparring for breath. Grime and perspiration streaked their countenances. Duane Mallett wore a humorously tinted eye and a prehensile upper lip; Scott's nose had again yielded to the coy persuasion of a left-handed jab and the proud blood of the Seagraves once more offended high heaven on that April day.

Geraldine, one arm imprisoning Naida's waist, walked coolly in between them:

"Don't let's fight any more. The thing to do is to get Mrs. Bramton to give you enough for four to eat and bring it back here. Scott, please shake hands with Duane."

"I wasn't licked," muttered Scott.

"Neither was I," said Duane.

"Nobody was licked by anybody," announced Geraldine. "Do get something to eat, Scott; Naida and I are starving!"

After some hesitation the boys touched gloves respectfully, and Scott shook off his mitts, and started for the kitchen.

And there, to his horror and surprise, he was confronted by Mrs. Severn, black hat, crape veil, and gloves still on, evidently that instant arrived from those occult and, as the children supposed, distant bournes of Staten Island, where the supreme mystery of all had been at work.

"Oh, Scott!" she exclaimed tremulously, "what on earth has happened? What is all this that Mrs. Farren and Howker have been telling me?"

The boy stood petrified. Then there surged over him the memory of his brief happiness in these new companions - a happiness now to be snatched away ere scarcely tasted. Into the child's dirty, disfigured face came a hunted expression; he looked about for an avenue of escape, and Kathleen Severn caught him at the same instant and drew him to her.

"What is it, Scott? Tell me, darling!"

"Nothing.... Yes, there is something. I opened the front door and let a strange boy and girl in to play with us, and I've just been fighting with him, and we were having such good times - I -" his voice broke - "I can't bear to have them go - so soon -"

Kathleen looked at him for a moment, speechless with consternation. Then:

"Where are they, Scott?"

"In the - the hedge."

"Out *there*?"

"Yes."

"*Who* are they?"

"Their names are Duane Mallett and Naida Mallett. We got them to run away from their nurse. Duane's such a bully fellow." A sob choked him.

"Come with me at once," said Kathleen.

Behind the rhododendrons smiling peace was extending its pinions; Duane had produced a pocketful of jack-stones, and the three children were now seated on the grass, Naida manipulating the jacks with soiled but deft fingers.

Duane was saying to Geraldine:

"It's funny that you didn't know you were rich. Everybody says so, and all the nurses in the Park talk about it every time you and Scott walk past."

"If I'm rich," said Geraldine, "why don't I have more money?"

"Don't they let you have as much as you want?"

"No - only twenty-five cents every month.... It's my turn, Naida! Oh, bother! I missed. Go on, Duane -"

And, glancing up, her tongue clove to the roof of her mouth as Kathleen Severn, in her mourning veil and gown, came straight up to where they sat.

"Geraldine, dear, the grass is too damp to sit on," said Mrs. Severn quietly. She turned to the youthful guests, who had hastily risen.

"You are Naida Mallett, it seems; and you are Duane? Please

come in now and wash and dress properly, because I am going to telephone to your mother and ask her if you may remain to luncheon and play in the nursery afterward."

Dazed, the children silently followed her; one of her arms lay loosely about the shoulders of her own charges; one encircled Naida's neck. Duane walked cautiously beside his sister.

In the house the nurses took charge; Geraldine, turning on the stairs, looked back at Kathleen Severn.

"Are you really going to let them stay?"

"Yes, I am, darling."

"And - and may we play together all alone in the nursery?"

"I think so.... I think so, dear."

She ran back down the stairs and impetuously flung herself into Kathleen's arms; then danced away to join the others in the blessed regions above.

Mrs. Severn moved slowly to the telephone, and first called up and reassured Mrs. Mallett, who, however, knew nothing about the affair, as the nurse was still scouring the Park for her charges.

Then Mrs. Severn called up the Half Moon Trust Company and presently was put into communication with Colonel Mallett, the president. To him she told the entire story, and added:

"It was inevitable that the gossip of servants should enlighten the children sooner or later. The irony of it all is that this gossip filtered in here through your son, Duane. That is how the case stands, Colonel Mallett; and I have used my judgment and permitted the children this large liberty which they have long needed, believe me, long, long needed. I hope that your trust officer, Mr. Tappan, will approve."

"Good Lord!" said Colonel Mallett over the wire. "Tappan won't stand for it! You know that he won't, Mrs. Severn. I suppose, if he consults us, we can call a directors' meeting and consider this new phase of the case."

"You ought to; the time is already here when the children should no longer suffer such utter isolation. They *must* make acquaintances, they must have friends, they should go to parties like other children - they ought to be given outside schooling sooner or later. All of which questions must be taken up by your directors as soon as possible, because my children are fast getting out of hand - fast getting away from me; and before I know it I shall have a young man and a young girl to account for - and to account to, colonel -"

"I'll sift out the whole matter with Mr. Tappan; I'll speak to Mr. Grandcourt and Mr. Beekman to-night. Until you hear from us, no more visitors for the children. By the way, is that matter - the one we talked over last month - definitely settled?"

"Yes. I can't help being worried by the inclination she displays. It frightens me in such a child."

"Scott doesn't show it?"

"No. He hates anything like that."

"Do the servants thoroughly understand your orders?"

"I'm a little troubled. I have given orders that no more brandied peaches are to be made or kept in the house. The child was perfectly truthful about it. She admitted filling her cologne bottle with the syrup and sipping it after she was supposed to be asleep."

"Have you found out about the sherry she stole from the kitchen?"

"Yes. She told me that for weeks she had kept it hidden and soaked a lump of sugar in it every night.... She is absolutely truthful, colonel. I've tried to make her understand the danger."

"All right. Good-bye." Kathleen Severn hung up the receiver with a deep indrawn breath.

From the nursery above came a joyous clamour and trampling and shouting.

Suddenly she covered her face with her black-gloved hands.

CHAPTER II

IN TRUST

The enfranchisement of the Seagrave twins proceeded too slowly to satisfy their increasing desire for personal liberty and their fast-growing impatience of restraint.

Occasionally, a few carefully selected and assorted children were permitted to visit them in relays, and play in the nursery for limited periods without the personal supervision of Kathleen or the nurses; but no serious innovation was attempted, no radical step taken without authority from old Remsen Tappan, the trust officer of the great Half Moon Trust Company.

There could be no arguing with Mr. Tappan.

Shortly before Anthony Seagrave died he had written to his old friend Tappan:

> "If I live, I shall see to it that my grandchildren know nothing of the fortune awaiting them until they become of age - which will be after I am ended. Meanwhile, plain food and clothing, wholesome home seclusion from the promiscuity of modern child life, and an exhaustive education in every grace, fashion, and accomplishment of body and intellect is the training I propose for the development in them of the only thing in the world worth cultivating - unterrified individualism.

"The ignorance which characterises the conduct of modern institutes of education reduces us all to one mindless level, reproducing *ad nauseam* what is known as 'average citizens.' This nation is already crawling with them; art, religion, letters, government, business, human ideals remain embryonic because the 'average citizen' can conceive nothing higher, can comprehend nothing loftier even when the few who have escaped the deadly levelling grind of modern methods of education attempt to teach the masses to think for themselves.

"That is bad enough in itself - but add to cut-and-dried pedagogy the outrageous liberty which modern pupils are permitted in school and college, and add to that the unheard-of luxury in which they live - and the result is stupidity and utter ruin.

"My babies must have discipline, system, frugality, and leisure for individual development drilled into them. I do not wish them to be ignorant of one single modern grace and accomplishment; mind and body must be trained together like a pair of Morgan colts.

"But I will not have them victims of pedagogy; I will not have them masters of their time and money until they are of age; I will not permit them to choose companions or pursuits for their leisure until they are fitted to do so.

"If there is in them, latent, any propensity toward viciousness - any unawakened desire for that which has been my failing - hard work from dawn till dark is the antidote. An exhausted child is beyond temptation.

"If I pass forward, Tappan, before you - and it is likely because I am twenty years older and I have lived unwisely - I shall arrange matters in such shape that you can carry out something of what I have tried to begin, far better than I, old friend; for I am strong in theory and very weak in practice; they are such dear little things! And when they cry to be taken up - and a modern trained nurse says 'No! let them cry!' good God! Remsen, I sometimes sneak into their thoroughly modern and scientifically arranged nursery, which resembles an operating room in a brand-new hospital, and I take up my babies and rock them in my arms, terrified lest that modern and highly trained nurse discover my infraction of sanitary rule and precept.

"I don't know; babies were born, and survived cradles and mothers' arms and kisses long before sterilised milk and bacilli were invented.

"You see I *am* weak in more ways than one. But I do mean to give them every chance. It isn't that these old arms ache for them, that this rather tired heart weakens when they cry for God knows what, and modern science says let them *cry*! - it is that, deep in me, Tappan, a heathenish idea persists that what they need more than hygienics and scientific discipline is some of that old-fashioned love - love which rocks them when it is not good for them - love which overfeeds them sometimes so that they yell with old-fashioned colic - love which ventures a bacilli-laden kiss. Friend, friend - I am very unfit! It will be well for them when I move on. Only try to love them, Tappan. And if you ever doubt, kill them with indulgence, rather than with hygiene!"

He died of pneumonia a few weeks later. He had no chance. Remsen Tappan picked up the torch from the fallen hand and, blowing it into a brisk blaze, shuffled forward to light a path through life for the highly sterilised twins.

So the Half Moon Trust became father and mother to the Seagrave children; and Mr. Tappan as dry nurse prescribed the brand of intellectual pap for them and decided in what manner it should be administered.

Now home tuition and the "culture of the indiwidool" was a personal hobby of Mr. Tappan, and promiscuous schools his abomination. Had not his own son, Peter Stuyvesant Tappan, been reared upon unsteady legs to magnificent physical and intellectual manhood under this theory?

So there was to be no outside education for the youthful Seagraves; from the nursery schoolroom no chance of escape remained. As they grew older they became wild to go to school; stories of schoolrooms and playgrounds and studies and teachers and jolly fellowship and vacations, brought to them from outside by happier children, almost crazed them with the longing for it.

It was hard for them when their little friends the Malletts were sent abroad to school; Naida, now aged twelve, to a convent, and Duane, who was now fifteen, three years older than the Seagrave twins, accompanied his mother and a tutor, later to enter some school of art in Paris and develop whatever was in him. For like all parents, Duane's had been terribly excited over his infantile efforts at picture-making - one of the commonest and earliest developed of talents, but which never fails to amaze and delight less gifted parents and which continues to overstock the world with mediocre artists.

So it was arranged that Colonel Mallett should spend every summer abroad with his wife to watch the incubation of Duane's Titianesque genius and Naida's unbelievable talent for music; and when the children came to bid good-bye to the Seagrave twins, they seized each other with frantic embraces, vowing lifelong fidelity. Alas! it is those who depart who forget first; and at the end of a year, Geraldine's and Scott's letters remained unanswered.

At the age of thirteen, after an extraordinary meeting of the directors of the Half Moon Trust Company, it was formally decided that a series of special tutors should now be engaged to carry on to the bitter end the Tappan-Seagrave system of home culture; and the road to college was definitely closed.

"I want my views understood," said Mr. Tappan, addressing

the board of solemn-visaged directors assembled in session to determine upon the fate of two motherless little children. "Indiwidoolism is nurtured in excloosion; the elimination of the extraneous is necessary for the dewelopment of indiwidoolism. I regard the human indiwidool as sacred. Like a pearl" - he pronounced it "poil" - "it can grow in beauty and symmetry and purity and polish only when nourished in seclusion. Indiwidoolism is a poil without price; and the natal mansion, gentlemen - if I may be permitted the simulcritude - is its oyster.

"My old friend, Anthony Seagrave, shared with me this unalterable conwiction. I remember in the autumn of 1859 -"

The directors settled themselves in their wadded arm-chairs; several yawned; some folded their hands over their ample stomachs. The June atmosphere was pleasantly conducive to the sort of after-luncheon introspection which is easily soothed by monotones of the human voice.

And while Mr. Tappan droned on and on, some of the directors watched him with one eye half open, thinking of other things, and some listened, both eyes half closed, thinking of nothing at all.

Many considered Mr. Tappan a very terrible old man, though why terrible, unless the most rigid honesty and bigoted devotion to duty terrifies, nobody seemed to know.

Long Island Dutch - with all that it implies - was the dull stock he rooted in. Born a poor farmer's son, with a savage passion for learning, he almost destroyed his eyesight in lonely study under the flicker of tallow dips. All that had ever come to him of knowledge came in these solitary vigils. Miry and sweating from the plough he mastered the classics, law, chemistry, engineering; and finally emerging heavily from the reek of Long Island fertiliser, struck with a heavy surety at Fortune and brought her to her knees amidst a shower of gold. And all alone he gathered it in.

On Coenties Slip his warehouse still bore the legend: "R. Tappan: Iron." All that he had ever done he had done alone. He knew of no other way; believed in no other way.

Plain living, plainer clothing, tireless thinking undisturbed - that had been his childhood; and it had suited him.

Never but once had he made any concession to custom and nature, and that was only when, desiring an heir, he was obliged to enter into human partnership to realise the wish.

His son was what his father had made him under the iron cult of solitary development; and now, the father, loyal in his own way to the memory of his old friend Anthony Seagrave, meant to do his full duty toward the orphaned grandchildren.

So it came to pass that tutors and specialists replaced Kathleen in the schoolroom; and these ministered to the twin "poils," who were now fretting through their thirteenth year, mad with desire for boarding-school.

Four languages besides their own were adroitly stuffed into them; nor were letters, arts, and sciences neglected, nor the mundane and social patter, accomplishments, and refinements, including poise, pose, and deportment.

Specialists continued to guide them indoors and out; they rode every morning at eight with a specialist; they drove in the Park between four and five with the most noted of four-in-hand specialists; fencing, sparring, wrestling, swimming, gymnastics, were all supervised by specialists in those several very important and scientific arts; and specialists also taught them hygiene: how to walk, sit, breathe; how to masticate; how to relax after the manner of the domestic cat.

They had memory lessons; lessons in personal physiology, and in first aid to themselves.

Specialists cared for their teeth, their eyes, their hair, their skin, their hands and feet.

Everything that was taught them, done for them, indirectly educated them in the science of self-consideration and deepened an unavoidably natural belief in their own overwhelming importance. They had not been born so.

But in the house of Seagrave everything revolved around and centred in them; everything began for them and ended for them alone. They had no chance.

True, they were also instructed in theology and religion; they became well grounded in the elements of both, - laws, by-laws, theory, legends, proverbs, truisms, and even a few abstract truths. But there was no meaning in either to these little prisoners of self. Seclusion is an enemy to youth; solitude its destruction.

When the twins were fifteen they went to their first party. A week of superficial self-restraint and inward delirium was their preparation, a brief hour of passive bewilderment the realisation. Dazed by the sight and touch and clamor of the throng, they moved and spoke as in a vision. The presence of their own kind in such numbers confused them; overwhelmed, they found no voices to answer the call of happiness. Their capacity to respond was too limited.

As in a dream they were removed earlier than anybody else - taken away by a footman and a maid with decorous pomp and circumstance, carefully muffled in motor robes, and embedded in a limousine.

The daily papers, with that lofty purpose which always characterises them, recorded next morning the important fact that the famous Seagrave twins had appeared at their first party.

* * * * *

Between the ages of fifteen and sixteen the twins might have entered Harvard, for the entrance examinations were tried on both children, and both passed brilliantly.

For a year or two they found a substitute for happiness in pretending that they were really at college; they simulated, day by day, the life that they supposed was led there; they became devoted to their new game. Excited through tales told by tutor and friend, they developed a passionate loyalty for their college and class; they were solemnly elected to coveted societies, they witnessed Harvard victories, they strove fiercely for honours; their ideals were lofty, their courage clean and high.

So completely absorbed in the pretence did they become that their own tutors ventured to suggest to Mr. Tappan that such fiercely realistic mimicry deserved to be rewarded. Unfortunately, the children heard of this; but the Trust Officer's short answer killed their interest in playing at happiness, and their junior year began listlessly and continued without ambition. There was no heart in the pretence. Their interest had died. They studied mechanically because they were obliged to; they no longer cared.

That winter they went to a few more parties - not many. However, they were gingerly permitted to witness their first play, and later, the same year, were taken to "Lohengrin" at the opera.

During the play, which was a highly moral one, they sat watching, listening, wide-eyed as children.

At the opera Geraldine's impetuous soul soared straight up to paradise with the first heavenly strains, and remained there far above the rigid, breathless little body, bolt upright in its golden sarcophagus of the grand tier.

Her physical consciousness really seemed to have fled. Until the end she sat unaware of the throngs, of Scott and Kathleen whispering behind her, of several tall, broad-shouldered, shy young fellows who came into their box between the acts and tried to discuss anything at all with her, only to find her blind, deaf, and dumb.

These were the only memories of her first opera - confused, chaotic brilliancy, paradise revealed: and long, long afterward, the carriage flying up Fifth Avenue through darkness all gray with whirling snow.

* * * * *

Their eighteenth year dragged, beginning in physical and intellectual indifference, but promised stormily as they became more accustomed to glimpses of an outside world - a world teeming with restless young people in unbelievable quantities.

Scott had begun to develop two traits: laziness and a tendency to sullen, unspoken wrath. He took more liberty than was officially granted him - more than Geraldine dared take - and came into collision with Kathleen more often now. He boldly overstayed his leave in visiting his few boy friends for an afternoon; he returned home alone on foot after dusk, telling the chauffeur to go to the devil. Again and again he remained out to dinner without permission, and, finally, one afternoon quietly and stealthily cut his studies, slipped out of the house, and reappeared about dinner-time, excited, inclined to be boisterously defiant, admitting that he had borrowed enough money from a friend to go to a matinee with some other boys, and that he would do it again if he chose.

Also, to Kathleen's horror, he swore deliberately at table when Mr. Tappan's name was mentioned; and Geraldine looked up with startled brown eyes, divining in her brother something new - something that unconsciously they both had long, long waited for - the revolt of youth ere youth had been crushed for ever from the body which encased it.

"Damn him," repeated Scott, a little frightened at his own words and attitude; "I've had enough of this baby business; I'm eighteen and I want two things: some friends to go about with freely, and some money to do what other boys do. And you can tell Mr. Tappan, for all I care."

"What would you buy with money that is not already provided for, Scott?" asked Kathleen, gently ignoring his excited profanity.

"I don't know; there is no pleasure in using things which that fool of a Trust Company votes to let you have. Anyway, what I want is liberty and money."

"What would you do with what you call liberty, dear?"

"Do? I'd - I'd - well, I'd go shooting if I wanted to. I'd buy a gun and go off somewhere after ducks."

"But your father's old club on the Chesapeake is open to you. Shall I ask Mr. Tappan?"

"Oh, yes: I know," he sneered, "and Mr. Tappan would send some chump of a tutor there to teach me. I don't want to be taught how to hit ducks. I want to find out for myself. I don't care for that sort of thing," he repeated savagely; "I just ache to go off somewhere with a boy of my own age where there's no club and no preserve and no tutor; and where I can knock about and get whatever there is to get without anybody's help."

Geraldine said: "You have more liberty now than I have, Scott. What are you howling for?"

"The only real liberty I have I take! Anyway, you have enough for a girl of your age. And you'd better shut up."

"I won't shut up," she retorted irritably. "I want liberty as much as you do. If I had any, I'd go to every play and opera in New York. And I'd go about with my friends and I'd have gowns fitted, and I'd have tea at Sherry's, and I'd shop and go to matinees and to the Exchange, and I'd be elected a member of the Commonwealth Club and play basket-ball there, and swim, and lunch and - and then have another fitting -"

"Is that what you'd do with your liberty?" he sneered. "Well, I don't wonder old Tappan doesn't give you any money."

"I do need money and decent gowns. I'm sick of the frumpy prunes-and-prisms frocks that Kathleen makes me wear -"

Kathleen's troubled laugh interrupted her:

"Dearest, I do the best I can on the allowance made you by Mr. Tappan. His ideas on modern feminine apparel are perhaps not yours or mine."

"I should say not!" returned Geraldine angrily. "There isn't a girl of my age who dresses as horridly as I do. I tell you, Mr. Tappan has got to let me have money enough to dress decently. If he doesn't, I - I'll begin to give him as much trouble as Scott does - more, too!"

She set her teeth and stared at her glass of water.

"What about my coming-out gown?" she asked.

"I have written him about your debut," said Kathleen soothingly.

"Oh! What did the old beast say?"

"He writes," began Kathleen pleasantly, "that he considers eighteen an unsuitable age for a young girl to make her bow to New York society."

"Did he say that?" exclaimed Geraldine, furious. "Very well; I shall write to Colonel Mallett and tell him I simply will not endure it any longer. I've had enough education; I'm suffocated with it! Besides, I dislike it. I want a dinner-gown and a ball-gown and my hair waved and dressed on top of my head instead of bunched half way! I want to have an engagement pad - I want to have places to go to - people expecting me; I want silk stockings and pretty underclothes! Doesn't that old fool understand what a girl wants and needs?"

She half rose from her seat at the table, pushing away the fruit which a servant offered; and, laying her hands flat on the cloth, leaned forward, eyes flashing ominously.

"I'm getting tired of this," she said. "If it goes on, I'll probably run away."

"So will I," said Scott, "but I've good reasons. They haven't done anything to you. You're making a terrible row about nothing."

"Yes, they have! They've suppressed me, stifled me, bottled me up, tinkered at me, overgroomed me, dressed me ridiculously, and stuffed my mind. And I'm starved all the time! O Kathleen, I'm hungry! hungry! Can't you understand?

"They've made me into something I was not. I've never yet had a chance to be myself. Why couldn't they let me be it? I know - I *know* that when at last they set me free because they have to - I - I'll act like a fool; I'll not know what to do with my liberty - I'll not know how to use it - how to understand or be understood.... Tell Mr. Tappan that! Tell him that it is all silly and wrong! Tell him that a young girl never forgets when other girls laugh at her because she never had any money, and dresses like a frump, and wears her hair like a baby!... And if he doesn't listen to us, some day Scott and I will show him and the others how we feel about it! I can make as much trouble as Scott can; I'll do it, too -"

"Geraldine!"

"Very well. I'm boiling inside when I think of - some things. The injustice of a lot of hateful, snuffy old men deciding on what sort of underclothes a young girl shall wear!... And I *will* make my debut! I will! I will!"

"Dearest -"

"Yes, I will! I'll write to them and complain of Mr. Tappan's stingy, unjust treatment of us both -"

"Let me do the writing, dear," said Kathleen quietly. And she rose from the table and left the dining-room, both arms around the necks of the Seagrave twins, drawing them close to her sides - closer when her sidelong glance caught the sullen bitterness on the darkening features of the boy, and when on the girl's fair face she saw the flushed, wide-eyed, questioning stare.

When the young, seeking reasons, gaze questioningly at nothing, it is well to divine and find the truthful answer, lest their *other* selves, evoked, stir in darkness, counselling folly.

The answer to such questions Kathleen knew; who should know better than she? But it was not for her to reply. All she could do was to summon out of the vasty deep the powers that ruled her wards and herself; and these, convoked in solemn assembly because of conflict with their Trust Officer, might decide in becoming gravity such questions as what shall be the proper quality and cost of a young girl's corsets; and whether or not real lace and silk are necessary for attire more intimate still.

* * * * *

During the next two years the steadily increasing friction between Remsen Tappan and his wards began seriously to disturb the directors of the Half Moon Trust. That worthy old line company viewed with uneasiness the revolutionary tendencies of the Seagrave twins as expressed in periodical and passionate letters to Colonel Mallett. The increasing frequency of these appeals for justice and for intervention fore-shadowed the desirability of a conference. Besides, there was a graver matter to consider, which implicated Scott.

When Kathleen wrote, suggesting a down-town conference to decide delicate questions concerning Geraldine's under-garments and Scott's new gun, Colonel Mallett found it more convenient to appoint the Seagrave house as rendezvous.

And so it came to pass one pleasant Saturday afternoon in late October that, in twos and threes, a number of solemn old gentlemen, faultlessly attired, entered the red drawing-room of the Seagrave house and seated themselves in an impressive semicircle upon the damask chairs.

They were Colonel Stuart Mallett, president of the institution, just returned from Paris with his entire family; Calvin McDermott, Joshua Hogg, Carl Gumble, Friedrich Gumble; the two vice-presidents, James Cray and Daniel Montross; Myndert Beekman, treasurer; Augustus Varick, secretary; the Hon. John D. Ellis; Magnelius Grandcourt 2d, and Remsen Tappan, Trust Officer.

If the pillars of the house of Seagrave had been founded upon millions, the damask and rosewood chairs in the red drawing-room now groaned under the weight of millions. Power, authority, respectability, and legitimate affluence sat there majestically enthroned in the mansion of the late Anthony Seagrave, awaiting in serious tribunal the appearance of the last of that old New York family.

Mrs. Severn came in first; the directors rose as one man, urbane, sprightly, and gallant. She was exceedingly pretty; they recognised it. They could afford to.

Compositely they were a smooth, soft-stepping, soft-voiced, company. An exception or two, like Mr. Tappan, merely accented the composite impression of rosy-cheeked, neatly shaven, carefully dressed prosperity. They all were cautious of voice, moderate of speech, chary of gesture. There was always an impressive pause before a director of the Half Moon Trust answered even the most harmless question addressed to him. Some among them made it a conservative rule to swallow nothing several times before speaking at all. It was a safe habit to acquire. *Aut prudens aut nullus.*

Geraldine's starched skirts rustled on the stairway. When she came into the room the directors of the Half Moon Trust were slightly astonished. During the youth of the twins, the wives of several gentlemen present had called at intervals to inspect the growth of Anthony Seagrave's grandchildren, particularly those worthy and acquisitive ladies who had children themselves. The far-sighted reap rewards. Some day these baby twins would be old enough to marry. It was prudent to remember such details. A position as an old family friend might one day prove of thrifty advantage in this miserably mercenary world where dog eats dog, and dividends are sometimes passed. God knows and pities the sorrows of the rich.

Geraldine, her slim hand in Colonel Mallett's, courtesied with old-time quaintness, then her lifted eyes swept the rosy, rotund countenances before her. To each she courtesied and spoke, offering the questioning hand of amity.

The thing that seemed to surprise them was that she had grown since they had seen her. Time flies when hunting safe investments. The manners she retained, like her fashion of wearing her hair, and the cut and length of her apparel were clearly too childish to suit the tall, slender, prettily rounded figure - the mature oval of the face, the delicately firm modelling of the features.

This was no child before them; here stood adorable adolescence, a hint of the awakening in the velvet-brown eyes which were long and slightly slanting at the corners; hints, too, in the vivid lips, in the finer outline of the profile, in faint bluish shadows under the eyes, edging the curved cheeks' bloom.

They had not seen her in two years or more, and she had grown up. They had merely stepped down-town for a hasty two years' glance at the market, and, behind their backs, the child had turned into a woman.

Hitherto they had addressed her as "Geraldine" and "child," when a rare interview had been considered necessary. Now, two years later, unconsciously, it was "Miss Seagrave," and considerable embarrassment when the subject of intimate attire could no longer be avoided.

But Geraldine, unconscious of such things, broached the question with all the directness characteristic of her.

"I am sorry I was rude in my last letter," she said gravely, turning to Mr. Tappan. "Will you please forgive me?... I am glad you came. I do not think you understand that I am no longer a little girl, and that things necessary for a woman are necessary for me. I want a quarterly allowance. I need what a young woman needs. Will you give these things to me, Mr. Tappan?"

Mr. Tappan's dry lips cracked apart; he swallowed grimly several times, then his long bony fingers sought the meagre ends of his black string tie:

"In the cultiwation of the indiwidool," he began harshly, and checked himself, when Geraldine flushed to her ear tips and stamped her foot. Self-control had gone at last.

"I won't listen to that!" she said, breathless; "I've listened to it for ten years - as long as I can remember. Answer me honestly, Mr. Tappan! Can I have what other women have - silk underwear and stockings - real lace on my night dresses - and plenty of it? Can I have suitable gowns and furs, and have my hair dressed properly? I want you to answer; can I make my debut this winter and have the gowns I require - and the liberty that girls of my age have?" She turned on Colonel Mallett: "The liberty that Naida has had is all I want; the sort of things you let her have all I ask for." And appealing to Magnelius Grandcourt, who stood pursing his thick lips, puffed out like a surprised pouter pigeon: "Your daughter Catherine has more than I ask; why do you let her have what you consider bad for me? *Why*?"

Mr. Grandcourt swallowed several times, and spoke in an undertone to Joshua Hogg. But he did not reply to Geraldine.

Remsen Tappan turned his iron visage toward Colonel Mallett - ignoring Geraldine's questions.

"In the cultiwation of the indiwidool," he began again dauntlessly -

"Isn't there anybody to answer me?" asked Geraldine, turning from one to another.

"Concerning the cultiwation -"

"Answer me!" she flashed back. There were tears in her voice, but her eyes blazed.

"Miss Seagrave," interposed old Mr. Montross gravely, "I beg of you to remember -"

"Let him answer me first! I asked him a perfectly plain question. It - it is silly to ignore me as though I were a foolish child - as though I didn't know my mind."

"I think, Mr. Tappan, perhaps if you could give Miss Seagrave a qualified answer to her questions - make some preliminary statement -" began Mr. Cray cautiously.

"Concerning what?" snapped Tappan with a grim stare.

"Concerning my stockings and my underwear," said Geraldine fiercely. "I'm tired of dressing like a servant!"

Mr. Tappan's rugged jaw opened and shut with another snap.

"I'm opposed to any such innovation," he said.

"And - my coming out this winter? And my quarterly allowance? Answer me!"

"Time enough when you turn twenty-one, Miss Seagrave. Cultiwation of mind concerns you now, not cultiwation of raiment."

"That - that -" stammered Geraldine, "is s-su-premely s-silly." The tears reached her eyes; she brushed them away angrily.

Mallett coughed and glanced at Myndert Beekman, then past the secretary, Mr. Varick, directly at Mr. Tappan.

"If you could see your way to - ah - accede to some - a number - perhaps, in a measure, to all of Miss Seagrave's not unreasonable requests, Mr. Tappan -"

He hesitated, looked dubiously at Mr. Montross, who nodded. Mr. Cray, also, made an almost imperceptible sign of concurrence. Magnelius Grandcourt, the sixty-year *enfant terrible* of the company, dreaded for his impulsive outbursts - though the effect of these outbursts was always very carefully considered before-hand - stepped jauntily across the floor, and lifting Geraldine's hand to his rather purplish lips, saluted it with a flourish.

"Oh, I say, Tappan, let Miss Seagrave have what she wants!" he exclaimed with a hearty disregard of caution, which outwardly disturbed but inwardly deceived nobody except Geraldine and Mrs. Severn.

Colonel Mallett thought: "The acquisitive beast is striking attitudes on his fool of a son's account."

Mr. Tappan's small iron-gray eyes bored two holes through the inward motives of Mr. Grandcourt, and his mouth tightened till the seamed lips were merely a line.

"I think, Magnelius," said Colonel Mallett coldly, "that it is, perhaps, the sense of our committee that the time has practically arrived for some change - perhaps radical change - in the - in the - ah - the hitherto exceedingly wise regulations -"

"*May* I have real lace?" cried Geraldine - "Oh, I *beg* your pardon, Colonel Mallett, for interrupting, but I was perfectly crazy to know what you were going to say."

Other people have been crazier and endured more to learn what hope the verdict of ponderous authority might hold for them.

Colonel Mallett, a trifle ruffled at the interruption, swallowed several times and then continued without haste to rid himself of a weighty opinion concerning the debut and the petticoats of the Half Moon's ward. He might have made the child happy in one word. It took him twenty minutes.

Concurring opinions were then solemnly delivered by every director in turn except Mr. Tappan, who spoke for half an hour, doggedly dissenting on every point.

But the days of the old regime were evidently numbered. He understood it. He looked across at the crackled portrait of his old friend Anthony Seagrave; the faded, painted features were obliterated in a bar of slanting sunlight.

So, concluding his dissenting opinion, and having done his duty, he sat down, drawing the skirts of his frock-coat close around his bony thighs. He had done his best; his reward was this child's hatred - which she already forgot in the confused delight of her sudden liberation.

Dazed with happiness, to one after another Geraldine courtesied and extended the narrow childlike hand of amity -

even to him. Then, as though treading on invisible pink clouds, she floated out and away up-stairs, scarcely conscious of passing her brother on the stairway, who was now descending for his turn before the altar of authority.

* * * * *

When Scott returned he appeared to be unusually red in the face. Geraldine seized him ecstatically:

"Oh, Scott! I *am* to come out, after all - and I'm to have my quarterly, and gowns, and everything. I could have hugged Mr. Grandcourt - the dear! I was so frightened - frightened into rudeness - and then that beast of a Tappan scared me terribly. But it is all right now - and *what* did they promise you, poor dear?"

Scott's face still remained flushed as he stood, hands in his pockets, head slightly bent, tracing with the toe of his shoe the carpet pattern.

"You want to know what they promised me?" he asked, looking up at his sister with an unpleasant laugh. She poured a few drops of cologne onto a lump of sugar, placed it between her lips, and nodded:

"They *did* promise you something - didn't they?"

"Oh, certainly. They promised to make it hot for me if I ever again borrowed money on notes."

"Scott! did you do that?"

"Give my note? Certainly. I needed money - I've told old tabby Tappan so again and again. In a year I'll have all the money I need - so what's the harm if I borrow a little and promise to pay when I'm of age?"

Geraldine considered a moment: "It's curious," she reflected, "but do you know, Scott, I never thought of doing that. It never occurred to me to do it! Why didn't you tell me?"

"Because," said her brother with an embarrassed laugh, "it's not exactly a proper thing to do, I believe. Anyway, they raised a terrible row about it. Probably that's why they have at last given me a decent quarterly allowance; they think it's safer, I suppose - and they're right. The stingy old fossils."

The boyish boast, the veiled hint of revolt and reprisal vaguely disturbed Geraldine's sense of justice.

"After all," she said, "they have meant to be kind. They didn't know how, that's all. And, Scott, do let us try to be better now. I'm ashamed of my rudeness to them. And I'm going to be very, very good to Kathleen and not do one single thing to make her unhappy or even to bother Mr. Tappan.... And, oh, Scott! my silks and laces! my darling clothes! All is coming true! Do you hear? And, Scott! Naida and Duane are back and I'm dying to see them. Duane is twenty-three, think of it!"

She seized him and spun him around.

"If you don't hug me and tell me you're fond of me, I shall go mad. Tell me you're fond of me, Scott! You do love me, don't you?"

He kissed his sister with preoccupied toleration: "Whew!" he said, "your breath reeks of cologne!

"As for me," he added, half sullenly, "I'm going to have a few things I want, now.... And do a few things, too."

But what these things were he did not specify. Nor did Geraldine have time to speculate, so occupied was she now with preparations for the wonderful winter which was to come true at last - which was already beginning to come true with exciting visits to that magic country of brilliant show-windows which, like an enchanted city by itself, sparkles from Madison

Square to the Plaza between Fourth Avenue and Broadway.

* * * * *

Into this sparkling metropolitan zone she hastened with Kathleen; all day long, week after week, she flitted from shop to shop, never satisfied, always eager to see, to explore. Yet two things Kathleen noticed: Geraldine seemed perfectly happy and contented to view the glitter of vanity fair without thought of acquiring its treasures for herself; and, when reminded that she was there to buy, she appeared to be utterly ignorant of the value of money, though a childhood without it was supposed to have taught her its rarity and preciousness.

The girl's personal tastes were expensive; she could linger in ecstasy all the morning over piles of wonderful furs without envy, without even thinking of them for herself; but when Kathleen mentioned the reason of their shopping, Geraldine always indicated sables as her choice, any single piece of which would have required half her yearly allowance to pay for.

And she was for ever wishing to present things to Kathleen; silks that were chosen, model gowns that they examined together, laces, velvets, jewels, always her first thought seemed to be that Kathleen should have what they both enjoyed looking at so ardently; and many a laughing contest they had as to whether her first quarterly allowance should be spent upon herself or her friends.

On the surface it would appear that unselfishness was the key to her character. That was impossible; she had lived too long alone. Yet Geraldine was clearly not acquisitive; though, when she did buy, her careless extravagance worried Kathleen. Spendthrift - in that she cared nothing for the money value of anything - her bright, piquant, eager face was a welcome sight to the thrifty metropolitan shopkeeper at Christmas-tide. A delicate madness for giving obsessed her; she bought a pair of guns for Scott, laces and silks for Kathleen, and for the servants everything she could think of. Nobody was forgotten, not even

Mr. Tappan, who awoke Christmas morning to gaze grimly upon an antique jewelled fob all dangling with pencils and seals. In the first flush of independence it gave her more pleasure to give than to acquire.

Also, for the first time in her life, she superintended the distribution of her own charities, flying in the motor with Kathleen from church to mission, eager, curious, pitiful, appalled, by turns. Sentiment overwhelmed her; it was a new kind of pleasure.

* * * * *

One night she arose shivering from her warm bed, and with ink and paper sat figuring till nearly dawn how best to distribute what fortune she might one day possess, and live an exalted life on ten dollars a week.

Kathleen found her there asleep, head buried in the scattered papers, limbs icy to the knees; and there ensued an interim of bronchitis which threatened at one time to postpone her debut.

But the medical profession of Manhattan came to the rescue in battalions, and Geraldine was soon afoot, once more drifting ecstatically among the splendours of the shops, thrilling with the nearness of the day that should set her free among unnumbered hosts of unknown friends.

Who would these unknown people turn out to be? What hearts were at that very moment destined to respond in friendship to her own?

Often lying awake, nibbling her scented lump of sugar, the darkness reddening, at intervals, as embers of her bedroom fire dropped glowing to the hearth, she pictured to herself this vast, brilliant throng awaiting to welcome her as one of them. And her imagination catching fire, through closed lids she seemed to see heavenly vistas of youthful faces - a thousand arms outstretched in welcome; and she, advancing, eyes dim with happiness, giving herself to this world of youth and friendship - crossing the threshold - leaving for ever behind her the past with its loneliness and isolation.

It was of friendships she dreamed, and the blessed nearness of others, and the liberty to seek them. She promised herself she would never, never again permit herself to be alone. She had no definite plans, except that. Life henceforth must be filled with the bright shapes of comrades. Life must be only pleasure. Never again must sadness come near her. A miraculous capacity for happiness seemed to fill her breast, expanding with the fierce desire for it, until under the closed lids tears stole out, and there, in the darkness, she held out her bare arms to the world - the kind, good, generous, warm-hearted world, which was waiting, just beyond her threshold, to welcome her and love her and companion her for ever.

CHAPTER III

THE THRESHOLD

She awoke tired; she had scarcely closed her eyes that night. The fresh odour of roses filled her room when her maid arrived with morning gifts from Kathleen and Scott.

She lay abed until noon. They started dressing her about three. After that the day became unreal to her.

*   *   *   *   *

Manhattan was conventionally affable to Geraldine Seagrave, also somewhat curious to see what she looked like. Fifth Avenue and the neighbouring side streets were jammed with motors and carriages on the bright January afternoon that Geraldine made her bow, and the red and silver drawing-rooms, so famous a generation ago, were packed continually.

What people saw was a big, clumsy house expensively overdecorated in the appalling taste of forty years ago, now screened by forests of palms and vast banks of flowers; and they saw a number of people popularly identified with the sort of society which newspapers delight to revere; and a few people of real distinction; and a young girl, noticeably pale, standing beside Kathleen Severn and receiving the patronage of dowagers and beaux, and the impulsive clasp of fellowship from fresh-faced young girls and nice-looking, well-mannered young fellows.

The general opinion seemed to be that Geraldine Seagrave possessed all the beauty which rumour had attributed to her as her right by inheritance, but the animation of her clever mother was lacking. Also, some said that her manners still smacked of the nursery; and that, unless it had been temporarily frightened out of her, she had little personality and less charm.

Nothing, as a matter of fact, had been frightened out of her; for weeks she had lived in imagination so vividly through that day that when the day really arrived it found her physically and mentally unresponsive; the endless reiteration of names sounded meaninglessly in her ears, the crowding faces blurred. She was passively satisfied to be there, and content with the touch of hands and the pleasant-voiced formalities of people pressing toward her from every side.

* * * * *

Afterward few impressions remained; she remembered the roses' perfume, and a very fat woman with a confusing similarity of contour fore and aft who blocked the lines and rattled on like a machine-gun saying dreadfully frank things about herself, her family, and everybody she mentioned.

Naida Mallett, whom she had not seen in many years, she had known immediately, and now remembered. And Naida had taken her white-gloved hand shyly, whispering constrained formalities, then had disappeared into the unreality of it all.

Duane, her old playmate, may have been there, but she could not remember having seen him. There were so many, many youths of the New York sort, all dressed alike, all resembling one another - many, many people flowing past her where she stood submerged in the silken ebb eddying around her.

* * * * *

These were the few hazy impressions remaining - she was

recalling them now while dressing for her first dinner dance. Later, when her maid released her with a grunt of Gallic disapproval, she, distraite, glanced at her gown in the mirror, still striving to recall something definite of the day before.

"*Was* Duane there?" she asked Kathleen, who had just entered.

"No, dear.... Why did you happen to think of Duane Mallett?"

"Naida came.... Duane was such a splendid little boy.... I had hoped -"

Mrs. Severn said coolly:

"Duane isn't a very splendid man. I might as well tell you now as later."

"What in the world do you mean, Kathleen?"

"I mean that people say he was rather horrid abroad. Some women don't mind that sort of thing, but I do."

"Horrid? How?"

"He went about Europe with unpleasant people. He had too much money - and that is ruinous for a boy. I hate to disillusion you, but for several years people have been gossipping about Duane Mallett's exploits abroad; and they are not savoury."

"What were they? I am old enough to know."

"I don't propose to tell you. He was notoriously wild. There were scandals. Hush! here comes Scott."

"For Heaven's sake, pinch some colour into your cheeks!" exclaimed her brother; "we're not going to a wake!"

And Kathleen said anxiously: "Your gown is perfection, dear;

are you a trifle tired? You do look pale."

"Tired?" repeated Geraldine - "not in the least, dearest.... If I seem not to be excited, I really am, internally; but perhaps I haven't learned how to show it.... Don't I look well? I was so preoccupied with my gown in the mirror that I forgot to examine my face."

Mrs. Severn kissed her. "You and your gown are charming. Come, we are late, and that isn't permitted to debutantes."

* * * * *

It was Mrs. Magnelius Grandcourt who was giving the first dinner and dance for Geraldine Seagrave. In the cloak-room she encountered some very animated women of the younger married set, who spoke to her amiably, particularly a Mrs. Dysart, who said she knew Duane Mallett, and who was so friendly that a bit of colour warmed Geraldine's pallid cheeks and still remained there when, a few minutes later, she saluted her heavily jewelled hostess and recognised in her the fat fore-and-aft lady of the day before.

Mrs. Magnelius Grandcourt, glittering like a South American scarab, detained her with the smallest and chubbiest hands she had ever seen inside of gloves.

"My dear, you look ghastly," said her hostess. "You're probably scared to death. This is my son, Delancy, who is going to take you in, and I'm wondering about you, because Delancy doesn't get on with debutantes, but that can't be helped. If he's pig enough not to talk to you, it wouldn't surprise me - and it's just as well, too, for if he likes anybody he compromises them, but it's no use your ever liking a Grandcourt, for all the men make rotten husbands - I'm glad Rosalie Dysart threw him over for poor Jack Dysart; it saved her a divorce! I'd get one if I could; so would Magnelius. My husband was a judge once, but he resigned because he couldn't send people up for the things he was doing himself."

Mrs. Grandcourt, still gabbling away, turned to greet new arrivals, merely switching to another subject without interrupting her steady stream of outrageous talk. She was celebrated for it - and for nothing else.

Geraldine, bewildered and a little horrified, looked at her billowy, bediamonded hostess, then at young Delancy Grandcourt, who, not perceptibly abashed by his mother's left-handed compliments, lounged beside her, apparently on the verge of a yawn.

"My mother says things," he explained patiently; "nobody minds 'em.... Shall we exchange nonsense - or would you rather save yourself until dinner?"

"Save myself what?" she asked nervously.

"The nuisance of talking to me about nothing. I'm not clever."

Geraldine reddened.

"I don't usually talk about nothing."

"I do," he said. "I never have much to say."

"Is that because you don't like debutantes?" she asked coldly.

"It's because they don't care about me.... If you would talk to me, I'd really be grateful."

He flushed and stepped back awkwardly to allow room for a slim, handsome man to pass between them. The very ornamental man did not pass, however, but calmly turned toward Geraldine, and began to talk to her.

She presently discovered his name to be Dysart; and she also discovered that Mr. Dysart didn't know her name; and, for a moment after she had told him, surprise and a confused sense of resentment silenced her, because she was quite certain now that they had never been properly presented.

That negligence of conventions was not unusual in this new world she was entering, she had already noticed; and this incident was evidently another example of custom smilingly ignored. She looked up questioningly, and Dysart, instantly divining the trouble, laughed in his easy, attractive fashion - the fashion he usually affected with women.

“You seemed so fresh and cool and sweet all alone in this hot corner that I simply couldn't help coming over to hear whether your voice matched the ensemble. And it surpasses it. Are you going to be resentful?”

“I'm too ignorant to be - or to laugh about it as you do.... Is it because I look a simpleton that you come to see if I really am?”

“Are you planning to punish me, Miss Seagrave?”

“I'm afraid I don't know how.”

“Fate will, anyway, unless I am placed next you at dinner,” he said with his most reassuring smile, and rose gracefully.

“I'm going to fix it,” he added, and, pushing his way toward his hostess, disappeared in the crush.

Later young Grandcourt reappeared from the crush to take her in. Every table seated eight, and, sure enough, as she turned involuntarily to glance at her neighbour on the right, it was Dysart's pale face, cleanly cut as a cameo, that met her gaze. He nodded back to her with unfeigned satisfaction at his own success.

“That's the way to manage,” he said, “when you want a thing very much. Isn't it, Miss Seagrave?”

“You did not ask me whether I wanted it,” she said.

"Don't you want me here? If you don't -" His features fell and he made a pretence of rising. His pale, beautifully sculptured face had become so fearfully serious that she coloured up quickly.

"Oh, you *wouldn't* do such a thing - now! to embarrass me."

"Yes, I would - I'd do anything desperate."

But she had already caught the flash of mischief, and realising that he had been taking more or less for granted in tormenting her, looked down at her plate and presently tasted what was on it.

"I know you are not offended," he murmured. "Are you?"

She knew she was not, too; but she merely shrugged. "Then why do you ask me, Mr. Dysart?"

"Because you have such pretty shoulders," he replied seriously.

"What an idiotic reply to make!"

"Why? Don't you think you have?"

"What?"

"Pretty shoulders."

"I don't think anything about my shoulders!"

"You would if there was anything the matter with them," he insisted.

Once or twice he turned his handsome dark gaze on her while she was dissecting her terrapin.

"They tip up a little - at the corners, don't they?" he inquired anxiously. "Does it hurt?"

"Tip up? What tips up?" she demanded.

"Your eyes."

She swung around toward him, confused and exasperated; but no seriousness was proof against the delighted malice in Dysart's face; and she laughed a little, and laughed again when he did. And she thought that he was, perhaps, the handsomest man she had ever seen. All debutantes did.

Young Grandcourt turned from the pretty, over-painted woman who, until that moment, had apparently held him interested when his food failed to monopolise his attention, and glanced heavily around at Geraldine.

All he saw was the back of her head and shoulders. Evidently she was not missing him. Evidently, too, she was having a very good time with Dysart.

"What are you laughing about?" he asked wistfully, leaning forward to see her face.

Geraldine glanced back across her shoulder.

"Mr. Dysart is trying to be impertinent," she replied carelessly; and returned again to the impertinent one, quite ready for more torment now that she began to understand how agreeable it was.

But Dysart's expression had changed; there was something vaguely caressing in voice and manner as he murmured:

"Do you know there is something almost divine in your face."

"What did you say?" asked Geraldine, looking up from her ice in its nest of spun sugar.

"You so strenuously reject the truthful compliments I pay you, that perhaps I'd better not repeat this one."

"Was it really more absurd flattery?"

"No, never mind...." He leaned back in his chair, absently turning the curious, heavily chiselled ring on his little finger, but every few moments his expressive eyes reverted to her. She was eating her ice with all the frank enjoyment of a schoolgirl.

"Do you know, Miss Seagrave, that you and I are really equipped for better things than talking nonsense."

"I know that I am," she observed.... "Isn't this spun sugar delicious!"

"Yes; and so are you."

But she pretended not to hear.

He laughed, then fell silent; his dreamy gaze shifted from vacancy to her - and, casually, across the room, where it settled lightly as a butterfly on his wife, and there it poised for a moment's inexpressive examination. Scott Seagrave was talking to Rosalie; she did not notice her husband.

After that, with easy nonchalance approaching impudence, he turned to his own neglected dinner partner, Sylvia Quest, who received his tardy attentions with childish irritation. She didn't know any better. And there was now no time to patch up matters, for the signal to rise had been given and Dysart took Sylvia to the door with genuine relief. She bored him dreadfully since she had become sentimental over him. They always did.

Lounging back through the rising haze of tobacco-smoke he encountered Peter Tappan and stopped to exchange a word.

"Dancing?" he inquired, lighting his cigarette.

Tappan nodded. "You, too, of course." For Dysart was one of those types known in society as a "dancing man." He also led cotillions, and a morally blameless life as far as the more virile Commandments were concerned.

He said: “That little Seagrave girl is rather fetching.”

Tappan answered indifferently:

“She resembles the general run of this year's output. She's weedy. They all ought to marry before they go about to dinners, anyway.”

“Marry whom?”

“Anybody - Delancy, here, for instance. You know as well as I do that no woman is possible unless she's married,” yawned Tappan. “Isn't that so, Delancy?” clapping Grandcourt on the shoulder.

Grandcourt said “yes,” to be rid of him; but Dysart turned around with his usual smile of amused contempt.

“You think so, too, Delancy,” he said, “because what is obvious and ready-made appeals to you. You think as you eat - heavily - and you miss a few things. That little Seagrave girl is charming. But you'd never discover it.”

Grandcourt slowly removed the fat cigar from his lips, rolled it meditatively between thick forefinger and thumb:

“Do you know, Jack, that you've been saying that sort of thing to me for a number of years?”

“Yes; and it's just as true now as it ever was, old fellow.”

“That may be; but did it ever occur to you that I might get tired hearing it.... And might, possibly, resent it some day?”

For a long time Dysart had been uncomfortably conscious that Grandcourt had had nearly enough of his half-sneering, half-humourous frankness. His liking for Grandcourt, even as a schoolboy, had invariably been tinged with tolerance and good-humoured contempt. Dysart had always led in everything; taken what he chose without considering Grandcourt - sometimes out of sheer perversity, he had taken what Grandcourt wanted - not really wanting it himself - as in the case of Rosalie Dene.

"What are you talking about resenting? - my monopolising your dinner partner?" asked Dysart, smiling. "Take her; amuse yourself. I don't want her."

Grandcourt inspected his cigar again. "I'm tired of that sort of thing, too," he said.

"What sort of thing?"

"Contenting myself with what you don't want."

Dysart lit a cigarette, still smiling, then shrugged and turned as though to go. Around them through the smoke rose the laughing clamour of young men gathering at the exit.

"I want to tell you something," said Grandcourt heavily. "I'm an ass to do it, but I want to tell you."

Dysart halted patiently.

"It's this," went on Grandcourt: "between you and my mother, I've never had a chance; she makes me out a fool and you have always assumed it to be true."

Dysart glanced at him with amused contempt.

A heavy flush rose to Grandcourt's cheek-bones. He said slowly:

"I want my chance. You had better let me have it when it comes."

"What chance do you mean?"

"I mean - a woman. All my life you've been at my elbow to step in. You took what you wanted - your shadow always falls between me and anybody I'm inclined to like.... It happened to-night - as usual.... And I tell you now, at last, I'm tired of it."

"What a ridiculous idea you seem to have of me," began Dysart, laughing.

"I'm afraid of you. I always was. Now - let me alone!"

"Have you ever known me, since I've been married -" He caught Grandcourt's eye, stammered, and stopped short. Then: "You certainly are absurd. Delancy! I wouldn't deliberately interfere with you or disturb a young girl's peace of mind. The trouble with you is -"

"The trouble with *you* is that women take to you very quickly, and you are always trying to see how far you can arouse their interest. What's the use of risking heartaches to satisfy curiosity?"

"Oh, I don't have heartaches!" said Dysart, intensely amused.

"I wasn't thinking of you. I suppose that's the reason you find it amusing.... Not that I think there's any real harm in you -"

"Thanks," laughed Dysart; "it only needed that remark to damn me utterly. Now go and dance with little Miss Seagrave, and don't worry about my trying to interfere."

Grandcourt looked sullenly at him. "I'm sorry I spoke, now," he said. "I never know enough to hold my tongue to you."

He turned bulkily on his heel and left the dining-hall. There were others, in throngs, leaving - young, eager-faced fellows, with a scattering of the usual "dancing" men on whom everybody could always count, and a few middle-aged gentlemen and women of the younger married set to give stability to what was, otherwise, a debutante's affair.

Dysart, strolling about, booked a dance or two, performed creditably, made his peace, for the sake of peace, with Sylvia Quest, whose ignorant heart had been partly awakened under his idle investigations. But this was Sylvia's second season, and she would no doubt learn several things of which she heretofore had been unaware. Just at present, however, her heart was very full, and life's outlook was indeed tragic to a young girl who believed herself wildly in love with a married man, and who employed all her unhappy wits in the task of concealing it.

A load of guilt lay upon her soul; the awful fact that she adored him frightened her terribly; that she could not keep away from him terrified her still more. But most of all she dreaded that he might guess her secret.

"I don't know why you thought I minded your not - not talking to me during dinner," she faltered. "I was having a perfectly heavenly time with Peter Tappan."

"Do you mean that?" murmured Dysart. He could not help playing his part, even when it no longer interested him. To murmur was as natural to him as to breathe.

She looked up piteously. "I would rather have talked to you," she said. "Peter Tappan is only an overgrown boy. If you had really cared to talk to me -" She checked herself, flushing deeply.

O Lord! he thought, contemplating in the girl's lifted eyes the damage he had not really expected to do. For it had, as usual, surprised him to realise, too late, how dangerous it is to say too much, and look too long, and how easy it is to awaken hearts asleep.

Dancing was to be general before the cotillion. Sylvia would have given him as many dances as he asked for; he danced once with her as a great treat, resolving never to experiment any more with anybody.... True, it might have been amusing to see how far he could have interested the little Seagrave girl - but he would renounce that; he'd keep away from everybody.

But Dysart could no more avoid making eyes at anything in petticoats than he could help the tenderness of his own smile or the caressing cadence of his voice, or the subtle, indefinite something in him which irritated men but left few women indifferent and some greatly perturbed as he strolled along on his amusing journey through the world.

He was strolling on now, having managed to leave Sylvia planted; and presently, without taking any particular trouble to find Geraldine, discovered her eventually as the centre of a promising circle of men, very young men and very old men - nothing medium and desirable as yet.

For a while, amused, Dysart watched her at her first party. Clearly she was inexperienced; she let these men have their own way and their own say; she was not handling them skilfully; yet there seemed to be a charm about this young girl that detached man after man from the passing throng and added them to her circle - which had now become a half circle, completely cornering her.

Animated, shyly confident, brilliant-eyed, and flushed with the excitement of attracting so much attention, she was beginning to lose her head a little - just a little. Dysart noticed it in her nervous laughter; in a slight exaggeration of gesture with fan and flowers; in the quick movement of her restless little head, as though it were incumbent upon her to give to every man confronting her his own particular modicum of attention - which was not like a debutante, either; and Dysart realised that she was getting on.

So he sauntered up, breaking through the circle, and reminded

Geraldine of a dance she had not promised him.

She knew she had not promised, but she was quite ready to give it - had already opened her lips to assent - when a young man, passing, swung around abruptly as though to speak to her, hesitating as Geraldine's glance encountered his without recognition.

But, as he started to move on, she suddenly knew him; and at the same moment Kathleen's admonition rang in her ears. Her own voice drowned it.

"Oh, Duane!" she exclaimed, stretching out her hand across Dysart's line of advance.

"You *are* Geraldine Seagrave, are you not?" he asked smilingly, retaining her hand in such a manner as practically to compel her to step past Dysart toward him.

"Of course I am. You might have known me had you been amiable enough to appear at my coming out."

He laughed easily, still retaining her hand and looking down at her from his inch or two of advantage. Then he casually inspected Dysart, who, not at all pleased, returned his gaze with a careless unconcern verging on offence. Few men cared for Dysart on first inspection - or on later acquaintance; Mallett was no exception.

Geraldine said, with smiling constraint:

"It has been so very jolly to see you again." And withdrew her hand, adding: "I hope - some time -"

"Won't you let me talk to you now for a moment or two? You are not going to dismiss me with that sort of come-back - after all these years - are you?"

He seemed so serious about it that the girl coloured up.

"I - that is, Mr. Dysart was going to - to -" She turned and looked at Dysart, who remained planted where she had left him, exceedingly wroth at experiencing the sort of casual treatment he had so often meted out to others. His expression was peevish. Geraldine, confused, began hurriedly:

"I thought Mr. Dysart meant to ask me to dance."

"*Meant* to?" interrupted Mallett, laughing; "*I* mean to ask for this dance, and I do."

Once more she turned and encountered Dysart's darkening gaze, hesitated, then with a nervous, gay little gesture to him, partly promise, partly adieu, she took Mallett's arm.

It was the first glimmer of coquetry she had ever deliberately displayed; and at the same instant she became aware that something new had been suddenly awakened in her - something which stole like a glow through her veins, exciting her with its novelty.

"Do you know," she said, "that you have taken me forcibly away from an exceedingly nice man?"

"I don't care."

"Oh - but might I not at least have been consulted?"

"Didn't you want to come?" he asked, stopping short. There was something overbearing in his voice and his straight, unwavering gaze.

She didn't know how to take it, how to meet it. Voice and manner required some proper response which seemed to be beyond her experience.

She did not answer; but a slight pressure of her bare arm set him in motion again.

The phenomenon interested her; to see what control over this abrupt young man she really had she ventured a very slight retrograde arm-pressure, then a delicate touch to right, to left, and forward once more. It was most interesting; he backed up, guided right and left, and started forward or halted under perfect control. What had she been afraid of in him? She ventured to glance around, and, encountering a warmly personal interest in his gaze, instantly assumed that cold, blank, virginal mask which the majority of young girls discard at her age.

However, her long-checked growth in the arts of womanhood had already recommenced. She had been growing fast, feverishly, and was just now passing that period where the desire for masculine admiration innocently rules all else, but where the discovery of it chills and constrains.

She passed it at that moment. The next time their glances met she smiled a little. A new epoch in her life had begun.

"Where are you taking me?" she asked. "Are we not going to dance?"

"I thought we might sit out a dance or two in the conservatory - one or two -"

"One," she said decidedly. "Here are some palms. Why not sit here?"

There were a number of people about; she saw them, too, noted his hesitation, understood it.

"We'll sit here," she said, and stood smilingly regarding him while he lugged up two chairs to the most retired corner.

Slowly waving her fan, she seated herself and surveyed the room.

It is quite true that reunion after many years usually ends in constraint and indifference. If she felt slightly bored, she certainly looked it. Neither of them resembled the childish recollections or preconceived notions of the other. They found themselves inspecting one another askance, as though furtively attempting to surprise some familiar feature, some resemblance to a cherished memory.

But the changes were too radical; their eyes, looking for old comrades, encountered the unremembered eyes of strangers - for they were strangers - this tall young man, with his gray eyes, pleasantly fashioned mouth, and cleanly moulded cheeks; and this long-limbed girl, who sat, knees crossed, one long, slim foot nervously swinging above its shadow on the floor.

In spite of his youth there was in his manner, if not in his voice, something tinged with fatigue. She thought of what Kathleen had said about him; looked up, instinctively questioning him with curious, uncomprehending eyes; then her gaze wandered, became lost in smiling retrospection as she thought of Dysart, peevish; and she frankly regretted him and his dance.

Young Mallett stirred, passed a rather bony hand over his shaven upper lip, and said abruptly: "I never expected you'd grow up like this. You've turned into a different kind of girl. Once you were chubby of cheek and limb. Do you remember how you used to fight?"

"Did I?"

"Certainly. You hit me twice in the eye because I lost my temper sparring with Scott. Your hands were small but heavy in those days.... I imagine they're heavier now."

She laughed, clasped both pretty hands over her knee, and tilted back against the palm, regarding him from dark, velvety eyes.

"You were a curiously fascinating child," he said. "I remember how fast you could run, and how your hair flew - it was thick and dark, with rather sunny high lights; and you were always running - always on the go.... You were a remarkably just girl; that I remember. You were absolutely fair to everybody."

"I was a very horrid little scrub," she said, watching him over her gently waving fan, "with a dreadful temper," she added.

"Have you it now?"

"Yes. I get over it quickly. Do you find Scott very much changed?"

"Well, not as much as you. Do you find Naida changed?"

"Not nearly as much as you."

They smiled. The slight embarrassment born of polite indifference brightened into amiable interest, tinctured by curiosity.

"Duane, have you been studying painting all these years?"

"Yes. What have you been doing all these years?"

"Nothing." A shadow fell across her face. "It has been lonely - until recently. I began to live yesterday."

"You used to tell me you were lonely," he nodded.

"I was. You and Naida were godsends." Something of the old thrill stirred her recollection. She leaned forward, looking at him curiously; the old memory of him was already lending him something of the forgotten glamour.

"How tall you are!" she said; "how much thinner and - how very impressively grown-up you are, Duane. I didn't expect you to be entirely a man so soon - with such a - an odd - expression -"

He asked, smiling: “What kind of an expression have I, Geraldine?”

“Not a boyish one; entirely a man's eyes and mouth and voice - a little too wise, as though, deep inside, you were tired of something; no, not exactly that, but as though you had seen many things and had lived some of them -”

She checked herself, lips softly apart; and the memory of what she had heard concerning him returned to her.

Confused, she continued to laugh lightly, adding: “I believe I was afraid of you at first. Ought I to be, still? You know more than I do - you know different kinds of things: your face and voice and manner show it. I feel humble and ignorant in the presence of so distinguished a European artist.”

They were laughing together now without a trace of constraint; and she was aware that his interest in her was unfeigned and unmistakably the interest of a man for a woman, that he was looking at her as other men had now begun to look at her, speaking as other men spoke, frankly interested in her as a woman, finding her agreeable to look at and talk to.

In the unawakened depths of her a conviction grew that her old playmate must be classed with other men - man in the abstract - that indefinite and interesting term, hinting of pleasures to come and possibilities unimagined.

“Did you paint pictures all the time you were abroad?” she asked.

“Not every minute. I travelled a lot, went about, was asked to shoot in England and Austria.... I had a good time.”

“Didn't you work hard?”

“No. Isn't it disgraceful!”

"But you exhibited in three salons. What were your pictures?"

"I did a portrait of Lady Bylow and her ten children."

"Was it a success?"

He coloured. "They gave me a second medal."

"Oh, I am so glad!" she exclaimed warmly. "And what were your others?"

"A thing called 'The Witch.' Rather painful."

"What was it?"

"Life size. A young girl arrested in bed. Her frightened beauty is playing the deuce with the people around. I don't know why I did it - the painting of textures - her flesh, and the armour of the Puritan guard, the fur of the black cat - and - well, it was academic and I was young."

"Did they reward you?"

"No."

"What was the third picture?"

"Oh, just a girl," he said carelessly.

"Did they give you a prize for it?"

"Y-yes. Only a mention."

"Was it a portrait?"

"Yes - in a way."

"What was it? Just a girl?"

"Yes."

"Who was she?"

"Oh, just a girl -"

"Was she pretty?"

"Yes. Shall we dance this next -"

"No. Was she a model?"

"She posed -"

Geraldine, lips on the edge of her spread fan, regarded him curiously.

"That is a very romantic life, isn't it?" she murmured.

"What?"

"Yours. I don't know much about it; Kathleen took me to hear 'La Boheme'; and I found Murger's story in the library. I have also read 'Trilby.' Did *you* - were you - was life like that when you studied in the Latin Quarter?"

He laughed. "Not a bit. I never saw that species of life off the stage."

"Oh, wasn't there any romance?" she asked forlornly.

"Well - as much as you find in New York or anywhere."

"Is there any romance in New York?"

"There is anywhere, isn't there? If only one has the instinct to recognise it and a capacity to comprehend it."

"Of course," she murmured, "there are artists and studios and models and poverty everywhere.... I suppose that without poverty real romance is scarcely possible."

He was still laughing when he answered:

"Financial conditions make no difference. Romance is in one's self - or it is nowhere."

"Is it in - you?" she asked audaciously.

He made no pretence of restraining his mirth.

"Why, I don't know, Geraldine. Lots of people have the capacity for it. Poverty, art, a studio, a velvet jacket, and models are not essentials.... You ask if it is in *me*. I think it is. I think it exists in anybody who can glorify the commonplace. To make people look with astonished interest at something which has always been too familiar to arrest their attention - only your romancer can accomplish this."

"Please go on," she said as he ended. "I'm listening very hard. You *are* glorifying commonplaces, you know."

They both laughed; he, a little red, disconcerted, piqued, and withal charmed at her dainty thrust at himself.

"I *was* talking commonplaces," he admitted, "but how was I to know enough not to? Women are usually soulfully receptive when a painter opens a tin of mouldy axioms.... I didn't realise I was encountering my peer -"

"You may be encountering more than that," she said, the excitement of her success with him flushing her adorably.

"Oh, I've heard how terribly educated you and Scott are. No doubt you can floor me on anything intellectual. See here, Geraldine, it's simply wicked! - you are so soft and pretty, and nobody could suspect you of knowing such a lot and pouncing out on a fellow for trying a few predigested platitudes on you -"

"I *don't* know *anything*, Duane! How perfectly horrid of you!"

"Well, you've scared me!"

"I haven't. You're laughing at me. You know well enough that I don't know the things you know."

"What are they, in Heaven's name?"

"Things - experiences - matters that concern life - the world, men, everything!"

"You wouldn't be interesting if you knew such things," he said. She thought there was the same curious hint of indifference, something of listlessness, almost fatigue in the expression of his eyes. And again, apparently apropos of nothing, she found herself thinking of what Kathleen had said about this man.

"I don't understand you," she said, looking at him.

He smiled, and the ghost of a shadow passed from his eyes.

"I was talking at random."

"I don't think you were."

"Why not?"

She shook her head, drawing a long, quiet breath. Silent, lips resting in softly troubled curves, she thought of what Kathleen had said about this man. *What* had he done to disgrace himself?

A few moments later she rose with decision.

"Come," she said, unconsciously imperious.

He looked across the room and saw Dysart.

"But I haven't begun to tell you -" he began; and she interrupted smilingly:

"I know enough about you for a while; I have learned that you are a very wonderful young man and that I'm inclined to like you. You will come to see me, won't you?... No, I can't remain here another second. I want to go to Kathleen. I want you to ask her to dance, too.... Please don't urge me, Duane. I - this is my first dinner dance - yes, my very first. And I *don't* intend to sit in corners - I wish to dance; I desire to be happy. I want to see lots and lots of men, not just one.... You don't know all the lonely years I must make up for every minute now, or you wouldn't look at me in such a sulky, bullying way.... Besides - do you think I find you a compensation for all those delightful people out yonder?"

He glanced up and saw Dysart still watching them. Suddenly he dropped his hand over hers.

"Perhaps you may find that compensation in me some day," he said. "How do you know?"

"What a silly thing to say! Don't paw me, Duane; you hurt my hand. Look at what you've done to my fan!"

"It came between us. I'm sorry for anything that comes between us."

Both were smiling fixedly; he said nothing for a moment; their gaze endured until she flinched.

"Silly," she said, "you are trying to tyrannise over me as you did when we were children. I remember now -"

"*You* did the bullying then."

"Did I? Then I'll continue."

"No, you won't; it's my turn."

"I will if I care to!"

"Try it."

"Very well. Take me to Kathleen."

"Not until I have the dances I want!"

Again their eyes met in silence. Dark little lights glimmered in hers; his narrowed. The fixed smile died out.

"The dances *you* want!" she repeated. "How do you propose to secure them? By crushing my fingers or dragging me about by my hair? I want to tell you something, Duane: these blunt, masterful men are very amusing on the stage and in fiction, but they're not suitable to have tagging at heel -"

"I won't do any tagging at heel," he said; "don't count on it."

"I have no inclination to count on you at all," she retorted, thoroughly irritated.

"You will have it some day."

"Oh! Do you think so?"

"Yes.... I didn't mean to speak the way I did. Won't you give me a dance or two?"

"No. I had no idea how horrid you could be.... I was told you were.... Now I can believe it. Take me to Kathleen; do you hear me?"

After a step or two he said, not looking at her:

"I'm really sorry, Geraldine. I'm not a brute. Something about that fellow Dysart upset me."

"Please don't talk about it any more."

"No.... Only I *am* glad to see you again, and I do care for your regard."

"Then earn it," she said unevenly, as her anger subsided. "I don't know very much about men in the world, but I know enough to understand when they're offensive."

"Was I?"

"Yes.... Because you carried me away with a high hand, you thought it the easiest way to take with me on every occasion.... Duane, do you know, in some ways, we are somewhat alike? And that is why we used to fight so."

"I believe we are," he said slowly. "But - I was never able to keep away from you."

"Which makes our outlook rather stormy, doesn't it?" she said, turning to him with all of her old sweet friendly manner. "*Do* let us agree, Duane. Mercy on us! we ought to adore each other - unless we have forgotten the quarrelsome but adorable friendship of our childhood. *I* thought you were the perfection of all boys."

"I thought there was no girl to equal you, Geraldine."

She turned audaciously, not quite knowing what she was saying:

"Think so now, Duane! It will be good for us both."

"Do you mean it?"

"Not - seriously," she said.... "And, Duane, please don't be too serious with me. I am - you make me uncertain - you make me uncomfortable. I don't know just what to say to you or just how it will be taken. You mustn't be - that way - with *me*; you won't, will you?"

He was silent for a moment; then his face lighted up. "No," he said, laughing; "I'll open another can of platitudes.... You're a dear to forgive me."

* * * * *

Dancing had been general before the cotillion; debutantes continued to arrive in shoals from other dinners, a gay, rosy, eager throng, filling drawing-rooms, conservatory, and library with birdlike flutter and chatter, overflowing into the breakfast-room, banked up on the stairs in bright-eyed battalions.

The cotillion, led by Jack Dysart dancing alone, was one of those carefully thought out intellectual affairs which shakes New York society to its intellectual foundations.

In one figure Geraldine came whizzing into the room in a Palm Beach tricycle-chair trimmed with orchids and propelled by Peter Tappan; and from her seat amid the flowers she distributed favours - live white cockatoos, clinging, flapping, screeching on gilded wands; fans spangled with tiny electric jewels; parasols of pink silk set with incandescent lights; crystal cages containing great, pale-green Luna moths alive and fluttering; circus hoops of gilt filled with white tissue paper, through which the men jumped.

There was also a Totem-pole figure - and other things, including supper and champagne, and the semi-obscurity of conservatory and stairs; and there was the usual laughter to cover heart-aches, and the inevitable torn gowns and crushed flowers; and a number of young men talking too loud and too much in the cloak-room, and Rosalie Dysart admitting to Scott Seagrave in the conservatory that nobody really understood her; and Delancy Grandcourt edging about the outer borders of the flowery, perfumed vortex, following Geraldine and losing her a hundred times.

On one of these occasions she was captured by Duane Mallett

and convoyed to the supper-room, where later she became utterly transfigured into a laughing, blushing, sparkling, delicious creature, small ears singing with her first venturesome glass of champagne.

All the world seemed laughing with her; life itself was only an endless bubble of laughter, swelling the gay, unending chorus; life was the hot breeze from scented fans stirring a thousand roses; life was the silken throng and its whirling and its feverish voices crying out to her to live!

Her childhood's playmate had come back a stranger, but already he was being transformed, through the magic of laughter, into the boy she remembered; awkwardness of readjusting her relations with him had entirely vanished; she called him dear Duane, laughed at him, chatted with him, appealed, contradicted, rebuked, tyrannised, until the young fellow was clean swept off his feet.

Then Dysart came, and for the second time the note of coquetry was struck, clearly, unmistakably, through the tension of a moment's preliminary silence; and Duane, dumb, furious, yielded her only when she took Dysart's arm with a finality that became almost insolent as she turned and looked back at her childhood's comrade, who followed, scowling at Dysart's graceful back.

Confused by his hurt and his anger, which seemed out of all logical proportion to the cause of it, he turned abruptly and collided with Grandcourt, who had edged up that far, waiting for the opportunity of which Dysart, as usual, robbed him.

Grandcourt apologised, muttering something about Mrs. Severn wishing him to find Miss Seagrave. He stood, awkwardly, looking after Geraldine and Dysart, but not offering to follow them.

"Lot of debutantes here - the whole year's output," he said vaguely. "What a noisy supper-room - eh, Mallett? I'm rather afraid champagne is responsible for some of it."

Duane started forward, halted.

"Did you say Mrs. Severn wants Miss Seagrave?"

"Y - yes.... I'd better go and tell her, hadn't I?"

He flushed heavily, but made no movement to follow Geraldine and Dysart, who had now entered the conservatory and disappeared.

For a full minute, uncomfortably silent, the two men stood side by side; then Duane said in a constrained voice:

"I'll speak to Miss Seagrave, if you'll find her brother and Mrs. Severn"; and walked slowly toward the palm-set rotunda.

When he found them - and he found them easily, for Geraldine's overexcited laughter warned and guided him - Dysart, her fan in his hands, looked up at Duane intensely annoyed, and the young girl tossed away a half-destroyed rose and glanced up, the laughter dying out from lips and eyes.

"Kathleen sent for you," said Duane drily.

"I'll come in a minute, Duane."

"In a moment," repeated Dysart insolently, and turned his back.

The colour surged into Mallett's face; he turned sharply on his heel.

"Wait!" said Geraldine; "Duane - do you hear me?"

"I'll take you back," began Dysart, but she passed in front of him and laid her hand on Mallett's arm.

"Won't you wait for me, Duane?"

And suddenly things seemed to be as they had been in their childhood, the resurgence swept them both back to the old and stormy footing again.

"Duane!"

"What?"

"I tell you to wait for me - *here*!" She stamped her foot.

He scowled - but waited. She turned on Dysart:

"Good-night!" - offering her hand with decision.

Dysart began: "But I had expected -"

"*Good-night!*"

Dysart stared, took the offered hand, hesitated, started to speak, thought better of it, made a characteristically graceful obeisance, and an excellent exit, all things considered.

Geraldine drew a deep breath, moved forward through the flower-set dimness a step or two, halted, and, as Mallett came up, passed her arm through his.

"Duane," she said, "the champagne has gone to my head."

"Nonsense!"

"It *has*! My cheeks are queer - the skin fits too tight. My legs don't belong to me - but they'll do."

She laughed and turned toward him; her feverish breath touched his cheek.

"My first dinner! Isn't it disgraceful? But how could I know?"

"You mustn't let it scare you."

"It doesn't. I don't care. I knew something would go wrong. I - the truth is, that I don't know how to act - how to accept my liberty. I don't know how to use it. I'm a perfect fool.... Do you think Kathleen will notice this? Isn't it terrible! She never dreamed I would touch any wine. Do I look - queer?"

"No. It isn't so, anyway - and you'll simply lean on me -"

"Oh, my knees are perfectly steady. It's only that they don't seem to belong to me. I'm - I'm excited - I've laughed too much - more than I have ever laughed in all the years of my life put together. You don't know what I mean, do you, Duane? But it's true; I've talked to-night more than I ever have in any one week.... And it's gone to my head - all this - all these people who laugh with me over nothing - follow me, tell me I am pretty, ask me for dances, favours, beg me for a word with them - as though I would need asking or urging! - as though my impulse is not to open my heart to every one of them - open my arms to them - thank them on my knees for being here - for being nice to me - all these boys who make little circles around me - so funny, so quaint in their formality -"

She pressed his arm tighter.

"*Let* me rattle on - let me babble, Duane. I've years of silence to make up for. Let me talk like a fool; *you* know I'm not one.... Oh, the happiness of this one night! - the happiness of it! I never shall have enough dancing, never enough of pleasure.... I - I'm perfectly mad over pleasure; I like men.... I suppose the champagne makes me frank about it - but I don't care - I do like men -"

"*That* one?" demanded Mallett, halting her on the edge of the palms which screened the conservatory doors.

"You mean Mr. Dysart? Yes - I - do like him."

"Well, he's married, and you'd better not," he snapped.

"C-can't I *like* him?" in piteous astonishment which set the colour flying into his face.

"Why, yes - of course - I didn't mean -"

"*What* did you mean? Isn't it - shouldn't he be -"

"Oh, it's all right, Geraldine. Only he's a sort of a pig to keep you away from - others -"

"Other - *pigs*?"

He turned sharply, seized her, and forcibly turned her toward the light. She made no effort to control her laughter, excusing it between breaths:

"I didn't mean to turn what you said into ridicule; it came out before I meant it.... Do let me laugh a little, Duane. I simply cannot care about anything serious for a while - I want to be frivolous -"

"Don't laugh so loud," he whispered.

She released his arm and sank down on a marble seat behind the flowering oleanders.

"Why are you so disagreeable?" she pouted. "I know I'm a perfect fool, and the champagne has gone to my silly head - and you'll never catch me this way again.... Don't scowl at me. Why don't you act like other men? Don't you know how?"

"Know how?" he repeated, looking down into the adorably flushed face uplifted. "Know how to do what?"

"To flirt. I don't. Everybody has tried to teach me to-night - everybody except you ... Duane.... I'm ready to go home; I'll go. Only my head is whirling so - Tell me - *are* you glad to see me again?... Really?... And you don't mind my folly? And my tormenting you?... And my - my turning *your* head a little?"

"You've done *that*," he said, forcing a laugh.

"Have I?... I knew it.... You see, I am horridly truthful to-night. *In vino veritas!* ... Tell me - did I, all by myself, turn that too-experienced head of yours?"

"You're doing it now," he said.

She laughed deliciously. "Now? Am I? Yes, I know I am. I've made a lot of men think hard to-night.... I didn't know I could; I never before thought of it.... And - even *you*, too?... You're not very serious, are you?"

"Yes, I am. I tell you, Geraldine, I'm about as much in love with you as -"

"In *love*!"

"Yes -"

"No!"

"Yes, I am -"

But she would not have it put so crudely.

"You dear boy," she said, "we'll both be quite sane to-morrow.... No, I don't mind your kissing my hand - I'm dreadfully tired, anyway.... We'll find Kathleen, shall we? My head doesn't buzz much."

"Geraldine," he said, deliberately encircling her waist, "you are only the same small girl I used to know, after all."

"Y-yes, I'm afraid so."

"And you're not really old enough to really care for anybody, are you?"

"Care?"

"Love."

"No, I'm not. Don't talk to me that way, Duane."

He drew her suddenly into his arms and kissed her on the cheek twice, and again on the mouth, as, crimson, breathless, she strained away from him.

"Duane!" she gasped - "why did you?" Then the throbbing of her body and crushed lips made her furious. "Why did you do that?" she cried fiercely - but her voice ended in a dry sob; she covered her head and face with bare arms; her hands tightened convulsively and clenched.

"Oh," she said, "how could you! - when I came to you - feeling - afraid of myself! I know you now. You are what they say you are."

"What do they say I am?" he stammered.

"Horrid - I don't know - wild! - whatever that implies.... I didn't care - I didn't care even to understand, because I thought you generous and nice to me - and I was so confident of you that I came with you and told you I had had some champagne which made my head swim.... And you - did this! It - it was contemptible."

He bit his lip, but said nothing.

"Why did you do it?" she demanded, dropping her arms from her face and staring at him. "Is that the sort of thing you did abroad?"

"Can't you see I'm in love with you?" he said.

"Oh! Is *that* love? Then keep it for your models and - and Bohemian grisettes! A decent man couldn't have done such a thing to me. I - I loathe myself for being silly and weak enough to have touched that wine, but I have more contempt for you than I have for myself. What you did was cowardly!"

Much of the colour had fled from her face; her eyes, bluish underneath the lower lids, turned wearily, helplessly in search of Kathleen.

"I knew I was unfit for liberty," she said, half to herself. "What an ending to my first pleasure!"

"For Heaven's sake, Geraldine," he broke out, "don't take an accident so tragically -"

"I want Kathleen. Do you hear?"

"Very well; I'll find her.... And, whatever you say or think, I *am* in love with you," he added fiercely.

His voice, his words, were meaningless; she was conscious only of the heavy pulse in throat and temple, of the desire for her room and darkness. Lights, music, the scent of dying flowers, laughter, men, all had become abhorrent. Something within her lay bruised and stunned; and, as never before, the vast and terrible phantom of her loneliness rose like a nightmare to menace her.

Later Kathleen came and took her away.

CHAPTER IV

THE YEAR OF DISCRETION

Her first winter resembled, more or less, the first winter of the average debutante.

Under the roof of the metropolitan social temple there was a niche into which her forefathers had fitted. Within the confines of this she expected, and was expected, to live and move and have her being, and ultimately wing upward to her God, leaving the consecrated cubby-hole reserved for her descendants.

She did what her sister debutantes did, and some things they did not do, was asked where they were asked, decorated the same tier of boxes at the opera, appeared in the same short-skirted entertainments of the Junior League, saw what they saw, was seen where they were seen, chattered, danced, and flirted with the same youths, was smitten by the popular "dancing" man, convalesced in average time, smoked her first cigarette, fell a victim to the handsome and horrid married destroyer, recovered with a shock when, as usual, he overdid it, played at being engaged, was kissed once or twice, adored Sembrich, listened ignorantly but with intuitive shudders to her first scandals, sent flowers to Ethel Barrymore, kept Lent with the pure fervour of a conscience troubled and untainted, drove four in the coaching parade, and lunched afterward at the Commonwealth Club, where her name was subsequently put up for election.

Spectacular charities lured her from the Plaza to Sherry's, from Sherry's to the St. Regis; church work beguiled her; women's suffrage, led daintily in a series of circles by Fashion and Wealth, enlisted her passive patronage. She even tried the slums, but the perfume was too much for her.

All the small talk and epigrams of the various petty impinging circles under the social dome passed into and out of her small ears - gossip, epigrams, aphorisms, rumours, apropos surmises, asides, and off-stage observations, subtle with double entendre, harmless and otherwise.

She met people of fashion, of wealth, and both; and now and then encountered one or two of those men and women of real distinction whose names and peregrinations are seldom chronicled in the papers.

She heard the great artists of the two operas sing in private; was regaled with information concerning the remarkable decency or indecency of their private careers. She saw fashionable plays which instructed the public about squalor, murder, and men's mistresses, which dissected very skilfully and artistically the ethics of moral degradation. And being as healthy and curious as the average girl, she found in the theatres material with which to inform herself about certain occult mysteries concerning which, heretofore, she had been left mercifully in doubt.

In spite of Kathleen, it was inevitable that she should acquire from the fashionable in literature, music, and the drama, that sorry and unnecessary wisdom which ages souls.

And if what she saw or heard ever puzzled her, there was always somebody, young or old, to enlighten her innocent perplexity; and with each illumination she shrank a little less aloof from this shabby wisdom gilded with "art," which she could not choose but accept as fact, but the depravity of which she never was entirely able to comprehend.

In March the Seagrave twins arrived at the alleged age of discretion. On their twenty-first birthday the Half Moon Trust Company went solemnly into court and rendered an accounting of its stewardship; the yearly reports which it had made during the term of its trusteeship were brought forward, examined by the court, and the great Half Moon Trust Company was given an honourable discharge. It had done its duty. The twins were masters of their financial and moral fate.

It was about that moribund period of the social solstice when the fag end of the season had fizzled out like a wet firecracker in the April rains; and Geraldine and Kathleen were tired, mentally and bodily. And Scott was buying polo ponies from a British friend and shotguns from a needy gentleman from Long Island.

It had been rather trying work to rid Geraldine of the aspirants for her fortune; during the winter she was proposed to under almost every conceivable condition and circumstance. Kathleen had been bored and badgered and bothered and importuned to the verge of exhaustion; Scott was used, shamelessly, without his suspecting it, and he generally had in tow a string of financially spavined aspirants who linked arms with him from club to club, from theatre to opera, from grille to grille, until he was pleasantly bewildered at his own popularity.

Geraldine was surprised, confused, shamed, irritated in turn with every new importunity. But she remained sensible enough to be quite frank and truthful with Kathleen, except for an exciting secret engagement with Bunbury Gray which lasted for two weeks. And Kathleen was given strength sufficient for each case as it presented itself; and now the fag end of the season died out; the last noble and indigent foreigner had been eluded; the last old beau foiled; the last squab-headed dancing man successfully circumvented. And now the gallinaceous half of the world was leaving town in noisy and glittering migration, headed for temporary roosts all over the globe, from Newport to Nova Scotia, from Kineo to Kara Dagh.

Country houses were opening throughout the Western Hemisphere; Long Island stirred from its long winter lethargy, stung into active life by the Oyster Bay mosquito; town houses closed; terrace, pillar, portico, and windows were already being boarded over; lace curtains came down; textiles went to the cleaners; the fresh scent of camphor and lavender lingered in the mellow half-light of rooms where furniture and pictures loomed linen-shrouded and the polished floor echoed every footstep.

In the sunny gloom of the Seagrave house Geraldine found a grateful retreat from the inspiring glare and confused racket of her first winter; ample time for rest, reverie, and reflection, with only a few intimates to break her meditations, only informality to reckon with, and plenty of leisure to plan for the summer.

Around the house, trees and rhododendrons were now in freshest bloom, flower-beds fragrant, grass tenderly emerald. The moving shadows of maple leaves patterned the white walls of her bedroom; wind-blown gusts of wistaria fragrance, from the long, grapelike, violet-tinted bunches swaying outside the window, puffed out her curtains every morning.

At night subtler perfumes stole upward from the dark garden; the roar of traffic from the avenues was softened; carriage lights in the purpling dusk of the Park moved like firebugs drifting through level wooded vistas. Across the reservoir lakes the jewelled night-zone of the West Side sparkled, reflected across the water in points of trembling flame; south, a gemmed bar of topaz light, upright against the sky, marked the Plaza; beyond, sprinkled into space like constellations dusting endless depths, the lights of the city receded far as the eye could see.

In the zenith the sky is always tinted with the strange, sinister night-glow of the metropolis, red as fire-licked smoke when fog from the bay settles, pallid as the very shadow of light when nights are clear; but it is always there - always will be there after the sun goes down into the western seas, and the eyes of the monstrous iron city burn on through the centuries.

* * * * *

One morning late in April Geraldine Seagrave rode up under the porte-cochere with her groom, dismounted, patted her horse sympathetically, and regarded with concern the limping animal as the groom led him away to the stables. Then she went upstairs.

To Kathleen, who was preparing to go out, she said:

"I had scarcely entered the Park, my dear, when poor Bibi pulled up lame. No, I told Redmond not to saddle another; I suppose Duane will be furious. Where are you going?"

"I don't know. Shall I wait for you? I've ordered a victoria."

"No, thanks. You look so pretty this morning, Kathleen. Sometimes you appear younger than I do. Scott was pig enough to say so the other day when I had a headache. It's true enough, too," she added, smiling.

Kathleen Severn laughed; she looked scarcely more than twenty-five and she knew it.

"You pretty thing!" exclaimed Geraldine, kissing her, "no wonder you attract the really interesting men and leave me the dreadful fledglings! It's bad of you; and I don't see why I'm stupid enough to have such an attractive woman for my closest" - a kiss - "dearest friend! Even Duane is villain enough to tell me that he finds you overwhelmingly attractive. Did you know it?"

Geraldine's careless gaiety seemed spontaneous enough; yet there was the slightest constraint in Kathleen's responsive smile:

"Duane isn't to be taken seriously," she said.

"Not by any means," nodded Geraldine, twirling her crop.

"I'm glad you understand him," observed Kathleen, gazing at the point of her sunshade. She looked up presently and met Geraldine's dark gaze. Again there came that almost imperceptible hesitation; then:

"I certainly do understand Duane Mallett," said Geraldine carelessly.

"Shall I wait for you?" asked Kathleen. "We can lunch out together and drive in the Park later."

"I'm too lazy even to take off my boots and habit. Where's that volume of Mendez you thought fit to hide from me, you wretch?"

"Why on earth did you buy it?"

"I bought it because Rosalie Dysart says Mendez is a great modern master of prose -"

"And Rosalie is a great modern mistress of pose. Don't read Mendez."

"Isn't it necessary for a girl to read -"

"No, it isn't!"

"I don't want to be ignorant. Besides, I'm - curious to know -"

"Be decently curious, dearest. There's a danger mark; don't cross it."

"I don't wish to."

She stretched out her arms, crop in hand, doubled them back, and head tipped on one side, yawned shamelessly at her own laziness.

"Scott is becoming very restless," she said.

"About going away?"

"Yes. I really do think, Kathleen, that we ought to have some respectable country place to go to. It would be nice for Scott and the servants and the horses; and you and I need not stay there if it bores us -"

"Is he still thinking of that Roya-Neh place? It's horridly expensive to keep up. Oh, I knew quite well that Scott would bully you into consenting -"

"Roya-Neh seems to suit us both," admitted the girl indifferently. "The shooting and fishing naturally attract Scott; they say it's secluded enough for you and me to recuperate in; and if we ever want any guests, it's big enough to entertain dozens in.... I really don't care one way or the other; you know I never was very crazy about the country - and poison ivy, and mosquitoes and oil-smelling roads, and hot nights, and the perfume of fertilisers -"

"You poor child!" laughed Kathleen; "you don't know anything about the country except where you've been on Long Island in the immediate vicinity of your grandfather's horrid old place."

"Is it any more agreeable up there near Canada?"

"Roya-Neh is very lovely - of course - but - it's certainly not a wise investment, dear."

"Well, if Scott and I buy it, we'd never wish to sell it -"

"Suppose you were obliged to?"

Geraldine's velvet eyes widened lazily:

"Obliged to? Oh - yes - you mean if we went to smash."

Then her gaze became remote as she stood slowly tapping her gloved palm with her riding-crop.

"I think I'll dress," she said absently.

"Good-bye, then," nodded Kathleen.

"Good-bye," said the girl, turning lightly away across the hall. Kathleen's eyes followed the slender retreating figure, so slimly compact in its buoyancy. There was always something fascinatingly boyish in Geraldine's light, free carriage - just a touch of carelessness in the poise - almost a swing at times to the step. Duane had once said: "She has a bully walk!" Kathleen thought of it as, passing a mirror, she caught sight of herself. And the sudden glimpse of her own warm, rich beauty in all its exquisite maturity startled her. Surely she seemed to be growing younger.

She was. Dark-violet eyes, ruddy hair, a superb figure, a skin so white that it looked fragrant, made Kathleen Severn amazingly attractive. Men found her, to their surprise, rather unresponsive. She was amiable enough, nicely formal, and perfectly bred, it is true, but inclined to that sort of aloofness which is marked by lapses of inattention and the smiling silences of preoccupation.

She had married, very young, an army officer convalescing from Texan fever. He died suddenly on the very eve of their postponed wedding-trip. This was enough to account for lapses of inattention in any woman.

But Kathleen Severn had never been demonstrative. She was slow to care for people. Besides, the responsibility of bringing up the Seagrave twins had been sufficient to subdue anybody's spirits. She was only nineteen and a widow of a month when her distant relative, Magnelius Grandcourt, found her the position as personal guardian of the twins, then aged nine. Now they were twenty-one and she thirty-one; twelve years of service, twelve years of steady fidelity, which long ago had become a changeless and passionate devotion, made up of all she might have given to the dead, and of the unborn happiness she had never known. What other sort of love, if there was any, lay within her undeveloped, nobody knew because nobody had ever aroused it.

Sunshine transformed into great golden transparencies the lowered shades in the living room where Geraldine stood, pensive, distraite, idly twirling her crop by the loop. Presently it flew off her gloved forefinger and fell clattering across the carpetless floor. She bathed and dressed leisurely; later, when luncheon was brought to her, she dropped into a low, wide chair and, ignoring everything except the strawberries, turned her face to the breeze which was softly rattling the southern curtains.

Errant thoughts, light as summer fleece, drifted across her mind. Often, in such moments, she strove to realise that she was now mistress of herself; but never could completely.

"For example: if I want to buy Roya-Neh," she mused, biting into an enormous strawberry, "I can do it.... All I have to do is to say that I'll buy it.... And I can live there if I choose - as long as I choose.... It's a very agreeable sensation.... I can have anything I fancy, without asking Mr. Tappan.... It's rather odd that I don't want anything."

She crossed her ankles and lay back watching the sun-moats floating.

"Suppose," she murmured with perverse humour, "that I wished to build a bungalow in Timbuctoo ... or stand on my head, now, this very moment! Nobody on earth could stop me.... I believe I *will* stand on my head for a change."

The sudden smile made the curve of her cheek delicious. She sprang to her feet, spread her napkin on the polished floor, then gravely bending double, placed both palms flat on the square of damask, balanced and raised her body until the straight, slim limbs were rigidly pointed toward heaven.

Down tumbled her hair; her cheeks crimsoned; then dainty as a lithe and spangled athlete, she turned clean over in the air, landing lightly on both feet breathing fast.

"It's disgraceful!" she murmured; "I am certainly out of condition. Late hours are my undoing. Also cigarettes. I wish I didn't like to smoke."

She lighted one and strolled about the room, knotting up her dark hair, heels clicking sharply over the bare, polished floor.

Lacking a hair-peg, she sauntered off to her own apartments to find one, where she remained, lolling in the chaise-longue, alternately blowing smoke rings into the sunshine and nibbling a bonbon soaked in cologne. Only a girl can accomplish such combinations. How she ever began this silly custom of hers she couldn't remember, except that, when a small child, somebody had forbidden her to taste brandied peach syrup, which she adored; and the odour of cologne being similarly pleasant, she had tried it on her palate and found that it produced agreeable sensations.

It had become a habit. She was conscious of it, but remained indifferent because she didn't know anything about habits.

So all that sunny afternoon she lay in the chaise-longue, alternately reading and dreaming, her scented bonbons at her elbow. Later a maid brought tea; and a little later Duane Mallett was announced. He sauntered in, a loosely knit, graceful figure, still wearing his riding-clothes and dusty boots of the morning.

Geraldine Seagrave had had time enough to discover, during the past winter, that her old playfellow was not at all the kind of man he appeared to be. Women liked him too easily and he liked them without effort. There was always some girl in love with him until he was found kissing another. His tastes were amiably catholic; his caress instinctively casual. Beauty when responsive touched him. No girl he knew needed to remain unconsoled.

The majority of women liked him; so did Geraldine Seagrave. The majority instinctively watched him; so did she. In close acquaintance the man was a disappointment. It seemed as though there ought to be something deeper in him than the lightly humourous mockery with which he seemed to regard his very great talent - a flippancy that veiled always what he said and did and thought until nobody could clearly understand what he really thought about anything; and some people doubted that he thought at all - particularly the thoughtless whom he had carelessly consoled.

Women were never entirely indifferent concerning him; there remained always a certain amount of curiosity, whether they found him attractive or otherwise.

His humourous indifference to public opinions, bordering on effrontery, was not entirely unattractive to women, but it always, sooner or later, aroused their distrust.

The main trouble with Duane Mallett seemed to be his gaily cynical willingness to respond to any advance, however slight, that any pretty woman offered. This responsive partiality was disconcerting enough to make him dreaded by ambitious mothers, and an object of uneasy interest to their decorative offspring who were inclined to believe that a rescue party of one might bring this derelict into port and render him seaworthy for the voyage of life under their own particular command.

Besides, he was a painter. Women like them when they are carefully washed and clothed.

* * * * *

As Duane Mallett strolled into the living-room, Geraldine felt again, as she so often did, a slight sense of insecurity mingle with her liking for the man, or what might have been liking if she could ever feel absolute confidence in him. She had been, at times, very close to caring a great deal for him, when now and again it flashed over her that there must be in him something serious under his brilliant talent and the idle perversity which mocked at it.

But now she recognised in his smile and manner everything that kept her from ever caring to understand him - the old sense of insecurity in his ironical formality; and her outstretched hand fell away from his with indifference.

"I didn't have the happiness of riding with you, after all," he said, serenely seating himself and dropping one lank knee over the other. "Promises wouldn't be valuable unless somebody broke a lot now and then."

"You probably had the happiness of riding with some other woman."

He nodded.

"Who, this time?"

"Rosalie Dysart."

Rumour had been busy with their names recently. The girl's face became expressionless.

"Sorry you didn't come," he said, looking out of the window where the flapping shade revealed a lilac in bloom.

"How long did you wait for me?"

"About a minute. Then Rosalie passed -"

"Rosalies will always continue to pass through your career, my omnivorous friend.... Did it even occur to you to ride over here and find out why I missed our appointment?"

"No; why didn't you come?"

"Bibi went lame. I'd have had another horse saddled if I hadn't seen you, over my shoulder, join Mrs. Dysart."

"Too bad," he commented listlessly.

"Why? You had a perfectly good time without me, didn't you?"

"Oh, yes, pretty good. Delancy Grandcourt was out after luncheon, and when Rosalie left he stuck to me and talked about you until I let my horse bolt, and it stirred up a few mounted policemen and riding-schools, I can tell you!"

"Oh, so you lunched with Mrs. Dysart?"

"Yes. Where is Kathleen?"

"Driving," said the girl briefly. "If you don't care for any tea, there is mineral water and a decanter over there."

He thanked her, rose and mixed himself what he wanted, and began to walk leisurely about, the ice tinkling in the glass which he held. At intervals he quenched his thirst, then resumed his aimless promenade, a slight smile on his face.

"Has anything particularly interesting happened to you, Duane?" she asked, and somehow thought of Rosalie Dysart.

"No."

"How are your pictures coming on?"

"The portrait?" he asked absently.

"Portrait? I thought all the very grand ladies you paint had left town. Whose portrait are you painting?"

Before he answered, before he even hesitated, she knew.

"Rosalie Dysart's," he said, gazing absently at the lilac-bush in flower as the wind-blown curtain revealed it for a moment.

She lifted her dark eyes curiously. He began to stir the ice in his glass with a silver paper-cutter.

"She is wonderfully beautiful, isn't she?" said the girl.

"Overwhelmingly."

Geraldine shrugged and gazed into space. She didn't exactly know why she had given that little hitch to her shoulders.

"I'd like to paint Kathleen," he observed.

A flush tinted the girl's cheeks. She said nervously:

"Why don't you ask her?"

"I've meant to. Somehow, one doesn't ask things lightly of Kathleen."

"One doesn't ask things of some women at all," she remarked.

He looked up; she was examining her empty teacup with fixed interest.

"Ask what sort of thing?" he inquired, walking over to the table and resting his glass on it.

"Oh, I don't know what I meant. Nothing. What is that in your glass? Let me taste it.... Ugh! It's Scotch!"

She set back the glass with a shudder. After a few moments she picked it up again and tasted it disdainfully.

"Do you like this?" she demanded with youthful contempt.

"Pretty well," he admitted.

"It tastes something like brandied peaches, doesn't it?"

"I never noticed that it did."

And as he remained smilingly aloof and silent, at intervals, tentatively, uncertain whether or not she exactly cared for it, she tasted the iced contents of the tall, frosty glass and watched him where he sat loosely at ease flicking at sun-moats with the loop of his riding-crop.

"I'd like to see a typical studio," she said reflectively.

"I've asked you to mine often enough."

"Yes, to tea with other people. I don't mean that way. I'd like to see it when it's not all dusted and in order for feminine inspection. I'd like to see a man's studio when it's in shape for work - with the gr-r-reat painter in a fine frenzy painting, and the model posing madly -"

"Come on, then! If Kathleen lets you, and you can stand it, come down and knock some day unexpectedly."

"O Duane! I *couldn't*, could I?"

"Not with propriety. But come ahead."

"Naturally, impropriety appeals to you."

"Naturally. To you, too, doesn't it?"

"No. But wouldn't it astonish you if you heard a low, timid knocking some day when you and your Bohemian friends were carousing and having a riotous time there -"

"Yes, it would, but I'm afraid that low, timid knocking couldn't be heard in the infernal uproar of our usual revelry."

"Then I'd knock louder and louder, and perhaps kick once or twice if you didn't come to the door and let me in."

He laughed. After a moment she laughed, too; her dark eyes were very friendly now. Watching the amusement in his face, she continued to sip from his tall, frosted glass, quite unconscious of any distaste for it. On the contrary, she experienced a slight exhilaration which was gradually becoming delightful to her.

"Scotch-and-soda is rather nice, after all," she observed. "I had no idea - *What* is the matter with you, Duane?"

"You haven't swallowed all that, have you?"

"Yes, is it much?"

He stared, then with a shrug: "You'd better cut out that sort of thing."

"What?" she asked, surprised.

"What you're doing."

"Tasting your Scotch? Pooh!" she said, "it isn't strong. Do you think I'm a baby?"

"Go ahead," he said, "it's your funeral."

Legs crossed, chin resting on the butt of his riding-crop, he lay back in his chair watching her.

Women of her particular type had always fascinated him; Fifth Avenue is thronged with them in sunny winter mornings - tall, slender, faultlessly gowned girls, free-limbed, narrow of wrist and foot; cleanly built, engaging, fearless-eyed; and Geraldine was one of a type characteristic of that city and of the sunny Avenue where there pass more beautiful women on a December morning than one can see abroad in half a dozen years' residence.

How on earth this hemisphere has managed to evolve them out of its original material nobody can explain. And young Mallett, recently from the older hemisphere, was still in a happy trance of surprise at the discovery.

Lounging there, watching her where she sat warmly illumined by the golden light of the window-shade, he said lazily:

"Do you know that Fifth Avenue is always thronged with you, Geraldine? I've nearly twisted my head off trying not to miss the assorted visions of you which float past afoot or driving. Some day one of them will unbalance me. I'll leap into her victoria, ask her if she'd mind the temporary inconvenience of being adored by a stranger; and if she's a good sport she'll take a chance. Don't you think so?"

"It's more than I'd take with you," said the girl.

"You've said that several times."

He laughed, then looked up at her half humorously, half curiously.

"*You* would be taking no chances, Geraldine."

"I'd be taking chances of finding you holding some other girl's hands within twenty-four hours. And you know it."

"Hasn't anybody ever held yours?"

Displeasure tinted her cheeks a deeper red, but she merely shrugged her shoulders.

It was true that in the one evanescent and secret affair of her first winter she had not escaped the calf-like transports of Bunbury Gray. She had felt, if she had not returned them, the furtively significant pressure of men's hands in the gaiety and whirl of things; ardent and chuckle-headed youth had declared itself in conservatories and in corners; one impetuous mauling from a smitten Harvard boy of eighteen had left her furiously vexed with herself for her passive attitude while the tempest passed. True, she had vigorously reproved him later. She had, alas, occasion, during her first season, to reprove several demonstrative young men for their unconventionally athletic manner of declaring their suits. She had been far more severe with the humble, unattractive, and immobile, however, than with the audacious and ornamental who had attempted to take her by storm. A sudden if awkward kiss followed by the fiery declaration of the hot-headed disturbed her less than the persistent stare of an enamoured pair of eyes. As a child the description of an assault on a citadel always interested her, but she had neither sympathy nor interest in a siege.

Now, musing there in the sunlight on the events of her first winter, she became aware that she had been more or less instructed in the ways of men; and, remembering, she lifted her disturbed eyes to inspect this specimen of a sex which often perplexed but always interested her.

"What are you smiling about, Duane?" she asked defiantly.

"Your arraignment of me when half the men in town have been trying to marry you all winter. You've made a reputation for yourself, too, Geraldine."

"As what?" she asked angrily.

"A head-twister."

"Do you mean a flirt?"

"Oh, Lord! Only the French use that term now. But that's the idea, Geraldine. You are a born one. I fell for the first smile you let loose on me."

"You seem to have been a sort of general Humpty Dumpty for falls all your life, Duane," she said with dangerous sweetness.

"Like that immortal, I've had only one which permanently shattered me."

"Which was that, if you please?"

"The fall you took out of me."

"In other words," she said disdainfully, "you are beginning to make love to me again."

"No.... I *was* in love with you."

"You were in love with yourself, young man. You are on such excellent terms with yourself that you sympathise too ardently with any attractive woman who takes the least and most innocent notice of you."

He said, very much amused: "I was perfectly serious over you, Geraldine."

"The selfish always take themselves seriously."

It was she, however, who now sat there bright-eyed and unsmiling, and he was still laughing, deftly balancing his crop on one finger, and glancing at her from time to time with that glimmer of ever-latent mockery which always made her restive at first, then irritated her with an unreasoning desire to hurt him somehow. But she never seemed able to reach him.

"Sooner or later," she said, "women will find you out, thoroughly."

"And then, just think what a rush there will be to marry me!"

"There will be a rush to avoid you, Duane. And it will set in before you know it -" She thought of the recent gossip coupling his name with Rosalie's, reddened and bit her lip in silence. But somehow the thought irritated her into speech again:

"Fortunately, I was among the first to find you out - the first, I think."

"Heavens! when was that?" he asked in pretended concern, which infuriated her.

"You had better not ask me," she flashed back. "When a woman suddenly discovers that a man is untrustworthy, do you think she ever forgets it?"

"Because I once kissed you? What a dreadful deed!"

"You forget the circumstances under which you did it."

He flushed; she had managed to hurt him, after all. He began patiently:

"I've explained to you a dozen times that I didn't know -"

"But I *told* you!"

"And I couldn't believe you -"

"But you expect me to believe *you*?"

He could not exactly interpret her bright, smiling, steady gaze.

"The trouble with you is," she said, "that there is nothing to you but good looks and talent. There was once, but it died - over in Europe - somewhere. No woman trusts a man like you. Don't you know it?"

His smile did not seem to be very genuine, but he

answered lightly:

"When I ask people to have confidence in me, it will be time for them to pitch into me."

"Didn't you once ask me for your confidence - and then abuse it?" she demanded.

"I told you I loved you - if that is what you mean. And you doubted it so strenuously that, perhaps I might be excused for doubting it myself.... What is the use of talking this way, Geraldine?"

There was a ring of exasperation in her laughter. She lifted his glass, sipped a little, and, looking over it at him:

"I drink to our doubts concerning each other: may nothing ever occur to disturb them."

Her cheeks had begun to burn, her eyes were too bright, her voice unmodulated.

"Whether or not you ever again take the trouble to ask me to trust you in that way," she said, "I'll tell you now why I don't and why I never could. It may amuse you. Shall I?"

"By all means," he replied amiably; "but it seems to me as though you are rather rough on me."

"You were rougher with me the first time I saw you, after all those years. I met you with perfect confidence, remembering what you once were. It was my first grown-up party. I was only a fool of a girl, merely ignorant, unfit to be trusted with a liberty I'd never before had.... And I took one glass of champagne and it - you know what it did.... And I was bewildered and frightened, and I told you; and - you perhaps remember how my confidence in my old play-fellow was requited. Do you?"

Reckless impulse urged her on. Heart and pulses were beating very fast with a persistent desire to hurt him. Her animation, brilliant colour, her laughter seemed to wing every word like an arrow. She knew he shrank from what she was saying, in spite of his polite attention, and her fresh, curved cheek and parted lips took on a brighter tint. Something was singing, seething in her veins. She lifted her glass, set it down, and suddenly pushed it from her so violently that it fell with a crash. A wave of tingling heat mounted to her face, receded, swept back again. Confused, she straightened up in her chair, breathing fast. *What* was coming over her? Again the wave surged back with a deafening rush; her senses struggled, the blood in her ran riot. Then terror clutched her. Neither lips nor tongue were very flexible when she spoke.

"Duane - if you don't mind - would you go away now? I've a wretched headache."

He shrugged and stood up.

"It's curious," he said reflectively, "how utterly determined we seem to be to misunderstand each other. If you would give me half a chance - well - never mind."

"I wish you would go," she murmured, "I really am not well." She could scarcely hear her own voice amid the deafening tumult of her pulses. Fright stiffened the fixed smile on her lips. Her plight paralysed her for a moment.

"Yes, I'll go," he answered, smiling. "I usually am going somewhere - most of the time."

He picked up hat, gloves, and crop, looked down at her, came and stood at the table, resting one hand on the edge.

"We're pretty young yet, Geraldine.... I never saw a girl I cared for as I might have cared for you. It's true, no matter what I have done, or may do.... But you're quite right, a man of that sort isn't to be considered" - he laughed and pulled on one glove - "only - I knew as soon as I saw you that it was to be you or - everybody. First, it was anybody; then it was you - now it's everybody. Good-bye."

"Good-bye," she managed to say. The dizzy waves swayed her; she rested her cheeks between both hands and, leaning there heavily, closed her eyes to fight against it. She had been seated on the side of a lounge; and now, feeling blindly behind her, she moved the cushions aside, turned and dropped among them, burying her blazing face. Over her the scorching vertigo swept, subsided, rose, and swept again. Oh, the horror of it! - the shame, the agonised surprise. What was this dreadful thing that, for the second time, she had unwittingly done? And this time it was so much more terrible. How could such an accident have happened to her? How could she face her own soul in the disgrace of it?

Fear, loathing, frightened incredulity that this could really be herself, stiffened her body and clinched her hands under her parted lips. On them her hot breath fell irregularly.

Rigid, motionless, she lay, breathing faster and more feverishly. Tears came after a long while, and with them relaxation and lassitude. She felt that the dreadful thing which had seized and held her was letting go its hold, was freeing her body and mind; and as it slowly released her and passed on its terrible silent way, she awoke and sat up with a frightened cry - to find herself lying on her own bed in utter darkness.

A moment later her bedroom door opened without a sound and the lightfrom the hall streamed over Kathleen's bare shoulders and braided hair.

"Geraldine?"

The girl scarcely recognised Kathleen's altered voice. She lay listening, silent, motionless, staring at the white figure.

"Dearest, I thought you called me. May I come in?"

"I am not well."

But Kathleen entered and stood beside the bed, looking down at her in the dim light.

"Dearest," she began tremulously, "Duane told me you had a headache and had gone to your room to lie down, so I didn't disturb you -"

"Duane," faltered the girl, "is he here? What did he say?"

"He was in the library before dinner when I came in, and he warned me not to waken you. Do you know what time it is?"

"No."

"It is after midnight.... If you feel ill enough to lie here, you ought to be undressed. May I help you?"

There was no answer. For a moment Kathleen stood looking down at the girl in silence; then a sudden shivering seized her; she strove to control it, but her knees seemed to give way under it and she dropped down beside the bed, throwing both arms around Geraldine's neck.

"Oh, don't, *don't*!" she whimpered. "It is too terrible! It ruined your father and your grandfather! Darling, I couldn't bear to tell you this before, but now I've got to tell you! It is in your blood. Seagraves die of it! Do you understand?"

"W-what?" stammered the girl.

"That all their lives they did what - what you have done to-day - that you have inherited their terrible inclinations. Even as a little child you frightened me. Have you forgotten what you and I talked over and cried over after your first party?"

The girl said slowly: "I don't know how - it - happened, Kathleen. Duanecame in.... I tasted what he had in his glass....

I don't know why I did it. I wish I were dead!"

"There is only one thing to do - never to touch anything - anything -"

"Y-yes, I know that I must not. But how was I to know before? Will you tell me?"

"You understand *now*, thank God!"

"N-not exactly.... Other girls seem to do as they please without danger.... It is amazing that such a horrible thing should happen to me -"

"It is a shameful thing that it should happen to any woman. And the horror of it is that almost every hostess in town lets girls of your age run the risk. Darling, don't you know that the only chance a woman has with the world is in her self-control? When that goes, her chances go, every one of them! Dear - we have latent in us much the same vices that men have. We have within us the same possibilities of temptations, the same capacity for excesses, the same capabilities for resistance. Because you are a girl, you are not immune from unworthy desires."

"I know it. The - the dreadful thing about it is that I do desire such things. Perhaps I had better not even nibble sugar scented with cologne -"

"Do you do *that*?" faltered Kathleen.

"I did not know there was any danger in it," sobbed the girl. "You have scared me terribly, Kathleen."

"Is that true about the cologne?"

"Y-yes."

"You don't do it now, do you?"

"Yes."

"You don't do it every day, do you?"

"Yes, several times."

"How long" - Kathleen's lips almost refused to move - "how long have you done this?"

"For a long time. I've been ashamed of it. It's - it's the alcohol in it that I like, isn't it? I never thought of it in that way till now."

Kathleen, on her knees by the bedside, was crying silently. The girl slipped from her arms, turned partly over, and lying on her back, stared upward through the darkness.

So this was the secret reason that, unsuspected, had long been stirring her to instinctive uneasiness, which had made her half ashamed, half impatient with this silly habit which already inconvenienced her. Yet even now she could not feel any real alarm; she could not understand that the fangs of a habit can poison when plucked out. Of course there was now only one thing to do - keep aloof from everything. That would be easy. The tingling warmth of the perfume was certainly agreeable, but she must not risk even such a silly indulgence as that. Really, it was a very simple matter. She sat up, supporting her weight on one arm.

"Kathleen, darling," she whispered, bending forward and drawing the elder woman up onto the bed, "you mustn't be frightened about me. I've learned some things I didn't know. Do you think Duane -" In the darkness the blood scorched her face, the humiliation almost crushed her. But she went on: "Do you think Duane suspects that - that -"

"I don't think Duane suspects anything," said Kathleen, striving to steady her voice. "You came in here as soon as you felt - ill; didn't you?"

"I - yes -"

She could say no more. How she came to be on her bed in her own room she could not remember. It seemed to her as though she had fallen asleep on the lounge. Somehow, after Duane had gone, she must have waked and gone to her own room. But she could not recollect doing it.

Now she realised that she was tired, wretched, feverish. She suffered Kathleen to undress her, comb her hair, bathe her, and dry the white, slender body and limbs in which the veins still burned and throbbed.

When at length she lay between the cool sheets, silent, limp, heavy-lidded, Kathleen turned out the electric brackets and lighted the candle.

"Dear," she said, trying to speak cheerfully, "do you know what your brother has done?"

"What?" asked Geraldine drowsily.

"He has bought Roya-Neh, if you please, and he invites you to draw a check for half of it and to move there next week. As for me, I was furious with him. What do you think?"

Her voice softened to a whisper; she bent over the girl, looking closely at the closed lids. Under them a faint bluish tint faded into the whiteness of the cheek.

"Darling, darling!" whispered Kathleen, bending closer over the sleeping girl, "I love you so - I love you so!" And even as she said it, between the sleeper's features and her own floated the vision of Scott's youthfully earnest face; and she straightened suddenly to her full height and laid her hand on her breast in consternation. Under the fingers' soft pressure her heart beat faster. Again, with new dismay, this incredible sensation was stealing upon her, threatening to transform itself into something real, something definite, something not to be stifled or ignored.

She extinguished the candle; as she felt her way out of the darkness, arms extended, far away in the house she heard a door open and shut, and she bent over the balustrade to listen.

"Is that you, Scott?" she called softly.

"Yes; Duane and I did some billiards at the club." He looked up at her, the same slight pucker between his brows, boyishly slender in his evening dress. "You're not going to bed at once, are you, Kathleen, dear?"

"Yes, I am," she said briefly, backing into her own room, but holding the door ajar so that she could look out at him.

"Oh, come out and talk to a fellow," he urged; "I'm quite excited about this Roya-Neh business -"

"You're a perfect wretch, Scott. I don't want to talk about your unholy extravagance."

The boy laughed and stood at ease looking at the pretty face partly disclosed between door and wall with darkness for a velvety background.

"Just come out into the library while I smoke one cigarette," he began in his wheedling way. "I'm dying to talk to you about the game-preserve -"

"I can't; I'm not attired for a tete-a-tete with anything except my pillow."

"Then put on one of those fetching affairs you wear sometimes -"

"Oh, Scott, you are a nuisance!"

When, a few moments later, she came into the library in a delicate shimmering thing and little slippers of the same elusive tint, Scott jumped up and dragged a big chair forward.

“You certainly are stunning, Kathleen,” he said frankly; “you look twenty with all the charm of thirty. Sit here; I've a map of the Roya-Neh forest to show you.”

He drew up a chair for himself, lifted a big map from the table, and, unrolling it, laid it across her knees. Then he began to talk enthusiastically about lake and stream and mountain, and about wild boar and deer and keepers and lodges; and she bent her pretty head over the map, following his moving pencil with her eyes, sometimes asking a question, sometimes tracing a road with her own delicate finger.

Once or twice it happened that their hands touched en passant; and at the light contact, she was vaguely aware that somewhere, deep within her, the same faint dismay awoke; that in her, buried in depths unsuspected, something incredible existed, stirred, threatened.

“Scott, dear,” she said quietly, “I am glad you are happy over Roya-Neh forest, but it *was* too expensive, and it troubles me; so I'm going to sleep to dream over it.”

“You sweet little goose!” laughed the boy impulsively, passing his arm around her. He had done it so often to this nurse and mother.

They both rose abruptly; the map dropped; his arm fell away from her warm, yielding body.

He gazed at her flushed face rather stupidly, not realising yet that the mother and nurse and elder sister had vanished like a tinted bubble in that strange instant - that Kathleen was gone - that, in her calm, sweet, familiar guise stood a woman - a stranger, exquisite, youthful, with troubled violet eyes and vivid lips, looking at him as though for the first time she had met his gaze across the world.

She recovered her composure instantly.

“I'm sorry, Scott, but I'm too sleepy to talk any more. Besides, Geraldine isn't very well, and I'm going to doze with one eye open. Good-night, dear.”

“Good-night,” said the boy vacantly, not offering the dutiful embrace to which he and she had so long and so lightly been accustomed.

CHAPTER V

ROYA-NEH

Late on a fragrant mid-June afternoon young Seagrave stood on the Long Terrace to welcome a guest whose advent completed a small house-party of twelve at Roya-Neh.

"Hello, Duane!" cried the youthful landowner in all the pride of new possession, as Mallett emerged from the motor; "frightfully glad to see you, old fellow! How is it in town? Did you bring your own rods? There are plenty here. What do you think of my view? Isn't that rather fine?" - looking down through the trees at the lake below. "There are bass in it. Those things standing around under the oaks are only silly English fallow deer. Sorry I got 'em. What do you think of my house? It's merely a modern affair worked up to look old and colonial.... Yes, it certainly does resemble the real thing, but it isn't. No Seagraves fit and bled here. Those are Geraldine's quarters up there behind the leaded windows. Those are Kathleen's where the dinky woodbine twineth. Mine face the east, and yours are next. Come on out into the park -"

"Not much!" returned young Mallett. "I want a bath!"

"The park," interrupted Scott excitedly, "is the largest fenced game-preserve in America! It's only ten minutes to the Sachem's Gate, if we walk fast."

"I want a bath and fresh linen."

"Don't you care to see the trout? Don't you want to try to catch a glimpse of a wild boar? I should think you'd be crazy to see -"

"I'm crazy about almost any old thing when I'm well scrubbed; otherwise, I'm merely crazy. That was a wild trip up. I'm all over cinders."

A woman came quietly out onto the terrace, and Duane instantly divined it, though his back was toward her and her skirts made no sound.

"Oh, is that you, Kathleen?" he cried, pivoting. "How d'ye do?" with a vigorous handshake. "Every time I see you you're three times as pretty as I thought you were when I last saw you."

"Neat but involved," said Kathleen Severn. "You have a streak of cinder across that otherwise fascinating nose."

"I don't doubt it! I'm going. Where's Geraldine?"

"Having her hair done in your honour; return the compliment by washing your face. There's a maid inside to show you."

"Show me how to wash my face!" exclaimed Duane, delighted. "This is luxury -"

"I want him to see the Gray Water before it's too late, with the sunlight on the trees and the big trout jumping," protested Scott.

"I'll do my own jumping if you'll furnish the tub," observed Duane. "Where's that agreeable maid who washes your guests' faces?"

Kathleen nodded an amused dismissal to them. Arm in arm they entered the house, which was built out of squared blocks of field stone. Scott motioned the servants aside and did the piloting himself up a broad stone stairs, east along a wide sunny corridor full of nooks and angles and antique sofas and potted flowers.

"Not that way," he said; "Dysart is in there taking a nap. Turn to the left."

"Dysart?" repeated Duane. "I didn't know there was to be anybody else here."

"I asked Jack Dysart because he's a good rod. Kathleen raised the deuce about it when I told her, but it was too late. Anyway, I didn't know she had no use for him. He's certainly clever at dry-fly casting. He uses pneumatic bodies, not cork or paraffine."

"Is his wife here?" asked Duane carelessly.

"Yes. Geraldine asked her as soon as she heard I'd written to Jack. But when I told her the next day that I expected you, too, she got mad all over, and we had a lively talk-fest. What was there wrong in my having you and the Dysarts here at the same time? Don't you get on?"

"Charmingly," replied Duane airily.... "It will be very interesting, I think. Is there anybody else here?"

"Delancy Grandcourt. Isn't he the dead one? But Geraldine wanted him. And there's that stick of a Quest girl, and Bunbury Gray. Naida came over this afternoon from the Tappans' at Iron Hill - thank goodness -"

"I didn't know my sister was to be here."

"Yes; and you make twelve, counting Geraldine and me and the Pink 'uns."

"You didn't tell me it was to be a round-up," repeated Duane, absently surveying his chintz-hung quarters. "This is a pretty place you've given me. Where do you get all your electric lights? Where do you get fancy plumbing in this wilderness?"

"Our own plant," explained the boy proudly. "Isn't that corking water? Look at it - heavenly cold and clear, or hot as hell, whichever way you're inclined -" turning on a silver spigot chiselled like a cherub. "That water comes from Cloudy Lake, up there on that dome-shaped mountain. Here, stand here beside me, Duane, and you can see it from your window. That's the Gilded Dome - that big peak. It's in our park. There are a few elk on it, not many, because they'd starve out the deer. As it is, we have to cut browse in winter. For Heaven's sake, hurry, man! Get into your bath and out again, or we'll miss the trout jumping along Gray Water and Hurryon Brook."

"Let 'em jump!" retorted Duane, forcibly ejecting his host from the room and locking the door. Then, lighting a cigarette, he strolled into the bath room and started the water running into the porcelain tub.

He was in excellent spirits, quite undisturbed by the unexpected proximity of Rosalie Dysart or the possible renewal of their hitherto slightly hazardous friendship. He laid his cigarette aside for the express purpose of whistling while undressing.

Half an hour later, bathed, shaved, and sartorially freshened, he selected a blue corn-flower from the rural bouquet on his dresser, drew it through his buttonhole, gave a last alluring twist to his tie, surveyed himself in the mirror, whistled a few bars, was perfectly satisfied with himself, then, unlocking the door, strolled out into the corridor. Having no memory for direction, he took the wrong turn.

A distractingly pretty maid laid aside her sewing and rose from her chair to set him right; he bestowed upon her his most courtly thanks. She was unusually pretty, so he thanked her again, and she dimpled, one hand fingering her apron's edge.

"My child," said he gravely, "are you by any fortunate chance as good as you are ornamental?"

She replied that she thought she was.

"In that case," he said, "this is one of those rare occasions in a thankless world where goodness is amply and instantly rewarded."

She made a perfunctory resistance, but looked after him, smiling, as he sauntered off down the hallway, rearranging the blue corn-flower in his button-hole. At the turn by the window, where potted posies stood, he encountered Rosalie Dysart in canoe costume - sleeves rolled up, hair loosened, becomingly tanned, and entirely captivating in her thoughtfully arranged disarray.

"Why, Duane!" she exclaimed, offering both her hands with that impulsively unstudied gesture she carefully cultivated for such occasions.

He took them; he always took what women offered.

"This is very jolly," he said, retaining the hands and examining her with unfeigned admiration. "Tell me, Mrs. Dysart, are you by any fortunate chance as good as you are ornamental?"

"I heard you ask that of the maid around the corner," said Rosalie coolly. "Don't let the bucolic go to your head, Mr. Mallett." And she disengaged her hands, crossed them behind her, and smiled back at him. It was his punishment. Her hands were very pretty hands, and well worth holding.

"That maid," he said gravely, "has excellent manners. I merely complimented her upon them.... What else did you - ah - hear, Mrs. Dysart?"

"What one might expect to hear wherever you are concerned. I don't mind. The things you do rather gracefully seem only offensive when other men do them.... Have you just arrived?"

"An hour ago. Did you know I was coming?"

"Geraldine mentioned it to everybody, but I don't think anybody swooned at the news.... My husband is here."

She still confronted him, hands behind her, with an audacity which challenged - her whole being was always a delicate and perpetual challenge. There are such women. Over her golden-brown head the late summer sunlight fell, outlining her full, supple figure and bared arms with a rose light.

"Well?" she asked.

"If only you *were* as good as you are ornamental," he said, looking at her impudently. "But I'm afraid you're not."

"What would happen to me if I were?"

"Why," he said with innocent enthusiasm, "you would have *your* reward, too, Mrs. Dysart."

"The sort of reward which I heard you bestow a few moments ago upon that maid? I'm no longer the latter, so I suppose I'm not entitled to it, am I?"

The smile still edged her pretty mouth; there was an instant when matters looked dubious for her; but a door opened somewhere, and, still smiling, she slipped by him and vanished into a neighbouring corridor.

Howker, the old butler, met him at the foot of the stairs.

"Tea is served on the Long Terrace, sir. Mr. Seagrave wishes to know whether you would care to see the trout jumping on the Gray Water this evening? If so, you are please not to stop for tea, but go directly to the Sachem's Gate. Redmond will guide you, sir."

"All right, Howker," said Duane absently; and strolled on along the hall, thinking of Mrs. Dysart.

The front doors swung wide, opening on the Long Terrace, which looked out across a valley a hundred feet below, where a small lake glimmered as still as a mirror against a background of golden willows and low green mountains.

There were a number of young people pretending to take tea on the terrace; and some took it, and others took other things. He knew them all, and went forward to greet them. Geraldine Seagrave, a new and bewitching coat of tan tinting cheek and neck, held out her hand with all the engaging frankness of earlier days. Her clasp was firm, cool, and nervously cordial - the old confident affection of childhood once more.

"I am *so* glad you came, Duane. I've really missed you." And sweeping the little circle with an eager glance; "You know everybody, I think. The Dysarts have not yet appeared, and Scott is down at the Gate Lodge. Come and sit by me, Duane."

Two or three girls extended their hands to him - Sylvia Quest, shy and quiet; Muriel Wye, white-skinned, black-haired, red-lipped, red-cheeked, with eyes like melted sapphires and the expression of a reckless saint; and his blond sister, Naida, who had arrived that afternoon from the Tappans' at Iron Hill, across the mountain.

Delancy Grandcourt, uncouth and highly coloured, stood up to shake hands; Bunbury Gray, a wiry, bronzed little polo-playing squadron man, hailed Duane with enthusiasm.

"Awfully glad to see you, Bunny," said Duane, who liked him immensely - "oh, how are you?" offering his hand to Reginald Wye, a hard-riding, hard-drinking, straight-shooting young man, who knew nothing on earth except what concerned sport and the drama. He and his sister of the sapphire eyes and brilliant cheeks were popularly known as the Pink 'uns.

Jack Dysart arrived presently, graceful, supple, always smilingly, elaborate of manner, apparently unconscious that he was not cordially admired by the men who returned his greeting. Later, Rosalie, came, enchantingly demure in her Greuze-like beauty. Chardin might have made her; possibly Fragonard. She did not resemble the Creator's technique. Dresden teacups tinkled, ice clattered in tall glasses, the two fountains splashed away bravely, prettily modulated voices made agreeable harmony on the terrace, blending with the murmur of leaves overhead as the wind stirred them to gossip. Over all spread a calm evening sky.

"Tea, dear?" asked Geraldine, glancing up at Mrs. Dysart. Rosalie shook her head with a smile.

Lang, the second man, was flitting about, busy with a decanter of Scotch. A moment later Rosalie signified her preference for it with a slight nod. Geraldine, who sat watching indifferently the filling of Mrs. Dysart's glass, suddenly leaned back and turned her head sharply, as though the aroma from glass and decanter were distasteful to her. In a few minutes she rose, walked over to the parapet, and stood leaning against the coping, apparently absorbed in the landscape.

The sun hung low over the flat little tree-clad mountains, which the lake, now inlaid with pink and gold, reflected. A few fallow deer moved quietly down there, ruddy spots against the turf.

Duane, carrying his glass with him, rose and stepped across the strip of grass to her side, and, glancing askance at her, was on the point of speaking when he discovered that her eyes were shut and her face colourless and rigid.

"What is it?" he asked surprised. "Are you feeling faint, Geraldine?"

She opened her eyes, velvet dark and troubled, but did not turn around.

"It's nothing," she answered calmly. "I was thinking of several things."

"You look so white -"

"I am perfectly well. Bend over the parapet with me, Duane. Look at those rocks down there. What a tumble! What a death!"

He placed his glass between them on the coping, and leaned over. She did not notice the glass for a moment. Suddenly she wheeled, as though he had spoken, and her eyes fell on the glass.

"What *is* the matter?" he demanded, as she turned on her heel and moved away.

"I'm a trifle nervous, I believe. If you want to see the big trout breaking on Hurryon, you'd better come with me."

She was walking swiftly down the drive to the south of the house. He overtook her and fell into slower step beside her.

The sun had almost disappeared behind the mountains; bluish haze veiled the valley; a horizon of dazzling yellow flecked with violet faded upward to palest turquoise. High overhead a feathered cloud hung, tinged with rose.

The south drive was bordered deep in syringas, all over snowy bloom; and as they passed they inhaled the full fragrance of the flowers with every breath.

"It's like heaven," said Duane; "and you are not incongruous in the landscape, either."

She looked around at him; the smile that curved her mouth had the faintest suspicion of tenderness about it.

She said slowly:

"Do you realise that I am genuinely glad to see you? I've been horrid to you. I don't yet really believe in you, Duane. I detest some of the things you are and say and do; but, after all, I've missed you. Incredible as it sounds, I've been a little lonely without you."

He said gaily: "When a woman becomes accustomed to chasing the family cat out of the parlour with the broom, she misses the sport when the cat migrates permanently."

"Have you migrated - permanently? O Duane! I thought you *did* care for me - in your own careless fashion -"

"I do. But I'm not hopelessly enamoured of your broom-stick!"

Her laugh was a little less spontaneous, as she answered:

"I know I have been rather free with my broom. I'm sorry."

"You *have* made some sweeping charges on that cat!" he said, laughing.

"I know I have. That was two months ago. I don't think I am the morally self-satisfied prig I was two months ago.... I'd be easier on anything now, even a cat. But don't think I mean more than I do mean, Duane," she added hastily. "I've missed you a little. I want you to be nice to me.... After all, you're the oldest friend I have except Kathleen."

"I'll be as nice as you'll let me," he said. They turned from the driveway and entered a broad wood road. "As nice as you'll let me," he repeated.

"I won't let you be sentimental, if that's what you mean," she observed.

"Why?"

"Because you are you."

"In a derogatory sense?"

"Somewhat. I might be like you if I were a man, and had your easy, airy, inconsequential way with women. But I won't let you have it with me, my casual friend. Don't hope for it."

"What have I ever done -"

"Exactly what you're doing now to Rosalie - what you did to a dozen women this winter - what you did to me" - she turned and looked at him - "the first time I ever set eyes on you since we were children together. I know you are not to be taken seriously; almost everybody knows that! And all the same, Duane, I've thought about you a lot in these two months up here, and - I'm happy that you've come at last.... You won't mistake me and try to be sentimental with me, will you?"

She laid her slim, sun-tanned hand on his arm; they walked on together through the woodland where green bramble sprays glimmered through clustering tree trunks and the fading light turned foliage and undergrowth to that vivid emerald which heralds dusk.

"Duane," she said, "I'm dreadfully restless and I cannot account for it.... Perhaps motherless girls are never quite normal; I don't know. But, lately, the world has seemed very big and threatening around me.... Scott is nice to me, usually; Kathleen adorable.... I - I don't know what I want, what it is I miss."

Her hand still rested lightly on his arm as they walked forward. She was speaking at intervals almost as though talking in an undertone to herself:

"I'm in - perplexity. I've been troubled. Perhaps that is what makes me tolerant of you; perhaps that's why I'm glad to see you.... Trouble is a new thing to me. I thought I had troubles - perhaps I had as a child. But this is deeper, different, disquieting."

"Are you in love?" he asked.

"No."

"Really?"

"Really."

"Then what -"

"I can't tell you. Anyway, it won't last. It can't, ... Can it?"

She looked around at him, and they both laughed a little at her inconsequence.

"I feel better for pretending to tell you, anyway," she said, as they halted before high iron gates hung between two granite posts from which the woven wire fence of the game park, ten feet high, stretched away into the darkening woods on either hand.

"This is the Sachem's Gate," she said; "here is the key; unlock it, please."

Inside they crossed a stream dashing between tanks set with fern and tall silver birches.

"Hurryon Brook," she said. "Isn't it a beauty? It pours into the Gray Water a little farther ahead. We must hasten, or it will be too dark to see the trout."

Twice again they crossed the rushing brook on log bridges. Then through the trees stretching out before them they caught sight of the Gray Water, crinkling like a flattened sheet of hammered silver.

Everywhere the surface was starred and ringed and spattered by the jumping fish; and now they could hear them far out, splash! slap! clip-clap! splash! - hundreds and hundreds jumping incessantly, so that the surface of the water was constantly broken over the entire expanse.

Now and then some great trout, dark against the glimmer, leaped full length into the air; everywhere fish broke, swirled, or rolled over, showing "colour."

"There is Scott," she whispered, attuning her voice to the forest quiet - "out there in that canoe. No, he hasn't taken his rod; he seldom does; he's perfectly crazy over things of this sort. All day and half the night he's out prowling about the woods, not fishing, not shooting, just mousing around and listening and looking. And for all his dreadfully expensive collection of arms and rods, he uses them very little. See him out there drifting about with the fish breaking all around - some within a foot of his canoe! He'll never come in to dress for dinner unless we call him."

And she framed her mouth with both hands and sent a long, clear call floating out across the Gray Water.

"All right; I'll come!" shouted her brother. "Wait a moment!"

They waited many moments. Dusk, lurking in the forest, peered out, casting a gray net over shore and water. A star quivered, another, then ten, and scores and myriads.

They had found a seat on a fallen log; neither seemed to have very much to say. For a while the steady splashing of the fish sounded like the uninterrupted music of a distant woodland waterfall. Suddenly it ceased as if by magic. Not another trout rose; the quiet was absolute.

"Is not this stillness delicious?" she breathed.

"It is sweeter when you break it."

"Please don't say such things.... *Can't* you understand how much I want you to be sincere to me? Lately, I don't know why, I've seemed to feel so isolated. When you talk that way I feel more so. I - just want - a friend."

There was a silence; then he said lightly:

"I've felt that way myself. The more friends I make the more solitary I seem to be. Some people are fashioned for a self-imprisonment from which they can't break out, and through which no one can penetrate. But I never thought of you as one of those."

"I seem to be at times - not exactly isolated, but unable to get close to - to Kathleen, for example. Do you know, Duane, it might be very good for me to have you to talk to."

"People usually like to talk to me. I've noticed it. But the curious part of it is that they have nothing to give me in exchange for my attention."

"What do you mean?"

He laughed. "Oh, nothing. I amuse people; I know it. You - and everybody - say I am all cleverness and froth - not to be taken seriously. But did it ever occur to you that what you see in me you evoke. Shallowness provokes shallowness, levity, lightness, inconsequence - all are answered by their own echo.... And you and the others think it is I who answer."

He laughed, not looking at her:

"And it happens that you - and the others - are mistaken. If I appear to be what you say I am, it is merely a form of self-defence. Do you think I could endure the empty nonsense of a New York winter if I did not present to it a surface like a sounding-board and let Folly converse with its own echo - while, behind it, underneath it, Duane Mallett goes about his own business."

Astonished, not clearly understanding, she listened in absolute silence. Never in all her life had she heard him speak in such a manner. She could not make out whether bitterness lay under his light and easy speech, whether a maliciously perverse humour lurked there, whether it was some new mockery.

He said carelessly: "I give what I receive. And I have never received any very serious attention from anybody. I'm only Duane Mallett, identified with the wealthy section of society you inhabit, the son of a wealthy man, who went abroad and dabbled in colour and who paints pictures of pretty women. Everybody and the newspapers know me. What I see of women is a polished coquetry that mirrors my fixed smirk; what I see of men is less interesting."

He looked out through the dusk at the darkening water:

"You say you are beginning to feel isolated. Can anybody with any rudiment of intellect feel otherwise in the social environment you and I inhabit - where distinction and inherited position count for absolutely nothing unless propped up by wealth - where any ass is tolerated whose fortune and lineage pass inspection - where there is no place for intelligence and talent, even when combined with breeding and lineage, unless you are properly ballasted with money enough to forget that you have any?"

He laughed.

"So you feel isolated? I do, too. And I'm going to get out. I'm tired of decorating a set where the shuttle-cock of conversation is worn thin, frayed, ragged! Where the battledore is fashionable scandal and the players half dead with ennui and their neighbour's wives -"

"Duane!"

"Oh, Lord, you're a world-wise graduate at twenty-two! Truth won't shock you, more's the pity.... As for the game - I'm done with it; I can't stand it. The amusement I extract doesn't pay.

Good God! and you wonder why I kiss a few of you for distraction's sake, press a finger-tip or two, brush a waist with my sleeve!"

He laughed unpleasantly, and bent forward in the darkness, clasped hands hanging between his knees.

"Duane," she said in astonishment, "what do you mean? Are you trying to quarrel with me, just when, for the first time, something in this new forest country seemed to be drawing us together, making us the comrades we once were?"

"We're too old to be comrades. That's book rubbish. Men and women have nothing in common, intellectually, unless they're in love. For company, for straight conversation, for business, for sport, a man would rather be with men. And either you and I are like everybody else or we're going to really care for each other. Not for your pretty face and figure, or for my grin, my six feet, and thin shanks; I can care for face and figure in any woman. What's the use of marrying for what you'll scarcely notice in a month?... If you *are you*, Geraldine, under all your attractive surface there's something else which you have never given me."

"Wh - what?" she asked faintly.

"Intelligent interest in me."

"Do you mean," she said slowly, "that you think I underestimate you?"

"Not as I am. I don't amount to much; but I might if you cared."

"Cared for you?"

"No, confound it! Cared for what I could be."

"I - I don't think I understand. What could you be?"

"A man, for one thing. I'm a thing that dances. A fashionable portrait painter for another. The combination is horrible."

"You are a successful painter."

"Am I? Geraldine, in all the small talk you and I have indulged in since my return from abroad, have you ever asked me one sincere, intelligent, affectionate question about my work?"

"I - yes - but I don't know anything about -"

He laughed, and it hurt her.

"Don't you understand," she said, "that ordinary people are very shy about talking art to a professional -"

"I don't want you to talk art. Any little thing with blue eyes and blond curls can do it. I wanted you to see what I do, say what you think, like it or damn it - only do something about it! You've never been to my studio except to stand with the perfumed crowd and talk commonplaces in front of a picture."

"I can't go alone."

"Can't you?" he asked, looking closely at her in the dusk, so close that she could see every mocking feature.

"Yes," she said in a low, surprised voice, "I could go alone - anywhere - with you.... I didn't realise it before, Duane."

"You never tried. You once mistook an impulse of genuine passion for the sort of thing I've done since. You made a terrific fuss about being kissed when I saw, as soon as I saw you, that I wanted to win you, if you'd let me. Since then you've chosen the key-note of our relations, not I, and you don't like my interpretation of my part."

For a while she sat silent, preoccupied with this totally new revelation of a man about whom she supposed she had long ago made up her mind.

"I'm glad we've had this talk," she said at last.

"I am, too. I haven't asked you to fall in love with me; I haven't asked for your confidence. I've asked you to take an intelligent, affectionate interest in what I might become, and perhaps you and I won't be so lonely if you do."

He struck a match in the darkness and lighted a cigarette. Close inshore Scott Seagrave's electric torch flashed. They heard the velvety scraping of the canoe, the rattle and thump as he flung it, bottom upward, on the sandy point.

"Hello, you people! Where are you?" - sweeping the wood's edge with his flash-light - "oh, there you are. Isn't this glorious? Did you ever see such a sight as those big fellows jumping?"

"Meanwhile," said his sister, rising, "our guests are doubtless yelling with hunger. What time is it, Duane? Half-past eight? Please hurry, Scott; we've got to get back and dress in five minutes!"

"I can do it easily," announced her brother, going ahead to light the path. And all the way home he discussed aloud upon the stripping, hatching, breeding, care, and diseases of trout, never looking back, and quite confident that they were listening attentively to his woodland lecture.

"Duane," she said, lowering her voice, "do you think all our misunderstandings are ended?"

"Certainly," he replied gaily. "Don't you?"

"But how am I going to make everybody think you are not frivolous?"

"I am frivolous. There's lots of froth to me - on top. You know that sort of foam you see on grass-stems in the fields. Hidden away inside is a very clever and busy little creature. He uses the froth to protect himself."

"Are you going to froth?"

"Yes - until -"

"Until what?"

"You -"

"Go on."

"Shall I say it?"

"Yes."

"Well, then, unless you and I find each other intellectually satisfactory."

"You said only a man - in love with a woman - could find her interesting in that way."

"Yes. What of it?"

"Nothing.... Only I'm afraid you'll have to froth, then," she said, laughing. "I haven't any intention of falling in love with you, Duane, and you'll find me stupid if I don't. Do you know that what you intimate is very horrid?"

"Why?"

"Yes, it is. Besides, it's a sort of threat -"

"A threat?"

"Certainly. You threaten to - you know perfectly well what you threaten to do unless I immediately consider the possibility of our - caring for each other - sentimentally."

"But what do you care if you don't care?"

"I - don't. All the same it's horrid and - and unfair. Suppose I was frothy and behaved -"

"Misbehaved?"

"Yes. Just because you wouldn't agree to take a sentimental interest in me?"

"I *would* agree! I'll agree now!"

"Suppose you wouldn't?"

"I can't imagine -"

"Oh, Duane, be honest! And I'll tell you flatly - if you do misbehave. Just because I don't particularly desire to rush into your arms -"

"But I haven't threatened to."

Unconsciously she laid her hand on his arm again, slipping it a little way under.

"You're just as you were years ago - just the dearest of playmates. We're not too old to play, are we?"

"I can't with you; it's too dangerous."

"What nonsense! Yes, you can. You like me for my intelligence in spite of what you say about men and women -"

"I wouldn't care for your intelligence if I were not in -"

"Duane, stop, please!"

"In danger," he continued blandly, "of proving my proposition."

"You are insufferable. I am as intelligent as you."

"I know it, but it wouldn't attract me unless -"

"It ought to," she said hastily. "And, Duane, I'm going to make you take me into account. I'm going to exercise a man's privilege with you by - by saying frankly - several things -"

"What things?"

The amused mockery in his voice gave her courage.

"For one thing, I'm going to tell you that people - gossip - that there are - are -"

"Rumours?" he asked in pretended anxiety.

"Yes.... About you and - of course they are silly and contemptible; but what's the use of being attentive enough to a woman - careless enough to give colour to them?"

After an interval he said: "Perhaps you'll tell me who beside myself these rumours concern?"

"You know, don't you?"

"There might be several," he said coolly. "Who is it?"

For a moment a tiny flash of anger made her cheeks hot. Then she said:

"You know perfectly well it's Rosalie. I think we have become good enough comrades for me to use a man's privilege -"

"Men wouldn't permit themselves that sort of privilege," he said, laughing.

"Aren't men frank with their friends?" she demanded hotly.

"About as frank as women."

"I thought -" She hesitated, tingling with the old desire to hurt him, flick him in the raw, make him wince in his exasperating complacency. Then, "I've said it anyhow. I'm trying to show an interest in you - as you asked me to do -"

He turned in the darkness, caught her hand:

"You dear little thing," he whispered, laughing.

CHAPTER VI

ADRIFT

During the week the guests at Roya-Neh were left very much to their own devices. Nobody was asked to do anything; there were several good enough horses at their disposal, two motor cars, a power-boat, canoes, rods, and tennis courts and golf links. The chances are they wanted sea-bathing. Inland guests usually do.

Scott Seagrave, however, concerned himself little about his guests. All day long he moused about his new estate, field-glasses dangling, cap on the back of his head, pockets bulging with untidy odds and ends until the increasing carelessness of his attire and manners moved Kathleen Severn to protest.

"I don't know what is the matter with you, Scott," she said. "You were always such a fastidious boy - even dandified. Doesn't anybody ever cut your hair? Doesn't somebody keep your clothes in order?"

"Yes, but I tear 'em again," he replied, carefully examining a small dark-red newt which he held in the palm of one hand. "I say, Kathleen, look at this little creature. I was messing about under the ledges along Hurryon Brook, and found this amphibious gentleman occupying the ground-floor apartment of a flat stone."

Kathleen craned her dainty neck over the shoulder of his

ragged shooting coat.

"He's red enough to be poisonous, isn't he? Oh, do be careful!"

"It's only a young newt. Take him in your hand; he's cool and clammy and rather agreeable."

"Scott, I won't touch him!"

"Yes, you will!" He caught her by the arm; "I'm going to teach you not to be afraid of things outdoors. This lizard-like thing is perfectly harmless. Hold out your hand!"

"Oh, Scott, don't make me -"

"Yes, I will. I thought you and I were going to be in thorough accord and sympathy and everything else."

"Yes, but you mustn't bully me."

"I'm not. I merely want you to get over your absurd fear of live things, so that you and I can really enjoy ourselves. You said you would, Kathleen."

"Can't we be in perfect sympathy and roam about and - and everything, unless I touch such things?"

He said reproachfully, balancing the little creature on his palm: "The fun is in being perfectly confident and fearless. You have no idea how I like all these things. You said you were going to like 'em, too."

"I do - rather."

"Then take this one and pet it."

She glanced at the boy beside her, realising how completely their former relations were changing.

Long ago she had given all her heart to the Seagrave children - all the unspent passion in her had become an unswerving devotion to them. And now, a woman still young, the devotion remained, but time was modifying it in a manner sometimes disquieting. She tried not to remember that now, in Scott, she had a man to deal with, and tried in vain; and dealt with him weakly, and he was beginning to do with her as he pleased.

"You do like to bully me, don't you?" she said.

"I only want you to like to do what I like to do."

She stood silent a moment, then, with a shudder, held out her hand, fingers rigid and wide apart.

"Oh!" she protested, as he placed the small dark-red amphibian on the palm, where it crinkled up and lowered its head.

"That's the idea!" he said, delighted. "Here, I'll take it now. Some day you'll be able to handle snakes if you'll only have patience."

"But I don't want to." She stood holding out the contaminated hand for a moment, then dropped on her knees and scrubbed it vigorously in the brook.

"You see," said Scott, squatting cheerfully beside her, "you and I don't yet begin to realise the pleasure that there is in these woods and streams - hidden and waiting for us to discover it. I wouldn't bother with any other woman, but you've always liked what I like, and its half the fun in having you see these things. Look here, Kathleen, I'm keeping a book of field notes." He extracted from his stuffed pockets a small leather-covered book, fished out a stylograph, and wrote the date while she watched over his shoulder.

"Discovered what seems to be a small dark-red newt under a stone near Hurryon Brook. Couldn't make it bite me, so let

Kathleen hold it. Query: Is it a land or water lizard, a salamander, or a newt; and what does it feed on and where does it deposit its eggs?"

Kathleen's violet eyes wandered to the written page opposite.

"Did you really see an otter, Scott?"

"Yes, I did!" he exclaimed. "Out in the Gray Water, swimming like a dog. That was yesterday afternoon. It's a scarce creature here. I'll tell you what, Kathleen; we'll take our luncheon and go out and spend the day watching for it."

"No," she said, drying her hands on her handkerchief, "I can't spend every minute of the day with you. Ask some other woman."

"What other woman?" She was gazing out at the sunlit ripples. A little unquiet thrill leaped through her veins, but she went on carelessly:

"Take some pretty woman out with you. There are several here -"

"Pretty woman," he repeated. "Do you think that's the only reason I want you to come?"

"Only reason? What a silly thing to say, Scott. I am not a pretty woman to you - in that sense -"

"You are the prettiest I ever saw," he said, looking at her; and again the unquiet thrill ran like lightning through her veins. But she only laughed carelessly and said:

"Oh, of course, Geraldine and I expect our big brother to say such things."

"It has nothing to do with Geraldine or with brothers," he said doggedly. She strove to laugh, caught his gaze, and, discountenanced, turned toward the stream.

"We can cross on the stepping stones," she suggested. And after a moment: "Are you coming?"

"See here, Kathleen," he said, "you're not acting squarely with me."

"What do you mean?"

"No, you're not. I'm a man, and you know it."

"Of course you are, Scott."

"Then I wish you'd recognise it. What's the use of mortifying me when I act - speak - behave as any man behaves who - who - is - fond of a - person."

"But I don't mean to - to mortify you. What have I done?"

He dug his hands into the pockets of his riding breeches, took two or three short turns along the bank, came back to where she was standing.

"You probably don't remember," he said, "one night this spring when - when -" He stopped short. The vivid tint in her cheeks was his answer - a swift, disconcerting answer to an incomplete question, the remainder of which he himself had scarcely yet analysed.

"Scott, dear," she said steadily, in spite of her softly burning cheeks, "I will be quite honest with you if you wish. I do know what you've been trying to say. I am conscious that you are no longer the boy I could pet and love and caress without embarrassment to either of us. You are a man, but try to remember that I am several years older – "

"Does that matter!" he burst out.

"Yes, dear, it does.... I care for you - and Geraldine - more than for anybody in the world. I understand your loyalty to me, Scott, and I - I love it. But don't confuse it with any serious sentiment."

"I do care seriously."

"You make me very happy. Care for me very, very seriously; I want you to; I - I need it. But don't mistake the kind of affection that we have for each other for anything deeper, will you?"

"Don't you want to care for me - that way?"

"Not *that* way, Scott."

"Why?"

"I've told you. I am so much older -"

"*Couldn't* you, all the same?"

She was trembling inwardly. She leaned against a white birch-tree and passed one hand across her eyes and upward through the thick burnished hair.

"No, I couldn't," she whispered.

The boy walked to the edge of the brook. Past him hurried the sun-tipped ripples; under them, in irregular wedge formation, little ones ahead, big ones in the rear, lay a school of trout, wavering silhouettes of amber against the bottom sands.

One arm encircling the birch-tree, she looked after him in silence, waiting. And after a while he turned and came back to her:

"I suppose you knew I fell in love with you that night when - when - you remember, don't you?"

She did not answer.

"I don't know how it happened," he said: "something about you did it. I want to say that I've loved you ever since. It's made me serious.... I haven't bothered with girls since. You are the only woman who interests me. I think about you most of the time when I'm not doing something else," he explained naively. "I know perfectly well I'm in love with you because I don't dare touch you - and I've never thought of - of kissing you good-night as we used to before that night last spring.... You remember that we didn't do it that night, don't you?"

Still no answer, and Kathleen's delicate, blue-veined hands were clenched at her sides and her breath came irregularly.

"That was the reason," he said. "I don't know how I've found courage to tell you. I've often been afraid you would laugh at me if I told you.... If it's only our ages - you seem as young as I do...." He looked up, hopefully; but she made no response.

The boy drew a long breath.

"I love you, anyway," he said. "And that's how it is."

She neither spoke nor stirred.

"I suppose," he went on, "because I was such a beast of a boy, you can never forget it."

"You were the sweetest, the best -" Her voice broke; she swung about, moved away a few paces, stood still. When he halted behind her she turned.

"Dearest," she said tremulously, "let me give you what I can - love, as always - solicitude, companionship, deep sympathy in your pleasures, deep interest in your amusements.... Don't ask for more; don't think that you want more. Don't try to change the loyalty and love you have always had for something you - neither of us understand - neither of us ought to desire - or even think of -"

"Why?"

"Can't you understand? Even if I were not too old in years, I dare not give up what I have of you and Geraldine for this new - for anything more hazardous.... Suppose it were so - that I could venture to think I cared for you that way? What might I put in peril? - Geraldine's affection for me - perhaps her relations with you.... And the world is cynical, Scott, and you are wealthy even among very rich men, and I was your paid guardian - quite penniless - engaged to care for and instruct -"

"Don't say such things!" he said angrily.

"The world would say them - your friends - perhaps Geraldine might be led to doubt - Oh, Scott, dear, I know, I know! And above all - I am afraid. There are too many years between us - too many blessed memories of my children to risk.... Don't try to make me care for you in any other way."

A quick flame leaped in his eyes.

"*Could* I?"

"No!" she exclaimed, appalled.

"Then why do you ask me not to try? I believe I could!"

"You cannot! You cannot, believe me. Won't you believe me? It must not happen; it is all wrong - in every way -"

He stood looking at her with a new expression on his face.

"If you are so alarmed," he said slowly, "you must have already thought about it. You'll think about it now, anyway."

"We are both going to forget it. Promise that you will!" She added hurriedly: "Drop my hand, please; there is Geraldine -

and Mr. Grandcourt, too!... Tell me - do my eyes look queer? Are they red and horrid?... Don't look at me that way. For goodness' sake, don't display any personal interest in me. Go and turn over some flat rocks and find some lizards!"

Geraldine, bare-armed and short-skirted, came swinging along the woodland path, Delancy Grandcourt dogging her heels, as usual, carrying a pair of rods and catching the artificial flies in the bushes at every step.

"We're all out of trout at the house!" she called across to the stream to her brother. "Jack Dysart is fishing down the creek with Naida and Sylvia. Where is Duane?"

"Somewhere around, I suppose," replied Scott sulkily. His sister took a running jump, cleared the bank, and alighted on a rock in the stream. Poised there she looked back at Grandcourt, laughed, sprang forward from stone to stone, and leaped to the moss beside Kathleen.

"Hello, dear!" she nodded. "Where did you cross? And where is Duane?"

"We crossed by the log bridge below," replied Kathleen. She added: "Duane left us half an hour ago. Wasn't it half an hour ago, Scott?" with a rising inflection that conveyed something of warning, something of an appeal. But on Scott's face the sullen disconcerted expression had not entirely faded, and his sister inspected him curiously. Then without knowing why, exactly, she turned and looked at Kathleen.

There was a subdued and dewy brilliancy in Kathleen's eyes, a bright freshness to her cheeks, radiantly and absurdly youthful; and something else - something so indefinable, so subtle, that only another woman's instinct might divine it - something invisible and inward, which transfigured her with a youthful loveliness almost startling.

They looked at one another. Geraldine, conscious of

something she could not understand, glanced again at her sulky brother.

"What's amiss, Scott?" she asked. "Has anything gone wrong anywhere?"

Scott, pretending to be very busy untangling Grandcourt's cast from the branches of a lusty young birch, said, "No, of course not," and the girl, wondering, turned to Kathleen, who sustained her questioning eyes without a tremor.

"What's the matter with Scott?" asked his sister. "He's the guiltiest-looking man - why, it's absurd, Kathleen! Upon my word, the boy is blushing!"

"What!" exclaimed Scott so furiously that everybody laughed. And presently Geraldine asked again where Duane was.

"Rosalie Dysart is canoeing on the Gray Water, and she hailed him and he left us and went down to the river," said Kathleen carelessly.

"Did Duane join her?"

"I think so -" She hesitated, watching Geraldine's sombre eyes. "I really don't know," she added. And, in a lower voice: "I wish either Duane or Rosalie would go. They certainly are behaving unwisely."

Geraldine turned and looked through the woods toward the Gray Water.

"It's their affair," she said curtly. "I've got to make Delancy fish or we won't have enough trout for luncheon. Scott!" calling to her brother, "your horrid trout won't rise this morning. For goodness' sake, try to catch something beside lizards and water-beetles!"

For a moment she stood looking around her, as though

perplexed and preoccupied. There was sunlight on the glade and on the ripples, but the daylight seemed to have become duller to her.

She walked up-stream for a little distance before she noticed Grandcourt plodding faithfully at her heels.

"Oh!" she said impatiently, "I thought you were fishing. You must catch something, you know, or we'll all go hungry."

"Nothing bites on these bally flies," he explained.

"Nothing bites because your flies are usually caught in a tree-top. Trout are not arboreal. I'm ashamed of you, Delancy. If you can't keep your line free in the woods" - she hesitated, then reddening a little under her tan - "you had better go and get a canoe and find Duane Mallett and help him catch - something worth while."

"Don't you want me to stay with you?" asked the big, awkward fellow appealingly. "There's no fun in being with Rosalie and Duane."

"No, I don't. Look! Your flies are in that bush! Untangle them and go to the Gray Water."

"Won't you come, too, Miss Seagrave?"

"No; I'm going back to the house.... And don't you dare return without a decent brace of trout."

"All right," he said resignedly. The midges bothered him; he mopped his red face, tugged at the line, but the flies were fast in a hazel bush.

"Damn this sort of thing," he muttered, looking piteously after Geraldine. She was already far away among the trees, skirts wrapped close to avoid briers, big straw hat dangling in one hand.

As she walked toward the Sachem's Gate she was swinging her hat and singing, apparently as unconcernedly as though care rested lightly upon her young shoulders.

Out on the high-road a number of her guests whizzed past in one of Scott's motors; there came a swift hail, a gust of wind-blown laughter, and the car was gone in a whirl of dust. She stood in the road watching it recede, then walked forward again toward the house.

Her accustomed elasticity appeared to have left her; the sun was becoming oppressive; her white-shod feet dragged a little, which was so unusual that she straightened her head and shoulders with nervous abruptness.

"What on earth is the matter with me?" she said, half aloud, to herself.

During these last two months, and apparently apropos of nothing at all, an unaccustomed sense of depression sometimes crept upon her.

At first she disregarded it as the purely physical lassitude of spring, but now it was beginning to disquiet her. Once a hazy suspicion took shape - hastily dismissed - that some sense, some temporarily suppressed desire was troubling her. The same idea had awakened again that evening on the terrace when the faint odour from the decanter attracted her. And again she suspected, and shrank away into herself, shocked, frightened, surprised, yet still defiantly incredulous.

Yet her suspicions had been correct. It was habit, disturbed by the tardiness of accustomed tribute, that stirred at moments, demanding recognition.

Since that night in early spring when fear and horror of herself had suddenly checked a custom which she had hitherto supposed to be nothing worse than foolish, twice - at times inadvertently, at times deliberately - she had sought relief from sleepless nervousness and this new depression in the old and apparently harmless manner of her girlhood. For weeks now she had exercised little control of herself, feeling immune, yet it scared her a little to recognise again in herself the restless premonitions of desire. For here, in the sunshine of the forest-bordered highway, that same dull uneasiness was stirring once more.

It was true, other things had stirred her to uneasiness that morning - an indefinable impression concerning Kathleen - a definite one which concerned Rosalie Dysart and Duane, and which began to exasperate her.

All her elasticity was gone now; tired without reason, she plodded on along the road in her little white shoes, head bent, brown eyes brooding, striving to fix her wandering thoughts on Duane Mallett to fight down the threatening murmurs of a peril still scarcely comprehended.

"Anyway," she said half aloud, "even if I ever could care for him, I dare not let myself do it with this absurd inclination always threatening me."

She had said it! Scarcely yet understanding the purport of her own words, yet electrified, glaringly enlightened by them, she halted. A confused sense that something vital had occurred in her life stilled her heart and her breathing together.

After a moment she straightened up and walked forward, turned across the lawn and into the syringa-bordered drive.

There was nobody in the terrace except Bunbury Gray in a brilliant waistcoat, who sat smoking a very large faience pipe and reading a sporting magazine. He got up with alacrity when he saw her, fetched her a big wicker chair, evidently inclined to let her divert him.

"Oh, I'm not going to," she observed, sinking into the cushions. For a moment she felt rather limp, then a quiver passed through her, tightening the relaxed nerves.

"Bunbury," she said, "do you know any men who ever get tired of idleness and clothes and their neighbours' wives?"

"Sure," he said, surprised, "I get tired of those things all right. I've got enough of this tailor, for example," looking at his trousers. "I'm tired of idleness, too. Shall we do something and forget the cut of my clothes?"

"What do you do when you tire of people and things?"

"Change partners or go away. That's easy."

"You can't change yourself - or go away from yourself."

"But I don't get tired of myself," he explained in astonishment. She regarded him curiously from the depths of her wicker chair.

"Bunbury, do you remember when we were engaged?"

He grinned. "Rather. I wouldn't mind being it again."

"Engaged?"

"Sure thing. Will you take me on again, Geraldine?"

"I thought you cared for Sylvia Quest."

"I do, but I can stop it."

She still regarded him with brown-eyed curiosity.

"Didn't you really tire of our engagement?"

"You did. You said that my tailor is the vital part of me."

She laughed. "Well, you *are* only a carefully groomed

combination of New York good form and good nature, aren't you?"

"I don't know. That's rather rough, isn't it? Or do you really mean it that way?"

"No, Bunny dear. I only mean that you're like the others. All the men I know are about the same sort. You all wear too many ties and waistcoats; you are, and say, and do too many kinds of fashionable things. You play too much tennis, drink too many pegs, gamble too much, ride and drive too much. You all have too much and too many - if you understand that! You ask too much and you give too little; you say too much which means too little. Is there none among you who knows something that amounts to something, and how to say it and do it?"

"What the deuce are you driving at, Geraldine?" he asked, bewildered.

"I'm just tired and irritable, Bunny, and I'm taking it out on you.... Because you were always kind - and even when foolish you were often considerate.... That's a new waistcoat, isn't it?"

"Well - I don't - know," he began, perplexed and suspicious, but she cut him short with a light little laugh and reached out to pat his hand.

"Don't mind me. You know I like you.... I'm only bored with your species. What do you do when you don't know what to do, Bunny?"

"Take a peg," he said, brightening up. "Do you - shall I call somebody -"

"No, please."

She extended her slim limbs and crossed her feet. Lying still there in the sunshine, arms crooked behind her head, she gazed straight out ahead. Light breezes lifted her soft bright hair; the same zephyrs bore from tennis courts on the east the far laughter and calling of the unseen players.

"Who are they?" she inquired.

"The Pink 'uns, Naida, and Jack Dysart. There's ten up on every set," he added, "and I've side obligations with Rosalie and Duane. Take you on if you like; odds are on the Pink 'uns. Or I'll get a lump of sugar and we can play 'Fly Loo.'"

"No, thanks."

A few moments later she said:

"Do you know, somehow, recently, the forest world - all this pretty place of lakes and trees -" waving her arm toward the horizon - "seems to be tarnished with the hard living and empty thinking of the people I have brought into it.... I include myself. The region is redolent of money and the things it buys. I had a better time before I had any or heard about it."

"Why, you've always had it -"

"But I didn't know it. I'd like to give mine away and do something for a living."

"Oh, every girl has that notion once in a lifetime."

"Have they?" she asked.

"Sure. It's hysteria. I had it myself once. But I found I could keep busy enough doing nothing without presenting my income to the Senegambians and spending life in a Wall Street office. Of course if I had a pretty fancy for the artistic and useful - as Duane Mallett has - I suppose I'd get busy and paint things and sell 'em by the perspiration of my brow -"

She said disdainfully: "If you were never any busier than

Duane, you wouldn't be very busy."

"I don't know. Duane seems to keep at it, even here, doesn't he?"

She looked up in surprise: "Duane hasn't done any work since he's been here, has he?"

"Didn't you know? What do you suppose he's about every morning?"

"He's about - Rosalie," she said coolly. "I've never seen any colour box or easel in their outfit."

"Oh, he keeps his traps at Hurryon Lodge. He's made a lot of sketches. I saw several at the Lodge. And he's doing a big canvas of Rosalie down there, too."

"At Hurryon Lodge?"

"Yes. Miller lets them have the garret for a studio."

"I didn't know that," she said slowly.

"Didn't you? People are rather catty about it."

"Catty?"

Sheer surprise silenced her for a while, then hurt curiosity drove her to questions; but little Bunbury didn't know much more about the matter, merely shrugging his shoulders and saying: "It's casual but it's all right."

Later the tennis players, sunburned and perspiring, came swinging up from the courts on their way to the showers. Bunbury began to settle his obligations; Naida and the Pink 'uns went indoors; Jack Dysart, handsome, dishevelled, sat down beside Geraldine, fastening his sleeves.

"I lost twice twenty," he observed. "Bunny is in fifty, I believe. Duane and Rosalie lose."

"Is that all you care about the game?" she asked with a note of contempt in her voice.

"Oh, it's good for one's health," he said.

"So is confession, but there's no sport in it. Tell me, Mr. Dysart, don't you play any game for it's own sake?"

"Two, mademoiselle," he said politely.

"What two?"

"Chess is one."

"What is the other?"

"Love," he replied, smiling at her so blandly that she laughed. Then she thought of Rosalie, and it was on the tip of her tongue to say something impudent. But "Do you do that game very well?" was all she said.

"Would you care to judge how well I do it?"

"As umpire? Yes, if you like."

He said: "We will umpire our own game, Miss Seagrave."

"Oh, we couldn't do that, could we? We couldn't play and umpire, too." Suddenly the thought of Duane and Rosalie turned her bitter and she said:

"We'll have two perfectly disinterested umpires. I choose your wife for one. Whom do you choose?"

Over his handsome face the slightest muscular change passed, but far from wincing he nodded coolly.

"One umpire is enough," he said. "When our game is well on you may ask Rosalie to judge how well I've done it - if you care to."

The bright smile she wore changed. Her face was now only a lovely dark-eyed mask, behind which her thoughts had suddenly begun racing - wild little thoughts, all tumult and confusion, all trembling, too, with some scarcely understood hurt lashing them to recklessness.

"We'll have two umpires," she insisted, scarcely knowing what she said. "I'll choose Duane for the second. He and Rosalie ought to be able to agree on the result of our game."

Dysart turned his head away leisurely, then looked around again unsmiling.

"Two umpires? Soit! But that means you consent to play."

"Play?"

"Certainly."

"With you?"

"With me."

"I'll consider it.... Do you know we have been talking utter nonsense?"

"That's part of the game."

"Oh, then - do you assume that the - the game has already begun?"

"It usually opens that way, I believe."

"And where does it end, Mr. Dysart?"

"That is for you to say," he replied in a lower voice.

"Oh! And what are the rules?"

"The player who first falls really in love loses. There are no stakes. We play as sportsmen - for the game's sake. Is it understood?"

She hesitated, smiling, a little excited, a little interested in the way he put things.

At that same moment, across the lawn, Rosalie and Duane strolled into view. She saw them, and with a nervous movement, almost involuntary, she turned her back on them.

Neither she nor Dysart spoke. She gazed very steadily at the horizon, as though there were sounds beyond the green world's rim. A few seconds later a shadow fell over the terrace at her feet - two shadows intermingled. She saw them on the grass at her feet, then quietly lifted her head.

"We caught no trout," said Rosalie, sitting down on the arm of the chair that Duane drew forward. "I fussed about in that canoe until Duane came along, and then we went in swimming."

"Swimming?" repeated Geraldine, dumfounded.

Rosalie balanced herself serenely on her chair-arm.

"Oh, we often do that."

"Swim - where?"

"Why across the Gray Water, child!"

"But - there are no bath houses -"

Rosalie laughed outright.

"Quite Arcadian, isn't it? Duane has the forest on one side of the Gray Water for a dressing-room, and I the forest on the other side. Then we swim out and shake hands in the middle. Our bathing dresses are drying on Miller's lawn. Please do tell me somebody is scandalised. I've done my best to brighten up this house party."

Dysart, really discountenanced, but not showing it, lighted a cigarette and asked pleasantly if the water was agreeable.

"It's magnificent," said Duane; "it was like diving into a lake of iced Apollinaris. Geraldine, why on earth don't you build some bath houses on the Gray Waters?"

Perhaps she had not heard his question. She began to talk very animatedly to Rosalie about several matters of no consequence. Dysart rose, stretched his sunburned arms with over-elaborate ease, tossed away his cigarette, picked up his tennis bat, and said: "See you at luncheon. Are you coming, Rosalie?"

"In a moment, Jack." She went on talking inconsequences to Geraldine; her husband waited, exchanging a remark or two with Duane in his easy, self-possessed fashion.

"Dear," said Rosalie at last to Geraldine, "I must run away and dry my hair. How did we come out at tennis, Jack?"

"All to the bad," he replied serenely, and nodding to Geraldine and Duane he entered the house, his young wife strolling beside him and twisting up her wet hair.

Duane seated himself and crossed his lank legs, ready for an amiable chat before he retired to dress for luncheon; but Geraldine did not even look toward him. She was lying deep in the chair, apparently relaxed and limp; but every nerve in her was at tension, every delicate muscle taut and rigid, and in her heart was anger unutterable, and close, very close to the lids which shadowed with their long fringe the brown eyes' velvet, were tears.

"What have you been up to all the morning?" he asked. "Did you try the fishing?"

"Yes."

"Anything doing?"

"No."

"I thought they wouldn't rise. It's too clear and hot. That's why I didn't keep on with Kathleen and Scott. Two are enough on bright water. Don't you think so?"

She said nothing.

"Besides," he added, "I knew you had old Grandcourt running close at heel and that made four rods on Hurryon. So what was the use of my joining in?"

She made no reply.

"You didn't mind, did you?" he asked carelessly.

"No."

"Oh, all right," he nodded, not feeling much relieved.

The strange blind anger still possessed her. She lay there immobile, expressionless, enduring it, not trying even to think why; yet her anger was rising against him, and it surged, receded helplessly, flushed her veins again till they tingled. But her lids remained closed; the lashes rested softly on the curve of her cheeks; not a tremor touched her face.

"I am wondering whether you are feeling all right," he ventured uneasily, conscious of the tension between them.

With an effort she took command of herself.

"The sun was rather hot. It's a headache; I walked back by the road."

"*With* the faithful one?"

"No," she said evenly, "Mr. Grandcourt remained to fish."

"He went to worship and remained to fish," said Duane, laughing. The girl lifted her face to look at him - a white little face so strange that the humour died out in his eyes.

"He's a good deal of a man," she said. "It's one of my few pleasant memories of this year - Mr. Grandcourt's niceness to me - and to all women."

She set her elbow on the chair's edge and rested her cheek in her hollowed hand. Her gaze had become remote once more.

"I didn't know you took him so seriously," he said in a low voice. "I'm sorry, Geraldine."

All her composure had returned. She lifted her eyes insolently.

"Sorry for what?"

"For speaking as I did."

"Oh, I don't mind. I thought you might be sorry for yourself."

"Myself?"

"And your neighbour's wife," she added.

"Well, what about myself and my neighbour's wife?"

"I'm not familiar with such matters." Her face did not change, but the burning anger suddenly welled up in her again. "I don't know anything about such affairs, but if you think I ought to I might try to learn."

She laughed and leaned back into the depths of her chair. "You and I are such intimate friends it's a shame I shouldn't understand and sympathise with what most interests you."

He remained silent, gazing down at his shadow on the grass, hands clasped loosely between his knees. She strove to study him calmly; her mind was chaos; only the desire to hurt him persisted, rendered sterile by the confused tumult of her thoughts.

Presently, looking up:

"Do you doubt that things are not right between - my neighbour's wife - and me?" he inquired.

"The matter doesn't interest me."

"Doesn't it?"

"No."

"Then I have misunderstood you. What is the matter that does interest you, Geraldine?"

She made no reply.

He said, carelessly good-humoured: "I like women. It's curious that they know it instinctively, because when they're bored or lonely they drift toward me.... Lonely women are always adrift, Geraldine. There seems to be some current that sets in toward me; it catches them and they drift in, linger, and drift on. I seem to be the first port they anchor in.... Then a day comes when they are gone - drifting on at hazard through the years -"

"Wiser for their experience at Port Mallett?"

"Perhaps. But not sadder, I think."

"A woman adrift has no regrets," she said with contempt.

"Wrong. A woman who is in love has none."

"That is what I mean. The hospitality of Port Mallett ought to leave them with no regrets."

He laughed. "But they are not loved," he said. "They know it. That's why they drift on."

She turned on him white and tremulous.

"Haven't you even the excuse of caring for her?"

"Who?"

"A neighbour's wife - who comes drifting into your hospitable haven!"

"I don't pretend to love her, if that is what you mean," he said pleasantly.

"Then you make her believe it - and that's dastardly!"

"Oh, no. Women don't love unless made love to. You've only read that in books."

She said a little breathlessly: "You are right. I know men and women only through books. It's time I learned for myself."

CHAPTER VII

TOGETHER

The end of June and of the house party at Roya-Neh was now near at hand, and both were to close with a moonlight fete and dance in the forest, invitations having been sent to distant neighbours who had been entertaining similar gatherings at Iron Hill and Cloudy Mountain - the Grays, Beekmans, Ellises, and Grandcourts.

Silks and satins, shoe buckles and powdered hair usually mark the high tide of imaginative originality among this sort of people. So it was to be the inevitable Louis XVI fete - or as near to it as attenuated, artistic intelligence could manage, and they altered Duane's very clever and correct sketches to suit themselves, careless of anachronism, and sent the dainty water-colour drawings to town in order that those who sweat and sew in the perfumed ateliers of Fifth Avenue might use them as models.

"The fun - if there's any in dressing up - ought to lie in making your own costumes," observed Duane. But nobody displayed any inclination to do so. And now, on hurry orders, the sewers in the hot Fifth Avenue ateliers sewed faster. Silken and satin costumes, paste jewelry and property small-swords were arriving by express; maids flew about the house at Roya-Neh, trying on, fussing with lace and ribbon, bodice and flowered pannier, altering, retrimming, adjusting. Their mistresses met in one another's bedrooms for mysterious confabs over head-dress and coiffure, lace scarf, and petticoat.

As for the men, they surreptitiously tried on their embroidered coats and breeches, admired themselves in secrecy, and let it go at that, returning with embarrassed relief to cards, tennis, and the various forms of amiable idleness to which they were accustomed. Only Englishmen can masquerade seriously.

Later, however, the men were compelled to pay some semblance of attention to the general preparations, assemble their foot-gear, head-gear, stars, orders, sashes, swords, and try them on for Duane Mallett - to that young man's unconcealed dissatisfaction.

"You certainly resemble a scratch opera chorus," he observed after passing in review the sheepish line-up in his room. "Delancy, you're the limit as a Black Mousquetier - and, by the way, there weren't any in the reign of Louis XVI, so perhaps that evens up matters. Dysart is the only man who looks the real thing - or would if he'd remove that monocle. As for Bunny and the Pink 'un, they ought to be in vaudeville singing la-la-la."

"That's really a compliment to our legs," observed Reggie Wye to Bunbury Gray, flourishing his property sword and gracefully performing a *pas seul a la Genee.*

Dysart, who had been sullen all day, regarded them morosely.

Scott Seagrave, in his conventional abbe's costume of black and white, excessively bored, stood by the window trying to catch a glimpse of the lake to see whether any decent fish were breaking, while Scott walked around him critically, not much edified by his costume or the way he wore it.

"You're a sad and self-conscious-looking bunch," he concluded. "Scott, I suppose you'll insist on wearing your mustache and eyeglasses."

"You bet," said Scott simply.

"All right. And kindly beat it. I want to try on my own plumage in peace."

So the costumed ones trooped off to their own quarters with the half-ashamed smirk usually worn by the American male who has persuaded himself to frivolity. Delancy Grandcourt tramped away down the hall banging his big sword, jingling his spurs, and flapping his loose boots. The Pink 'un and Bunbury Gray slunk off into obscurity, and Scott wandered back through the long hall until a black-and-red tiger moth attracted his attention, and he forgot his annoying appearance in frantic efforts to capture the brilliant moth.

Dysart, who had been left alone with Duane in the latter's room, contemplated himself sullenly in the mirror while Duane, seated on the window sill, waited for him to go.

"You think I ought to eliminate my eye-glass?" asked Dysart, still inspecting himself.

"Yes, in deference to the conventional prejudice of the times. Nobody wore 'em at that period."

"You seem to be a stickler for convention - of the Louis XVI sort more than for the XIX century variety," remarked Dysart with a sneer.

Duane looked up from his bored contemplation of the rug.

"You think I'm unconventional?" he asked with a smile.

"I believe I suggested something of the sort to my wife the other day."

"Ah," said Duane blandly, "does she agree with you, Dysart?"

"No doubt she does, because your tendencies toward the

unconventional have been the subject of unpleasant comment recently."

"By some of your debutante conquests? You mustn't believe all they tell you."

"My own eyes and ears are competent witnesses. Do you understand me now?"

"No. Neither do you. Don't rely on such witnesses, Dysart; they lack character to corroborate them. Ask your wife to confirm me - if you ever find time enough to ask her anything."

"That's a damned impudent thing to say," returned Dysart, staring at him. A dull red stained his face, then faded.

Duane's eyebrows went up - just a shade - yet so insolently that the other stepped forward, the corners of his mouth white and twitching.

"I can speak more plainly," he said. "If you can't appreciate a pleasant hint I can easily accommodate you with the alternative."

There was silence for a moment.

"Dysart," said Duane, "what chance do you think you'd have in landing the - alternative?"

"That concerns me," said Dysart; and the pinched muscles around the mouth grew whiter and the man looked suddenly older. Duane had never before noticed how gray his temples were growing.

He said in a voice under perfect control: "You're right; the chances you care to take with me concern yourself. As for your ill-humour, I suppose I have earned it by being attentive to your wife. What is it you wish; that my hitherto very harmless attentions should cease?"

"Yes," said Dysart, and his square jaw quivered.

"Well, they won't. It takes the sort of man you are to strike classical attitudes. And, absurd as the paradox appears - and even taking into consideration your notorious indifference to your wife and your rather silly reputation as a debutante chaser - I do believe, Dysart, that, deep inside of you somewhere, there is enough latent decency to have inspired this resentment toward me - a resentment perfectly natural in any man who acts squarely toward his wife - but rather far fetched in your case."

Dysart, pallid, menacing, laid his hand on a chair.

The other laughed.

"As bad as that?" he asked contemptuously. "Don't do it, Dysart; it isn't in your line. You're only a good-looking, popular, dancing man; all your deviltry is in your legs, and I'd be obliged if they'd presently waft you out of my room."

"I suppose," said Dysart unsteadily, "that you would make yourself noisily ridiculous if I knocked your blackguard head off."

"It's only in novels that people are knocked down successfully and artistically," admitted the other. "In everyday life they resent it. Yes - if you do anything hysterical there will be some sort of a disgraceful noise, I suppose. It's shoot or suit in these unromantic days, Dysart, otherwise the newspapers laugh at you."

Dysart's well-shaped fists relaxed, the chair dropped, but even when he let it go murder danced in his eyes.

"Yes," he said, "it's shoot or a suit in these days; you're perfectly right, Mallett. And we'll let it go at that for the present."

He stood a moment, straight, handsome, his clearly stencilled eyebrows knitted, watching Duane. Whatever in the man's face and figure was usually colourless, unaccented, irresolute, disappeared as he glared rigidly at the other.

For there is no resentment like the resentment of the neglectful, no jealousy like the jealousy of the faithless.

"To resume, in plain English," he said, "keep away from my wife, Mallett. You comprehend that, don't you?"

"Perfectly. Now get out!"

Dysart hesitated for the fraction of a second longer, as though perhaps expecting further reply, then turned on his heel and walked out.

Later, while Duane was examining his own costume preparatory to trying it on, Scott Seagrave's spectacled and freckled visage protruded into the room. He knocked as an after-thought.

"Rosalie sent me. She's dressed in all her gimcracks and wants your expert opinion. I've got to go -"

"Where is she?"

"In her room. I'm going out to the hatchery with Kathleen -"

"Come and see Rosalie with me, first," said Duane, passing his arm through Scott's and steering him down the sunny corridor.

When they knocked, Mrs. Dysart admitted them, revealing herself in full costume, painted and powdered, the blinds pulled down, and the electric lights burning behind their rosy shades.

"It's my final dress rehearsal," she explained. "Mr. Mallett, *is* my hair sufficiently a la Lamballe to suit you?"

"Yes, it is. You're a perfect little porcelain figurette! There's not an anachronism in you or your make-up. How did you do it?"

"I merely stuck like grim death to your sketches," she said demurely.

Scott eyed her without particular interest. "Very corking," he said vaguely, "but I've got to go down to the hatchery with Kathleen, so you won't mind if I leave -"

He closed the door behind him before anybody could speak. Duane moved toward the door.

"It's a charming costume," he said, "and most charmingly worn; your hair is exactly right - not too much powder, you know -"

"Where shall I put my patch? Here?"

"Higher."

"Here?"

He came back to the centre of the room where she stood.

"Here," he said, indenting the firm, cool ivory skin with one finger, "and here. Wear two."

"And my rings - do you think that my fingers are overloaded?" She held out her fascinating smooth little hands. He supported them on his upturned palms and examined the gems critically.

They talked for a few moments about the rings, then: "Thank you so much," she said, with a carelessly friendly pressure. "How about my shoes? Are the buckles of the period?"

One of her hands encountered his at hazard, lingered, dropped, the fingers still linked lightly in his. She bent over, knees straight, and lifted the hem of her petticoat, displaying her Louis XVI footwear.

“Shoes and buckles are all right,” he said; “faultless, true to the period - very fascinating.... I've got to go - one or two things to do -”

They examined the shoes for some time in silence; still bending over she turned her dainty head and looked around and up at him. There was a moment's pause, then he kissed her.

“I was afraid you'd do that - some day,” she said, straightening up and stepping back one pace, so that their linked hands now hung pendant between them.

“I was sure of it, too,” he said. “Now I think I'd better go - as all things are en regle, even the kiss, which was classical - pure - Louis XVI.... Besides, Scott was idiot enough to shut the door. That's Louis XVI, too, but too much realism is never artistic.”

“We could open the door again - if that's why you're running away from me.”

“What's the use?”

She glanced at the door and then calmly seated herself.

“Do you think that we are together too much?” she asked.

“Hasn't your husband made similar observations?” he replied, laughing.

“It isn't for him to make them.”

“Hasn't he objected?”

"He has suddenly and unaccountably become disagreeable enough to make me wish he had some real grounds for his excitement!" she said coolly, and closed her teeth with a little click. She added, between them: "I'm inclined to give him something real to howl about."

He said: "You're adrift. Do you know it?"

"Certainly I know it. Are you prepared to offer salvage? I'm past the need of a pilot."

He smiled. "You haven't drifted very far yet - only as far as Mallett Harbour. That's usually the first port - for derelicts. Anchors are dropped rather frequently there - but, Rosalie, there's no safe mooring except in the home port."

Her pretty, flushed face grew very serious as she looked up questioningly.

"Isn't there an anchorage near you, Duane? Are you quite sure?"

"Why, no, dear, I'm not sure. But let me tell you something: it isn't in me to love again. And that isn't square to you."

After a silence she repeated: "Again? Have you been in love?"

"Yes."

"Are you embittered? I thought only callow fledglings moped."

"If I were embittered I'd offer free anchorage to all comers. That's the fledgling idea - when blighted - be a 'deevil among the weemin,'" he said, laughing.

"You have that hospitable reputation now," she persisted, unsmiling.

"Have I? Judge for yourself then - because no woman I ever

knew cares anything for me now."

"You mean that if any of them had anything intimate to remember they'd never remain indifferent?"

"Well - yes."

"They'd either hate you or remember you with a certain tenderness."

"Is that what happens?" he asked, amused.

"I think so," she said thoughtfully.... "As for what you said, you are right, Duane; I am adrift.... You - or a man like you could easily board me - take me in tow. I'm quite sure that something about me signals a pilot; and that keen eyes and bitter tongues have noted it. And I don't care. Nor do I know yet what my capabilities for evil are.... Do you care to - find out?"

"It wouldn't be a square deal to you, Rosalie."

"And - if I don't care whether it's a square deal or not?"

"Why, dear," he said, covering her nervous, pretty hand with both of his, "I'd break your heart in a week."

He laughed, dropped her fingers, stepped back to the door, and, laying his hand on the knob, said evenly:

"That husband of yours is not the sort of man I particularly take to, but I believe he's about the average if you'd care to make him so."

She coloured with surprise. Then something in her scornful eyes inspired him with sudden intuition.

"As a matter of fact," he said lightly, "you care for him still."

"I can very easily prove the contrary," she said, walking slowly up to him, close, closer, until the slight tremor of contact halted her and her soft, irregular breath touched his face.

"What a girl like you needs," he laughed, taking her into his arms, "is a man to hold her this way - every now and then, and" - he kissed her - "tell her she is incomparable - which I cannot truthfully tell you, dear." He released her at arms' length.

"I don't know whose fault it is," he went on: "I don't know whether he still really cares for you in spite of his weak peregrinations to other shrines; but you still care for him. And it's up to you to make him what he can be - the average husband. There are only two kinds, Rosalie, the average and the bad."

She looked straight into his eyes, but the deep, mantling colour belied her audacity.

"Do you know," she said, "that we haven't - lived together for two years?"

"I don't want to know such things," he said gently.

"Well, you do know now. I - am - very much alone. You see I have already become capable of saying anything - and of doing it, too."

There came a reckless glimmer into her eyes; she set her teeth - a trick of hers; the fresh lips parted slightly under her rapid breathing.

"Do you think," she said unevenly, "that I'm going on all my life like this - without anything more than the passing friendship of men to balance the example he sets me?"

"No, I think something is bound to happen, Rosalie. May I suggest what ought to happen?"

She nodded thoughtfully; only the quiver of her lower lip betrayed the tension of self-control.

"Take him back," he said.

"I no longer care for him."

"You are mistaken."

After a moment she said: "I don't think so; truly I don't. All consideration for him has died in me. His conduct doesn't matter - doesn't hurt me any more -"

"Yes, it does. He's just a plain ass - an average ass - ownerless, and, like all asses, convinced that he can take care of himself. Go and put the halter on him again."

"Go - and - what do you mean?"

"Tether him. You did once. It's up to you; it's usually up to a woman when a man wanders untethered. What one woman, or a dozen, can do with a man his wife can do in the same fashion! What won him in the beginning always holds good until he thinks he has won you. Then the average man flourishes his heels. He is doing it. What won him was not you alone, or love, alone; it was his uncertainty of both that fascinated him. That's what charms him in others; uncertainty. Many men are that way. It's a sporting streak in us. If you care for him now - if you could ever care for him, take him as you took him first.... Do you want him again?"

She stood leaning against the door, looking down. Much of her colour had died out.

"I don't know," she said.

"I do."

"Well - *do* I?"

"Yes."

"You think so? Why?"

"Because he's adrift, too. And he's rather weak, rather handsome, easily influenced - unjust, selfish, vain, wayward - just the average husband. And every wife ought to be able to manage these lords of creation, and keep them out of harm.... And keep them in love, Rosalie. And the way to do it is the way you did it first.... Try it." He kissed her gaily, thinking he owed that much to himself.

And through the door which had swung gently ajar, Geraldine Seagrave saw them, and Rosalie saw her.

For a moment the girl halted, pale and rigid, and her heart seemed to cease its beating; then, as she passed with averted head, Rosalie caught Duane's wrists in her jewelled grasp and released herself with a wrench.

"You've given me enough to think over," she said. "If you want me to love you, stay - and close that door - and we'll see what happens. If you don't - you had better go at once, Duane. And leave my door open - to see what else fate will send me." She clasped her hands behind her back, laughing nervously.

"It's like the old child's game - 'open your mouth and close your eyes and see what God will send you?' - usually something not at all resembling the awaited bonbon.... Good-bye, my altruistic friend - and thank you for your XXth Century advice, and your Louis XVI assistance."

"Good-bye," he returned smilingly, and sauntered back toward his room where his own untried finery awaited him.

Ahead, far down the corridor, he caught sight of Geraldine, and called to her, but perhaps she did not hear him for he had to put on considerable speed to overtake her.

"In these last few days," he said laughingly, "I seldom catch a glimpse of you except when you are vanishing into doorways or down corridors."

She said nothing, did not even turn her head or halt; and, keeping pace with her, he chatted on amiably about nothing in particular until she stopped abruptly and looked at him.

"I am in a hurry. What is it you want, Duane?"

"Why - nothing," he said in surprise.

"That is less than you ask of - others." And she turned to continue her way.

"Is there anything wrong, Geraldine?" he asked, detaining her.

"Is there?" she replied, shaking off his hand from her arm.

"Not as far as I'm concerned."

"Can't you even tell the truth?" she asked with a desperate attempt to laugh.

"Wait a minute," he said. "Evidently something has gone all wrong -"

"Several things, my solicitous friend; I for one, you for another. Count the rest for yourself."

"What has happened to you, Geraldine?"

"What has always threatened."

"Will you tell me?"

"No, I will not. So don't try to look concerned and interested in a matter that regards me alone."

"But what is it that has always threatened you?" he insisted gently, coming nearer - too near to suit her, for she backed away toward the high latticed window through which the sun poured over the geraniums on the sill. There was a seat under it. Suddenly her knees threatened to give way under her; she swayed slightly as she seated herself; a wave of angry pain swept through her setting lids and lips trembling.

"Now I want you to tell me what it is that you believe has always threatened you."

"Do you think I'd tell you?" she managed to say. Then her self-possession returned in a flash of exasperation, but she controlled that, too, and laughed defiantly, confronting him with pretty, insolent face uptilted.

"What do you want to know about me? That I'm in the way of being ultimately damned like all the rest of you?" she said. "Well, I am. I'm taking chances. Some people take their chances in one way - like you and Rosalie; some take them in another - as I do.... Once I was afraid to take any; now I'm not. Who was it said that self-control is only immorality afraid?"

"Will you tell me what is worrying you?" he persisted.

"No, but I'll tell you what annoys me if you like."

"What?"

"Fear of notoriety."

"Notoriety?"

"Certainly - not for myself - for my house."

"Is anybody likely to make it notorious?" he demanded, colouring up.

"Ask yourself.... I haven't the slightest interest in your personal conduct" - there was a catch in her voice - "except when it threatens to besmirch my own home."

The painful colour gathered and settled under his cheek-bones.

"Do you wish me to leave?"

"Yes, I do. But you can't without others knowing how and why."

"Oh, yes, I can -"

"You are mistaken. I tell you *others* will know. Some do know already. And I don't propose to figure with a flaming sword. Kindly remain in your Eden until it's time to leave - with Eve."

"Just as you wish," he said, smiling; and that infuriated her.

"It ought to be as I wish! That much is due me, I think. Have you anything further to ask, or is your curiosity satisfied?"

"Not yet. You say that you think something threatens you? What is it?"

"Not what threatens *you*," she said in contempt.

"That is no answer."

"It is enough for you to know."

He looked her hard in the eyes. "Perhaps," he said in a low voice, "I know more about you than you imagine I do, Geraldine - *since last April.*"

She felt the blood leave her face, the tension crisping her muscles; she sat up very straight and slender among the cushions and defied him.

"What do you - think you know?" she tried to sneer, but her voice shook and failed.

He said: "I'll tell you. For one thing, you're playing fast and loose with Dysart. He's a safe enough proposition - but what is that sort of thing going to arouse in you?"

"What do you mean?" Her voice cleared with an immense relief. He noted it.

"It's making you tolerant," he said quietly, "familiar with subtleties, contemptuous of standards. It's rubbing the bloom off you. You let a man who is married come too close to you - you betray enough curiosity concerning him to do it. A drifting woman does that sort of thing, but why do you cut your cables? Good Lord, Geraldine, it's a fool business - permitting a man an intimacy -"

"More harmless than his wife permits you!" she retorted.

"That is not true."

"You are supposed to lie about such things, aren't you?" she said, reddening to the temples. "Oh, I am learning your rotten code, you see - the code of all these amiable people about me. You've done your part to instruct me that promiscuous caresses are men's distraction from ennui; Rosalie evidently is in sympathy with that form of amusement - many men and women among whom I live in town seem to be quite as casual as you are.... I did have standards once, scarcely knowing what they meant; I clung to them out of instinct. And when I went out into the world I found nobody paying any attention to them."

"You are wrong."

"No, I'm not. I go among people and see every standard I set up, ignored. I go to the theatre and see plays that embody everything I supposed was unthinkable, let alone unutterable.

But the actors utter everything, and the audience thinks everything - and sometimes laughs. I can't do that - yet. But I'm progressing."

"Geraldine -"

"Wait!... My friends have taught me a great deal during this last year - by word, precept, and example. Things I held in horror nobody notices enough to condone. Take treachery, for example. The marital variety is all around me. Who cares, or is even curious after an hour's gossip has made it stale news? A divorce here, a divorce there - some slight curiosity to see who the victims may marry next time - that curiosity satisfied - and so is everybody. And they go back to their business of money-getting and money-spending - and that's what my friends have taught me. Can you wonder that my familiarity with it all breeds contempt enough to seek almost any amusement in sheer desperation - as you do?"

"I have only one amusement," he said.

"What?"

"Painting."

"And your model," she nodded with a short laugh. "Don't forget her. Your pretences are becoming tiresome, Duane. Your pretty model, Mrs. Dysart, poses less than you do."

Another wave of heart-sickness and anger swept over her; she felt the tears burning close to her lids and turned sharply on him:

"It's all rotten, I tell you - the whole personnel and routine - these people, and their petty vices and their idleness and their money! I - I do want to keep myself above it - clean of it - but what am I to do? One can't live without friends. If I don't gamble I'm left alone; if I don't flirt I'm isolated. If one stands aloof from everything one's friends go elsewhere. What can

I do?"

"Make decent friends. I'm going to."

He bent forward and struck his knee with his closed fist.

"I'm going to," he repeated. "I've waited as long as I can for you to stand by me. I could have even remained among these harmless simians if you had cared for me. You're all the friend I need. But you've become one of them. It isn't in you to take an intelligent interest in me, or in what I care for. I've stood this sort of existence long enough. Now I'm all through with it."

She stared. Anger, astonishment, exasperation moved her in turn. Bitterness unlocked her lips.

"Are you expecting to take Mrs. Dysart with you to your intellectual solitude?"

"I would if I - if we cared for each other," he said, calmly seating himself.

She said, revolted: "Can't you even admit that you are in love with her? Must I confess that I could not avoid seeing you with her in her own room - half an hour since? Will *that* wring the truth out of you?"

"Oh, is that what you mean?" he said wearily. "I believe the door was open.... Well, Geraldine, whatever you saw won't harm anybody. So come to your own conclusions.... But I wish you were out of all this - with your fine insight and your clear intelligence, and your sweetness - oh, the chances for happiness you and I might have had!"

"A slim chance with you!" she said.

"Every chance; perhaps the only chance we'll ever have. And we've missed it."

"We've missed nothing" - a sudden and curious tremor set her heart and pulses beating heavily - "I tell you, Duane, it doesn't matter whom people of our sort marry because we'll always sicken of our bargain. What chance for happiness would I run with such a man as you? Or you with a girl like me?"

She lay back among the cushions, with a tired little laugh. "We are like the others of our rotten sort, only less aged, less experienced. But we have, each of us, our own heritage, our own secret depravity." She hesitated, reddening, caught his eye, stammered her sentence to a finish and flinched, crimsoning to the roots of her hair.

He stood up, paced the room for a few moments, came and stood beside her.

"Once," he said very low, "you admitted that you dare go anywhere with me. Do you remember?"

"Yes."

"Those are your rooms, I believe," pointing to a closed door far down the south corridor.

"Yes."

"Take me there now."

"I - cannot do that -"

"Yes, you can. You must."

"Now? - Duane."

"Yes, now - *now*! I tell you our time is now if it ever is to be at all. Don't waste words."

"What do you want to say to me that cannot be said here?" she asked in consternation.

He made no answer, but she found herself on her feet and moving slowly along beside him, his hand just touching her arm as guide.

"What is it, Duane?" she asked fearfully, as she laid her hand on the knob and turned to look at his altered face.

He made no answer. She hesitated, shivered, opened the door, hesitated again, slowly crossed the threshold, turned and admitted him.

The western sun flooded the silent chamber of rose and gray; a breeze moved the curtains, noiselessly; the scent of flowers freshened the silence.

There was a divan piled with silken cushions; he placed several for her; she stood irresolute for a moment, then, with a swift, unquiet side glance at him, seated herself.

"What is it?" she asked, looking up, her face beginning to reflect the grave concern in his.

"I want you to marry me, Geraldine."

"Is - is *that* what -"

"Partly. I want you to love me, too. But I'll attend to that if you'll marry me - I'll guarantee that. I - I will guarantee - more than that."

She was still looking up, searching his sombre face. She saw the muscles tighten along the jaw; saw the grave lines deepening. A sort of bewildered fear possessed her.

"I - am not in love with you, Duane." She added hastily, "I don't trust you either. How could I -"

"Yes, you do trust me."

"After what you have done to Rosalie -"

"You know that all is square there. Say so!"

She gazed at the floor, convinced, but not answering.

"Do you believe I love you?"

She shook her head, eyes still on the floor.

"Tell me the truth! Look at me!"

She said with an effort: "You think you care for me.... You believe you do, I suppose -"

"And *you* believe it, too! Give me my chance - take your own!"

"*My* chance?" - with a flash of anger.

"Yes; take it, and give me mine. I tell you, Geraldine, we are going to need each other desperately some day. I need you now - to-morrow you'll need me more; and the day after, and after that in perilous days to follow our need will be the greater for these hours wasted - can't you understand by this time that we've nothing to hold us steady through the sort of life we're born to except - each other -"

His voice suddenly broke; he dropped down on the couch beside her, imprisoning her clasped hands on her knees. His emotion, the break in his voice, excited them both.

"Are you trying to frighten me and take me by storm?" she demanded, forcing a smile. "What is the matter, Duane? What do you mean by peril?... You are scaring me -"

"Little Geraldine - my little comrade! Can't you understand? It isn't only my selfish desire for you - it isn't all for myself! - I care more for you than that. I love you more deeply than a mere lover! Must I say more to you? Must I even hurt you?

Must I tell you what I know - of you?"

"W-what?" she asked, startled.

He looked at her miserably. In his eyes she read a meaning that terrified her.

"Duane - I don't - understand," she faltered.

"Yes you do. Let's face it now!"

"F-face what?" Her voice was only a whisper.

"I can tell you if you'll love me. Will you?"

"I don't understand," she repeated in white-lipped distress. "Why do you look at me so strangely? And you tell me that I - know.... What is it that I know? Couldn't you tell me? I am -" Her voice failed.

"Dear - do you remember - once - last April that you were - ill?... And awoke to find yourself on your own bed?"

"Duane!" It was a cry of terror.

"Dearest! Dearest! Do you think I have not known - since then - what has troubled you - here -"

She stared at him in crimsoned horror for an instant, then with a dry sob, bowed her head and covered her face with desperate hands. For a moment her whole body quivered, then she collapsed. On his knees beside her he bent and touched with trembling lips her arms, her knees, the slim ankles desperately interlocked, the tips of her white shoes.

"Dearest," he whispered brokenly, "I know - I know - believe me. I have fought through worse, and won out. You said once that something had died out in me - while I was abroad. It did not die of itself, dear. But it left its mark.... You say self-control is only depravity afraid.... That is true; but I have made my depravity fear me. I can do what I please with it now; I can tempt it, laugh at it, silence it. But it cost me something to make a slave of it - what you saw in my face is the claw-mark it left fighting me to the death."

Very straight on his knees beside her he bent again, pressing her rigid knees with his lips.

"I need you, Geraldine - I need all that is best in you; you must love me - take me as an ally, dear, against all that is worst in you. I'll love you so confidently that we'll kill it - you and I together - my strength and yours, my bitter and deep understanding and your own sweet contempt for weakness wherever it may be, even in yourself."

He touched her; and she shuddered under the light caress, still bent almost double, and covering her face with both hands. He bent over her, one knee on the divan.

"Let's pull ourselves together and talk sense, Geraldine," he said with an effort at lightness.

"Don't you remember that bully little girl who swung her fists in single combat and uppercut her brother and me whenever her sense of fairness was outraged? The time has come when you, who were so fair to others, are going to be fair to yourself by marrying me -"

She dropped both hands and stared at him out of wide, tear-wet eyes.

"Fair to myself - at your expense, Duane?"

"What do you mean? I love you."

"Am I to let you - you marry me - knowing - what you know? Is that what you call my sense of fairness?" And, as he attempted to speak:

"Oh, I have thought about it already! - I must have been conscious that this would happen some day - that - that I was capable of caring for you - and it alarmed me -"

"Are you capable of loving me?"

"Duane, you must not ask me that!"

"Tell me!"

But she pushed him back, and they faced each other, her hands remaining on his shoulders. She strove piteously to endure his gaze, flinched, strove to push him from her again - but the slender hands lay limply against him. So they remained, her hands at intervals nervously tightening and relaxing on his shoulders, her tearful breath coming faster, the dark eyes closing, opening, turning from him, toward him, searching, now in his soul, now in her own, her self-command slipping from her.

"It is cowardly in me - if I do it," she said in the ghost of a voice.

"Do what?"

"Let you risk - what I m-might become."

"You little saint!"

"Some saints *were* depraved at first - weren't they?" she said without a smile. "Oh, Duane, Duane, to think I could ever be here speaking to you about - about the horror that has happened to me - looking into your face and giving up my dreadful secret to you - laying my very soul naked before you! How can I look at you -"

"Because I love you. Now give me the right to your lips and heart!"

There was a long silence. Then she tried to smile.

"My - my lips? I - thought you took such things - lightly -"

She hesitated, glanced up at him, then began to tremble.

"Duane - if you are in earnest about our - about an engagement - promise me that I may be released if I - think best -"

"Why?"

"I - I might fail -"

"The more need of me. But you can't fail -"

"Yes, but if I should, dear. Will you release me? I cannot - I will not engage myself to you - unless you promise to let me go if I think it best. You know what my word means. Give it back to me if matters go wrong with me. Will you?"

"But I am going to marry you now!" he said with a short, excited laugh.

"Now!" she repeated, appalled.

"Certainly, to make sure of you. We don't need a license in this State. There's a parson at West Gate Village.... I intend to make sure of you now. You can keep it a secret if you like. When you return to town we can have everything en regle - engagement announced, cards, church wedding, and all that. Meanwhile I'm going to be sure of you."

"W-when?"

"This afternoon."

His excitement thrilled her; a vivid colour surged over neck and brow.

"Duane, I did not dream that you cared so much, so truly - Oh, I - I do love you then! - I love you, Duane! I love you!"

He drew her suddenly into his arms, close, closer; she lifted her face; he kissed her; and she gave him her heart with a sob.

"You will wait for m-me, won't you?" she stammered, striving to keep her reason through the delicious tumult that swept her senses. "Before I m-marry you I must be quite certain that you take no risk -"

She looked up into his steady eyes; a passion of tenderness overwhelmed her, and her locked arms tightened around his neck.

"Oh," she whispered, "you *are* the boy I loved so long, so long ago - my comrade Duane - my own little boy! How was I to know I loved you this way, too? How could I understand!"

Already the glamour of the past was transfiguring the man for her, changing him back into the lad she had ruled so long ago, glorifying him - drawing them together into that golden age where her ears already caught the far cries and laughter of the past.

Now, her arms around him, she looked at him and looked at him as though she had not set eyes on him since then.

"Of course, I love you," she said impatiently, as though surprised and hurt that he or she had ever doubted it. "You always were mine; you are *mine*! Nobody else could ever have had you - no matter what you did - or what I did.... And nobody except you could ever, ever have had me. That is perfectly plain now.... Oh, you - you darling" - she murmured, drawing his face against hers. Tears sprang to her brown eyes; her mouth quivered.

"You *will* love me, won't you? Because I'm going quite mad about you, Duane.... I don't think I know just what I'm saying

- or what I'm doing."

She drew him closer; he caught her, crushing her in his arms, and she yielded, clung to him for a moment, drew back in flushed resistance, still bewildered by her own passion. Then, into her eyes came that divine beauty which comes but once on earth - innocence awakened; and the white lids drooped a little, and the mouth quivered, surrendering with a sigh.

* * * * *

"You never have, never could love any other man? Say it. I know it, but - say it, sweetheart!"

"Only you, Duane."

"Are you happy?"

"I am in heaven."

She closed her eyes - opening them almost immediately and passing one hand across his face as though afraid he might have vanished.

"You are there yet," she murmured with a faint smile.

"So are you," he whispered, laughing - "my little dream girl - my little brown-eyed, brown-haired, long-legged, swift-running, hard-hitting -"

"Oh, *do* you remember that dreadful blow I gave you when we were sparring in the library? *Did* it hurt you, my darling - I was sure it did, but you never would admit it. Tell me now," she coaxed, adorable in her penitence.

"Well - yes, it did." He laughed under his breath - "I don't mind telling you now that it fractured the bridge of my nose."

"What!" - in horror. "That perfectly delicious straight nose of yours!"

"Oh, I had it fixed," he said, laughing. "If you deal me no more vital blows than that I'll never mind -"

"I - deal you a - a blow, Duane! *I*!"

"For instance, by not marrying me right away -"

"Dear - I can't."

The smile had died out in her eyes and on her lips.

"You know I can't, don't you?" she said tenderly. "You know I've got to be fair to you." Her face grew graver. "Dear - when I stop and try to think - it dismays me to understand how much in love with you I am.... Because it is too soon.... It would be safer to wait before I start to love you - this way. There is a cowardly streak in me - a weak streak -"

"What blessed nonsense you do talk, don't you?"

"No, dear."

She moved slightly toward him, settling close, as though within the circle of his arms lay some occult protection.

For a while she lay very close to him, her pale face pressed against his shoulder, brown eyes remote. Neither spoke. After a long time she laid her hands on his arms, gently disengaging them, and, freeing herself, sprang to her feet. A new, lithe and lovely dignity seemed to possess her - an exquisite, graceful, indefinable something which lent a hint of splendour to her as she turned and looked down at him.

Then, mischievously tender, she stooped and touched her childish mouth to his - her cheek, her throat, her hair, her lids, her hands, in turn all brushed his lips with fragrance - the very ghost of contact, the exquisite mockery of caress.

"If you don't go at once," she murmured, "I'll never let you go at all. Wait - let me see if anybody is in the corridor -"

She opened the door and looked out.

"Not a soul," she whispered, "our reputations are still intact. Good-bye - I'll put on a fresh gown and meet you in ten minutes!... Where? Oh, anywhere - *anywhere*, Duane. The Lake. Oh, that is too far away! Wait here on the stairs for me - that isn't so far away - just sit on the stairs until I come. Do you promise? *Truly*? Oh, you angel boy!... Yes - but only one more, then - to be quite sure that you won't forget to wait on the stairs for me...."

CHAPTER VIII

AN AFTERGLOW

Deliciously weary, every fibre in her throbbing with physical fatigue, she had nevertheless found it impossible to sleep.

The vivid memory of Duane holding her in his arms, while she gave her heart to him with her lips, left her tremulous and confused by emotions of which she yet knew little.

Toward dawn a fever of unrest drove her from her hot, crushed pillows to the cool of the open casements. The morning was dark and very still; no breeze stirred; a few big, widely scattered stars watched her. For a long while she stood there trying to quiet the rapid pulse and fast breathing; and at length, with an excited little laugh, she sank down among the cushions on the window-seat and lay back very still, her head, with its glossy, disordered hair, cradled in her arms.

"Is *this* love?" she said to herself. "Is this what it is doing to me? Am I never again going to sleep?"

But she could not lie still; her restless hands began groping about in the darkness, and presently the fire from a cigarette glimmered red.

She remained quiet for a few moments, elbow among the pillows, cheek on hand, watching the misty spirals float through the open window. After a while she sat up nervously and tossed the cigarette from her. Like a falling star the spark whirled earthward in a wide curve, glowed for a few seconds on the lawn below, and slowly died out.

Then an inexplicable thing occurred. Unthinkingly she had turned over and extended her arm, searching in the darkness behind her. There came a tinkle, a vague violet perfume, and the starlight fell on her clustering hair and throat as she lifted and drained the brimming glass.

Suddenly she stood up; the frail, crystal glass fell from her fingers, splintering on the stone sill; and with a quick, frightened intake of breath, lips still wet and scented, and the fire of it already stealing through her veins, she awoke to stunned comprehension of what she had done.

For a moment only startled astonishment dominated her. That she could have done this thing so instinctively and without forethought or intent, seemed impossible. She bowed her head in her hands, striving desperately to recollect the circumstances; she sprang to her feet and paced the darkened room, trying to understand. A terrified and childish surprise possessed her, which changed slowly to anger and impatience as she began to realise the subtle treachery that habit had practised on her - so stealthy is habit, betraying the body unawares.

Overwhelmed with consternation, she seated herself to consider the circumstances; little flashes of alarm assisted her. Then a sort of delicate madness took possession of her, deafening her ears to the voice of fear. She refused to be afraid.

As she sat there, both hands unconsciously indenting her breast, the clamour and tumult of her senses drowned the voice within.

No, she would not be afraid! - though the burning perfume was mounting to her head with every breath and the glow grew steadily in her body, creeping from vein to vein. No, she would not be afraid. It could never happen again. She would be on her guard after this.... Besides, the forgetfulness had been so momentary, the imprudence so very slight ... and it had helped her, too - it was already making her sleepy ... and she had needed something to quiet her - needed sleep....

After a long while she turned languidly and picked up the little crystal flask from the dresser - an antique bit of glass which Rosalie had given her.

Dawn whitened the edges of the sky; the birds were becoming very noisy. She lifted the curiously cut relic; an imprisoned fluid glimmered with pale-violet light - some scented French distillation which Rosalie affected because nobody else had ever heard of it - an aromatic, fiery essence, faintly perfumed.

For a moment the girl gazed at it curiously. Then, on deliberate impulse, she filled another glass.

"One thing is certain," she said to herself; "if I am capable of controlling myself at all, I must begin now. If I should touch this it would be excess.... I would like to, but" - she flung the contents from the window - "I won't. And *that* is the way I am able to control myself."

She smiled, set the glass aside, and raised her eyes to the paling stars. When at last she stretched herself out on the bed, dawn was already lighting the room, but she fell asleep at once.

It was a flushed and rather heavy slumber, not perfectly natural; and when Kathleen entered at nine o'clock, followed by Geraldine's maid with the breakfast-tray, the girl still lay with face buried in her hair, breathing deeply and irregularly, her lashes wet with tears.

The maid retired; Kathleen bent low over the feverishly parted lips, kissed them, hesitated, drew back sharply, and cast a rapid glance around the room. Then she went over to the dressing-table and lifted Rosalie's antique flacon; and set it back slowly, as the girl turned her face on the pillow and opened her eyes.

"Is that you, Kathleen?"

"Yes, dear."

For a few seconds she lay quite motionless, then, rising on one elbow, she passed the backs of her fingers across her lids, laughed sleepily, and straightened up, freeing her eyes from the confusion of her hair.

"I've had horrid dreams. I've been crying in my sleep. Come here," she said, stretching out her arms, and Kathleen went slowly.

The girl pulled her head down, linking both arms around her neck:

"You darling, can you ever guess what miracle happened to me yesterday?"

"No.... What?"

"I promised to marry Duane Mallett!"

There was no reply. The girl clung to her excitedly, burying her face against Kathleen's cheek, then released her with a laugh, and saw her face - saw the sorrowful amazement in it, the pain.

"Kathleen!" she exclaimed, startled, "what is the matter?"

Mrs. Severn dropped down on the bed's edge, her hands loosely clasped. Geraldine's brown eyes searched hers in hurt astonishment.

"Aren't you glad for me, Kathleen? What is it? Why do you -" And all at once she divined, and the hot colour stained her from brow to throat. Kathleen bent forward swiftly and caught her in her arms with a smothered cry; but the girl freed herself and leaned back, breathing fast.

"Duane knows about me," she said. "I told him."

"He knew before you told him, my darling."

Another wave of scarlet swept Geraldine's face.

"That is true.... He found out - last April.... But he and I are not afraid. I promised him -" And her voice failed as the memory of the night's indulgence flashed in her brain.

Kathleen began: "You promised me, too -" And her voice also failed.

There was a silence; the girl's eyes turned miserably toward the dressing-table, closed with a slow, inward breath which ended like a sob; and again she was in Kathleen's arms - struggled from them only to drop her head on Kathleen's knees and lie, tense face hidden, both hands clenched. The wave of grief and shame swept her and passed.

After a while she spoke in a hard little voice:

"It is foolish to say I cannot control myself.... I did not think what I was doing last night - that was all. Duane knows my danger - tendency, I mean. He isn't worried; he knows that I can take care of myself -"

"Don't marry him until *you* know you can."

"But I am perfectly certain of myself now!"

"Only prove it, darling. Be frank with me. Who in the world loves you as I do, Geraldine? Who desires happiness for you as I do? What have I in life besides you and Scott?... And lately, dearest - I *must* speak as I feel - something - some indefinable constraint seems to have grown between you and me - something - I don't exactly know what - that threatens our intimate understanding -"

"No, there is nothing!"

"Be honest with me, dear. What is it?"

The girl lay silent for a while, then:

"I don't know myself. I have been - worried. It may have been that."

"Worried about yourself, you poor lamb?"

"A little.... And a little about Duane."

"But, darling, if Duane loves you, that is all cleared up, isn't it?"

"Yes.... But for a long time he and Rosalie made me perfectly wretched.... I didn't know I was in love with him, either.... And I couldn't sleep very much, and I - I simply couldn't tell you how unhappy they were making me - and I - sometimes - now and then - in fact, very often, I - formed the custom of - doing what I ought not to have done - to steady my nerves - in fact, I simply let myself go - badly."

"Oh, my darling! My darling! Couldn't you have told me - let me sit with you, talk, read to you - *love* you to sleep? Why did you do this, Geraldine?"

"Nothing - very disgraceful - ever happened. It only helped me to sleep when I was excited and miserable.... I - I didn't care what I did - Duane and Rosalie made me so wretched. And there seemed no use in my trying to be different from others, and I thought I might as well be as rotten as everybody. But I tried and couldn't - I tried, for instance, to misbehave with Jack Dysart, but I couldn't - and I only hated myself and him and Rosalie and Duane!"

She sat up, flushed, dishevelled, lips quivering. "I want to confess! I've been horribly depraved for a week! I gambled with the Pink 'uns and swore as fashionably as I knew how! I scorched my tongue with cigarettes; I sat in Bunny Gray's room with the door bolted and let him teach me how to make silver fizzes and Chinese juleps out of Rose wine and saki! I let Jack Dysart retain my hand - and try to kiss me - several times -"

"Geraldine!"

"I *did*. I wanted to be horrid."

She sat there breathing fast, her big brown eyes looking defiantly at Kathleen, but the child's mouth quivered beyond control and the nervous hands tightened and relaxed.

"How bad have I been, Kathleen? It sounds pretty bad to tell it. But Muriel says 'damn!' and Rosalie says 'the devil!' and when anything goes wrong and I say, 'Oh, fluff!' I mean swearing, so I thought I'd do it.... And almost every woman I know smokes and has her favourite cocktail, and they all bet and play for stakes; and from what I hear talked about, nobody's conduct is modified because anybody happens to be married -"

The horror in Kathleen's blue eyes checked her; she hid her face in her hands for a moment, then flung out her arms and crushed Kathleen to her breast.

"I'm going to tell Duane how I've behaved. I couldn't rest until he knows the very worst ... how fearfully common and bad a girl I can be. Darling, don't break down. I don't want to go any closer to the danger line than I've been. And, oh, I'm so ashamed, so humiliated - I - I wish I could go to Duane as - as clean and sweet and innocent as he would have me. For he is the dearest boy - and I love him so, Kathleen. I'm so silly about him.... I've got to tell him how I behaved, haven't I?"

"Are - are you going to?"

"Of course I am!" ... She drew away and sat up very straight in bed, serious, sombre-eyed, hands clasped tightly about her knees.

"Do you know," she said, as though to herself, "it is curious that a trivial desire for anything like that" - pointing to Rosalie's gift - "should make me restless - annoy me, cause me discomfort. I can't understand why it should actually torment me. It really does, sometimes."

"That is the terrible part of it," faltered Kathleen. "For God's sake, keep clear of anything with even the faintest odour of alcohol about it.... Where did you find that cut-glass thing?"

"Rosalie gave it to me."

"What is in it?"

"I don't know - creme de something or other."

Kathleen took the girl's tightly clasped hands in hers:

"Geraldine, you've got to be square to Duane. You can't marry him until you cleanse yourself, until you scour yourself free of this terrible inclination for stimulants."

"H-how can I? I don't intend, ever again, to -"

"Prove it then. Let sufficient time elapse -"

"How long? A - year?"

"Dear, if you will show a clean record of self-control for a year I ask no more. It ought not to be difficult for you to dominate this silly weakness. Your will-power is scarcely tainted. What fills me with fear is this habit you have formed of caressing danger - this childish trifling with something which is still asleep in you - with all that is weak and ignoble. It is there - it is in all of us - in you, too. Don't rouse it; it is still asleep -

merely a little restless in its slumber - but, oh, Geraldine! Geraldine! - if you ever awake it! - if you ever arouse it to its full, fierce consciousness -"

"I won't," said the girl hastily. "Oh, I won't, I won't, Kathleen, darling. I do know it's in me - I feel that if I ever let myself go I could be reckless and wicked. But truly, truly, I won't. I - darling, you mustn't cry - please, don't - because you are making me cry. I cried in my sleep, too.... I ought to be very happy -" She forced a laugh through the bright tears fringing her lashes, bent forward swiftly, kissed Kathleen, and sprang from the bed.

"I want my bath and breakfast!" she cried. "If I'm to be a Louis XVI doll this week, it's time my face was washed and my sawdust reinforced. Do fix my tray, dear, while I'm in the bath - and ring for my maid.... And when you go down you may tell Duane to wait for me on the stairs. It's good discipline; he'll find it stupid because I'll be a long time - but, oh, Kathleen, it is perfectly heavenly to bully him!"

* * * * *

Later she sent a note to him by her maid:

> "TO THE ONLY MAN IN THE WORLD,
> ON THE STAIRS.
>
> "*Patient Sir*: If you will go to the large beech-tree beyond Hurryon Gate and busy yourself by carving upon it certain initials intertwined within the circumscribed outlines of a symbol popularly supposed to represent a human heart, your industry will be presently and miraculously rewarded by the apparition of her who presumably occupies no inconsiderable place in your affections."

At the Hurryon Gate Duane found Rosalie trying to unlock it, a dainty, smiling Rosalie, fresh as a blossom, and absurdly like a schoolgirl with her low-cut collar, snowy neck, and the thick braid of hair. Under her arm she carried her bathing-dress.

"I'm going for a swim; I nearly perished with the heat last night.... id you sleep well, Duane?"

"Rather well."

She hesitated, looked up: "Are you coming with me?"

"I have an appointment."

"Oh!... Are you going to let me go alone?"

He laughed: "I've no choice; I really have an appointment this morning."

She inspected him, drew a step nearer, laid both hands lightly on his shoulders.

"Duane, dear," she said, "are you really going to let me drift past you out to sea - after all?"

"What else can I do? Besides, you are not going to drift."

"Yes, I am. You were very nice to me yesterday."

"It was you who were very sweet to me.... But I told you how matters stand. You care for your husband."

"Yes, you did tell me. But it is not true. I thought about it all night long; I find that I do not care for him - as you told me I did."

He said, smiling: "Nor do you really care for me."

"I could care."

Her hands still lay lightly on his shoulders; he smilingly

disengaged them, saluted the finger tips, and swung them free.

"No, you couldn't," he said - "nor could I."

She clasped her hands behind her, confronting him with that gaily audacious allure which he knew so well:

"Does a man really care whether or not he is in love with a woman before he makes love to her?"

"Do you want an honest answer?"

"Please."

"Well, then - if she is sufficiently attractive, a man doesn't usually care."

"Am I sufficiently attractive?"

"Yes."

"Then - why do you hesitate?... I know the rules of the game. When one wearies, the other must pretend to.... And then they make their adieux very amiably.... Isn't that a man's ideal of an affair with a pretty woman?"

He laughed: "I suppose so."

"So do I. You are no novice, are you - as I am?"

"Are you a novice, Rosalie?"

"Yes, I am. You probably don't believe it. It is absurd, isn't it, considering these lonely years - considering what he has done - that I haven't anything with which to reproach myself."

"It is very admirable," he said.

"Oh, yes, theoretically. I was too fastidious - perhaps a little bit too decent. It's curious how inculcated morals and early precepts make mountains out of what is really very simple travelling. If a woman ceases to love her husband, she is going to miss too much in life if she's afraid to love anybody else.... I suppose I have been afraid."

"It's rather a wholesome sort of fear," he said.

"Wholesome as breakfast-food. I hate it. Besides, the fear doesn't exist any more," shaking her head. "Like the pretty girls in a very popular and profoundly philosophical entertainment, I've simply got to love somebody" - she smiled at him - "and I'd prefer to fall honestly and disgracefully in love with you - if you'd give me the opportunity." There was a pause. "Otherwise," she concluded, "I shall content myself with doing a mischief to your sex where I can. I give you the choice, Duane - I give you the disposal of myself. Am I to love - you? - or be loved by God knows whom - and make him suffer for it" - she set her little even teeth - "and pay back to men what man has done to me?"

"Nonsense," he said good-humouredly; "isn't there anything except playing at love that counts in the world?"

"Nothing counts without it. I've learned that much."

"Some people have done pretty well without it."

"You haven't. You might have been a really good painter if you cared for a woman who cared for you. There's no tenderness in your work; it's all technique and biceps."

He said gravely: "You are right."

"Am I?... Do you think you could try to care for me - even for that reason, Duane - to become a better painter?"

"I'm afraid not," he said pleasantly.

There was a silence; her expression changed subtly, then the colour came back and she smiled and nodded adieu.

"Good-bye," she said; "I'm going to get into all sorts of mischief. The black flag is hoisted. *Malheur aux hommes!*"

"There's one now," said Duane, laughing as Delancy Grandcourt's bulk appeared among the trees along Hurryon Water. "Lord! what a bungler he is on a trout-stream!"

Rosalie turned and gazed at the big, clumsy young man who was fishing with earnestness and method every unlikely pool in sight.

"Does he belong to anybody?" she asked, considering him. "I want to do real damage. He is usually at Geraldine's heels, isn't he?"

"Oh, let him alone," said Duane; "he's an awfully decent fellow. If a man of that slow, plodding, faithful species ever is thoroughly aroused by a woman, it will be a lively day for his tormentor."

Rosalie's blue eyes sparkled: "Will it?"

"Yes, it will. You had better not play hob with Delancy. Are you intending to?"

"I don't know. Look at the man! That's the fourth time he's landed his line in a bush! He'll fall into that pool if he's not - mercy! - there he goes! Did you ever see such a genius for clumsiness?"

She was moving forward through the trees as she spoke; Duane called after her in a warning voice:

"Don't try to do anything to disturb him. It's not good sport; he's a mighty decent sort, I tell you."

"I won't play any tricks on your good young man," she said with a shrug of contempt, and sauntered off toward the Gray Water. Her path, however, crossed Grandcourt's, and as she stepped upon the footbridge she glanced down, where, wading gingerly in mid-stream, Delancy floundered and panted and barely contrived to maintain a precarious footing, while sending his flies sprawling down the rapids.

"Good-morning," she nodded, as he caught sight of her. He attempted to take off his cap, slipped, wallowed, and recovered his balance by miracle alone.

"There's a thumping big trout under that bridge," he informed her eagerly; "he ran downstream just now, but I can't seem to raise him."

"You splash too much. You'd probably raise him if you raised less of something else."

"Is that it?" he inquired innocently. "I try not to, but I generally manage to raise hell with every pool before I get a chance to fish it. I'll show you just where he lies. Watch!"

His cast of flies whistled wildly; there was a quick pang of pain in her shoulder and she gave a frightened cry.

"Good Lord! Have I got *you*?" he exclaimed, aghast.

"You certainly have," she retorted, exasperated, "and you had better come up and get this hook out! You'll need it if you want to fish any more."

Dripping and horrified, he scrambled up the bank to the footbridge; she flinched, but made no sound, as he freed her from the hook; a red stain appeared on the sleeve of her waist, above the elbow.

"It's fortunate that it was a b-barbless hook," he stammered, horribly embarrassed and contemplating with dismay the damage he had accomplished; "otherwise," he added, "we would have had to cut out the hook. We're rather lucky, I think. Is it very painful?"

"Sufficiently," she said, disgusted. "But I suppose this sort of thing is nothing unusual for you."

"I've hooked one or two people," he admitted, reddening. "I suppose you won't bother to forgive me, but I'm terribly sorry. If you'll let me put a little mud on it -"

She disdained to reply. He hovered about her, clumsily solicitous, and whichever way she turned, he managed to get underfoot, until, thoroughly vexed, she stood stock-still and opened her arms with a hopeless gesture:

"What *are* you trying to do, Delancy? Do you want to embrace me? I wish you wouldn't leap about me like a great Dane puppy!"

The red surged up into his face anew:

"I beg your pardon," he said. "I'm very sorry."

She looked at him curiously: "I beg yours - you big, silly boy. Don't blush at me. Great Danes are exceedingly desirable property, you know.... Did you wish to be forgiven for anything? What on earth are you doing with that horrid fistful of muck?"

"I only want to put some mud on that wound, if you'll let me. It's good for hornet stings -"

She laughed and backed away: "Do you believe there is any virtue in mud, Delancy? - good, deep mire - when one is bruised and sore and lonely and desperate? Oh, don't try to understand - what a funny, confused, stupid way you have of looking at me! I remember you used to look at me that way sometimes - oh, long ago - before I was married, I think."

The heavy colour which surged so readily to his temples began to amuse her; she leaned back against the bridge rail and contemplated him with smiling disdain.

"Do you know," she said, "years ago, I had a slight, healthy suspicion that you were on the verge of falling in love with me."

He tried to smile, but the colour died out in his face.

"Yes, I was on the verge," he contrived to answer.

"Why didn't you fall over?"

"I suppose it was because you married Jack Dysart," he said simply.

"Was *that* all?"

"All?" He thought he perceived the jest, and managed to laugh again.

"Really, I am perfectly serious," repeated Rosalie. "Was that all that prevented you from falling in love with me - because I was married?"

"I think so," he said. "Wasn't it reason enough?"

"I didn't know it was enough for a man. I don't believe I know exactly how men consider such matters.... You've managed to hook that fly into my gown again! And now you've torn the skirt hopelessly! What a devastating sort of creature you are, Delancy! You used to step on my slippers at dancing school, and, oh, Heaven! how I hated you.... Where are you going?" for he had begun to walk away, reeling in his wet line as he moved, his grave, highly coloured face lowered, troubled eyes intent on what he was doing.

When she spoke, he halted and raised his head, and she saw

the muscles flexed under the bronze skin of the jaw - saw the lines of pain appear where his mouth tightened. All of the clumsy boy in him had vanished; she had never troubled herself to look at him very closely, and it surprised her to see how worn his face really was under the eyes and cheek-bones - really surprised her that there was much of dignity, even of a certain nobility, in his quiet gaze.

"I asked you where you are going?" she repeated with a faint smile.

"Nowhere in particular."

"But you are going *somewhere*, I suppose."

"I suppose so."

"In my direction?"

"I think not."

"That is very rude of you, Delancy - when you don't even know where my direction lies. Do you think," she demanded, amused, "that it is particularly civil of a man to terminate an interview with a woman before she offers him his conge?"

He finished reeling in his line, hooked the drop-fly into the reel-guide, shifted his creel, buttoned on the landing-net, and quietly turned around and inspected Mrs. Dysart.

"I want to tell you something," he said. "I have never, even as a boy, had from you a single word which did not in some vague manner convey a hint of your contempt for me. Do you realise that?"

"W-what!" she faltered, bewildered.

"I don't suppose you do realise it. People generally feel toward me as you feel; it has always been the fashion to tolerate me. It is a legend that I am thick-skinned and stupidly slow to take offence. I am not offended now.... Because I could not be with you.... But I am tired of it, and I thought it better that you should know it - after all these years."

Utterly confounded, she leaned back, both hands tightening on the hand-rail behind her, and as she comprehended the passionless reproof, a stinging flush deepened over her pretty face.

"Had you anything else to say to me?" he asked, without embarrassment.

"N-no."

"Then may I take my departure?"

She lifted her startled blue eyes and regarded him with a new and intense curiosity.

"Have I, by my manner or speech, ever really hurt you?" she asked. "Because I haven't meant to."

He started to reply, hesitated, shook his head, and his pleasant, kindly smile fascinated her.

"You haven't intended to," he said. "It's all right, Rosalie -"

"But - have I been horrid and disagreeable? Tell me."

In his troubled eyes she could see he was still searching to excuse her; slowly she began to recognise the sensitive simplicity of the man, the innate courtesy so out of harmony with her experience among men. What, after all, was there about him that a woman should treat with scant consideration, impatience, the toleration of contempt? His clumsy manner? His awkwardness? His very slowness to exact anything for himself? Or had it been the half-sneering, half-humourous attitude of her husband toward him which had insensibly coloured her attitude?

She had known Delancy Grandcourt all her life - that is, she had neglected to know him, if this brief revelation of himself warranted the curiosity and interest now stirring her.

"Were you really ever in love with me?" she asked, so frankly that the painful colour rose to his hair again, and he stood silent, head lowered, like a guilty boy caught in his sins.

"But - good heavens!" she exclaimed with an uneasy little laugh, "there's nothing to be ashamed of in it! I'm not laughing at you, Delancy; I am thinking about it with - with a certain re -" She was going to say regret, but she substituted "respect," and, rather surprised at her own seriousness, she fell silent, her uncertain gaze continually reverting to him.

She had never before noticed how tall and well-built he was, in spite of the awkwardness with which he moved - a great, big powerful machine, continually checked and halted, as though by some fear that his own power might break loose and smash things. That seemed to be the root of his awkwardness - unskilful self-control - a vague consciousness of the latent strength of limb and body and will, which habit alone controlled, and controlled unskilfully.

She had never before known a man resembling this new revelation of Grandcourt. Without considering or understanding why, she began to experience an agreeable sense of restfulness and security in the silence which endured between them. He stood full in the sunlight, very deeply preoccupied with the contents of his fly-book; she leaned back on the sun-scorched railing of the bridge, bathing-suit tucked under one arm, listening to the melody of the rushing stream below. It seemed almost like the intimacy of old friendship, this quiet interval in the sun, with the moving shadows of leaves at their feet and the music of the water in their ears - a silence unbroken save by that, and the pure, sweet call-note of some woodland bird from the thickets beyond.

"What fly are you trying?" she asked, dreamily conscious of the undisturbed accord.

"Wood-ibis - do you think they might come to it?" he asked so naturally that a sudden glow of confidence in him, in the sunlit world around her, warmed her.

"Let me look at your book?"

He brought it. Together they fumbled the brilliantly patterned aluminum leaves, fumbling with tufted silks and feathers, until she untangled a most alluringly constructed fly and drew it out, presenting it to him between forefinger and thumb.

"Shall we try it?"

"Certainly," he said.

Duane, carving hieroglyphics on the bark of the big beech, raised his head and looked after them.

"That's a pretty low trick," he said to himself, as they sauntered away toward the Gray Water. And he scowled in silence and continued his carving.

CHAPTER IX

CONFESSION

So many guests were arriving from Iron Hill, Cloudy Mountain, and West Gate Village that the capacity of Roya-Neh was overtaxed. Room had to be made somehow; Geraldine and Naida Mallett doubled up; twin beds were installed for Dysart and Bunny Gray; Rosalie took in Sylvia Quest with a shrug, disdaining any emotion, even curiosity, concerning the motherless girl whose imprudences with Jack Dysart had furnished gossip sufficient to last over from the winter.

The Tappans appeared with their guests, old Tappan grimmer, rustier, gaunter than usual; his son and heir, Peter - he of the rambling and casual legs - more genial, more futile, more acquiescent than ever. The Crays, Beckmans, Ellises, and Grandcourts arrived; Catharine Grandcourt shared Mrs. Severn's room; Scott Seagrave went to quarters at the West Gate, and Duane was driven forth and a cot-bed set up for him in his studio at Hurryon Lodge.

The lawns and terraces of Roya-Neh were swarming with eager, laughing young people; white skirts fluttered everywhere in the sun; tennis-courts and lake echoed with the gay tumult, motors tooted, smart horses and showy traps were constantly drawing up or driving off; an army of men from West Gate Village were busy stringing lanterns all over the grounds, pitching pavilions in the glade beyond Hurryon Gate, and decorating everything with ribbons, until Duane suggested to Scott that they tie silk bows on the wild squirrels, as everything ought to be as Louis XVI as possible. He himself did actually so adorn several respectable Shanghai hens which he caught at their oviparous duties, and the spectacle left Kathleen weak with laughter.

As for Duane, he suddenly seemed to have grown years younger. All that was careless, inconsequential, irresponsible, seemed to have disappeared in a single night, leaving a fresh, boyish enthusiasm quite free from surface cynicism - quite innocent of the easy, amused mockery which had characterised him. The subtle element of self-consciousness had disappeared, too. If it had remained unnoticed, even undetected before, now its absence was noticeable, for there was no longer any attitude about him, no policy to sustain, nothing of that humourous, bantering sophistication which ignores conventionality. For it is always a conscious effort to ignore it, an attitude to disregard what custom has sanctioned.

Kathleen had never realised what a really sweet and charming fellow he was until that morning, when he took her aside and told her of his engagement.

"Do you know," he said, "it is as though life had stopped for me many years ago when Geraldine and I were playmates; it's exactly as though all the interval of years in between counted less than a dream, and now, at last, I am awake and taking up real life again.... You see, Kathleen, as a matter of fact, I'm incomplete by myself. I'm only half of a suit of clothes; Geraldine always wore the rest of me."

"However," said Kathleen mischievously, "you've been very tireless in trying on, they say. It's astonishing you never found a good fit -"

"That was all part of the dream interval," he interrupted, a little out of countenance, "everything was absurdly unreal. Are you going to be nice to me, Kathleen?"

"Of course I am, you blessed boy!" she said, taking him in her vigorous young arms and kissing him squarely and thoroughly. Then she held him at arms' length and looked him very gravely in the eyes:

"Love her a great deal, Duane," she said in a low voice; "she needs it."

"I could not help doing it."

But Kathleen repeated:

"Love her enough. She will be yours to make - yours to unmake, to mould, fashion, remould - with God's good help. Love her enough."

"Yes," he said, very soberly.

A slight constraint fell between them; they spoke of the fete, and Kathleen presently left to superintend details which never worried her, never disturbed the gay and youthful confidence which had always from the beginning marked her successful superintendence of the house of Seagrave.

Geraldine and Scott were very busy playing hostess and host, receiving new-comers, renewing friendships interrupted by half a summer's separation; but there was very little to do except to be affable, for Kathleen's staff of domestics was perfectly adequate - the old servants of the house of Seagrave, who were quite able by themselves to maintain the household traditions and whip into line of duty the new and less conscientious recruits below stairs.

A great many people were gathered on the terrace when Duane descended the stairs, on his way to inspect his temporary quarters in Miller's loft, at Hurryon Lodge.

He stopped and spoke to many, greeted Delancy Grandcourt's loquacious and rotund mother, politely listened to her scandalous budget of gossip, shook hands cordially with her big, handsome daughter, Catharine, a strapping girl, with the shyly honest eyes of her brother and the rather heavy but shapely body and limbs of an indolent Juno. A harsh voice pronounced his name; old Mr. Tappan extended a dry hand and bored him through with eyes like holes burnt in a blanket.

"And do you still cultiwate the fine arts, young man?" he inquired, as sternly as though he privately suspected Duane of maltreating them.

Duane shook hands with him.

"The school of the indiwidool," continued Mr. Tappan, "is what artists need. Woo the muses in solitude; cultiwate 'em in isolation. Didn't Benjamin West live out in the backwoods? And I guess he managed to make good without raising hell in the Eekole di Boze Arts with a lot of dissipated wagabonds at his elbow, inculcating immoral precepts and wasting his time and his father's money."

And he looked very hard at Duane, who winced, but agreed with him solemnly.

Geraldine, on the edge of a circle of newly arrived guests, leaned over and whispered mischievously:

"Is that what *you* did at the Ecole des Beaux Arts? Did you behave like all that or did you cultivate the indiwidool?"

He shook hands again, solemnly, with Mr. Tappan, stepped back, and joined her.

"Where on earth have you been hiding?" she inquired.

"You said that if I carved certain cabalistic signs on the big beech-tree you would presently appear to me in a pink cloud - you faithless little wretch!"

"How could I? Three motor-loads arrived from Iron Hill before I was half dressed, and ever since I've been doing my traditional duty; and," in a lower voice, "I was perfectly crazy to go to the beech-tree all the time. Did you wait long, you poor boy?"

"Man is born to wait. I came back just now to find you.... I told Kathleen," he added, radiant.

"What?" she whispered, flushing deliciously. "Oh, pooh! I told her about it this morning - the very first thing. We both snivelled. I didn't sleep at all last night.... There's something I wish to tell you -"

The gay smile suddenly died out in her eyes; a strange, wistful tenderness softened them, touching her lips, too, which always gave that very young, almost childish pathos to her expression. She put out her hand instinctively and touched him.

"I want to be alone with you, Duane - for a little while."

"Shall I go to the beech-tree and wait?"

She glanced around with a hopeless gesture:

"You see? Other people are arriving and I've simply got to be here. I don't see how I can get away before luncheon. Where were you going just now?"

"I thought I'd step over to the studio to see what sort of a shake-down you've given me to repose on."

"I wish you would. Poor child, I do hope you will be comfortable. It's perfectly horrid to send you out of the house -"

"Oh, I don't mind," he nodded, laughing, and she gave him a shy glance of adieu and turned to receive another guest.

In his extemporized studio at Hurryon Lodge he found that

old Miller had already provided him with a washstand and accessories, a new tin tub and a very comfortable iron bed.

The place was aromatic with the odour of paints, varnishes, turpentine, and fixative; he opened the big window, let in air and sunshine, and picked up a sheaf of brushes, soft and pliable from a fresh washing in turpentine and black soap.

Confronting him on a big improvised easel was the full-length, half-reclining portrait of Rosalie Dysart - a gay, fascinating, fly-away thing after the deliberately artificial manner of the French court painters who simpered and painted a hundred and fifty years ago. Ribbons fluttered from the throat and shoulder of this demure, fair-skinned, and blue-eyed creature, who was so palpably playing at masquerade. A silken parody of a shepherdess - a laughing, dainty, snowy-fingered aristocrat, sweet-lipped, provocative, half reclining under a purposely conventional oak, between the branches of which big white clouds rolled in a dark-blue sky - this was Rosalie as Duane had painted her with all the perversely infernal skill of a brush always tipped with a mockery as delicate as her small, bare foot, dropping below the flowered petticoat.

The unholy ease with which he had done it gave him a secret thrill of admiration. It was apparently all surface - the exquisite masquerader, the surrounding detail, the technical graciousness and flow of line and contour, the effortless brush-work. Yet, with an ease which demanded very respectful consideration, he had absorbed and transmitted the frivolous spirit of the old French masters, which they themselves took so seriously; the portrait was also a likeness, yet delightfully permeated with the charm of a light-minded epoch; and somehow, behind and underneath it all, a brilliant mockery sparkled - the half-amused, half-indifferent brilliancy of the painter himself. It was there for any who could appreciate it, and it was quite irresistible, particularly since he had, after a dazzling preliminary study or two from a gamekeeper's small, chubby son, added, fluttering in mid-air, a pair of white-winged Loves, chubby as cherubs but much more Gallic.

Nobody excepting Rosalie and himself had seen the picture. What he meant to do with it he did not know, half ashamed as he was of its satiric cleverness. Painters would hate it - stand hypnotised, spellbound the while - and hate it, for they are a serious sort, your painters of pictures, and they couldn't appreciate an art which made fun of art; they would execrate the uncanny mastery and utterly miss the gay perversity of the performance, and Duane knew it and laughed wickedly. What a shock! What would sober, seriously inclined people think if an actor who was eminently fitted to play *Lear*, should bow to his audience and earnestly perform a very complicated and perfect flip-flap?

Amused with his own disrespectful reflections, he stood before the picture, turning from it with a grin from time to time to compare it with some dozen vigorous canvases hanging along the studio wall - studies that he knew would instantly command the owlish respect of the truly earnest - connoisseurs, critics, and academicians in this very earnest land of ours.

There was a Sargent-like portrait of old Miller, with something of that great master's raucous colouring and perhaps intentional discords, and all of his technical effrontery; and here, too, lurked that shadow of mockery ever latent in the young man's brush - something far more subtle than caricature or parody - deeper than the imitation of manner - something like the evanescent caprice of a strong hand, which seems to threaten for a second, then passes on lightly, surely, transforming its menace into a caress.

There were two adorable nude studies of Miller's granddaughters, aged six and seven - quaintly and engagingly formal in their naïve astonishment at finding themselves quite naked. There was a fine sketch of Howker, wrinkled, dim-eyed, every inch a butler, every fibre in him the dignified and self-respecting, old-time servant, who added his dignity to that of the house he had served so long and well. The latter picture was masterly, recalling Gandara's earlier simplicity and

Whistler's single-minded concentration without that gentleman's rickety drawing and harmonious arrangements in mud.

For in Duane's work, from somewhere deep within, there radiated outward something of that internal glow which never entirely fades from the canvases of the old masters - which survives mould and age, the opacity of varnish, and the well-intentioned maltreatment of unbaked curators.

There was no mystery about it; he prepared his canvas with white-lead, gave it a long sun-bath, modelled in bone-black and an earth-red, gave it another bath in the sun, and then glazed. This, a choice of permanent colours, and oil as a medium, was the mechanical technique.

Standing there, thoughts remote, idly sorting and re-sorting his brushes, he heard the birds singing on the forest's edge, heard the wind in the pines blowing, with the sound of flowing water, felt the warmth of the sun, breathed the mounting freshness from the fields. Life was still very, very young; it had only begun since love had come, and that was yesterday.

And as he stood there, happy, a trifle awed as he began to understand what life might hold for him, there came quick steps on the stair, a knock, her voice outside his door:

"Duane! May I come in?"

He sprang to the door; she stepped inside, breathing rapidly, delicately flushed from her haste.

"I couldn't stand it any longer, so I left Scott to scrape and bow and pull his forelock. I've got to go back in a few minutes. Are you glad to see me?"

He took her in his arms.

"Dearest, dearest!" she murmured, looking at him with all her heart in her brown eyes.

So they stood for a little while, her mouth and body acquiescent to his embrace.

"Such a long, long time since I saw you. Nearly half an hour," he said.

"Yes." She drew away a little:

"Do you know," she said, looking about her, over his shoulder, "I have never been here since you took it as a studio."

She caught a glimpse of the picture on the easel, freed herself, and, retaining his hand in both of hers, gazed curiously at Rosalie's portrait.

"How perfectly charming!" she said. "But, Duane, there's a sort of exquisite impudence about what you've done! Did you mean to gently and disrespectfully jeer at our mincing friends, Boucher, Nattier, *et al.*?"

"I knew you'd understand!" he exclaimed, delighted. "Oh, you wonderful little thing - you darling!" He caught her to him again, but she twisted away and tucked one arm under his:

"Don't, Duane; I want to see these things. What a perfectly dear study of Miller's kiddies! Oh, it is too lovable, too adorable! You wouldn't sell that - would you?"

"Of course not; it's yours, Geraldine."

After a moment she looked up at him:

"Ours?" she asked; but the smile faded once more from eyes and lips; she suffered him to lead her from canvas to canvas, approved them or remained silent, and presently turned and glanced toward the small iron bed. Manner and gaze had become distrait.

"You think this will be comfortable, Duane?" she

inquired listlessly.

"Perfectly," he said.

She disengaged her hand from his, walked over to the lounge, turned, and signed for him to seat himself. Then she dropped to her knees and settled down on the rug at his feet, laying her soft cheek against his arm.

"I have some things to tell you," she said in a low voice.

"Very serious things?" he asked, smiling.

"Very."

"All right; I am listening."

"Very serious things," she repeated, gazing through the window, where green tree-tops swayed in the breezy sunlight; and she pressed her cheek closer to his arm.

"I have not been very - good," she said.

He looked at her, suppressed the smile that twitched at his mouth, and waited.

"I wish I could give myself to you as clean and sweet and untainted as - as you deserve.... I can't; and before we go any further I must tell you -"

"Why, you blessed child," he exclaimed, half laughing, half serious. "You are not going to confess to me, are you?"

"Duane, I've got to tell you everything. I couldn't rest unless I was perfectly honest with you."

"But, dear," he said, a trifle dismayed, "such confidences are not necessary. Nor am I fit to hear your list of innocent transgressions -"

"Oh, they are not very innocent. Let me tell you; let me cleanse myself as much as I can. I don't want to have any secrets from you, Duane. I want to go to you as guiltless as confession can make me. I want to begin clean. Let me tell you. Couldn't you let me tell you, Duane?"

"And I, dear? Do - do you expect me to tell *you*? Do you expect me to do as you do?"

She looked up at him surprised; she had expected it. Something in his face warned her of her own ignorance.

"I don't know very much about men, Duane. Are there things you cannot say to me?"

"One or two, dear."

"Do you mean until after we are married?"

"Not even then. There is no use in your knowing."

She had never considered that, either.

"But *ought* I to know, Duane?"

"No," he said miserably, "you ought not."

She sat upright for a few seconds longer, gazing thoughtfully at space, then pressed her pale face against his knee again in silent faith and confidence.

"Anyway, I know you will be fair to me in your own way," she said. "There is only one way that I know how to be fair to you. Listen."

And in a shamed voice she forced herself to recite her list of sins; repeating them as she had confessed them to Kathleen. She told him everything; her silly and common imprudence with Dysart, which, she believed, had bordered the danger mark; her ignoble descent to what she had always held aloof from, meaning demoralisation in regard to betting and gambling and foolish language; and last, but most shameful, her secret and perilous temporising with a habit which already was making self-denial very difficult for her. She did not spare herself; she told him everything, searching the secret recesses of her heart for some small sin in hiding, some fault, perhaps, overlooked or forgotten. All that she held unworthy in her she told this man; and the man, being an average man, listened, head bowed over her fragrant hair, adoring her, wretched in heart and soul with the heavy knowledge of all he dare not tell or forget or cleanse from him, kneeling repentant, in the sanctuary of her love and confidence.

She told him everything - sins of omission, childish depravities, made real only by the decalogue. Of indolence, selfishness, unkindness, she accused herself; strove to count the times when she had yielded to temptation.

He was reading the first human heart he had ever known - a heart still strangely untainted, amid a society where innocence was the exception, doubtful wisdom the rule, and where curiosity was seldom left very long in doubt.

His hands fell over hers as her voice ceased, but he did not speak.

She waited a little while, then, with a slight nestling movement, turned and hid her face on his knees.

"With God's help," she whispered, "I will subdue what threatens me. But I am afraid of it! Oh, Duane, I am afraid."

He managed to steady his voice.

"What is it, darling, that seems to tempt you," he asked; "is it the taste - the effect?"

"The - effect. If I could only forget it - but I can't help

thinking about it - I suppose just because it's forbidden - For days, sometimes, there is not the slightest desire; then something stirs it up in me, begins to annoy me; or the desire comes sometimes when I am excited or very happy, or very miserable. There seems to be some degraded instinct in me that seeks for it whenever my emotions are aroused.... I must be honest with you; I - I feel that way *now* - because, I suppose, I am a little excited."

He raised her and took her in his arms.

"But you won't, will you? Simply tell me that you won't."

She looked at him, appalled by her own hesitation. Was it possible, after the words she had just uttered, the exaltation of confession still thrilling her, that she could hesitate? Was it morbid over-conscientiousness in the horror of a broken promise to him that struck her silent?

"Say it, Geraldine."

"Oh, Duane! I've said it so often to Kathleen and myself! Let me promise myself again - and keep my word. Let me try that way, dear, before I - I promise you?"

There was a feverish colour in her face; she spoke rapidly, like one who temporises, trying to convince others and over-ride the inward voice; her slender hands were restless on his shoulders, her eyes lowered, avoiding his.

"Perhaps if you and Kathleen, and I, myself, were not so afraid - perhaps if I were not forbidden - if I had your confidence and my own that I would not abuse my liberty, it might be easier to refrain. Shall we try it that way, Duane?"

"Do you think it best?"

"I think - I might try that way. Dear, I have so much to sustain me now - so much more at stake! Because there is the dread of losing you - for, Duane, until I am mistress of myself, I will never, never marry you - and do you suppose I am going to risk our happiness? Only leave me free, dear; don't attempt to wall me in at first, and I will surely find my way."

She sprang up, trying to smile, hesitated, then slowly came back to where he was standing and put her arms around his neck.

"Good-bye until luncheon," she said. "I must go back to my neglected guests - I am going to run all the way as fast as my legs can carry me! Kathleen will be dreadfully mortified. Do you love me?... Even after my horrid confessions?... Oh, you darling!... Now that you know the very worst, I begin to feel as clean and fresh as though I had just stepped from the bath.... And I *will* try to be what you would have me, dear.... Because I am quite crazy about you - oh, completely mad!"

She bent impulsively and kissed his hands, freed herself with a breathless laugh, and turned and fled.

For a long time her lover stood there, motionless, downcast, clenched fists in his pockets, face to face with the past. And that which lay behind him was that which lies behind what is commonly known to the world as the average man.

CHAPTER X

DUSK

The Masked Dance was to begin at ten that evening; for that reason dinner had been served early at scores of small tables on the terrace, a hilarious and topsy-turvy, but somewhat rapid affair, because everybody required time for dressing, and already throughout the house maids and valets were scurrying around, unpacking masks and wigs and dainty costumes for the adorning of the guests at Roya-Neh.

Toward nine o'clock the bustle and confusion became distracting; corridors were haunted by graceful flitting figures in various stages of deshabille, in quest of paraphernalia feminine and maids to adjust the same. A continual chatter filled the halls, punctuated by smothered laughter and subdued but insistent appeals for aid in the devious complications of intimate attire.

On the men's side of the house there was less hubbub and some quiet swearing; much splashing in tubs, much cigarette smoke. Men entered each other's rooms, half-clad in satin breeches, silk stockings, and ruffled shirts, asking a helping hand in tying queue ribbons or adjusting stocks, and lingered to smoke and jest and gossip, and jeer at one another's finery, or to listen to the town news from those week-enders recently arrived from the city.

The talk was money, summer shows, and club gossip, but

financial rumours ruled.

Young Ellis, in pale blue silk and wig, perched airily, on a table, became gloomily prophetic concerning the steady retirement of capital from philanthropic enterprises hatched in Wall Street; Peter Tappan saw in the endlessly sagging market dire disaster for the future digestions of wealthy owners of undistributed securities.

"Marble columns and gold ceilings don't make a trust company," he sneered. "There are a few billionaire gamblers from the West who seem to think Wall Street is Coney Island. There'll be a shindy, don't make any mistake; we're going to have one hell of a time; but when it's over the corpses will all be shipped - ahem! - west."

Several men laughed uneasily; one or two old line trust companies were mentioned; then somebody spoke of the Minnisink, lately taken over by the Algonquin.

Duane lighted a cigarette and, watching the match still burning, said:

"Dysart is a director. You can't ask for any more conservative citizen than Dysart, can you?"

Several men looked around for Dysart, but he had stepped out of the room.

Ellis said, after a silence:

"That gambling outfit from the West has bedevilled one or two good citizens in Gotham town."

Dr. Bailey shrugged his big, fat shoulders.

"It's no secret, I suppose, that the Minnisink crowd is being talked about," he grunted.

Ellis said in a low but perfectly distinct voice:

"Neither is it any secret that Jack Dysart has been hit hard in National Ice."

Peter Tappan slipped from his seat on the table and threw away his cigarette:

"One thing is sure as soubrettes," he observed; "the Clearing House means to get rid of certain false prophets. The game law is off prophets - in the fall. There'll be some good gunning - under the laws of New Jersey."

"I hope they'll be careful not to injure any marble columns or ruin the gold-leaf on the ceilings," sneered Ellis. "Come on, some of you fellows, and fix the buckle in this cursed stock of mine."

"I thought fixing stocks was rather in your own line," said Duane to the foxy-visaged and celebrated manipulator, who joined very heartily in the general and unscrupulous laugh.

A moment later, Dysart, who had heard every word from the doorway, walked silently back to his own room and sat down, resting his temples between his closed fists.

The well-cut head was already silvery gray at the temples; one month had done it. When animated, his features still appeared firm and of good colour; relaxed, they were loose and pallid, and around the mouth fine lines appeared. Often a man's hands indicate his age, and his betrayed him, giving the lie to his lithe, straight, graceful figure. The man had aged amazingly in a month or two.

Matters were not going very well with him. For one thing, the Half-Moon Trust Company had finally terminated all dealings with the gorgeous marble-pillared temple of high finance of which he was a director. For another, he had met the men of the West, and for them he had done things which he did not always care to think about. For another, money was becoming disturbingly scarce, and the time was already past for selling securities.

During the last year he had been vaguely aware of some occult hostility to himself and his enterprises - not the normal hostility of business aggression - but something indefinable - merely negative at first, then more disturbing, sinister, foreboding; something in the very air to which he was growing more sensitive every day.

By all laws of finance, by all signs and omens, a serious reaction from the saturnalia of the last few years was already over-due. He had felt it, without alarm at first, for the men of the West laughed him to scorn and refused to shorten sail. They still refused. Perhaps they could not. One thing was certain: he could scarcely manage to take in a single reef on his own account. He was beginning to realise that the men with whom rumour was busy were men marked down by their letters; and they either would not or could not aid him in shortening sail.

For a month, now, under his bland and graceful learning among the intimates of his set, Dysart had been slowly but steadily going to pieces. At such moments as this it showed on the surface. It showed now in his loose jaw and flaccid cheeks; in the stare of the quenched eyes.

He was going to pieces, and he was aware of it. For one thing, he recognised the physical change setting in; for another, his cool, selfish, self-centred equanimity was being broken down; the rigorous bodily regime from which he had never heretofore swerved and which alone enabled him to perform the exacting social duties expected of him, he had recently neglected. He felt the impending bodily demoralisation, the threatened mental disintegration; he suspected its symptoms in a new nervous irritability, in lapses of self-command, in unaccountable excesses utterly foreign to his habitual self-control.

Dissolute heretofore only in the negative form, whatever it was that impended threatening him, seemed also to be driving him into an utter and monstrous lack of caution, and - God alone knew how - he had at last done the one thing that he never dreamed of doing. And the knowledge of it, and the fear of it, bit deeper into his shallow soul every hour of the day and night. And over all, vague, indefinite, hung something that menaced all that he cared for most on earth, held most sacred - his social position in the Borough of Manhattan and his father's pride in him and it.

* * * * *

After a while he stood up in his pale blue silken costume of that mincing, smirking century which valued a straight back and a well-turned leg, and very slowly, as though tired, he walked to the door separating his wife's dressing-room from his own.

"May I come in?" he asked.

A maid opened the door, saying that Mrs. Dysart had gone to Miss Quest's room to have her hair powdered. He seated himself; the maid retired.

For a while he sat there, absently playing with his gilt-hilted sword, sombre-eyed, preoccupied, listening to the distant joyous tumult in the house, until quick, light steps and a breezy flurry of satin at the door announced his wife's return.

"Oh," she said coolly; "you?"

That was her greeting; his was a briefer nod.

She went to her mirror and studied her face, trying a patch here, a hint of vermilion there, touching up brow and lashes and the sweet, curling corners of her mouth.

"Well?" she inquired, over her shoulder, insolently.

He got up out of the chair, shut the door, and returned to his seat again.

"Have you made up your mind about the *D* and *P* securities?" he asked.

"I told you I'd let you know when I came to any conclusion," she replied drily.

"Yes, I know what you said, Rosalie. But the time is shortening. I've got to meet certain awkward obligations -"

"So you intimated before."

He nodded and went on amiably: "All I ask of you is to deposit those securities with us for a few months. They are as safe with us as they are with the Half-Moon. Do you think I'd let you do it if I were not certain?"

She turned and scrutinised him insultingly:

"I don't know," she said, "how many kinds of treachery you are capable of."

"What do you mean?"

"What I say. Frankly, I don't know what you are capable of doing with my money. If I can judge by what you've done with my married life, I scarcely feel inclined to confide in you financially."

"There is no use in going over that again," he said patiently. "We differ little from ordinary people, I fancy. I think our house is as united as the usual New York domicile. The main thing is to keep it so. And in a time of some slight apprehension and financial uneasiness - perhaps even of possible future stress - you and I, for our own sakes, should stand firmly together to weather any possible gale."

"I think I am able to weather whatever I am responsible for," she said. "If you do the same, we can get on as well as we ever have."

"I don't believe you understand," he persisted, forcing a patient smile. "All business in the world is conducted upon borrowed capital. I merely -"

"Do you need more capital?" she inquired, so bluntly that he winced.

"Yes, for a few months. I may require a little additional collateral -"

"Why don't you borrow it, then?"

"There is no necessity if you will temporarily transfer -"

"*Can* you borrow it? Or is the ice in your trust company too rotten to stand the strain?"

He flushed darkly and the temper began to escape in his voice:

"Has anybody hinted that I couldn't? Have you been discussing my personal business affairs with any of the pups whom you drag about at your heels? No matter what your personal attitude toward me may be, only a fool would undermine the very house that -"

"I don't believe you understand, Jack," she said quietly; "I care absolutely nothing about your house."

"Well, you care about your own social status, I suppose!" he retorted sharply.

"Not very much."

"That's an imbecile thing to say!"

"Is it?" She turned to the mirror and touched her powdered hair lightly with both hands, and continued speaking with her back turned toward him:

"I married you for love. Remember that. There was even something of it alive in the roots, I think, until within a few days - in spite of what you are, what you have done to me. Now the thing is dead. I can tell you when it died, if you like."

And as he said nothing:

"It died when I came in late one evening, and, passing my corridor and a certain locked door, I heard a young girl sobbing. Then it died."

She turned on him, contemptuously indifferent, and surveyed him at her leisure:

"Your conduct to me has been such as to deliberately incite me to evil. Your attitude has been a constant occult force, driving me toward it. By the life you have led, and compelled me to lead, you have virtually set a premium upon my infidelity. What you may have done, I don't know; what you have done, even recently, I am not sure of. But I know this: you took my life and made a parody of it. I never lived; I have been tempted to. If the opportunity comes, I will."

Dysart rose, his face red and distorted:

"I thought young Mallett had taught you to live pretty rapidly!" he said.

"No," she replied, "you only thought other people thought so. That is why you resented it. Your jealousy is of that sort - you don't care what I am, but you do care what the world thinks I am. And that is all there ever was to you - all there ever will be: desperate devotion to your wretched little social status, which includes sufficient money and a chaste wife to make it secure."

She laughed; fastened a gardenia in her hair:

"I don't know about your money, and I don't care. As for your wife, she will remain chaste as long as it suits her, and not one fraction of a second longer."

"Are you crazy?" he demanded.

"Why, it does seem crazy to you, I suppose - that a woman should have no regard for the sacredness of your social status. I have no regard for it. As for your honour" - she laughed unpleasantly - "I've never had it to guard, Jack. And I'll be responsible for my own, and the tarnishing of it. I think that is all I have to say."

She walked leisurely toward the door, passing him with a civil nod of dismissal, and left him standing there in his flower-embroidered court-dress, the electric light shining full on the thin gray hair at his temples.

In the corridor she met Naida, charming in her blossom-embroidered panniers; and she took both her hands and kissed her, saying:

"Perhaps you won't care to have me caress you some day, so I'll take this opportunity, dear. Where is your brother?"

"Duane is dressing," she said. "What did you mean by my not wishing to kiss you some day?"

"Nothing, silly." And she passed on, turned to the right, and met Sylvia Quest, looking very frail and delicate in her bath-robe and powdered hair. The girl passed her with the same timid, almost embarrassed little inclination with which she now invariably greeted her, and Rosalie turned and caught her, turning her around with a laugh. "What is the matter, dear?"

"M-matter?" stammered Sylvia, trembling under the reaction.

"Yes. You are not very friendly, and I've always liked you. Have I offended you, Sylvia?"

She was looking smilingly straight into the blue eyes.

"No - oh, no!" said the girl hastily. "How can you think that, Mrs. Dysart?"

"Then I don't think it," replied Rosalie, laughing. "You are a trifle pale, dear. Touch up your lips a bit. It's very Louis XVI. See mine?... Will you kiss me, Sylvia?"

Again a strange look flickered in the girl's eyes; Rosalie kissed her gently; she had turned very white.

"What is your costume?" asked Mrs. Dysart.

"Flame colour and gold."

"Hell's own combination, dear," laughed Rosalie. "You will make an exquisite little demon shepherdess."

And she went on, smiling back at the girl in friendly fashion, then turned and lightly descended the stairway, snapping on her loup-mask before the jolly crowd below could identify her.

Masked figures here and there detained her, addressing her in disguised voices, but she eluded them, slipped through the throngs on terrace and lawn, ran down the western slope and entered the rose-garden. A man in mask and violet-gray court costume rose from a marble seat under the pergola and advanced toward her, the palm of his left hand carelessly balanced on his gilded hilt.

"So you did get my note, Duane?" she said, laying her pretty hand on his arm.

"I certainly did. What can I do for you, Rosalie?"

"I don't know. Shall we sit here a moment?"

He laughed, but continued standing after she was seated.

The air was heavy with the scent of rockets and phlox and ragged pinks and candy-tuft. Through the sweet-scented dusky silence some small and very wakeful bird was trilling. Great misty-winged moths came whirring and hovering among the blossoms, pale blurs in the darkness, and everywhere the drifting lamps of fireflies lighted and died out against the foliage.

The woman beside him sat with masked head bent and slightly turned from him; her restless hands worried her fan; her satin-shod feet were crossed and recrossed.

"What is the matter?" he asked.

"Life. It's all so very wrong."

"Oh," he said, smiling, "so it's life that is amiss, not we!"

"I suppose we are.... I suppose I am. But, Duane" - she turned and looked at him - "I haven't had much of a chance yet - to go very right or very wrong."

"You've had chances enough for the latter," he said with an unpleasant laugh. "In this sweet coterie we inhabit, there's always that chance."

"There are good women in it, good wives. Your sister is in it."

"Yes, and I mean to take her out," said Duane grimly. "Do you think I want Naida to marry some money-fattened pup in this set?"

"Where can you take her?"

"Where I'm going in future myself - among people whose

brains are not as obsolete as my appendix; where there still exist standards and old-fashioned things like principles and religion, and a healthy terror of the Decalogue!"

"Is anybody really still afraid of the Decalogue?" she asked curiously.

"Even we are, but some of us are more afraid of ennui. Fire and fear are the greatest purifiers in the world; it's fear of some sort or other, and only fear, that keeps the world as decent as it is."

"I'm not afraid," she said, playing with her fan. "I'm only afraid of dying before I have lived at all."

"What do you call living?"

"Being loved," she said, and looked up at him.

"You poor little thing!" he said, only partly in earnest.

"Yes, I'm sorry for the girl I was.... I was rather a nice girl, Duane. You remember me before I married."

"Yes, I do. You were a corker. You are still."

She nodded: "Yes, outwardly. Within is - nothing. I am very, very old; very tired."

He said no more. She sat listlessly watching the dusk-moths hovering among the pinks. Far away in the darkness rockets were rising, spraying the sky with fire; faint strains of music came from the forest.

"Their Fete Galante has begun," she said. "Am I detaining you too long, Duane?"

"No."

She smiled: "It is rather amusing," she observed, "my coming to you for my morals - to you, Duane, who were once supposed to possess so few."

"Never mind what I possess," he said, irritated. "What sort of advice do you expect?"

"Why, moral advice, of course."

"Oh! Are you on the verge of demoralisation?"

"I don't know. Am I?... There is a man -"

"Of course," he said, coming as near a sneer as he was capable. "I know what you've done. You've nearly twisted poor Grandcourt's head off his honest neck. If you want to know what I think of it, it's an abominable thing to do. Why, anybody can see that the man is in love with you, and desperately unhappy already, I told you to let him alone. You promised, too."

He spoke rapidly, sharply; she bent her fair head in silence until he ended.

"May I defend myself?" she asked.

"Of course."

"Then - I did not mean to make him care for me."

"You all say that."

"Yes; we are not always as innocent as I happen to be this time. I really did not try, did not think, that he was taking a little unaccustomed kindness on my part so seriously ... I overdid it; I'd been beastly to him - most women are rude to Delancy Grandcourt, somehow or other. I always was. And one day - that day in the forest - somehow something he said opened my eyes - hurt me.... And women are fools to believe him one.

Why, Duane, he's every inch a man - high-minded, sensitive, proud, generous, forbearing."

Duane turned and stared at her; and to her annoyance the blood mounted to her cheeks, but she went on:

"Of course he has affected me. I don't know how it might have been with me if I were not so - so utterly starved."

"You mean to say you are beginning to care for Delancy Grandcourt?"

"Care? Yes - in a perfectly nice way -"

"And otherwise?"

"I - don't know. I am honest with you, Duane; I don't know. A - a little devotion of that kind" - she tried to laugh - "goes to my head, perhaps. I've been so long without it.... I don't know. And I came here to tell you. I came here to ask you what I ought to do."

"Good Lord!" said Duane, "do you already care enough for him to worry about your effect on him?"

"I - do not wish him to be unhappy."

"Oh. But you are willing to be unhappy in order to save him any uneasiness. See here, Rosalie, you'd better pull up sharp."

"Had I?"

"Certainly," he said brutally. "Not many days ago you were adrift. Don't cut your cable again."

A vivid colour mounted to her temples:

"That is all over," she said. "Have I not come to you again in spite of the folly that sent me drifting to you before? And can I pay you a truer compliment, Duane, than to ask the hospitality of your forbearance and the shelter of your friendship?"

"You *are* a trump, Rosalie," he said, after a moment's scowling. "You're all right.... I don't know what to say.... If it's going to give you a little happiness to care for this man -"

"But what will it do to him, Duane?"

"It ought to do him good if such a girl as you gives him all of herself that she decently can. I don't know whether I'm right or wrong!" he added almost angrily. "Confound it! there seems no end to conjugal infelicity around us these days. I don't know where the line is - how close to the danger mark an unhappy woman may drift and do no harm to anybody. All I know is that I'm sorry - terribly sorry for you. You're a corker."

"Thanks," she said with a faint smile. "Do you think Delancy may safely agree with you without danger to his peace of mind?"

"Why not? After all, you're entitled to lawful happiness. So is he.... Only -"

"Only - what?"

"I've never seen it succeed."

"Seen what succeed?"

"What is popularly known as the platonic."

"Oh, this isn't *that*," she said naively. "He's rather in love already, and I'm quite sure I could be if I - I let myself."

Duane groaned.

"Don't come to me asking what to do, then," he said impatiently, "because I know what you ought to do and I don't know what I'd do under the circumstances. You know as well as I do where the danger mark is. Don't you?"

"I - suspect."

"Well, then -"

"Oh, we haven't reached it yet," she said innocently.

Her honesty appalled him, and he got up and began to pace the gravel walk.

"Do you intend to cross it?" he asked, halting abruptly.

"No, I don't.... I don't want to.... Do you think there is any fear of it?"

"My Lord!" he said in despair, "you talk like a child. I'm trying to realise that you women - some of you who appear so primed with doubtful, worldly wisdom - are practically as innocent as the day you married."

"I don't know very much about some things, Duane."

"I notice that," he said grimly.

She said very gravely: "This is the first time I have ever come very near caring for a man.... I mean since I married." And she rose and glanced toward the forest.

They stood together for a moment, listening to the distant music, then, without speaking, turned and walked toward the distant flare of light which threw great trees into tangled and grotesque silhouette.

"Tales of the Geneii," she murmured, fastening her loup; "Fate is the Sultan. Pray God nobody cuts my head off."

"You are much too amusing," he said as, side by side, they

moved silently on through the pale starlight, like errant phantoms of a vanished age, and no further word was said between them, nor did they look at each other again until, ahead, the road turned silvery under the rays of the Lodge acetylenes, and beyond, the first cluster of brilliant lanterns gleamed among the trees.

"And here we separate," she said. "Good-bye," holding out her hand. "It is my first rendezvous. Wish me a little happiness, please."

"Happiness and - good sense," he said, smiling. He retained her hand for a second, let it go and, stepping back, saluted her gaily as she passed before him into the blaze of light.

CHAPTER XI

FETE GALANTE

The forest, in every direction, was strung with lighted lanterns; tall torches burning edged the Gray Water, and every flame rippled straight upward in the still air.

Through the dark, mid-summer woodland music of violin, viola, and clarionet rang out, and the laughter and jolly uproar of the dancers swelled and ebbed, with now and then sudden intervals of silence slowly filled by the far noise of some unseen stream rushing westward under the stars.

Glade, greensward, forest, aisles, and the sylvan dancing floor, bounded by garlanded and beribboned pillars, swarmed with a gay company. Torchlight painted strange high lights on silken masks, touching with subdued sparkles the eyes behind the slanting eye-slits; half a thousand lanterns threw an orange radiance across the glade, bathing the whirling throngs of dancers, glimmering on gilded braid and sword hilt, on powdered hair, on fresh young faces laughing behind their masks; on white shoulders and jewelled throats, on fan and brooch and spur and lacquered heel. There was a scent of old-time perfume in the air, and, as Duane adjusted his mask and drew near, he saw that sets were already forming for the minuet.

He recognised Dysart, glorious in silk and powder, perfectly in his element, and doing his part with eighteenth-century elaboration; Kathleen, tres grande-dame, almost too exquisitely real for counterfeit; Delancy Grandcourt, very red in the face under his mask, wig slightly awry, conscientiously behaving as nearly like a masked gentleman of the period as he knew how; his sister Naida, sweet and gracious; Scott, masked and also spectacled, grotesque and preoccupied, casting patient glances toward the dusky solitudes that he much preferred, and from whence a distant owl fluted at intervals, inviting his investigations.

And there were the Pink 'uns, too, easily identified, having all sorts of a good time with a pair of maskers resembling Doucette Landon and Peter Tappan; and there in powder, paint, and patch capered the Beekmans, Ellises, and Montrosses - all the clans of the great and near-great of the country-side, gathering to join the eternal hunt for happiness where already the clarionets were sounding "Stole Away."

For the quarry in that hunt is a spectre; sighted, it steals away; and if one remains very, very still and listens, one may hear, far and faint, the undertone of phantom horns mocking the field that rides so gallantly.

"Stole away," whispered Duane in Kathleen's ear, as he paused beside her; and she seemed to know what he meant, for she nodded, smiling:

"You mean that what we hunt is doomed to die when we ride it down?"

"Let us be in at the death, anyway," he said. "Kathleen, you're charming and masked to perfection. It's only that white skin of yours that betrays you; it always looks as though it were fragrant. Is that Geraldine surrounded three deep - over there under that oak-tree?"

"Yes; why are you so late, Duane? And I haven't seen Rosalie, either."

He did not care to enlighten her, but stood laughing and twirling his sword-knot and looking across the glittering throng, where a daintily masked young girl stood defending herself with fan and bouquet against the persistence of her gallants. Then he shook out the lace at his gilded cuffs, dropped one palm on his sword-hilt, saluted Kathleen's finger-tips with graceful precision, and sauntered toward Geraldine, dusting his nose with his filmy handkerchief - a most convincing replica of the bland epoch he impersonated.

As for Geraldine, she was certainly a very lovely incarnation of that self-satisfied and frivolous century; her success had already excited her a little; men seemed suddenly to have gone quite mad about her; and this and her own beauty were taking effect on her, producing an effect the more vivid, perhaps, because it was a reaction from the perplexities and tears of yesterday and the passionate tension of the morning.

Within her breast the sense of impending pleasure stirred and fluttered deliciously with every breath of music; the confused happiness of being in love, the relief in relaxation from a sterner problem, the noisy carnival surging, rioting around her, men crowding about her, eager in admiration and rivalry, the knowledge of her own loveliness - all these set the warm blood racing through every vein, and tinted lip and cheek with a colour in brilliant contrast to the velvety masked eyes and the snow of the slender neck.

Through the gay tumult which rang ceaselessly around her, where she stood, plying her painted fan, her own laughter sounded at intervals, distinct in its refreshing purity, for it had always that crystalline quality under a caressing softness; but Duane, who had advanced now to the outer edge of the circle, detected in her voice no hint of that thrilling undertone which he had known, which he alone among men had ever awakened. Her gaiety was careless, irresponsible, childlike in its clarity; under her crescent mask the smiles on her smooth young face dawned and died out, brief as sun-spots flashing over snow. Briefer intervals of apparent detachment from everything succeeded them; a distrait survey of the lantern-lit dancers, a preoccupied glance at the man speaking to her, a lifting of the delicate eyebrows in smiling preoccupation. But always behind the black half-mask her eyes wandered throughout the throng as though seeking something hidden; and on her vivid lips the smile became fixed.

Whether or not she had seen him, Duane could not tell, but presently, as he forced a path toward her, she stirred, closed her fan, took a step forward, head a trifle lowered; and right of way was given her, as she moved slowly through the cluster of men, shaking her head in vexation to the whispered importunities murmured in her ear, answering each according to his folly - this man with a laugh, that with a gesture of hand or shoulder, but never turning to reply, never staying her feet until, passing close to Duane, and not even looking at him:

"Where on earth have you been, Duane?"

"How did you know me?" he said, laughing; "you haven't even looked at me yet."

"On peut voir sans regarder, Monsieur. Nous autres demoiselles, nous voyons tres bien, tres bien ... et nous ne regardons jamais."

She had paused, still not looking directly at him. Then she lifted her head.

"Everybody has asked me to dance; I've said yes to everybody, but I've waited for you," she said. "It will be that way all my life, I think."

"It has been that way with me, too," he said gaily. "Why should we wait any more?"

"Why are you so late?" she asked. She had missed Rosalie, too, but did not say so.

"I am rather late," he admitted carelessly; "can you give me this dance?"

She stepped nearer, turning her shoulder to the anxious lingerers, who involuntarily stepped back, leaving a cleared space around them.

"Make me your very best bow," she whispered, "and take me. I've promised a dozen men, but it doesn't matter."

He said in a low voice, "You darling!" and made her a very wonderful bow, and she dropped him a very low, very slow, very marvellous courtesy, and, rising, laid her fingers on his embroidered sleeve. Then turning, head held erect, and with a certain sweet insolence in the droop of her white lids, she looked at the men around her.

Gray said in a low voice to Dysart: "That's as much as to admit that they're engaged, isn't it? When a girl doesn't give a hoot what she does to other men, she's nailed, isn't she?"

Dysart did not answer; Rosalie, passing on Grandcourt's arm, caught the words and turned swiftly, looking over her shoulder at Geraldine.

But Geraldine and Duane had already forgotten the outer world; around them the music swelled; laughter and voice grew indistinct, receding, blending in the vague tumult of violins. They gazed upon each other with vast content.

"As a matter of fact," said Duane, "I don't remember very well how to dance a minuet. I only wanted to be with you. We'll sit it out if you're afraid I'll make a holy show of you."

"Oh, dear," said Geraldine in pretty distress, "and I let you beguile me when I'm dying to do this minuet. Duane, you *must* try to remember! *Everybody* will be watching us." And as her quick ear caught the preliminary bars of the ancient and stately measure:

"It's the Menuet d'Exaudet," she said hurriedly; "listen, I'll instruct you as we move; I'll sing it under my breath to the air of the violins," and, her hand in his, she took the first slow, dainty step in the old-time dance, humming the words as they moved forward:

"Gravement
Noblement
On s'avance;
On fait trois pas de cote
Deux battus, un jete
Sans rompre la cadence -"

Then whispered, smiling:

"You are quite perfect, Duane; keep your head level, dear:

"Chassez
Rechassez
En mesure!
Saluez -
Gravement
Noblement
On s'avance
Sans rompre la cadence.

"Quite perfect, my handsome cavalier! Oh, we are doing it most beautifully" - with a deep, sweeping reverence; then rising, as he lifted her finger-tips: "You are stealing the rest of my heart," she said.

"Our betrothal dance," he whispered. "Shall it be so, dear?"

They looked at each other as though they stood there alone; the lovely old air of the Menuet d'Exaudet seemed to exhale from the tremulous violins like perfume floating through the woods; figures of masked dancers passed and repassed them through the orange-tinted glow; there came a vast rustle of silk, a breezy murmur, the scented wind from opening fans, the rattle of swords, and the Menuet d'Exaudet ended with a dull roll of kettle-drums.

A few minutes later he had her in his arms in a deliciously wild waltz, a swinging, irresponsible, gipsy-like thing which set the blood coursing and pulses galloping.

Every succeeding dance she gave to him. Now and then a tiny cloud of powder-dust floated from her hair; a ribbon from her shoulder-knot whipped his face; her breath touched his lips; her voice, at intervals, thrilled and caressed his ears, a soft, breathless voice, which mounting exaltation had made unsteadily sweet.

"You know - dear - I'm dancing every dance with you - in the teeth of decency, the face of every convention, and defiance of every law of hospitality. I belong to my guests."

And again:

"Do you know, Duane, there's a sort of a delicious madness coming over me. I'm all trembling under my skin with the overwhelming happiness of it all. I tell you it's intoxicating me because I don't know how to endure it."

He caught fire at her emotion; her palm was burning in his, her breath came irregularly, lips and cheeks were aflame, as they came to a breathless halt in the torchlight.

"Dear," she faltered, "I simply *must* be decent to my guests.... I'm dying to dance with you again, but I can't be so rude.... Oh, goodness! here they come, hordes of them. I'll give them a dance or two - anybody who speaks first, and then you'll come and find me, won't you?... Isn't that enough to give them - two or three dances? Isn't that doing my duty as chatelaine sufficiently?"

"Don't give them any," he said with conviction. "They'll know we're engaged if you don't -"

"Oh, Duane! We are only - only provisionally engaged," she said. "I am only on probation, dear. You know it can't be announced until I - I'm fit to marry you -"

"What nonsense!" he interrupted, almost savagely. "You're winning out; and even if you are not, I'll marry you, anyway, and make you win!"

"We have talked that over -"

"Yes, and it is settled!"

"No, Duane -"

"I tell you it is!"

"No. Hush! Somebody might overhear us. Quick, dear, here comes Bunny and Reggie Wye and Peter Tappan, all mad as hatters. I've behaved abominably to them! Will you find me after the third dance? Very well; tell me you love me then - whisper it, quick!... Ah-h! Moi aussi, Monsieur. And, remember, after the third dance!"

She turned slowly from him to confront an aggrieved group of masked young men, who came up very much hurt, clamouring for justice, explaining volubly that it was up to her to keep her engagements and dance with somebody besides Duane Mallett.

"Mon Dieu, Messieurs, je ne demanderais pas mieux," she said gaily. "Why didn't somebody ask me before?"

"You promised us each a dance," retorted Tappan sulkily, "but you never made good. I'll take mine now if you don't mind -"

"I'm down first!" insisted the Pink 'un.

They squabbled over her furiously; Bunbury Gray got her; she swung away into a waltz on his arm, glancing backward at

Duane, who watched her until she disappeared in the whirl of dancers. Then he strolled to the edge of the lantern-lit glade, stood for a moment looking absently at the shadowy woods beyond, and presently sauntered into the luminous dusk, which became darker and more opaque as he left the glare of the glade behind.

Here and there fantastic figures loomed, moving slowly, two and two, under the fairy foliage; on the Gray Water canoes strung with gaudy paper lanterns drifted; clouds of red fire rolled rosy and vaporous along the water's edge; and in the infernal glow, hazy shapes passed and repassed, finding places among scores of rustic tables, where servants in old-time livery and powdered wigs hurried to and fro with ices and salads, and set the white-covered tables with silverware and crystal.

A dainty masked figure in demon red flitted across his path in the uncanny radiance. He hailed her, and she turned, hesitated, then, as though convinced of his identity, laughed, and hastened on with a nod of invitation.

“Where are you going, pretty mask?” he inquired, wending his pace and trying to recognise the costume in the uncertain cross light.

But she merely laughed and continued to retreat before him, keeping the distance between them, hastening her steps whenever he struck a faster gait, pausing and looking back at him with a mocking smile when his steps slackened; a gracefully malicious, tormenting, laughing creature of lace and silk, whose retreat was a challenge, whose every movement and gesture seemed instinct with the witchery of provocation.

On the edge of the ring of tables she paused, picked up a goblet, held it out to a passing servant, who immediately filled the glass.

Then, before Duane could catch her, she drained the goblet to his health and fled into the shadows, he hard on her heels, pressing her closer, closer, until the pace became too hot for her, and she turned to face him, panting and covering her masked face with her fan.

"Now, my fair unknown, we shall pay a few penalties," he said with satisfaction; but she defended herself so adroitly that he could not reach her mask.

"Be fair to me," she gasped at last; "why are you so rough with me when - when you need not be? I knew you at once, Jack."

And she dropped her arms, standing resistless, breathing fast, her masked face frankly upturned to be kissed.

"Now, who the devil," thought Duane, "have I got in my arms? And for whom does she take me?"

He gazed searchingly into the slitted eye-holes; the eyes appeared to be blue, as well as he could make out. He looked at the fresh laughing mouth, a young, sensitive mouth, which even in laughter seemed not entirely gay.

"Don't you really mind if I kiss you?" He spoke in a whisper to disguise his voice.

"Isn't it a little late to ask me that?" she said; and under her mask the colour stained her skin. "I think what we do now scarcely matters."

She was so confident, so plainly awaiting his caress, that for a moment he was quite ready to console her. And did not, could not, with the fragrant and yielding intimacy of Geraldine still warm in his quickened heart.

She stood quite motionless, her little hands warm in his, her masked face upturned. And, as he merely stared at her:

"What is the matter, Jack?" she breathed. "Why do you look at me so steadily?"

He ought to have let her go then; he hesitated, wondering which Jack she supposed him to be; and before he realised it her arms were on his shoulders, her mouth nearer to his.

"Jack, you frighten me! What is it?"

"N-nothing," he continued to stammer.

"Yes, there is. Does your - your wife suspect - anything -"

"No, she doesn't," said Duane grimly, trying to free himself without seeming to. "I've got an appointment -"

But the girl said piteously: "It isn't - Geraldine, is it?"

"*What*!"

"You - you admitted that she attracted you - for a little while.... Oh, I *did* forgive you, Jack; truly I did with all my miserable heart! I was so fearfully unhappy - I would have done anything." ... Her face flushed scarlet. "And I - did.... But you do love me, don't you?" And the next moment her lips were on his with a sob.

Duane reached back and quietly unclasped her fingers. Then very gently he forced her to a seat on a great fallen log. Still looking up at him, droopingly pathetic in contrast to her gay debut with him, she naively slipped up the mask over her forehead and passed her hand across her pretty blue eyes. Sylvia Quest!

The sinister significance of her attitude flashed over him, all doubt vanished, all the comedy of their encounter was gone in an instant. Over him swept a startled sequence of emotions - bitter contempt for Dysart, scorn of the wretchedly equivocal situation and of the society that bred it, a miserable desire to spare her, vexation at himself for what he had unwittingly stumbled upon. The last thought persisted, dominated; succeeded by a disgusted determination that she must be spared the shame and terror of what she had inadvertently revealed; that she must never know she had not been speaking to Dysart himself.

“If I tell you that all is well - and if I tell you no more than that,” he whispered, “will you trust me?”

“Have I not done so, Jack?”

The tragedy in her lifted eyes turned him cold with fury.

“Then wait here until I return,” he said. “Promise.”

“I promise,” she sighed, “but I don't understand. I'm a - a little frightened, dear. But I - believe you.”

He swung on his heel and made toward the lights once more, and a moment later the man he sought passed within a few feet of him, and Duane knew him by his costume, which was a blue replica of his own gray silks.

“Dysart!” he said sharply.

The masked figure swung gracefully around and stood still, searching the shadowy woodland inquiringly.

“I want a word with you. Here - not in the light, if you please. You recognise my voice, don't you?”

“Is that you, Mallett?” asked Dysart coldly, as the former appeared in the light for an instant and turned back again with a curt gesture.

“Yes. I want you to step over here among the trees, where nobody can interrupt us.”

Dysart followed more slowly; came to a careless halt:

“Well, what the devil do you want?” he demanded insolently.

"I'll tell you. I've had an encounter with a mask who mistook me for you.... And she has said - several things - under that impression. She still believes that I am you. I asked her to wait for me over there by those oaks. Do you see where I mean?" He pointed and Dysart nodded coolly. "Well, then, I want you to go back there - find her, and act as though it had been you who heard what she said, not I."

"What do you mean?"

"I mean exactly that. The girl ought never to know that what she said was heard and - and *understood*, Dysart, by any man in the world except the blackguard I'm telling this to. Now, do you understand?"

He stepped nearer:

"The girl is Sylvia Quest. *Now*, do you understand, damn you!"

A stray glimmer from the distant lanterns fell across Dysart's masked visage. The skin around the mouth was loose and ashy, the dry lips worked.

"That was a dirty trick of yours," he stammered; "a scoundrelly thing to do."

"Do you suppose that I dreamed for an instant that she was convicting herself and you?" said Duane in bitter contempt. "Go and manufacture some explanation of my conduct as though it were your own. Let her have that much peace of mind, anyway."

"You young sneak!" retorted Dysart. "I suppose you think that what you have heard will warrant your hanging around my wife. Try it and see."

"Good God, Dysart!" he said, "I never thought you were anything more vicious than what is called a 'dancing man.'

What are you, anyhow?"

"You'll learn if you tamper with my affairs," said Dysart. He whipped off his mask and turned a corpse-like visage on the younger man. Every feature of his face had altered: his good looks were gone, the youth in his eyes had disappeared, only a little evil lustre played over them; and out of the drawn pallor Duane saw an old man peering, an old man's lips twitching back from uneven and yellowed teeth.

"Mallett," he said, "you listen to me. Keep your investigating muzzle out of my affairs; forget what you've ferreted out; steer clear of me and mine. I want no scandal, but if you raise a breath of it you'll have enough concerning yourself to occupy you. Do you understand?"

"No," said Duane mechanically, staring at the man before him.

"Well, then, to be more precise, if you lift one finger to injure me you'll cut a figure in court.... And you can marry her later."

"Who?"

"My wife. I don't think Miss Seagrave will stand for what I'll drag you through if you don't keep clear of me!"

Duane gazed at him curiously:

"So *that* is what you are, Dysart," he said aloud to himself.

Dysart's temples reddened.

"Yes, and then some!... I understand that you have given yourself the privilege of discussing my financial affairs in public. Have you?"

Duane said in a dull voice: "The Algonquin Trust was mentioned, I believe. I did say that you are a director."

"You said I was hard hit and that the Clearing House meant to weed out a certain element that I represented in New York."

"I did not happen to say that," said Duane wearily, "but another man did."

"Oh. *you* didn't say it?"

"No. I don't lie, Dysart."

"Then add to that negative virtue by keeping your mouth shut," said Dysart between his teeth, "or you'll have other sorts of suits on your hands. I warn you now to keep clear of me and mine."

"Just what *is* yours?" inquired Duane patiently.

"You'll find out if you touch it."

"Oh. Is - is Miss Quest included by any hazard? Because if the right chance falls my way, I shall certainly interfere."

"If you do, I shall begin suit for alienation within twenty-four hours."

"Oh, no, you won't. You're horribly afraid, Dysart. This grimacing of yours is fear. All you want is to be let alone, to burrow through the society that breeds your sort. Like a maggot in a chestnut you feed on what breeds you. I don't care. Feed! What bred you is as rotten as you are. I'm done with it - done with all this," turning his head toward the flare of light. "Go on and burrow. What nourishes you can look out for itself.... Only" - he wheeled around and looked into the darkness where, unseen, Sylvia Quest awaited him - "only, in this set, the young have less chance than the waifs of the East Side."

He walked slowly up to Dysart and struck him across the face with open palm.

"Break with that girl or I'll break your head," he said.

Dysart was down on the leaves, struggling up to his knees, then to his feet, the thin blood running across his chin. The next instant he sprang at Duane, who caught him by both arms and forced him savagely into quivering inertia.

"Don't," he said. "You're only a thing that dances. Don't move, I tell you.... Wipe that blood off and go and set the silly girl's heart at rest.... And keep away from her afterward. Do you hear?"

He set his teeth and shook him so wickedly that Dysart's head rolled and his wig fell off.

"I know something of your sloppy record," he continued, still shaking him; "I know about your lap-dog fawning around Miss Seagrave. It is generally understood that you're as sexless as any other of your kind. I thought so, too. Now I know you. Keep clear of *me* and *mine*, Dysart.... And that will be about all."

He left him planted against a tree and walked toward the lights once more, breathing heavily and in an ugly mood.

On the edge of the glade, just outside the lantern glow, he stood sombre, distrait, inspecting the torn lace on his sleeve, while all around him people were unmasking amid cries of surprise and shouts of laughter, and the orchestra was sounding a march, and multicoloured Bengal fires rolled in clouds from the water's edge, turning the woods to a magic forest and the people to tinted wraiths.

Behind him he heard Rosalie's voice, caressing, tormenting by turns; and, glancing around for her victim, beheld Grandcourt at heel in calflike adoration.

Kathleen's laughter swung him the other way.

"Oh, Duane," she cried, the pink of excitement in her cheeks, "isn't it all too heavenly! It looks like Paradise afire with all those rosy clouds rolling under foot. Have you ever seen anything quite as charming?"

"It's rotten," said Duane brusquely, tearing the tattered lace free and tossing it aside.

"Wh-what!" she exclaimed.

"I say it's all rotten," he repeated, looking up at her. "All this - the whole thing - the stupidity of it - the society that's driven to these kind of capers, dreading the only thing it ever dreads - ennui! Look at us all! For God's sake, survey us damn fools, herded here in our pinchbeck mummery - forcing the sanctuary of these decent green woods, polluting them with smoke and noise and dirty little intrigues! I'm sick of it!"

"Duane!"

"Oh, yes; I'm one of 'em - dragging my idleness and viciousness and my stupidity and my money at my heels. I tell you, Kathleen, this is no good. There's a stench of money everywhere; there's a staler aroma in the air, too - the dubious perfume of decadence, of moral atrophy, of stupid recklessness, of the ennui that breeds intrigue! I'm deadly tired of it - of the sort of people I was born among; of their women folk, whose sole intellectual relaxation is in pirouetting along the danger mark without overstepping, and in concealing it when they do; of the overgroomed men who can do nothing except what can be done with money, who think nothing, know nothing, sweat nothing but money and what it can buy - like horses and yachts and prima donnas -"

She uttered a shocked exclamation, but he went on:

"Yes, prima donnas. Which of our friends was it who bought that pretty one that sang in 'La Esmeralda'?"

"Duane!" she exclaimed in consternation; but he took her protesting hands in his and held her powerless.

"You happen to be a darling," he said; "but you were not born to this environment. Geraldine was - and she is a darling. God bless her. Outside of my sister, Naida, and you two - with the exception of the newly fledged and as yet mercifully unregurgitated with vicious wisdom - who are all these people? Ciphers, save for their balances at their banks; nameless, save for the noisy reiteration of their hard-fisted forebears' names; without any ambition, except financial and social; without any objective, save the escape from ennui - without any taste, culture, inspiration, except that of physical gratification! Oh, Lord, I'm one of them, but I resign to-night."

"Duane, you're quite mad," she said, wrenching her hands free and gazing at him rather fearfully.

"I think he's dead sensible," said a calm voice at her elbow; and Scott Seagrave appeared, twirling his mask and blinking at them through his spectacles.

Duane laughed: "Of course I am, you old reptile-hunting, butterfly-chasing antediluvian! But, come on; Byzantium is gorging its diamond-swathed girth yonder with salad and champagne; and I'm hungry, even if Kathleen isn't -"

"I *am*!" she exclaimed indignantly. "Scott, can't you find Naida and Geraldine? Duane and I will keep a table until you return -"

"I'll find them," said Duane; and he walked off among the noisy, laughing groups, his progress greeted uproariously from table to table. He found Naida and Bunbury Gray, and they at once departed for the rendezvous indicated.

"Geraldine was here a little while ago," said Gray, "but she walked to the lake with Jack Dysart. My, but she's hitting it up," he added admiringly.

"Hitting it up?" repeated Duane.

"For a girl who never does, I mean. I imagine that she's a novice with champagne. Champagne and Geraldine make a very fetching combination, I can tell you."

"She took no more than I," observed Naida with a shrug; "one solitary glass. If a girl happens to be high strung and ventures to laugh a little, some wretched man is sure to misunderstand! Bunny, you're a gadabout!"

She made her way out from the maze of tables, Bunny following, somewhat abashed; and Duane walked toward the shore, where dozens of lantern-hung canoes bobbed, and the pasteboard cylinders of Bengal fire had burned to smouldering sparks.

In the dim light he came on the people he was looking for, seated on the rocks. Dysart, at her feet, was speaking in an undertone; Geraldine, partly turned away from him, hands clasped around her knees, was staring steadily across the water.

Neither rose as he came up; Dysart merely became mute; Geraldine looked around with a start; her lips parted in a soundless, mechanical greeting, then the flush in her cheeks brightened; and as she rose, Dysart got onto his feet and stood silently facing the new arrival.

"I said after the third dance, you know," she observed with an assumed lightness that did not deceive him. And, as he made no answer, he saw the faint flicker of fright in her eyes and the lower lip quiver.

He said pleasantly, controlling his voice: "Isn't this after the third dance? You are to be my partner for supper, I think."

"A long time after; and I've already sat at Belshazzar's feast, thank you. I couldn't very well starve waiting for you, could I?" And she forced a smile.

"Nevertheless, I must claim your promise," he said.

There was a silence; she stood for a moment gazing at nothing, with the same bright, fixed smile, then turned and glanced at Dysart. The glance was his dismissal and he knew it.

"If I must give you up," he said cheerfully, at his ease, "please pronounce sentence."

"I am afraid you really must, Mr. Dysart."

There was another interval of constraint; then Dysart spoke. His self-possession was admirable, his words perfectly chosen, his exit in faultless taste.

They looked after him until he was lost to view in the throngs beyond, then the girl slowly reseated herself, eyes again fixed on the water, hands clasped tightly upon her knee, and Duane found a place at her elbow. So they began a duet of silence.

The little wavelets came dancing shoreward out of the darkness, breaking with a thin, splashing sound against the shale at their feet. Somewhere in the night a restless heron croaked and croaked among the willows.

"Well, little girl?" he asked at last.

"Well?" she inquired, with a calmness that did not mislead him.

"I couldn't come to you after the third dance," he said.

"Why?"

He evaded the question: "When I came back to the glade the dancing was already over; so I got Kathleen and Naida to save a table."

"Where had you been all the while?"

"If you really wish to know," he said pleasantly, "I was talking to Jack Dysart on some rather important matters. I did not realise how the time went."

She sat mute, head lowered, staring out across the dark water. Presently he laid one hand over hers, and she straightened up with a tiny shock, turned and looked him full in the eyes.

"I'll tell you why you failed me - failed to keep the first appointment I ever asked of you. It was because you were so preoccupied with a mask in flame colour."

He thought a moment:

"Did you believe you saw me with somebody in a vermilion costume?"

"Yes; I did see you. It was too late for me to retire without attracting your attention. I was not a willing eavesdropper."

"Who was the girl you thought you saw me with?"

"Sylvia Quest. She unmasked. There is no mistake."

So he was obliged to lie, after all.

"It must have been Dysart you saw. His costume is very like mine, you know -"

"Does Jack Dysart stand for minutes holding Sylvia's hands - and is she accustomed to place her hands on his shoulders, as though expecting to be kissed? And does he kiss her?"

So he had to lie again: "No, of course not," he said, smiling. "So it could not have been Dysart."

"There are only two costumes like yours and Mr. Dysart's. Do you wish me to believe that Sylvia is common and depraved enough to put her arms around the neck of a man who is married?"

There was no other way: "No," he said, "Sylvia isn't that sort, of course."

"It was either Mr. Dysart or you."

He said nothing.

"Then it *was* you!" in hot contempt.

Still he said nothing.

"Was it?" with a break in her voice.

"Men can't admit things of that kind," he managed to say.

The angry colour surged up to her cheeks, the angry tears started, but her quivering lips were not under command and she could only stare at him through the blur of grief, while her white hands clinched and relaxed, and her fast-beating heart seemed to be driving the very breath from her body.

"Geraldine, dear -"

"It wasn't fair!" she broke out fiercely; "there is no honour in you - no loyalty! Oh, Duane! Duane! How could you - at the very moment we were nearer together than we had ever been! It isn't jealousy that is crying out in me; it is nothing common or ignoble in me that resents what you have done! It is the treachery of it! How *could* you, Duane?"

The utter hopelessness of clearing himself left him silent. How much was to be asked of him as sacrifice to code? How far was he expected to go to shield Sylvia Quest - this unhappy, demoralised girl, whose reputation was already at the mercy of two men?

"Geraldine," he said, "it was nothing but a carnival flirtation -

a chance encounter that meant nothing - the idlest kind of -"

"Is it idle to do what you did - and what she did? Oh, if I had only not seen it - if I only didn't know! I never dreamed of such a thing in you. Bunny Gray and I were taking a short cut to the Gray Water to sit out the rest of his dance - and he saw it, too - and he was furious - he must have been - because he's devoted to Sylvia." She made a hopeless gesture and dropped her hand to her side: "What a miserable night it has been for me! It's all spoiled - it's ended.... And I - my courage went.... I've done what I never thought to do again - what I was fighting down to make myself safe enough for you to marry - *you* to marry!" She laughed, but the mirth rang shockingly false.

"You mean that you had one glass of champagne," he said.

"Yes, and another with Jack Dysart. I'll have some more presently. Does it concern you?"

"I think so, Geraldine."

"You are wrong. Neither does what you've been doing concern me - the kind of man you've been - the various phases of degradation you have accomplished -"

"What particular species of degradation?" he asked wearily, knowing that Dysart was now bent on his destruction. "Never mind; don't answer, Geraldine," he added, "because there's no use in trying to set myself right; there's no way of doing it. All I can say is that I care absolutely nothing for Sylvia Quest, nor she for me; that I love you; that if I have ever been unworthy of you - as God knows I have - it is a bitterer memory to me than it could ever be to you."

"Shall we go back?" she said evenly.

"Yes, if you wish."

They walked back together in silence; a jolly company claimed them for their table; Geraldine laughingly accepted a glass of champagne, turning her back squarely on Duane.

Naida and Kathleen came across.

"We waited for you as long as we could," said his pretty sister, smothering a yawn. "I'm horribly sleepy. Duane, it's three o'clock. Would you mind taking me across to the house?"

He cast a swift, anxious glance at Geraldine; her vivid colour, the splendour of her eyes, her feverish laughter were ominous. With her were Gray and Sylvia, rather noisy in their gaiety, and the boisterous Pink 'uns, and Jack Dysart, lingering near, the make-up on his face in ghastly contrast to his ashen pallor and his fixed and unvaried grin.

"I'm waiting, Duane," said Naida plaintively.

So he turned away with her through the woods, where one by one the brilliant lantern flames were dying out, and where already in the east a silvery lustre heralded the coming dawn.

* * * * *

When he returned, Geraldine was gone. At the house somebody said she had come in with Kathleen, not feeling well.

"The trouble with that girl," said a man whom he did not know, "is that she's had too much champagne."

"You lie," said Duane quietly. "Is that perfectly plain to you?"

For a full minute the young man stood rigid, crimson, glaring at Duane. Then, having the elements of decency in him, he said:

"I don't know who you are, but you are perfectly right. I did lie. And I'll see that nobody else does."

CHAPTER XII

THE LOVE OF THE GODS

Two days later the majority of the people had left Roya-Neh, and the remainder were preparing to make their adieux to the young chatelaine by proxy; for Geraldine had kept her room since the night of the masked fete, and nobody except Kathleen and Dr. Bailey had seen her.

"Fashionable fidgets," said Dr. Bailey, in answer to amiable inquiries; "the girl has been living on her nerves, like the rest of you, only she can't stand as much as you can."

To Duane he said, in reply to persistent questions:

"As a plain and unromantic proposition, young man, it may be her liver. God alone knows with what young women stuff their bodies in those bucolic solitudes."

To Kathleen he said, after questioning her and listening in silence to her guarded replies:

"I don't know what is the matter, Mrs. Severn. The girl is extremely nervous. She acts, to me, as though she had something on her mind, but she insists that she hasn't. If I were to be here, I might come to some conclusion within the next day or two."

Which frightened Kathleen, and she asked whether anything

serious might be anticipated.

"Not at all," he said.

So, as he was taking the next train, there was nothing to do. He left a prescription and whizzed away to the railroad station with the last motor-load of guests.

There remained only Duane, Rosalie Dysart, Grandcourt, and Sylvia Quest, a rather subdued and silent group on the terrace, unresponsive to Scott's unfeigned gaiety to find himself comparatively alone and free to follow his own woodland predilections once more.

"A cordial host you are," observed Rosalie; "you're guests are scarcely out of sight before you break into inhuman chuckles."

"Speed the parting," observed Scott, in excellent spirits; "that's the truest hospitality."

"I suppose your unrestrained laughter will be our parting portion in a day or two," she said, amused.

"No; I don't mind a few people. Do you want to come and look for scarabs?"

"Scarabs? Do you imagine you're in Egypt, my poor friend?"

Scott sniffed: "Didn't you know we had a few living species around here? Regular scarabs. Kathleen and I found three the other day - one a regular beauty with two rhinoceros horns on the thorax and iridescent green and copper tinted wing-covers. Do you want to help me hunt for some more? You'll have to put on overshoes, for they're in the cow-yards."

Rosalie, intensely bored, thanked him and declined. Later she opened a shrimp-pink sunshade and, followed by Grandcourt, began to saunter about the lawn in plain sight, as people do preliminary to effacing themselves without exciting comment.

But there was nobody to comment on what they did; Duane was reading a sporting-sheet, souvenir of the departed Bunbury; Sylvia sat pallid and preoccupied, cheek resting against her hand, looking out over the valley. Her brother, her only living relative, was supposed to have come up that morning to take her to the next house party on the string which linked the days of every summer for her. But Stuyvesant had not arrived; and the chances were that he would turn up within a day or two, if not too drunk to remember her.

So Sylvia, who was accustomed to waiting for her brother, sat very colourless and quiet by the terrace parapet, pale blue eyes resting on the remoter hills - not always, for at intervals she ventured a furtive look at Duane, and there was something of stealth and of fright in the stolen glance.

As for Scott, he sat on the parapet, legs swinging, fussing with a pair of binoculars and informing the two people behind him - who were not listening - that he could distinguish a black-billed cuckoo from a thrasher at six hundred yards.

Which edified neither Sylvia nor Duane, but the boy continued to impart information with unimpaired cheerfulness until Kathleen came out from the house.

"How's Sis?" he inquired.

"I think she has a headache," replied Kathleen, looking at Duane.

"Could I see her?" he asked.

Kathleen said gently that Geraldine did not feel like seeing anybody at that time. A moment later, in obedience to Scott's persistent clamouring for scarabs, she went across the lawn with the young master of Roya-Neh, resigned to the inevitable in the shape of two-horned scarabs or black-billed cuckoos.

It had always been so with her; it would always be so. Long ago the Seagrave twins had demanded all she had to give; now, if Geraldine asked less, Scott exacted double. And she gave - how happily, only her Maker and her conscience knew.

Duane was still reading - or he had all the appearance of reading - when Sylvia lifted her head from her hand and turned around with an effort that cost her what colour had remained under the transparent skin of her oval face.

"Duane," she said, "it occurred to me just now that you might have really mistaken what I said and did the other night." She hesitated, nerving herself to encounter his eyes, lifted and levelled across the top of his paper at her.

He waited; she retained enough self-command to continue with an effort at lightness:

"Of course it was all carnival fun - my pretending to mistake you for Mr. Dysart. You understood it, didn't you?"

"Why, of course," he said, smiling.

She went on: "I - don't exactly remember what I said - I was trying to mystify you. But it occurred to me that perhaps it was rather imprudent to pretend to be on - on such impossible terms with Mr. Dysart – "

There was something too painful in her effort for him to endure. He said laughingly, not looking at her:

"Oh, I wasn't ass enough to be deceived, Sylvia. Don't worry, little girl." And he resumed the study of his paper.

Minutes passed - terrible minutes for one of them, who strove to find relief in his careless reassurance, tried desperately to believe him, to deceive that intuition which seldom fails her sex.

He, with the print blurred and meaningless before him, sat

miserable, dumb with the sympathy he could not show, hot with the anger he dared not express. He thought of Dysart as he had revealed himself, now gone back to town to face that little crop of financial rumours concerning the Algonquin that persisted so wickedly and would not be quieted. For the first time in his life, probably, Dysart was compelled to endure the discomforts of a New York summer - more discomforts this summer than mere dust and heat and noise. For men who had always been on respectful financial terms with Dysart and his string of banks and his Algonquin enterprise were holding aloof from him; men who had figured for years in the same columns of print where his name was so often seen as director and trustee and secretary - fellow-members who served for the honour of serving on boards of all sorts, charity boards, hospital, museum, civic societies - these men, too, seemed to be politely, pleasantly, even smilingly edging away from him in some indefinable manner.

Which seemed to force him toward certain comparatively newcomers among the wealthy financiers of the metropolis - brilliant, masterful, restless men from the West, whose friendship in the beginning he had sought, deeming himself farsighted.

Now that his vision had become normally adjusted he cared less for this intimacy which it was too late to break - at least this was not the time to break it with money becoming unbelievably scarcer every day and a great railroad man talking angrily, and another great railroad man preaching caution at a time when the caution of the man in the Street might mean something so serious to Dysart that he didn't care to think about it.

Dysart had gone back to New York in company with several pessimistic gentlemen - who were very open about backing their fancy; and their fancy fell on that old, ramshackle jade, Hard Times, by Speculation out of Folly. According to them there was no hope of her being scratched or left at the post.

"She'll run like a scared hearse-horse," said young Grandcourt gloomily. There was reason for his gloom. Unknown to his father he had invested heavily in Dysart's schemes. It was his father's contempt that he feared more than ruin.

So Dysart had gone to town, leaving behind him the utter indifference of a wife, the deep contempt of a man; and a white-faced girl alone with her memories - whatever they might be - and her thoughts, which were painful if one might judge by her silent, rigid abstraction, and the lower lip which, at moments, escaped, quivering, from the close-set teeth.

When Duane rose, folding his paper with a carelessly pleasant word or two, she looked up in a kind of naive terror - like a child startled at prospect of being left alone. It was curious how those adrift seemed always to glide his way. It had always been so; even stray cats followed him in the streets; unhappy dogs trotted persistently at his heels; many a journey had he made to the Bide-a-wee for some lost creature's sake; many a softly purring cat had he caressed on his way through life - many a woman.

As he strolled toward the eastern end of the terrace, Sylvia looked after him; and, suddenly, unable to endure isolation, she rose and followed as instinctively as her lesser sisters-errant.

It was the trotting of little footsteps behind him on the gravel that arrested him. A glance at her face was enough; vexed, shocked, yet every sympathy instantly aroused, he resigned himself to whatever might be required of him; and within him a bitter mirth stirred - acrid, unpleasant; but his smile indicated only charmed surprise.

"I didn't suppose you'd care for a stroll with me," he said; "it is exceedingly nice of you to give me the chance."

"I didn't want to be left alone," she said.

"It is rather quiet here since our gay birds have migrated," he said in a matter-of-fact way. "Which direction shall we take?"

"I - don't care."

"The woods?"

"No," with a shudder so involuntary that he noticed it.

"Well, then, we'll go cross country -"

She looked at her thin, low shoes and then at him.

"Certainly," he said, "that won't do, will it?"

She shook her head.

They were passing the Lodge now where his studio was and where he had intended to pack up his canvases that afternoon.

"I'll brew you a cup of tea if you like," he said; "that is, if it's not too unconventional to frighten you."

She smiled and nodded. Behind the smile her heavy thoughts throbbed on: How much did this man know? How much did he suspect? And if he suspected, how good he was in every word to her - how kind and gentle and high-minded! And the anguish in her smile caused him to turn hastily to the door and summon old Miller to bring the tea paraphernalia.

There was nothing to look at in the studio; all the canvases lay roped in piles ready for the crates; but Sylvia's gaze remained on them as though even the rough backs of the stretchers fascinated her.

"My father was an artist. After he married he did not paint. My mother was very wealthy, you know.... It seems a pity."

"What? Wealth?" he asked, smiling.

"N-no. I mean it seems a little tragic to me that father never continued to paint."

Miller's granddaughter came in with the tea. She was a very little girl with yellow hair and big violet eyes. After she had deposited everything, she went over to Duane and held up her mouth to be kissed. He laughed and saluted her. It was a reward for service which she had suggested when he first came to Roya-Neh; and she trotted away in great content.

Sylvia's indifferent gaze followed her; then she sipped the tea Duane offered.

"Do you remember your father?" he asked pleasantly.

"Why, yes. I was fourteen when he died. I remember mother, too. I was seven."

Duane said, not looking at her: "It's about the toughest thing that can happen to a girl. It's tough enough on a boy."

"It was very hard," she said simply.

"Haven't you any relatives except your brother Stuyvesant -" he began, and checked himself, remembering that a youthful aunt of hers had eloped under scandalous circumstances, and at least one uncle was too notorious even for the stomachs of the society that whelped him.

She let it pass in silence, as though she had not heard. Later she declined more tea and sat deep in her chair, fingers linked under her chin, lids lowered.

After a while, as she did not move or speak, he ventured to busy himself with collecting his brushes, odds and ends of studio equipment. He scraped several palettes, scrubbed up some palette-knives, screwed the tops on a dozen tubes of colour, and fussed and messed about until there seemed to be nothing further to do. So he came back and seated himself, and, looking up, saw the big tears stealing from under her closed lids.

He endured it as long as he could. Nothing was said. He leaned nearer and laid his hand over hers; and at the contact she slipped from the chair, slid to her knees, and laid her head on the couch beside him, both hands covering her face, which had turned dead white.

Minute after minute passed with no sound, no movement except as he passed his hand over her forehead and hair. He knew what to do when those who were adrift floated into Port Mallett. And sometimes he did more than was strictly required, but never less. Toward sundown she began to feel blindly for her handkerchief. He happened to possess a fresh one and put it into her groping hand.

When she was ready to rise she did so, keeping her back toward him and standing for a while busy with her swollen eyes and disordered hair.

"Before we go we must have tea together again," he said with perfectlymatter-of-fact cordiality.

"Y-yes." The voice was very, very small.

"And in town, too, Sylvia. I had no idea what a companionable girl you are - how much we have in common. You know silence is the great test of mutual confidence and understanding. You'll let me see you in town, won't you?"

"Yes."

"That will be jolly. I suppose now that you and I ought to be thinking about dressing for dinner."

She assented, moved away a step or two, halted, and, still with her back turned, held out her hand behind her. He took it, bent and kissed it.

"See you at dinner," he said cheerfully.

And she went out very quietly, his handkerchief pressed against her eyes.

He came back into the studio, swung nervously toward the couch, turned and began to pace the floor.

"Oh, Lord," he said; "the rottenness of it all - the utter rottenness."

* * * * *

Dinner that night was not a very gay function; after coffee had beenserved, the small group seemed to disintegrate as though by some prearrangement, Rosalie and Grandcourt finding a place for themselves in the extreme western shadow of the terrace parapet, Kathleen returning to the living-room, where she had left her embroidery.

Scott, talking to Sylvia and Duane, continued to cast restless glances toward the living-room until he could find the proper moment to get away. And in a few minutes Duane saw him seated, one leg crossed over the other, a huge volume on "Scientific Conservation of Natural Resources" open on his knees, seated as close to Kathleen as he could conveniently edge, perfectly contented, apparently, to be in her vicinity.

From moment to moment, as her pretty hands performed miracles in tinted silks, she lifted her eyes and silently inspected the boy who sat absorbed in his book. Perhaps old memories of a child seated in the schoolroom made tender the curve of her lips as she turned again to her embroidery; perhaps a sentiment more recent made grave the beautiful lowered eyes.

Sylvia, seated at the piano, idly improvising, had unconsciously drifted into the "Menuet d'Exaudet," and Duane's heart began to quicken as he stood listening and looking out through the open windows at the stars.

How long he stood there he did not know; but when, at length, missing the sound of the piano, he looked around, Sylvia was already on the stairs, looking back at him as she moved upward.

"Good-night," she called softly; "I am very tired," and paused as he came forward and mounted to the step below where she waited.

"Good-night, Miss Quest," he said, with that nice informality that women always found so engaging. "If you have nothing better on hand in the morning, let's go for a climb. I've discovered a wild-boar's nest under the Golden Dome, and if you'd like to get a glimpse of the little, furry, striped piglings, I think we can manage it."

She thanked him with her eyes, held out her thin, graceful hand of a schoolgirl, then turned slowly and continued her ascent.

As he descended, Kathleen, looking up from her embroidery, made him a sign, and he stood still.

"Where are you going?" asked Scott, as she rose and passed him.

"I'm coming back in a moment."

Scott restlessly resumed his book, raising his head from time to time as though listening for her return, fidgeting about, now examining the embroidery she had left on the lamp-lit table, now listlessly running over the pages that had claimed his close attention while she had been near him.

Across the hall, in the library, Duane stood absently twisting an unlighted cigar, and Kathleen, her hand on his shoulder, eyes lifted in sweet distress, was searching for words that seemed to evade her.

He cut the knot without any emotion:

"I know what you are trying to say, Kathleen. It is true that there has been a wretched misunderstanding, but if I know Geraldine at all I know that a mere misunderstanding will not do any permanent harm. It is something else that - worries me."

"Oh, Duane, I know! I know! She cannot marry you - in honour - until that - that terrible danger is eliminated. She will not, either. But - don't give her up! Be with her - with us in this crisis - during it! See us through it, Duane; she is well worth what she costs us both - and costs herself."

"She must marry me now," he said. "I want to fight this thing with all there is in me and in her, and in my love for her and hers for me. I can't fight it in this blind, aloof way - this thing that is my rival - that stands with its claw embedded in her body warning me back! The horror of it is in the blind, intangible, abstract force that is against me. I can't fight it aloof from her; I can't take her away from it unless I have her in my arms to guard, to inspire, to comfort, to watch. Can't you see, Kathleen, that I must have her every second of the time?"

"She will not let you run the risk," murmured Kathleen. "Duane, she had a dreadful night - she broke down so utterly that it scared me. She is horribly frightened; her nervous demoralisation is complete. For the first time, I think, she is really terrified. She says it is hopeless, that her will and nerve are undermined, her courage contaminated.... Hour after hour I sat with her; she made me tell her about her grandfather - about what I knew of the - the taint in her family."

"Those things are merely predispositions," he said. "Self-command makes them harmless."

"I told her that. She says that they are living sparks that will smoulder while life endures."

"Suppose they are," he said; "they can never flame unless nursed.... Kathleen, I want to see her -"

"She will not."

"Has she spoken at all of me?"

"Yes."

"Bitterly?"

"Y-yes. I don't know what you did. She is very morbid just now, anyway; very desperate. But I know that, unconsciously, she counts on an adjustment of any minor personal difficulty with you.... She loves you dearly, Duane."

He passed an unsteady hand across his eyes.

"She must marry me. I can't stand aloof from this battle any longer."

"Duane, she will not. I - she said some things - she is morbid, I tell you - and curiously innocent - in her thoughts - concerning herself and you. She says she can never marry."

"Exactly what did she say to you?"

Kathleen hesitated; the intimacy of the subject left her undecided; then very seriously her pure, clear gaze met his:

"She will not marry, for your own sake, and for the sake of any - children. She has evidently thought it all out.... I must tell you how it is. There is no use in asking her; she will never consent, Duane, as long as she is afraid of herself. And how to quiet that fear by exterminating the reason for it I don't know -" Her voice broke pitifully. "Only stand by us, Duane. Don't go away just now. You were packing to go; but please don't leave me just yet. Could you arrange to remain for a while?"

"Yes, I'll arrange it.... I'm a little troubled about my father -" He checked himself. "I could run down to town for a day or two and return – "

"Is Colonel Mallett ill?" she asked.

"N-no.... These are rather strenuous times - or threaten to be. Of course the Half-Moon is as solid as a rock. But even the very, very great are beginning to fuss.... And my father is not young, Kathleen. So I thought I'd like to run down and take him out to dinner once or twice - to a roof-garden or something, you know. It's rather pathetic that men of his age, grown gray in service, should feel obliged to remain in the stifling city this summer."

"Of course you must go," she said; "you couldn't even hesitate. Is your mother worried?"

"I don't suppose she has the slightest notion that there is anything to worry over. And there isn't, I think. She and Naida will be in the Berkshires; I'll go up and stay with them later - when Geraldine is all right again," he added cheerfully.

Scott, fidgeting like a neglected pup, came wandering into the hall, book in hand.

"For the love of Mike," he said impatiently, "what have you two got to talk about all night?"

"My son," observed Duane, "there are a few subjects for conversation which do not include the centipede and the polka-dotted dickey-bird. These subjects Kathleen and I furtively indulge in when we can arrange to elude you."

Scott covered a yawn and glanced at Kathleen.

"Is Geraldine all right?" he asked with all the healthy indifference of a young man who had never been ill, and was, therefore, incapable of understanding illness in others.

"Certainly, she's all right," said Duane. And to Kathleen: "I believe I'll venture to knock at her door -"

"Oh, no, Duane. She isn't ready to see anybody -"

"Well, I'll try -"

"Please, don't!"

But he had her at a disadvantage, and he only laughed and mounted the stairs, saying:

"I'll just exchange a word with her or with her maid, anyway."

When he turned into the corridor Geraldine's maid, seated in the window-seat sewing, rose and came forward to take his message. In a few moments she returned, saying:

"Miss Seagrave asks to be excused, as she is ready to retire."

"Ask Miss Seagrave if I can say good-night to her through the door."

The maid disappeared and returned in a moment.

"Miss Seagrave wishes you good-night, sir."

So he thanked the maid pleasantly and walked to his own room, now once more prepared for him after the departure of those who had temporarily required it.

Starlight made the leaded windows brilliant; he opened them wide and leaned out on the sill, arms folded. The pale astral light illuminated a fairy world of meadow and garden and spectral trees, and two figures moving like ghosts down by the fountain among the roses - Rosalie and Grandcourt pacing the gravel paths shoulder to shoulder under the stars.

Below him, on the terrace, he saw Kathleen and Scott - the latter carrying a butterfly net - examining the borders of white pinks with a lantern. In and out of the yellow rays swam multitudes of night moths, glittering like flakes of tinsel as the lantern light flashed on their wings; and Scott was evidently doing satisfactory execution, for every moment or two Kathleen uncorked the cyanide jar and he dumped into it from the folds of the net a fluttering victim.

"That last one is a Pandorus Sphinx!" he said in great excitement to Kathleen, who had lifted the big glass jar into the lantern light and was trying to get a glimpse of the exquisite moth, whose wings of olive green, rose, and bronze velvet were already beating a hazy death tattoo in the lethal fumes.

"A Pandorus! Scott, you've wanted one so much!" she exclaimed, enchanted.

"You bet I have. Pholus pandorus is pretty rare around here. And I say, Kathleen, that wasn't a bad net-stroke, was it? You see I had only a second, and I took a desperate chance."

She praised his skill warmly; then, as he stood admiring his prize in the jar which she held up, she suddenly caught him by the arm and pointed:

"Oh, quick! There is a hawk-moth over the pinks which resembles nothing we have seen yet!"

Scott very cautiously laid his net level, stole forward, shining the lantern light full on the darting, hazy-winged creature, which was now poised, hovering over a white blossom and probing the honeyed depths with a long, slim proboscis.

"I thought it might be only a Lineata, but it isn't," he said excitedly. "Did you ever see such a timid moth? The slightest step scares the creature."

"Can't you try a quick net-stroke sideways?"

Her voice was as anxious and unsteady as his own.

"I'm afraid I'll miss. Lord but it's a lightning flier! Where is it now?"

"Behind you. Do be careful! Turn very slowly."

He pivoted; the slim moth darted past, circled, and hung before a blossom, wings vibrating so fast that the creature was merely a gray blur in the lantern light. The next instant Gray's net swung; a furious fluttering came from the green silk folds; Kathleen whipped off the cover of the jar, and Duane deftly imprisoned the moth.

"Upon my word," he said shakily, "I believe I've got a Tersa Sphinx! - a sub-tropical fellow whose presence here is mere accident!"

"Oh, if you have!" she breathed softly. She didn't know what a Tersa Sphinx might be, but if its capture gave him pleasure, that was all she cared for in the world.

"It *is* a Tersa!" he almost shouted. "By George! it's a wonder."

Radiant, she bent eagerly above the jar where the strange, slender, gray-and-brown hawk-moth lay dying. Its recoiling proboscis and its slim, fawn-coloured legs quivered. The eyes glowed like tiny jewels.

"If we could only keep these little things alive," she sighed; then, fearful of taking the least iota from his pleasure, added: "but of course we can't, and for scientific purposes it's all right to let the lovely little creatures sink into their death-sleep."

A slight haze had appeared over the lake; a sudden cool streak grew in the air, which very quickly cleared the flower-beds of moths; and the pretty sub-tropical sphinx was the last specimen of the evening.

In the library Scott pulled out a card-table and Kathleen brought forceps, strips of oiled paper, pins, setting-blocks, needles, and oblong glass weights; and together, seated opposite each other, they removed the delicate-winged contents of the collecting jar.

Kathleen's dainty fingers were very swift and deft with the forceps. Scott watched her. She picked up the green-and-rose Pandorus, laid it on its back on a setting-block, affixed and pinned the oiled-paper strips, drew out the four wings with the setting-needle until they were symmetrical and the inner margin of the anterior pair was at right angles with the body.

Then she arranged the legs, uncoiled and set the proboscis, and weighted the wings with heavy glass strips.

They worked rapidly, happily there together, exchanging views and opinions; and after a while the brilliant spoils of the evening were all stretched and ready to dry, ultimately to be placed in plaster-of-Paris mounts and hermetically sealed under glass covers.

Kathleen went away to cleanse her hands of any taint of cyanide; Scott, returning from his own ablutions, met her in the hall, and so miraculously youthful, so fresh and sweet and dainty did she appear that, in some inexplicable manner, his awkward, self-conscious fear of touching her suddenly vanished, and the next instant she was in his arms and he had kissed her.

"Scott!" she faltered, pushing him from her, too limp and dazed to use the strength she possessed.

Surprised at what he had done, amazed that he was not afraid of her, he held her tightly, thrilled dumb at the exquisite trembling contact.

"Oh, what are you doing," she stammered, in dire consternation; "what have you done? We - you cannot - you must let me go, Scott -"

"You're only a girl, after all - you darling!" he said, inspecting her in an ecstacy of curiosity. "I wonder why I've been afraid of you for so long? - just because I love you!"

"You don't - you can't care for me that way -"

"I care for you in every kind of a way that anybody can care about anybody." She turned her shoulder, desperately striving to release herself, but she had not realised how tall and strong he was. "How small you are," he repeated wonderingly; "just a soft, slender girl, Kathleen. I can't see how I ever came to let you make me study when I didn't want to."

"Scott, dear," she pleaded breathlessly, "you must let me go. This - this is utterly impossible -"

"What is?"

"That you and I can - could care - this way -"

"Don't you?"

"I - no!"

"Is that the truth, Kathleen?"

She looked up; the divine distress in her violet eyes sobered him, awed him for a moment.

"Kathleen," he said, "there are only a few years' difference between our ages. I feel older than you; you look younger than I - and you are all in the world I care for - or ever have cared for. Last spring - that night -"

"Hush, Scott," she begged, blushing scarlet.

"I know you remember. That is when I began to love you. You must have known it."

She said nothing; the strain of her resisting arms against his breast had relaxed imperceptibly.

"What can a fellow say?" he went on a little wildly, checked at moments by the dryness of his throat and the rapid heartbeats that almost took his breath away when he looked at her. "I love you so dearly, Kathleen; there's no use in trying to live without loving you, for I couldn't do it!... I'm not really young; it makes me furious to think you consider me in that light. I'm a man, strong enough and old enough to love you - and make you love me! I *will* make you!" His arms tightened.

She uttered a little cry, which was half a sob; his boyish roughness sent a glow rushing through her. She fought against the peril of it, the bewildering happiness that welled up - fought against her heart that was betraying her senses, against the deep, sweet passion that awoke as his face touched hers.

"Will you love me?" he said fiercely.

"No!"

"Will you?"

"Yes.... Let me go!" she gasped.

"Will you love me in the way I mean? Can you?"

"Yes. I do. I - have, long since.... Let me go!"

"Then - kiss me."

She looked up at him a moment, slowly put both arms around his neck: "Now," she breathed faintly, "release me."

And at the same instant he saw Geraldine descending the stairs.

Kathleen saw her, too; saw her turn abruptly, re-mount and disappear. There was a moment's painful silence, then, without a word, she picked up her lace skirts, ran up the stairway, and continued swiftly on to Geraldine's room.

"May I come in?" She spoke and opened the door of the bedroom at the same time, and Geraldine turned on her, exasperated, hands clenched, dark eyes harbouring lightning:

"Have I gone quite mad, Kathleen, or have you?" she demanded.

"I think I have," whispered Kathleen, turning white and halting. "Geraldine, you will *have* to listen. Scott has told me that he loves me -"

"Is this the first time?"

"No.... It is the first time I have listened. I can't think clearly; I scarcely know yet what I've said and done. What must you think?... But won't you be a little gentle with me - a little forbearing - in memory of what I have been to you - to him - so long?"

"What do you wish me to think?" asked the girl in a hard voice. "My brother is of age; he will do what he pleases, I suppose. I - I don't know what to think; this has astounded me. I never dreamed such a thing possible -"

"Nor I - until this spring. I know it is all wrong; this is making me more fearfully unhappy every minute I live. There is nothing but peril in it; the discrepancy in our ages makes it hazardous - his youth, his overwhelming fortune, my position and means - the world will surely, surely misinterpret, misunderstand - I think even you, his sister, may be led to credit - what, in your own heart, you must know to be utterly and cruelly untrue."

"I don't know what to say or think," repeated Geraldine in a dull voice. "I can't realise it; I thought that our affection for you was so - so utterly different."

She stared curiously at Kathleen, trying to reconcile what she had always known of her with what she now had to reckon with - strove to find some alteration in the familiar features, something that she had never before noticed, some new, unsuspected splendour of beauty and charm, some undetected and subtle allure. She saw only a wholesome, young, and lovely woman, fresh-skinned, slender, sweet, and graceful - the same companion she had always known and, as she remembered, unchanged in any way since the years of childhood, when Kathleen was twenty and she and her brother were ten.

"I suppose," she said, "that if Scott is in love with you, there is only one thing to do."

"There are several," said Kathleen in a low voice.

"Will you not marry him?"

"I don't know; I think not."

"Are you not in love with him?"

"Does that matter?" asked Kathleen steadily. "Scott's happiness is what is important."

"But his happiness, apparently, depends on you."

Kathleen flushed and looked at her curiously.

"Dear, if I knew that was so, I would give myself to him.

Neither you nor he have ever asked anything of me in vain. Even if I did not love him - as I do - and he needed me, I would give myself to him. You and he have been all there was in life for me. But I am afraid that I may not always be all that life holds for him. He is young; he has had no chance yet; he has had little experience with women. I think he ought to have his chance."

She might have said the same thing of herself. A bride at her husband's death-bed, widowed before she had ever been a wife, what experience had she? All her life so far had been devoted to the girl who stood there confronting her, and to the brother. What did she know of men? - of whether she might be capable of loving some man more suitable? She had not given herself the chance. She never would, now.

There was no selfishness in Kathleen Severn. But there was much in the Seagrave twins. The very method of their bringing up inculcated it; they had never had any chance to be otherwise. The "cultiwation of the indiwidool" had driven it into them, taught them the deification of self, forced them to consider their own importance above anything else in the world.

And it was of that importance that Geraldine was now thinking as she sat on the edge of her bed, darkly considering these new problems that chance was laying before her one by one.

If Scott was going to be unhappy without Kathleen, it followed, as a matter of course, that he must have Kathleen. The chances Kathleen might take, what she might have to endure of the world's malice and gossip and criticism, never entered Geraldine's mind at all.

"If he is in love with you," she repeated, "it settles it, I think. What else is there to do but marry him?"

Kathleen shook her head. "I shall do what is best for him -

whatever that may be."

"You won't make him unhappy, I suppose?" inquired Geraldine, astonished.

"Dear, a woman may be truer to the man she loves - and kinder - by refusing him. Is not that what *you* have done - for Duane's sake?"

Geraldine sprang to her feet, face white, mouth distorted with anger:

"I made a god of Duane!" she broke out breathlessly. "Everything that was in me - everything that was decent and unselfish and pure-minded dominated me when I found I loved him. So I would not listen to my own desire for him, I would not let him risk a terrible unhappiness until I could go to him as clean and well and straight and unafraid as he could wish!" She laughed bitterly, and laid her hands on her breast. "Look at me, Kathleen! I am quite as decent as this god of mine. Why should I worry over the chances he takes when I have chances enough to take in marrying him? I was stupid to be so conscientious - I behaved like a hysterical schoolgirl - or a silly communicant - making him my confessor! A girl is a perfect fool to make a god out of a man. I made one out of Duane; and he acted like one. It nearly ended me, but, after all, he is no worse than I. Whoever it was who said that decency is only depravity afraid, is right. I *am* depraved; I *am* afraid. I'm afraid that I cannot control myself, for one thing; and I'm afraid of being unhappy for life if I don't marry Duane. And I'm going to, and let him take his chances!"

Kathleen, very pale, said: "That is selfishness - if you do it."

"Are not men selfish? He will not tell me as much of his life as I have told him of mine. I have told him everything. How do I know what risk I run? Yes - I do know; I take the risk of marrying a man notorious for his facility with women. And he lets me take that risk. Why should I not let him risk something?"

The girl seemed strangely excited; her quick breathing and bright, unsteady eyes betrayed the nervous tension of the last few days. She said feverishly:

"There is a lot of nonsense talked about self-sacrifice and love; about the beauties of abnegation and martyrdom, but, Kathleen, if I shall ever need him at all, I need him now. I'm afraid to be alone any longer; I'm frightened at the chances against me. Do you know what these days of horror have been to me, locked in here - all alone - in the depths of degradation for what - what I did that night - in distress and shame unutterable -"

"My darling -"

"Wait! I had more to endure - I had to endure the results of my education in the study of man! I had to realise that I loved one of them who has done enough to annihilate in me anything except love. I had to learn that he couldn't kill that - that I want him in spite of it, that I need him, that my heart is sick with dread; that he can have me when he will - Oh, Kathleen, I have learned to care less for him than when I denied him for his own sake - more for him than I did before he held me in his arms! And that is not a high type of love - I know it - but oh, if I could only have his arms around me - if I could rest there for a while - and not feel so frightened, so utterly alone! - I might win out; I might kill what is menacing me, with God's help - and his!"

She lay shivering on Kathleen's breast now, dry-eyed, twisting her ringless fingers in dumb anguish.

"Darling, darling," murmured Kathleen, "you cannot do this thing. You cannot let him assume a burden that is yours alone."

"Why not? What is one's lover for?"

"Not to use; not to hazard; not to be made responsible for a sick mind and a will already demoralised. Is it fair to ask him - to let him begin life with such a burden - such a handicap? Is it not braver, fairer, to fight it out alone, eradicate what threatens you - oh, my own darling! My little Geraldine! - is it not fairer to the man you love? Is he not worth striving for, suffering for? Have you no courage to endure if he is to be the reward? Is a little selfish weakness, a miserable self-indulgence to stand between you and life-long happiness?"

Geraldine looked up; her face was very white:

"Have you ever been tempted?"

"Have I not been to-night?"

"I mean by - something ignoble?"

"No."

"Do you know how it hurts?"

"To - to deny yourself?"

"Yes.... It is so - difficult - it makes me wretchedly weak.... I only thought he might help me.... You are right, Kathleen.... I must be terribly demoralised to have wished it. I - I will not marry him, now. I don't think I ever will.... You are right. I have got to be fair to him, no matter what he has been to me.... He has been fearfully unfair. After all, he is only a man.... I couldn't really love a god."

CHAPTER XIII

AMBITIONS AND LETTERS

Rosalie had departed; Grandcourt followed suit next day; Sylvia's brother, Stuyvesant, had at last found a sober moment at his disposal and had appeared at Roya-Neh and taken his sister away. Duane was all ready to go to New York to find out whether his father was worrying over anything, as the tone of his letters indicated.

The day he left, Kathleen and Geraldine started on a round of August house parties, ranging from Lenox to Long Island, including tiresome week ends and duty visits to some very unpretentious but highly intellectual relatives of Mrs. Severn. So Scott remained in solitary possession of Roya-Neh, with its forests, gardens, pastures, lakes and streams, and a staggering payroll and all the multiplicity of problems that such responsibility entails. Which pleased him immensely, except for the departure of Kathleen.

To play the intellectual country squire had been all he desired on earth except Kathleen. From the beginning White's "Selborne" had remained his model for all books, Kathleen for all women. He was satisfied with these two components of perfect happiness, and with himself, as he was, for the third ingredient in a contented and symmetrical existence.

He had accepted his answer from her with more philosophy than she quite expected or was prepared for, saying that if she made a particular point of it he would go about next winter and give himself a chance to meet as many desirable young girls as she thought best; that it was merely wasting time, but if it made her any happier, he'd wait and endeavour to return to their relations of unsentimental comradeship until she was satisfied he knew his mind.

Kathleen was, at first, a little dismayed at his complacency. It was only certainty of himself. At twenty-two there is time for anything, and the vista of life ahead is endless. And there was one thing more which Kathleen did not know. Under the covering of this Seagrave complacency and self-centred sufficiency, all alone by itself was developing the sprouting germ of consideration for others.

How it started he himself did not know - nor was he even aware that it had started. But long, solitary rambles and the quiet contemplation of other things besides himself had awakened first curiosity, then a dawning suspicion of the rights of others.

In the silence of forests it is difficult to preserve complacency; under the stars modesty is born.

It began to occur to him, by degrees, that his own personal importance among his kind *might* be due, in part, to his fortune. And from the first invasion of that shocking idea matters progressed rather rapidly with the last of the Seagraves.

He said uneasily to Duane, once: "Are you going in seriously for painting?"

"I *am* in," observed Duane drily.

"Professionally?"

"Sure thing. God hates an amateur."

"What are you after?" persisted Scott. "Fame?"

"Yes; I need it in my business."

"Are you contemplating a velvet coat and bow tie, and a bunch of the elect at your heels? - ratty men, and pop-eyed young women whose coiffure needs weeding?"

Duane laughed. "Are they any more deadly than our own sort? Why endure either? Because you are developing into a country squire, you don't have to marry Maud Muller." And he quoted Bret Harte:

"For there be women fair as she,
Whose verbs and nouns do more agree."

"You don't have to wallow in a profession, you know."

"But why the mischief do you want to paint professionally?" inquired Scott, with unsatisfied curiosity. "It isn't avarice, is it?"

"I expect to hold out for what my pictures are worth, if that's what you mean by avarice. What I'm trying to do," added Duane, striking his palm with his fist as emphasis, "is not to die the son of a wealthy man. If I can't be anything more, I'm not worth a damn. But I'm going to be. I can do it, Scott; I'm lazy, I'm undecided, I've a weak streak. And yet, do you know, with all my blemishes, all my misgivings, all my discouragements, panics, despondent moments, I am, way down inside, serenely and unaccountably certain that I can paint like the devil, and that I am going to do it. That sounds cheeky, doesn't it?"

"It sounds all right to me," said Scott. And he walked away thoughtfully, fists dug deep in his pockets.

And one still, sunny afternoon, standing alone on the dry granite crags of the Golden Dome, he looked up and saw, a quarter of a million miles above him, the moon's ghost swimming in azure splendour. Then he looked down and saw the map of the earth below him, where his forests spread out like moss, and his lakes mirrored the clouds, and a river belonging to him traced its course across the valley in a single silver thread. And a slight blush stung his face at the thought that, without any merit or endeavour of his own, his money had bought it all - his money, that had always acted as his deputy, fought for him, conquered for him, spoken for him, vouched for him - perhaps pleaded for him! - he shivered, and suddenly he realised that this golden voice was, in fact, all there was to him.

What had he to identify him on earth among mankind? Only his money. Wherein did he differ from other men? He had more money. What had he to offer as excuse for living at all? Money. What had he done? Lived on it, by it. Why, then, it was the money that was entitled to distinction, and he figured only as its parasite! Then he was nothing - even a little less. In the world there was man and there was money. It seemed that he was a little lower in the scale than either; a parasite - scarcely a thing of distinction to offer Kathleen Severn.

Very seriously he looked up at the moon.

It was the day following his somewhat disordered and impassioned declaration. He expected to receive his answer that evening; and he descended the mountain in a curiously uncertain and perplexed state of mind which at times bordered on a modesty painfully akin to humbleness.

Meanwhile, Duane was preparing to depart on the morrow. And that evening he also was to have his definite answer to the letter which Kathleen had taken to Geraldine Seagrave that morning.

> "Dear," he had written, "I once told you that my weakness needed the aid of all that is best in you; that yours required the best of courage and devotion that lies in me. It is surely so. Together we conquer the world - which is ourselves.

"For the little things that seem to threaten our separation do not really alarm me. Even if I actually committed the inconsequential and casual thing that so abruptly and so deeply offended you, there remains enough soundness in me at the core to warrant your charity and repay, in a measure, your forgiveness and a renewal of your interest in my behalf.

"Search your heart, Geraldine; question your intelligence; both will tell you that I am enough of a man to dare love you. And it takes something of a man to dare do it.

"There is a thing that I might say which would convince you, even against the testimony of your own eyes, that never in deed or in thought have I been really disloyal to you since you gave me your heart.... Yet I must not say it.... Can you summon sufficient faith in me to accept that statement - against the evidence of those two divine witnesses which condemn me - your eyes? Circumstantial evidence is no good in this case, dear. I can say no more than that.

"Dearest, what can compare to the disaster of losing each other?

"I ask you to let me have the right to stand by you in your present distress and despondency. What am I for if not for such moments?

"That night you were closer to the danger mark than you have ever been. I know that my conduct - at least your interpretation of it - threw you, for the moment off your guarded balance; but that your attitude toward such a crisis - your solution of such a situation - should be a leap forward toward self-destruction - a reckless surrender to anger and blind impulse, only makes me the more certain that we need each other now if ever.

"The silent, lonely, forlorn battle that has been going on

behind the door of your room and the doors of your heart during these last few days, is more than I can well endure. Open both doors to me; leagued we can win through!

"Give me the right to be with you by night as well as by daylight, and we two shall stand together and see 'the day break and the shadows flee away.'"

That same evening his reply came:

"My darling, Kathleen will give you this. I don't care what my eyes saw if you tell me it isn't true. I have loved you, anyway, all the while - even with my throat full of tears and my mouth bitter with anger, and my heart torn into several thousand tatters - oh, it is not very difficult to love you, Duane; the only trouble is to love you in the right way; which is hard, dear, because I want you so much; and it's so new to me to be unselfish. I began to learn by loving you.

"Which means, that I will not let you take the risk you ask for. Give me time; I've fought it off since that miserable night. Heaven alone knows why I surrendered - turning to my deadly enemy for countenance and comfort to support my childish and contemptible anger against you.

"Duane, there is an evil streak in me, and we both must reckon with it. Long, long before I knew I loved you, things you said and did often wounded me; and within me a perfectly unreasoning desire to hurt you - to make you suffer - always flamed up and raged.

"I think that was partly what made me do what you know I did that night. It would hurt you; that was my ignoble instinct. God knows whether it was also a hideous sort of excuse for my weakness - for I was blazing hot after the last dance - and the gaiety and uproar and laughter all overexcited me - and then what I had seen you do, and your not coming to me, and that ominous uneasy impulse stirring!

"That is the truth as I analyse it. The dreadful thing is that I could have been capable of dealing our chance of happiness such a cowardly blow.

"Well, it is over. The thing has fled for a while. I fought it down, stamped on it with utter horror and loathing. It - the encounter - tired me. I am weary yet - from honourable wounds. But I won out. If it comes back again - Oh, Duane! and it surely will - I shall face it undaunted once more; and every hydra-head that stirs I shall kill until the thing lies dead between us for all time.

"Then, dear, will you take the girl who has done this thing?

"GERALDINE SEAGRAVE."

This was his answer on the eve of his departure.

And on the morning of it Geraldine came down to say good-bye; a fresh, sweet, and bewildering Geraldine, somewhat slimmer than when he had last seen her, a little finer in feature, more delicate of body; and there was about her even a hint of the spirituel as a fascinating trace of what she had been through, locked in alone behind the doors of her room and heart.

She bade him good-morning somewhat shyly, offering her slim hand and looking at him with the slight uncertainty and bent brows of a person coming suddenly into a strong light.

He said under his breath: "You poor darling, how thin you are."

"Athletics," she said; "Jacob wrestled with an angel, but you know what I've been facing in the squared circle. Don't speak of it any more, will you? ... How sunburned you are! What have you been about since I've kept to my room?"

"I've painted Miller's kids in the open; I suppose the terrific influence of Sorolla has me in bondage for the moment." He laughed easily: "But don't worry; it will leave nothing except clean inspiration behind it. I'll think out my own way - grope it out through Pantheon and living maze. All I've really got to say in paint can be said only in my own way. I know that, even when realising that I've been sunstruck by Sorolla."

She listened demurely, watching him, her lips sensitive with understanding; and she laughed when he laughed away his fealty to the superb Spaniard, knowing himself and the untried strength within him.

"But when are you coming back to us, Duane?"

"I don't know. Father's letters perplex me. I'll write you every day, of course."

A quick colour tinted her skin:

"And I will write you every day. I will begin to-day. Kathleen and I expect to be here in September. But you will come back before that and keep Scott company; won't you?"

"I want to get into harness again," he said slowly. "I want to settle down to work."

"Can't you work here?"

"Not very well."

"Why?"

"To tell the truth," he admitted, smiling, "I require something more like a working studio than Miller's garret."

"That's what I thought," she said shyly, "and Scott and I have the plans for a studio all ready; and the men are to begin Monday, and Miller is to take the new gate cottage. Oh, the plans are really very wonderful!" she added hastily, as Duane looked grateful but dubious. "Rollins and Calvert drew them. I wrote to Billy Calvert and sent him the original plans for Hurryon Lodge. Duane, I thought it would please you -"

"It does, you dear, generous girl! I'm a trifle overwhelmed, that's all my silence meant. You ought not to do this for me -"

"Why? Aren't we to be as near each other as we can be until - I am ready - for something - closer?"

"Yes.... Certainly.... I'll arrange to work out certain things up here. As for models, if there is nothing suitable at Westgate village, you won't mind my importing some, will you?"

"No," she said, becoming very serious and gravely interested, as befitted the fiancee of a painter of consequence. "You will do what is necessary, of course; because I - few girls - are accustomed in the beginning to the details of such a profession as yours; and I'm very ignorant, Duane, and I must learn how to second you - intelligently" - she blushed - "that is, if I'm to amount to anything as an artist's wife."

"You dear!" he whispered.

"No; I tell you I am totally ignorant. A studio is an awesome place to me. I merely know enough to keep out of it when you are using models. That is safest, isn't it?"

He said, intensely amused: "It might be safer not to give pink teas while I am working from the nude."

"Duane! Do you think me a perfect ninny? Anyway, you're not *always* painting Venus and Ariadne and horrid Ledas, are you?"

"Not always!" he managed to assure her; and her pretty,

confused laughter mingled with his unembarrassed mirth as the motor-car swung up to carry him and his traps to the station.

They said good-bye; her dark eyes became very tragic; her lips threatened to escape control.

Kathleen turned away, manoeuvring Scott out of earshot, who knowing nothing of any situation between Duane and his sister, protested mildly, but forgot when Kathleen led him to an orange-underwing moth asleep on the stone coping of the terrace.

And when the unfortunate Catocala had been safely bottled and they stood examining it in the library, Scott's rapidly diminishing conceit found utterance:

"I say, Kathleen, it's all very well for me to collect these fascinating things, but any ass can do that. One can't make a particular name for one's self by doing what a lot of cleverer men have already done, and what a lot of idle idiots are imitating."

She raised her violet eyes, astonished:

"Do *you* want to make a name for yourself?"

"Yes," he said, reddening.

"Why not? I'm a nobody. I'm worse; I'm an amateur! You ought to hear what Duane has to say about amateurs!"

"But, Scott, you don't have to be anything in particular except what you are -"

"What am I?" he demanded.

"Why - yourself."

"And what's that?" He grew redder. "I'll tell you, Kathleen. I'm merely a painfully wealthy young man. Don't laugh; this is becoming deadly serious to me. By my own exertions I've never done one bally thing either useful or spectacular. I'm not distinguished by anything except an unfair share of wealth. I'm not eminent, let alone pre-eminent, even in that sordid class; there are richer men, plenty of them - some even who have made their own fortunes and have not been hatched out in a suffocating plethora of affluence like the larva of the Carnifex tumble-bug -"

"Scott!"

"And I!" he ended savagely. "Why, I'm not even pre-eminent as far as my position in the social puddle is concerned; there are sets that wouldn't endure me; there's at least one club into which I couldn't possibly wriggle; there are drawing-rooms where I wouldn't be tolerated, because I've nothing on earth to recommend me or to distinguish me from Algernon FitzNoodle and Montmorency de Sansgallette except an inflated income! What have I to offer anybody worth while for entertaining me? What have I to offer you, Kathleen, in exchange for yourself?"

He was becoming boyishly dramatic with sweeping gestures which amazed her; but she was conscious that it was all sincere and very real to him.

"Scott, dear," she began sweetly, uncertain how to take it all; "kindness, loyalty, and decent breeding are all that a woman cares for in a man -"

"You are entitled to more; you are entitled to a man of distinction, of attainment, of achievement -"

"Few women ask for that, Scott; few care for it; fewer still understand it -"

"You would. I've got a cheek to ask you to marry me - *me!* -

before I wear any tag to identify me except the dollar mark -"

"Oh, hush, Scott! You are talking utter nonsense; don't you know it?"

He made a large and rather grandiose gesture:

"Around me lies opportunity, Kathleen - every stone; every brook -"

The mischievous laughter of his listener checked him. She said: "I'm sorry; only it made me think of

> 'Sermons in stones,
> Books in the running brooks,'

and the indignant gentleman who said: 'What damn nonsense! It's "sermons in *books*, *stones* in the running brooks!"' Do go on, Scott, dear, I don't mean to be frivolous; it is fine of you to wish for fame -"

"It isn't fame alone, although I wouldn't mind it if I deserved it. It's that I want to do just one thing that amounts to something. I wish you'd give me an idea, Kathleen, something useful in - say in entomology."

Together they walked back to the terrace. Duane had gone; Geraldine sat sideways on the parapet, her brown eyes fixed on the road along which her lover had departed.

"Geraldine," said Kathleen, who very seldom relapsed into the vernacular, "this brother of yours desires to perform some startling stunt in entomology and be awarded Carnegie medals."

"That's about it," said Scott, undaunted. "Some wise guy put it all over the Boll-weevil, and saved a few billions for the cotton growers; another gentleman full of scientific thinks studied out the San Jose scale; others have got in good licks at mosquitoes and house-flies. I'd like to tackle something of that sort."

"Rose-beetles," said his sister briefly. In her voice was a suspicion of tears, and she kept her head turned from them.

"Nobody could ever get rid of Rose-beetles," said Kathleen. "But it *would* be exciting, wouldn't it, Scott? Think of saving our roses and peonies and irises every year!"

"I *am* thinking of it," said Scott gravely.

A few moments later he disappeared around the corner of the house, returning presently, pockets bulging with bottles and boxes, a field-microscope in one hand, and several volumes on Coleopte rain the other.

"They're gone," he said without further explanation.

"Who are gone?" inquired Kathleen.

"The Rose-beetles. They deposit their eggs in the soil. The larvae ought to be out by now. I'm going to begin this very minute, Kathleen." And he descended the terrace steps, entered the garden, and, seating himself under a rose-tree, spread out his paraphernalia and began a delicate and cautious burrowing process in the sun-dried soil.

"Fame is hidden under humble things," observed Geraldine with a resolute effort at lightness. "That excellent brother of mine may yet discover it in the garden dirt."

"Dirt breeds roses," said Kathleen. "Oh, look, dear, how earnest he is about it. What a boy he is, after all! So serious and intent, and so touchingly confident!"

Geraldine nodded listlessly, considering her brother's evolutions with his trowel and weeder where he lay flat on his stomach, absorbed in his investigations.

"Why does he get so grubby?" she said. "All his coat-pockets are permanently out of shape. The other day I was looking through them, at his request, to find one of my own handerchiefs which he had taken, and oh, horrors! a caterpillar, forgotten, had spun a big cocoon in one of them!"

She shuddered, but in Kathleen's laughter there was a tremor of tenderness born of that shy pride which arises from possession. For it was now too late, if it had not always been too late, for any criticism of this boy of hers. Perfect he had always been, wondrous to her, as a child, for the glimpses of the man developing in him; perfect, wonderful, adorable now for the glimpses of the child which she caught so constantly through the man's character now forming day by day under her loyal eyes. Everything masculine in him she loved or pardoned proudly - even his egotism, his slapdash self-confidence, his bullying of her, his domination, his exacting demands. But this new humility - this sudden humble doubt that he might not be worthy of her, filled her heart with delicious laughter and a delight almost childish.

So she watched him from the parapet, chin cupped in both palms, bright hair blowing, one shoulder almost hidden under the drooping scarlet nasturtiums pendant from the carved stone urn above; a fair, sweet, youthful creature, young as her guiltless heart, sweet as her conscience, fair as the current of her stainless life.

And beside her, seated sideways, brown eyes brooding, sat a young girl, delicately lovely, already harassed, already perplexed, already bruised and wearied by her first skirmishes with life; not yet fully understanding what threatened, what lay before - alas! what lay behind her - even to the fifth generation.

They were to motor to Lenox after luncheon. Before that - and leaving Scott absorbed in his grubbing, and Kathleen absorbed in watching him - Geraldine wandered back into the library and took down a book - a book which had both beguiled and horrified the solitude of her self-imprisonment. It was called "Simpson on Heredity."

There were some very hideous illustrated pages in that book; she turned to them with a fearful fascination which had never left her since she first read them. They dealt with the transission of certain tendencies through successive generations.

That the volume was an old one and amusingly out of date she did not realise, as her brown eyes widened over terrifying paragraphs and the soft tendrils of her glossy hair almost bristled.

She had asked Kathleen about it, and Kathleen had asked Dr. Bailey, who became very irritated and told Geraldine that anybody except a physician who ever read medical works was a fool. Desperation gave her courage to ask him one more question; his well-meant reply silenced her. But she had the book under her pillow. It is better to answer such questions when the young ask them.

And over it all she pondered and pored, and used a dictionary and shuddered, frightening herself into a morbid condition until, desperately scared, she even thought of going to Duane about it; but could not find the hardihood to do it or the vocabulary necessary.

Now Duane was gone; and the book lay there between her knees, all its technical vagueness menacing her with unknown terrors; and she felt that she could endure it alone no longer.

She wrote him:

> "You have not been gone an hour, and already I need you. I wish to ask you about something that is troubling me; I've asked Kathleen and she doesn't know; and Dr. Bailey was horrid to me, and I tried to find out from Scott whether he knew, but he wasn't much interested. So,

Duane, who else is there for me to ask except you? And I don't exactly know whether I may speak about such matters to you, but I'm rather frightened, and densely ignorant.

"It is this, dear; in a medical book which I read, it says that hereditary taints are transmissible; that sometimes they may skip the second generation but only to appear surely in the third. But it also says that the taint is very likely to appear in *every* generation.

"Duane, is this *true*? It has worried me sick since I read it. Because, my darling, if it is so, is it not another reason for our not marrying?

"Do you understand? I can and will eradicate what is threatening *me*, but if I marry you - you *do* understand, don't you? Isn't it all right for me to ask you whether, if we should have children, this thing would menace them? Oh, Duane - Duane! Have I any right to marry? Children come - God knows how, for nobody ever told me exactly, and I'm a fool about such things - but I summoned up courage to ask Dr. Bailey if there was any way to tell before I married whether I would have any, and he said I would if I had any notion of my duty and any pretence to self-respect. And I don't know what he means and I'm bewildered and miserable and afraid to marry you even when I myself become perfectly well. And that is what worries me, Duane, and I have nobody in the world to ask about it except you. Could you please tell me how I might learn what I ought to know concerning these things without betraying my own vital interest in them to whomever I ask? You see, Kathleen is as innocent as I.

"Please tell me all you can, Duane, for I am most unhappy."

* * * * *

"The house is very still and full of sunlight and cut flowers. Scott is meditating great deeds, lying flat in the dirt. Kathleen sits watching him from the parapet. And I am here in the library, with that ghastly book at my elbow, pouring out all my doubts and fears to the only man in the world - whom God bless and protect wherever he may be - Oh, Duane, Duane, how I love you!"

She hurriedly directed and sealed the letter and placed it in the box for outgoing mail; then, unquiet and apprehensive regarding what she had ventured to write, she began a restless tour of the house, upstairs and down, wandering aimlessly through sunny corridors, opening doors for a brief survey of chambers in which only the shadow-patterns of leaves moved on sunlit walls; still rooms tenanted only by the carefully dusted furniture which seemed to stand there watching attentively for another guest.

Duane had left his pipe in his bedroom. She was silly over it, even to the point of retiring into her room, shredding some cigarettes, filling the rather rank bowl, and trying her best to smoke it. But such devotion was beyond her physical powers; she rinsed her mouth, furious at being defeated in her pious intentions, and, making an attractive parcel of the pipe, seized the occasion to write him another letter.

"There is in my heart," she wrote, "no room for anything except you; no desire except for you; no hope, no interest that is not yours. You praise my beauty; you endow me with what you might wish I really possessed; and oh, I really am so humble at your feet, if you only knew it! So dazed by your goodness to me, so grateful, so happy that you have chosen me (I just jumped up to look at myself in the mirror; I *am* pretty, Duane, I've a stunning colour just now and there *is* a certain charm about me - even I can see it in what you call the upcurled corners of my mouth, and in my figure and hands) - and I am so happy that it is true - that you find me beautiful, that you care for my beauty.... It is so with a man, I believe; and a girl wishes to have him love her beauty, too.

"But, Duane, I don't think the average girl cares very much about that in a man. Of course you are exceedingly nice to look at, and I notice it sometimes, but not nearly as often as you notice what you think is externally attractive about me.

"In my heart, I don't believe it really matters much to a girl what a man looks like; anyway, it matters very little after she once knows him.

"Of course women do notice handsome men - or what we consider handsome - which is, I believe, not at all what men care for; because men usually seem to have a desire to kick the man whom women find good-looking. I know several men who feel that way about Jack Dysart. I think you do, for one.

"Poor Jack Dysart! To-day's papers are saying such horridly unpleasant things about the rich men with whom he was rather closely associated in business affairs several years ago. I read, but I do not entirely comprehend.

"The New York papers seem unusually gloomy this summer; nothing but predictions of hard times coming, and how many corporations the attorney-general is going to proceed against, and wicked people who loot metropolitan railways, and why the district-attorney doesn't do his duty - which you say he does - oh, dear; I expect that Scott and Kathleen and I will have to take in boarders this winter; but if nobody has any money, nobody can pay board, so everybody will be ruined and I don't very much care, for I could teach school, only who is to pay my salary if there's no money to pay it with? Oh, dear! what nonsense I am writing - only to keep on writing, because it seems to bring you a little nearer - my own - my Duane - my comrade - the same, same little boy who ran away from his nurse and came into our garden to fight my brother and - fall in love with his sister! Oh, Fate! Oh, Destiny! Oh, Duane Mallett!

"Here is a curious phenomenon. Listen:

"Away from you I have a woman's courage to tell you how I long for you, how my heart and my arms ache for you. But when I am with you I'm less of a woman and more of a girl - a girl not yet accustomed to some things - always guarded, always a little reticent, always instinctively recoiling from the contact I really like, always a little on the defensive against your lips, in spite of myself - against your arms - where, somehow, I cannot seem to stay long at a time - will not endure it - *cannot,* somehow.

"Yet, here, away from you, I so long for your embrace, and cannot imagine it too long, too close, too tender to satisfy my need of you.

"And this is my second letter to you within the hour - one hour after your departure.

"Oh, Duane, I do truly miss you so! I go about humming that air you found so quaint:

> "'Lisetto quittee la plaine,
> Moi perdi bonheur a moi,
> Yeux a moi semblent fontaine,
> Depuis moi pas mire toi,'

and there's a tear in every note of it, and I'm the most lonely girl on the face of the earth to-day.

"GERALDINE QUI PLEURE."

"P.S. - Voici votre pipe, Monsieur!"

CHAPTER XIV

THE PROPHETS

August in town found an unusual number of New York men at the clubs, at the restaurants, at the summer theatres. Men who very seldom shoved their noses inside the metropolitan oven during the summer baking were now to be met everywhere and anywhere within the financial district and without. The sky-perched and magnificent down-town "clubs" were full of men who under normal circumstances would have remained at Newport, Lenox, Bar Harbor, or who at least would have spent the greater portion of the summer on their yachts or their Long Island estates.

And in every man's hand or pocket was a newspaper.

They were scarcely worth reading for mere pleasure, these New York newspapers; indeed, there was scarcely anything in them to read except a daily record of the steady decline in securities of every description; paragraphs noting the passing of dividends; columns setting forth minutely the opinions of very wealthy men concerning the business outlook; chronicles in detail of suits brought against railroads and against great industrial corporations; accounts of inquiries by State and by Federal authorities into combinations resulting in an alleged violation of various laws.

Here and there a failure of some bucket-branded broker was noted - the reports echoing like the first dropping shots along the firing line.

Even to the most casual and uninterested outsider it was evident thatalready the metropolis was under a tension; that the tension was increasing almost imperceptibly day by day; that there seemed to be no very clear idea as to the reason of it, only a confused apprehension, an apparently unreassuring fear of some grotesque danger ahead, which daily reading of the newspapers was not at all calculated to allay.

Of course there were precise reasons for impending trouble given and reiterated by those amateurs of finance and politics whose opinions are at the disposal of the newspaper-reading public.

Prolixity characterised these solemn utterances, packed full of cant phrases such as "undigested securities" and "the treacherous attack on the nation's integrity."

Two principal reasons were given for the local financial uneasiness; and the one made the other ridiculous - first, that the nation's Executive was mad as Nero and had deliberately begun a senseless holocaust involving the entire nation; the other that a "panic" was due, anyway. It resembled the logic of the White Queen of immortal memory, who began screaming before she pricked her finger in order to save herself any emotion after the pin had drawn blood.

Men knew in their hearts that there was no real reason for impending trouble; that this menace was an unreal thing, intangible, without substance - only a shadow cast by their own assininity.

Yet shadows can be made real property when authority so ordains. Because there was once a man with a donkey who met a stranger in the desert.

The stranger bargained for and bought the donkey; the late owner shoved the shekels into his ample pockets and sat down in the mule's shadow to escape the sun; and the new owner brought suit to recover the rent due him for the occupation of the shadow cast by his donkey.

There was also a mule which waited seven years to kick.

There are asses and mules and all sorts of shadows. The ordinance of authority can affect only the shadow; the substance is immutable.

Among other serious gentlemen of consideration and means who had been unaccustomed to haunt the metropolis in the dog days was Colonel Alexander Mallett, President of the Half Moon Trust Company, and incidentally Duane's father.

His town-house was still open, although his wife and daughter were in the country. To it, in the comparative cool of the August evenings, came figures familiar in financial circles; such men as Magnelius Grandcourt, father of Delancy; and Remsen Tappan, and James Cray.

Others came and went, men of whom Duane had read in the newspapers - very great men who dressed very simply, very powerful men who dressed elaborately; and some were young and red-faced with high living, and one was damp of hair and long-nosed, with eyes set a trifle too close together; and one fulfilled every external requisite for a "good fellow"; and another was very old, very white, with a nut-cracker jaw and faded eyes, blue as an unweaned pup's, and a cream-coloured wig curled glossily over waxen ears and a bloodless and furrowed neck.

All these were very great men; but they and Colonel Mallett journeyed at intervals into the presence of a greater man who inhabited, all alone, except for a crew of a hundred men, an enormous yacht, usually at anchor off the white masonry cliffs of the seething city.

All alone this very great man inhabited the huge white steamer;

and they piped him fore and they piped him aft and they piped him over the side. Many a midnight star looked down at the glowing end of his black cigar; many a dawn shrilled with his boatswain's whistle. He was a very, very great man; none was greater in New York town.

It was said of him that he once killed a pompous statesman - by ridicule:

"I know who *you* are!" panted a ragged urchin, gazing up in awe as the famous statesman approached his waiting carriage.

"And who am I, my little man?"

"You are the great senator from New York."

"Yes - you are right. *But*" - and he solemnly pointed his gloved forefinger toward heaven - "but, remember, there is One even greater than I."

Duane had heard the absurd lampoon as a child, and one evening late inAugust, smoking his after-dinner cigar beside his father in the empty conservatory, he recalled the story, which had been one of his father's favorites.

But Colonel Mallett scarcely smiled, scarcely heard; and his son watched him furtively. The trim, elastic figure was less upright this summer; the close gray hair and cavalry mustache had turned white very rapidly since spring. For the first time, too, in all his life, Colonel Mallett wore spectacles; and the thin gold rims irritated his ears and the delicate bridge of his nose. Under his pleasant eyes the fine skin had darkened noticeably; thin new lines had sprung downward from the nostrils' clean-cut wings; but the most noticeable change was in his hands, which were no longer firm and fairly smooth, but were now the hands of an old man, restless if not tremulous, unsteady in handling the cigar which, unnoticed, had gone out.

They - father and son - had never been very intimate. An excellent understanding had always existed between them with nothing deeper in it than a natural affection and an instinctive respect for each other's privacy.

This respect now oppressed Duane because long habit, and the understood pact, seemed to bar him from a sympathy and a practical affection which, for the first time, it seemed to him his father might care for.

That his father was worried was plain enough; but how anxious and with how much reason, he had hesitated to ask, waiting for some voluntary admission, or at least some opening, which the older man never gave.

That night, however, he had tried an opening for himself, offering the old stock story which had always, heretofore, amused his father. And there had been no response.

In silence he thought the matter over; his sympathy was always quick; it hurt him to remain aloof when there might be a chance that he could help a little.

"It may amuse you," he said carelessly, "to know how much I've made since I came back from Paris."

The elder man looked up preoccupied. His son went on:

"What you set aside for me brings me ten thousand a year, you know. So far I haven't touched it. Isn't that pretty good for a start?"

Colonel Mallett sat up straighter with a glimmer of interest in his eyes.

Duane went on, checking off on his fingers:

"I got fifteen hundred for Mrs. Varick's portrait, the same for Mrs. James Cray's, a thousand each for portraits of Carl and

Friedrich Gumble; that makes five thousand. Then I had three thousand for the music-room I did for Mrs. Ellis; and Dinklespiel Brothers, who handle my pictures, have sold every one I sent; which gives me twelve thousand so far."

"I am perfectly astonished," murmured his father.

Duane laughed. "Oh, I know very well that sheer merit had nothing much to do with it. The people who gave me orders are all your friends. They did it as they might have sent in wedding presents; I am your son; I come back from Paris; it's up to them to do something. They've done it - those who ever will, I expect - and from now on it will be different."

"They've given you a start," said his father.

"They certainly have done that. Many a brilliant young fellow, with more ability than I, eats out his heart unrecognised, sterilised for lack of what came to me because of your influence."

"It is well to look at it in that way for the present," said his father. He sat silent for a while, staring through the dusk at the lighted windows of houses in the rear. Then:

"I have meant to say, Duane, that I - we" - he found a little difficulty in choosing his words - "that the Trust Company's officers feel that, for the present, it is best for them to reconsider their offer that you should undertake the mural decoration of the new building."

"Oh," said Duane, "I'm sorry! - but it's all right, father."

"I told them you'd take it without offence. I told them that I'd tell you the reason we do not feel quite ready to incur, at this moment, any additional expenses."

"Everybody is economising," said Duane cheerfully, "so I understand. No doubt - later -"

"No doubt," said his father gravely.

The son's attitude was careless, untroubled; he dropped one long leg over the other knee, and idly examining his cigar, cast one swift level look at the older man:

"Father?"

"Yes, my son."

"I - it just occurred to me that if you happen to have any temporary use for what you very generously set aside for me, don't stand on ceremony."

There ensued a long silence. It was his bedtime when Colonel Mallett stirred in his holland-covered armchair and stood up.

"Thank you, my son," he said simply; they shook hands and separated; the father to sleep, if he could; the son to go out into the summer night, walk to his nearest club, and write his daily letter to the woman he loved:

> "Dear, it is not at all bad in town - not that murderous, humid heat that you think I'm up against; and you must stop reproaching yourself for enjoying the delicious breezes in the Adirondacks. Women don't know what a jolly time men have in town. Follows the chronical of this August day:
>
> "I had your letter; that is breeze enough for me; it was all full of blue sky and big white clouds and the scent of Adirondack pines. Isn't it jolly for you and Kathleen to be at the Varicks' camp! And what a jolly crowd you've run into.
>
> "I note what you say about your return to the Berkshires, and that you expect to be at Berkshire Pass Inn with the motor on Monday. Give my love to Naida; I know you three and young Montross will have a bully tour through

the hill country.

"I also note your red-pencil cross at the top of the page - which always gives me, as soon as I open a letter of yours, the assurance that all is still well with you and that victory still remains with you. Thank God! Stand steady, little girl, for the shadows are flying and the dawn is ours.

"After your letter, breakfast with father - a rather silent one. Then he went down-town in his car and I walked to the studio. It's one of those stable-like studios which decorate the cross-streets in the 50's, but big enough to work in.

"A rather bothersome bit of news: the Trust Company reconsiders its commission; and I have three lunettes and three big mural panels practically completed. For a while I'll admit I had the blues, but, after all, some day the Trust Company is likely to take up the thing again and give me the commission. Anyway, I've had a corking time doing the things, and lots of valuable practice in handling a big job and covering large surfaces; and the problem has been most exciting and interesting because, you see, I've had to solve it, taking into consideration the architecture and certain fixed keys and standards, such as the local colour and texture of the marble and the limitations of the light area. Don't turn up your pretty nose; it's all very interesting.

"I didn't bother about luncheon; and about five I went to the club, rather tired in my spinal column and arm-weary.

"Nobody was there whom you know except Delancy Grandcourt and Dysart. The latter certainly looks very haggard. I do not like him personally, as you know, but the man looks ill and old and the papers are becoming bolder in what they hint at concerning him and the operations he was, and is still supposed to be, connected with; and it is deplorable to see such a physical change in any human being, guilty or innocent. I do not like to see pain; I never did. For Dysart I have no use at all, but he is suffering, and it is difficult to contemplate any suffering unmoved.

"There was a letter at the club for me from Scott. He says he's plugging away at the Rose-beetle's life history as a hors-d'oeuvre before tackling the appetising problem of his total extermination. Dear old Scott! I never thought that the boy I fought in your garden would turn into a spectacled savant. Or that his sister would prove to be the only inspiration and faith and hope that life holds for me!

"I talked to Delancy. He *is* a good young man, as you've always insisted. I know one thing; he's high-minded and gentle. Dysart has a manner of treating him which is most offensive, but it only reflects discredit on Dysart.

"Delancy told me that Rosalie is hostess in her own cottage this month and has asked him up. I heard him speaking rather diffidently to Dysart about it, and Dysart replied that he didn't 'give a damn who went to the house,' as he wasn't going.

"So much for gossip; now a fact or two: my father is plainly worried over the business outlook; and he's quite alone in the house; and that is why I don't go back to Roya-Neh just now and join your brother. I could do plenty of work there. Scott writes that the new studio is in good shape for me. What a generous girl you are! Be certain that at the very first opportunity I will go and occupy it and paint, no doubt, several exceedingly remarkable pictures in it which will sell for enormous prices and enable us to keep a maid-of-all-work when we begin our menage!

"Father has retired - poor old governor - it tears me all to pieces to see him so silent and listless. I am here at the club writing this before I go home to bed. Now I am going. Good-night, my beloved.

"DUANE."

"P.S. - An honour, or the chance of it, has suddenly confronted me, surprising me so much that I don't really dare to believe that it can possibly happen to me - at least not for years. It is this: I met Guy Wilton the other day; you don't know him, but he is a most charming and cultivated man, an engineer. I lunched with him at the Pyramid - that bully old club into which nothing on earth can take a man who has not distinguished himself in his profession. It is composed of professional and business men, the law, the army, navy, diplomatic and consular, the arts and sciences, and usually the chief executive of the nation.

"During luncheon Wilton said: 'You ought to be in here. You are the proper timber.'

"I was astounded and told him so.

"He said: 'By the way, the president of the Academy of Design is very much impressed with some work of yours he has seen. I've heard him, and other artists, also, discussing some pictures of yours which were exhibited in a Fifth Avenue gallery.'

"Well, you know, Geraldine, the breath was getting scarcer in my lungs every minute and I hadn't a word to say. And do you know what that trump of a mining engineer did? He took me about after luncheon and I met a lot of very corking old ducks and some very eminent and delightful younger ducks, and everybody was terribly nice, and the president of the Academy, who is startlingly young and amiable, said that Guy Wilton had spoken about me, and that it was customary that when anybody was proposed for membership, a man of his own profession should do it.

"And I looked over the club list and saw Billy Van Siclen's name, and now what do you think! Billy has proposed me, Austin, the marine painter, has seconded me, and no end of men have written in my behalf - professors, army men, navy men, business friends of father's, architects, writers - and I'm terribly excited over it, although my excitement has plenty of time to cool because it's a fearfully conservative club and a man has to wait years, anyway.

"This is the very great honour, dear, for it is one even to be proposed for the Pyramid. I know you will be happy over it.

"D."

The weather became hotter toward the beginning of September; his studio was almost unendurable, nor was the house very much better.

To eat was an effort; to sleep a martyrdom. Night after night he rose from his hot pillows to stand and listen outside his father's door; but the old endure heat better than the young, and very often his father was asleep in the stifling darkness which made sleep for him impossible.

The usual New York thunder-storms rolled up over Staten Island, covered the southwest with inky gloom, veined the horizon with lightning, then burst in spectacular fury over the panting city, drenched it to its steel foundations, and passed on rumbling up the Hudson, leaving scarcely any relief behind it.

In one of these sudden thunder-storms he took refuge in a rather modest and retired restaurant just off Fifth Avenue; and it being the luncheon hour he made a convenience of necessity and looked about for a table, and discovered Rosalie Dysart and Delancy Grandcourt en tete-a-tete over their peach and grapefruit salad.

There was no reason why they should not have been there; no reason why he should have hesitated to speak to them. But he did hesitate - in fact, was retiring by the way he came, when Rosalie glanced around with that instinct which divines a familiar presence, gave him a startled look, coloured promptly to her temples, and recovered her equanimity with a smile and a sign for him to join them. So he shook hands, but remained standing.

"We ran into town in the racer this morning," she explained. "Delancy had something on down-town and I wanted to look over some cross-saddles they made for me at Thompson's. Do be amiable and help us eat our salad. What a ghastly place town is in September! It's bad enough in the country this year; all the men wear long faces and mutter dreadful prophecies. Can you tell me, Duane, what all this doleful talk is about?"

"It's about something harder to digest than this salad. The public stomach is ostrichlike, but it can't stand the water-cure. Which is all Arabic to you, Rosalie, and I don't mean to be impertinent, only the truth is I don't know why people are losing confidence in the financial stability of the country, but they apparently are."

"There's a devilish row on down-town," observed Delancy, blinking, as an unusually heavy clap of thunder rattled the dishes.

"What kind of a row?" asked Duane.

"Greensleeve & Co. have failed, with liabilities of a million and microscopical assets."

Rosalie raised her eyebrows; Greensleeve & Co. were once brokers for her husband if she remembered correctly. Duane had heard of them but was only vaguely impressed.

"Is that rather a bad thing?" he inquired.

"Well - I don't know. It made a noise louder than that thunder. Three banks fell down in Brooklyn, too."

"What banks?"

Delancy named them; it sounded serious, but neither Duane nor Rosalie were any wiser.

"The Wolverine Mercantile Loan and Trust Company closed its doors, also," observed Delancy, dropping the tips of his long, highly coloured fingers into his finger-bowl as though to wash away all personal responsibility for these financial flip-flaps.

Rosalie laughed: "This is pleasant information for a rainy day," she said. "Duane, have you heard from Geraldine?"

"Yes, to-day," he said innocently; "she is leaving Lenox this morning for Roya-Neh. I hear that there is to be some shooting there Christmas week. Scott writes that the boar and deer are increasing very fast and must be kept down. You and Delancy are on the list, I believe."

Rosalie nodded; Delancy said: "Miss Seagrave has been good enough to ask the family. Yours is booked, too, I fancy."

"Yes, if my father only feels up to it. Christmas at Roya-Neh ought to be a jolly affair."

"Christmas anywhere away from New York ought to be a relief," observed young Grandcourt drily.

They laughed without much spirit. Coffee was served, cigarettes lighted. Presently Grandcourt sent a page to find out if the car had returned from the garage where Rosalie had sent it for a minor repair.

The car was ready, it appeared; Rosalie retired to readjust her hair and veil; the two men standing glanced at one another:

"I suppose you know," said Delancy, reddening with embarrassment, "that Mr. and Mrs. Dysart have separated."

"I heard so yesterday," said Duane coolly.

The other grew redder: "I heard it from Mrs. Dysart about half an hour ago." He hesitated, then frankly awkward: "I say, Mallett, I'm a sort of an ass about these things. Is there any impropriety in my going about with Mrs. Dysart - under the circumstances?"

"Why - no!" said Duane. "Rosalie has to go about with people, I suppose. Only - perhaps it's fairer to her if you don't do it too often - I mean it's better for her that any one man should not appear to pay her noticeable attention. You know what mischief can get into print. What's taken below stairs is often swiped and stealthily perused above stairs."

"I suppose so. I don't read it myself, but it makes game of my mother and she finds a furious consolation in taking it to my father and planning a suit for damages once a week. You're right; most people are afraid of it. Do you think it's all right for me to motor back with Mrs. Dysart?"

"Are *you* afraid?" asked Duane, smiling.

"Only on her account," said Grandcourt, so simply that a warm feeling rose in Duane's heart for this big, ungainly, vividly coloured young fellow whose direct and honest gaze always refreshed people even when they laughed at him.

"Are you driving?" asked Duane.

"Yes. We came in at a hell of a clip. It made my hair stand, but Mrs. Dysart likes it.... I say, Mallett, what sort of an outcome do you suppose there'll be?"

"Between Rosalie and Jack Dysart?"

"Yes."

"I know no more than you, Grandcourt. Why?"

"Only that - it's too bad. I've known them so long; I'm friendly with both. Jack is a curious fellow. There's much of good in him, Mallett, although I believe you and he are not on terms. He is a - I don't mean this for criticism - but sometimes his manner is unfortunate, leading people to consider him overbearing.

"I understand why people think so; I get angry at him, sometimes, myself - being perhaps rather sensitive and very conscious that I am not anything remarkable.

"But, somehow" - he looked earnestly at Duane - "I set a very great value on old friendships. He and I were at school. I always admired in him the traits I myself have lacked.... There is something about an old friendship that seems very important to me. I couldn't very easily break one.... It is that way with me, Mallett.... Besides, when I think, perhaps, that Jack Dysart is a trifle overbearing and too free with his snubs, I go somewhere and cool off; and I think that in his heart he must like me as well as I do him because, sooner or later, we always manage to drift together again.... That is one reason why I am so particular about his wife."

Another reason happened to be that he had been in love with her himself when Dysart gracefully shouldered his way between them and married Rosalie Dene. Duane had heard something about it; and he wondered a little at the loyalty to such a friendship that this young man so naively confessed.

"I'll tell you what I think," said Duane; "I think you're the best sort of an anchor for Rosalie Dysart. Only a fool would mistake your friendship. But the town's full of 'em, Grandcourt," he added with a smile.

"I suppose so.... And I say, Mallett - may I ask you something more?... I don't like to pester you with questions -"

"Go on, my friend. I take it as a clean compliment from a clean-cut man."

Delancy coloured, checked, but presently found voice to continue:

"That's very good of you; I thought I might speak to you about this Greensleeve & Co.'s failure before Mrs. Dysart returns."

"Certainly," said Duane, surprised; "what about them? They acted for Dysart at one time, didn't they?"

"They do now."

"Are you sure?"

"Yes, I am. I didn't want to say so before Mrs. Dysart. But the afternoon papers have it. I don't know why they take such a malicious pleasure in harrying Dysart - unless on account of his connections with that Yo Espero crowd - what's their names? - Skelton! Oh, yes, James Skelton - and Emanuel Klawber with his thirty millions and his string of banks and trusts and mines; and that plunger, Max Moebus, and old Amos Flack - Flack the hack stalking-horse of every bull-market, who laid down on his own brokers and has done everybody's dirty work ever since. How on earth, Mallett, do you suppose Jack Dysart ever got himself mixed up with such a lot of skyrockets and disreputable fly-by-nights?"

Duane did not answer. He had nothing good to say or think of Dysart.

Rosalie reappeared at that moment in her distractingly pretty pongee motor-coat and hat.

"Do come back with us, Duane," she said. "There's a rumble

and we'll get the mud off you with a hose."

"I'd like to run down sometimes if you'll let me," he said, shaking hands.

So they parted, he to return to his studio, where models booked long ahead awaited him for canvases which he was going on with, although the great Trust Company that ordered them had practically thrown them back on his hands.

That evening at home when he came downstairs dressed in white serge for dinner, he found his father unusually silent, very pale, and so tired that he barely tasted the dishes the butler offered, and sat for the most part motionless, head and shoulders sagging against the back of his chair.

And after dinner in the conservatory Duane lighted his father's cigar and then his own.

"What's wrong?" he asked, pleasantly invading the privacy of years because he felt it was the time to do it.

His father slowly turned his head and looked at him - seemed to study the well-knit, loosely built, athletic figure of this strong young man - his only son - as though searching for some support in the youthful strength he gazed upon.

He said, very deliberately, but with a voice not perfectly steady:

"Matters are not going very well, my boy."

"What matters, father?"

"Down-town."

"Yes, I've heard. But, after all, you people in the Half Moon need only crawl into your shell and lie still."

"Yes."

After a silence:

"Father, have you any outside matters that trouble you?"

"There are - some."

"You are not involved seriously?"

His father made an effort: "I think not, Duane."

"Oh, all right. If you were, I was going to suggest that I've deposited what I have, subject to your order, with your own cashier."

"That is - very kind of you, my son. I may - find use for it - for a short time. Would you take my note?"

Duane laughed. He went on presently: "I wrote Naida the other day. She has given me power of attorney. What she has is there, any time you need it."

His father hung his head in silence; only his colourless and shrunken hands worked on the arms of his chair.

"See here, father," said the young fellow; "don't let this thing bother you. Anything that could possibly happen is better than to have you look and feel as you do. Suppose the very worst happens - which it won't - but suppose it did and we all went gaily to utter smash.

"That is a detail compared with your going to smash physically. Because Naida and I never did consider such things vital; and mother is a brick when it comes to a show-down. And as for me, why, if the very worst hits us, I can take care of our bunch. It's in me to do it. I suppose you don't think so. But I can make money enough to keep us together, and, after all, that's the main thing."

His father said nothing.

"Of course," laughed Duane, "I don't for a moment suppose that anything like that is on the cards. I don't know what your fortune is, but judging from your generosity to Naida and me I fancy it's too solid to worry over. The trouble with you gay old capitalists," he added, "is that you think in such enormous sums! And you forget that little sums are required to make us all very happy; and if some of the millions which you cannot possibly ever use happen to escape you, the tragic aspect as it strikes you is out of all proportion to the real state of the case."

His father felt the effort his son was making; looked up wearily, strove to smile, to relight his cigar; which Duane did for him, saying:

"As long as you are not mixed up in that Klawber, Skelton, Moebus crowd, I'm not inclined to worry. It seems, as of course you know, that Dysart's brokers failed to-day."

"So I heard," said his father steadily. He straightened himself in his chair. "I am sorry. Mr. Greensleeve is a very old friend -"

The library telephone rang; the second man entered and asked if Colonel Mallett could speak to Mr. Dysart over the wire on a matter concerning the Yo Espero district.

Duane, astonished, sprang up asking if he might not take the message; then shrank aside as his father got to his feet. He saw the ghastly pallor on his face as his father passed him, moving toward the library; stood motionless in troubled amazement, then walked to the open window of the conservatory and, leaning there, waited.

His father did not return. Later a servant came:

"Colonel Mallett has retired, Mr. Duane, and begs that he be undisturbed, as he is very tired."

CHAPTER XV

DYSART

The possibility that his father could be involved in any of the spectacular schemes which had evidently caught Dysart, seemed so remote that Duane's incredulity permitted him to sleep that night, though the name Yo Espero haunted his dreams.

But in the morning, something he read in the paper concerning a vast enterprise, involving the control of the new radium mines in Southern California, startled him into trying to recollect what he had heard of Yo Espero and the Cascade Development and Securities Company. Tainting its title the sinister name of Moebus seemed to reoccur persistently in his confused imagination. Dysart's name, too, figured in it. And, somehow, he conceived an idea that his father once received some mining engineer's reports covering the matter; he even seemed to remember that Guy Wilton had been called into consultation.

Whatever associations he had for the name of the Cascade Development and Securities Company must have originated in Paris the year before his father returned to America. It seemed to him that Wilton had been in Spain that year examining the recent and marvellously rich radium find; and that his father and Wilton exchanged telegrams very frequently concerning a mine in Southern California known as Yo Espero.

His father breakfasted in his room that morning, but when he appeared in the library Duane was relieved to notice that his step was firmer and he held himself more erect, although his extreme pallor had not changed to a healthier colour.

"You know," said Duane, "you've simply got to get out of town for a while. It's all bally rot, your doing this sort of thing."

"I may go West for a few weeks," said his father absently.

"Are you going down-town?"

"No.... And, Duane, if you don't mind letting me have the house to myself this morning -"

He hesitated, glancing from his son to the telephone.

"Of course not," said Duane heartily. "I'm off to the studio -"

"I don't mean to throw you out," murmured his father with a painful attempt to smile, "but there's a stenographer coming from my office and several - business acquaintances."

The young fellow rose, patted his father's shoulder lightly:

"What is really of any importance," he said, "is that you keep your health and spirits. What I said last night covers my sentiments. If I can do anything in the world for you, tell me."

His father took the outstretched hand, lifted his faded eyes with a strange dumb look; and so they parted.

On Fifth Avenue and Fifty-ninth Street, Duane, swinging along at a good pace, turned westward, and half-way to Sixth Avenue encountered Guy Wilton going east, a packet under one arm, stick and hat in the other hand, the summer wind blowing the thick curly hair from his temples.

"Ah," observed Wilton, "early bird and worm, I suppose? Don't try to bolt me, Duane; I'm full of tough and undigested - er - problems, myself. Besides, I'm fermenting. Did you ever silently ferment while listening politely to a man you wanted to assault?"

Duane laughed, then his eye by accident, caught a superscription on the packet of papers under Wilton's arm: Yo Espero! His glance reverted in a flash to Wilton's face.

The latter said: "I want to write a book entitled 'Gentleman I Have Kicked.' Of course I've only kicked 'em mentally; but my! what a list I have! - all sorts, all nations - from certain domestic and predatory statesmen to the cad who made his beautiful and sensitive mistress notorious in a decadent novel! - all kinds, Duane, have I kicked mentally I've just used my foot on another social favorite -"

"Dysart!" said Duane, inspired, and, turning painfully red, begged Wilton's pardon.

"You've sure got a disconcerting way with you," admitted Wilton, very much out of countenance.

"It was rotten bad taste in me -"

Wilton grinned with a wry face: "Nobody is standing much on ceremony these days. Besides, I'm on to your trail, young man" - tapping the bundle under his arm - "your eye happened to catch that superscription; no doubt your father has talked to you; and you came to - a rather embarrassing conclusion."

Duane's serious face fell:

"My father and I have not talked on that subject, Guy. Are you going up to see him now?"

Wilton hesitated: "I suppose I am.... See here, Duane, how

much do you know about - anything?"

"Nothing," he said without humour; "I'm beginning to worry over my father's health.... Guy, don't tell me anything that my father's son ought not to know; but is there something I should know and don't? - anything in which I could possibly be of help to my father?"

Wilton looked carefully at a distant policeman for nearly a minute, then his meditative glance became focussed on vacancy.

"I - don't - know," he said slowly. "I'm going to see your father now. If there is anything to tell, I think he ought to tell it to you. Don't you?"

"Yes. But he won't. Guy, I don't care a damn about anything except his health and happiness. If anything threatens either, he won't tell me, but don't you think I ought to know?"

"You ask too hard a question for me to answer."

"Then can you answer me this? Is father at all involved in any of Jack Dysart's schemes?"

"I - had better not answer, Duane."

"You know best. You understand that it is nothing except anxiety for his personal condition that I thought warranted my butting into his affairs and yours."

"Yes, I understand. Let me think over things for a day or two. Now I've got to hustle. Good-bye."

He hastened on eastward; Duane went west, slowly, more slowly, halted, head bent in troubled concentration; then he wheeled in his tracks with nervous decision, walked back to the Plaza Club, sent for a cab, and presently rattled off up-town.

In a few minutes the cab swung east and came to a standstill a few doors from Fifth Avenue; and Duane sprang out and touched the button at a bronze grille.

The servant who admitted him addressed him by name with smiling deference and ushered him into a two-room reception suite beyond the tiny elevator.

There was evidently somebody in the second room; Duane had also noticed a motor waiting outside as he descended from his cab; so he took a seat and sat twirling his walking-stick between his knees, gloomily inspecting a room which, in pleasanter days, had not been unfamiliar to him.

Instead of the servant returning, there came a click from the elevator, a quick step, and the master of the house himself walked swiftly into the room wearing hat and gloves.

"What do you want?" he inquired briefly.

"I want to ask you a question or two," said Duane, shocked at the change in Dysart's face. Haggard, thin, snow-white at the temples with the light in his eyes almost extinct, the very precision and freshness of linen and clothing brutally accentuated the ravaged features.

"What questions?" demanded Dysart, still standing, and without any emotion whatever in either voice or manner.

"The first is this: are you in communication with my father concerning mining stock known as Yo Espero?"

"I am."

"Is my father involved in any business transactions in which you figure, or have figured?"

"There are some. Yes."

"Is the Cascade Development and Securities Co. one of them?"

"Yes, it is."

Duane's lips were dry with fear; he swallowed, controlled the rising anger that began to twitch at his throat, and went on in a low, quiet voice:

"Is this man - Moebus - connected with any of these transactions in which you and - and my father are interested?"

"Yes."

"Is Klawber?"

"Max Moebus, Emanuel Klawber, James Skelton, and Amos Flack are interested. Is that what you want to know?"

Duane looked at him, stunned. Dysart stepped nearer, speaking almost in a whisper:

"Well, what about it? Once I warned you to keep your damned nose out of my personal affairs -"

"I make some of them mine!" said Duane sharply; "when crooks get hold of an honest man, every citizen is a policeman!"

Dysart, face convulsed with fury, seized his arm in a vicelike grip:

"Will you keep your cursed mouth shut!" he breathed. "My father is in the next room. Do you want to kill him?"

At the same moment there came a stir from the room beyond, the tap-tap of a cane and shuffling steps across the polished parquet. Dysart's grip relaxed, his hand fell away, and he made a ghastly grimace as a little old gentleman came half-trotting, half-shambling to the doorway. He was small and dapper and pink-skinned under his wig; the pink was paint; his lips and eyes peered and simpered; from one bird-claw hand dangled a monocle.

Jack Dysart made a ghastly and supreme effort:

"I was just saying to Duane, father, that all this financial agitation is bound to blow over by December - Duane Mallett, father!" - as the old man raised his eye-glass and peeped up at the young fellow - "you know his father, Colonel Mallett."

"Yes, to be sure, yes, to be sure!" piped the old beau. "How-de-do! How-de-do-o-o! My son Jack and I motor every morning at this hour. It is becoming a custom - he! he! - every day from ten to eleven - then a biscuit and a glass of sherry - then a nap - te-he! Oh, yes, every day, Mr. Mallett, rain or fair - then luncheon at one, and the cigarette - te-he! - and a little sleep - and the drive at five! Yes, Mr. Mallett, it is the routine of a very old man who knew your grandfather - and all his set - when the town was gay below Bleecker Street! Yes, yes - te-he-he!"

Nervous spasms which passed as smiles distorted the younger Dysart's visage; the aged beau offered his hand to Duane, who took it in silence, his eyes fixed on the shrivelled, painted face:

"Your grandfather was a very fine man," he piped; "very fine! ve-ery fine! And so I perceive is his grandson - te-he! - and I flatter myself that my boy Jack is not unadmired - te-he-he! - no, no - not precisely unnoticed in New York - the town whose history is the history of his own race, Mr. Mallett - he is a good son to me - yes, yes, a good son. It is gratifying to me to know that you are his friend. He is a good friend to have, Mr. Mallett, a good friend and a good son."

Duane bent gently over the shrivelled hand.

"I won't detain you from your drive, Mr. Dysart. I hope you will have a pleasant one. It is a pleasure to know my grandfather's old friends. Good-bye."

And, erect, he hesitated a moment, then, for an old man's sake he held out his hand to Jack Dysart, bidding him good-bye in a pleasant voice pitched clear and decided, so that deaf ears might corroborate what half-blind and peering eyes so dimly beheld.

Dysart walked to the door with him, waved the servant aside, and, laying a shaking hand on the bronze knob, opened the door for his unbidden guest.

As Duane passed him he said:

"Thank you, Mallett," in a voice so low that Duane was half-way to his cab before he understood.

* * * * *

That day, and the next, and all that week he worked in his pitlike studio. Through the high sky-window a cloudless zenith brooded; the heat became terrific; except for the inevitable crush of the morning and evening migration south and north, the streets were almost empty under a blazing sun.

His father seemed to be physically better. Although he offered no confidences, it appeared to the son that there was something a little more cheerful in his voice and manner. It may have been only the anticipation of departure; for he was going West in a day or two, and it came out that Wilton was going with him.

The day he left, Duane drove him to the station. There was a private car, the "Cyane," attached to the long train. Wilton met them, spoke pleasantly to Duane; but Colonel Mallett did not invite his son to enter the car, and adieux were said where they stood.

As the young fellow turned and passed beneath the car-windows, he caught a glimpse above him of a heavy-jowled, red face into which a cigar was stuck - a perfectly enormous expanse of face with two little piglike eyes almost buried in the mottled fat.

“That's Max Moebus,” observed a train hand respectfully, as Duane passed close to him; “I guess there's more billions into that there private car than old Pip's crowd can dig out of their pants pockets on pay day.”

A little, dry-faced, chin-whiskered man with a loose pot-belly and thin legs came waddling along, followed by two red-capped negroes with his luggage. He climbed up the steps of the “Cyane”; the train man winked at Duane, who had turned to watch him.

“Amos Flack,” he said. “He's their 'lobbygow.'“ With which contemptuous information he spat upon the air-brakes and, shoving both hands into his pockets, meditatively jingled a bunch of keys.

* * * * *

The club was absolutely deserted that night; Duane dined there alone, then wandered into the great empty room facing Fifth Avenue, his steps echoing sharply across the carpetless floor. The big windows were open; there was thunder in the air - the sonorous stillness in which voices and footsteps in the street ring out ominously.

He smoked and watched the dim forms of those whom the heat drove forth into the night, men with coats over their arms and straw hats in their hands, young girls thinly clad in white, bare-headed, moving two and two with dragging steps and scarcely spirit left even for common coquetry or any response to the jesting oafs who passed.

Here and there a cruising street-dryad threaded the by-paths of the metropolitan jungle; here and there a policeman, gray helmet in hand, stood mopping his face, night-club tucked up snugly under one arm. Few cabs were moving; at intervals a creaking, groaning omnibus rolled past, its hurricane deck white with the fluttering gowns of women and young girls.

Somebody came into the room behind him; Duane turned, but could not distinguish who it was in the dusk. A little while later the man came over to where he sat, and he looked up; and it was Dysart.

There was silence for a full minute; Dysart stood by the window looking out; Duane paid him no further attention until he wheeled slowly and said:

"Do you mind if I have a word with you, Mallett?"

"Not if it is necessary."

"I don't know whether it is necessary."

"Don't bother about it if you are in the slightest doubt."

Dysart waited a moment, perhaps for some unpleasant emotion to subside; then:

"I'll sit down a moment, if you permit."

He dropped into one of the big, deep, leather chairs and touched the bell. A servant came; he looked across at Duane, hesitated to speak:

"Thank you," said Duane curtly. "I've cut it out."

"Scotch. Bring the decanter," murmured Dysart to the servant.

When it was served he drained the glass, refilled it, and turned in the rest of the mineral water. Before he spoke he emptied the glass again and rang for more mineral water. Then he looked at Duane and said in a low voice:

"I thought you were worried the other day when I saw you at

my house."

"What is that to you?"

Dysart said: "You were very kind - under provocation."

"I was not kind on your account."

"I understand. But I don't forget such things."

Duane glanced at him in profound contempt. Here was the stereotyped scoundrel with the classical saving trait - the one conventionally inevitable impulse for good shining like a diamond on a muck-heap - his apparently disinterested affection for his father.

"You were very decent to me that day," Dysart said. "You had something to say to me - but were good enough not to. I came over to-night to give you a chance to curse me out. It's the square thing to do."

"What do you know about square dealing?"

"Go on."

"I have nothing to add."

"Then I have if you'll let me." He paused; the other remained silent. "I've this to say: you are worried sick; I saw that. What worries you concerns your father. You were merciful to mine. I'll do what I can for you."

He swallowed half of what remained in his iced glass, set it back on the table with fastidious precision:

"The worst that can happen to your father is to lose control of the Yo Espero property. I think he is going to lose it. They've crowded me out. If I could have endured the strain I'd have stood by your father - for what you did for mine.... But I couldn't, Mallett."

He moistened his lips again; leaned forward:

"I think I know one thing about you, anyway; and I'm not afraid you'd ever use any words of mine against me -"

"Don't say them!" retorted Duane sharply.

But Dysart went on:

"You have no respect for me. You found out one thing about me that settled me in your opinion. Outside of that, however, you never liked me."

"That is perfectly true."

"I know it. And I want to say now that it was smouldering irritation from that source - wounded vanity, perhaps - coupled with worry and increasing cares, that led to that outburst of mine. I never really believed that my wife needed any protection from the sort of man you are. You are not that kind."

"That also is true."

"And I know it. And now I've cleared up these matters; and there's another." He bit his lip, thought a moment, then with a deep, long breath:

"When you struck me that night I - deserved it. I was half crazy, I think - with what I had done - with a more material but quite as ruinous situation developing here in town - with domestic complications - never mind where all the fault lay - it was demoralising me. Do you think that I am not perfectly aware that I stand very much alone among men? Do you suppose that I am not aware of my personal unpopularity as far as men are concerned? I have never had an intimate friend - except Delancy Grandcourt. And I've treated him like a beast.

There's something wrong about me; there always has been."

He slaked his thirst again; his hand shook so that he nearly dropped the glass:

"Which is preliminary," he went on, "to saying to you that no matter what I said in access of rage, I never doubted that your encounter with - Miss Quest - was an accident. I never doubted that your motive in coming to me was generous. God knows why I said what I did say. You struck me; and you were justified.... And that clears up that!"

"Dysart," said the other, "you don't have to tell me these things."

"Would you rather not have heard them?"

Duane thought a moment.

"I would rather have heard them, I believe."

"Then may I go on?"

"Is there anything more to explain between us?"

"No.... But I would like to say something - in my own behalf. Not that it matters to you - or to any man, perhaps, except my father. I would like to say it, Mallett."

"Very well."

"Then; I prefer that you should believe I am not a crook. Not that it matters to you; but I prefer that you do not believe it.... You have read enough in the papers to know what I mean. I'm telling you now what I have never uttered to any man; and I haven't the slightest fear you will repeat it or use it in any manner to my undoing. It is this:

"The men with whom I was unwise enough to become

partially identified are marked for destruction by the Clearing House Committee and by the Federal Government. I know it; others know it. Which means the ruthless elimination of anything doubtful which in future might possibly compromise the financial stability of this city.

“It is a brutal programme; the policy they are pursuing is bitterly unjust. Innocent and guilty alike are going to suffer; I never in all my life consciously did a crooked thing in business; and yet I say to you now that these people are bent on my destruction; that they mean to force us to close the doors of the Algonquin; that they are planning the ruin of every corporation, every company, every bank, every enterprise with which I am connected, merely because they have decreed the financial death of Moebus and Klawber!”

He made a trembling gesture with clenched hand, and leaned farther forward:

“Mallett! There is not one man to-day in Wall Street who has not done, and who is not doing daily, the very things for which the government officials and the Clearing House authorities are attempting to get rid of me. Their attacks on my securities will ultimately ruin me; but such attacks would ruin any financier, any bank in the United States, if continued long enough.

“Doesn't anybody know that when the government conspires with the Clearing House officials any security can be kicked out of the market? Don't they know that when bank examiners class any securities as undesirable, and bank officials throw them out from the loans of such institutions, that they're not worth the match struck to burn them into nothing?

“If they mean to close my companies and bring charges against me, I'll tell you now, Mallett, any official of any bank which to-day is in operation, can be indicted!”

He sat breathing fast, hands clasped nervously between his

knees. Duane, painfully impressed, waited. And after a moment Dysart spoke again:

"They mean my ruin. There is a bank examiner at work - this very moment while we're sitting here - on the Collect Pond Bank - which is mine. The Federal inquisitors went through it once; now a new one is back again. They found nothing with which to file an adverse report the first time. Why did they come back?

"And I'll tell you another thing, Mallett, which may seem a slight reason for my sullenness and quick temper; they've had secret-service men following me ever since I returned from Roya-Neh. They are into everything that I've ever been connected with; there is no institution, no security in which I am interested, that they have not investigated.

"And I tell you also, incredible as it may sound, that there is no security in which I am interested which is not now being attacked by government officials, and which, as a result of such attacks, is not depreciating daily. I tell you they've even approached the United States Court for its consent to a ruinous disposal of certain corporation notes in which I am interested! Will you tell me what you think of that, Mallett?"

Duane said: "I don't know, Dysart. I know almost nothing about such matters. And - I am sorry that you are in trouble."

The silence remained unbroken for some time; then Dysart stood up:

"I don't offer you my hand. You took it once for my father's sake. That was manly of you, Mallett.... I thought perhaps I might lighten your anxiety about your father. I hope I have.... And I must ask your pardon for pressing my private affairs upon you" - he laughed mirthlessly - "merely because I'd rather you didn't think me a crook - for my father's sake.... Good-night."

"Dysart," he said, "why in God's name have you behaved as you have to - that girl?"

Dysart stood perfectly motionless, then in a voice under fair control:

"I understand you. You don't intend that as impertinence; you're a square man, Mallett - a man who suffers under the evil in others. And your question to me meant that you thought me not entirely hopeless; that there was enough of decency in me to arouse your interest. Isn't that what you meant?"

"Yes, I think so."

"Well, then, I'll answer you. There isn't much left of me; there'll be less left of my fortune before long. I've made a failure of everything, fortune, friendship, position, happiness. My wife and I are separated; it is club gossip, I believe. She will probably sue for divorce and get it. And I ask you, because I don't know, can any amends be made to - the person you mentioned - by my offering her the sort and condition of man I now am?"

"You've got to, haven't you?" asked Duane.

"Oh! Is that it? A sort of moral formality?"

"It's conventional; yes. It's expected."

"By whom?"

"All the mess that goes to make up this compost heap we call society.... I think she also would expect it."

Dysart nodded.

"If you could make her happy it would square a great many things, Dysart."

The other looked up: "You?"

"I - don't know. Yes, in many ways; in that way at all events - if you made her happy."

Dysart stepped forward: "Would you be nice to her if I did? No other soul in the world knows except you. Other people would be nice to her. Would *you*? And would you have the woman you marry receive her?"

"Yes."

"That is square of you, Mallett.... I meant to do it, anyway.... Thank you.... Good-night."

"Good-night," said Duane in a low voice.

He returned to the house late that night, and found a letter from Geraldine awaiting him; the first in three days. Seated at the library table he opened the letter and saw at once that the red-pencilled cross at the top was missing.

Minutes passed; the first line blurred under his vacant gaze, for his eyes travelled no farther. Then the letter fell to the table; he dropped his head in his arms.

It was a curiously calm letter when he found courage to read it:

> "I've lost a battle after many victories. It went against me after a hard fight here alone at Roya-Neh. I think you had better come up. The fight was on again the next night - that is, night before last, but I've held fast so far and expect to. Only I wish you'd come.
>
> "It is no reproach to you if I say that, had you been here, I might have made a better fight. You couldn't be here; the shame of defeat is all my own.
>
> "Duane, it was not a disastrous defeat in one way. I held

out for four days, and thought I had won out. I was stupefied by loss of sleep, I think; this is not in excuse, only the facts which I lay bare for your consideration.

"The defeat was in a way a concession - a half-dazed compromise - merely a parody on a real victory for the enemy; because it roused in me a horror that left the enemy almost no consolation, no comfort, even no physical relief. The enemy is I myself, you understand - that other self we know about.

"She was perfectly furious, Duane; she wrestled with me, fought to make me yield more than I had - which was almost nothing - begged me, brutalised me, pleaded, tormented, cajoled. I was nearly dead when the sun rose; but I had gone through it.

"I wish you could come. She is still watching me. It's an armed truce, but I know she'll break it if the chance comes. There is no honour in her, Duane, no faith, no reason, no mercy. I know her.

"Can you not come? I won't ask it if your father needs you. Only if he does not, I think you had better come very soon.

"When may I restore the red cross to the top of my letters to you? I suppose I had better place it on the next letter, because if I do not you might think that another battle had gone against me.

"Don't reproach me. I couldn't stand it just now. Because I am a very tired girl, Duane, and what has happened is heavy in my heart - heavy on my head and shoulders like that monster Sindbad bore.

"Can you come and free me? One word - your arms around me - and I am safe.

"G.S."

As he finished, a maid came bearing a telegram on a salver.

"Tell him to wait," said Duane, tearing open the white night-message:

> "Your father is ill at San Antonio and wishes you to come at once. Notify your mother but do not alarm her. Your father's condition is favorable, but the outcome is uncertain.
>
> "WELLS, *Secretary*."

Duane took three telegram blanks from the note-paper rack and wrote:

> "My father is ill at San Antonio. They have just wired me, and I shall take the first train. Stand by me now. Win out for my sake. I put you on your honour until I can reach you."

And to his father:

> "I leave on first train for San Antonio. It's going to be all right, father."

And to his mother:

> "Am leaving for San Antonio because I don't think father is well enough to I'll write you and wire you. Love to you and Naida."

He gave the maid the money, turned, and unhooking the receiver of the telephone, called up the Grand Central Station.

CHAPTER XVI

THROUGH THE WOODS

The autumn quiet at Roya-Neh was intensely agreeable to Scott Seagrave. No social demands interfered with a calm and dignified contemplation of the Rose-beetle, *Melolontha subspinosa*, and his scandalous "Life History"; there was no chatter of girls from hall and stairway to distract the loftier inspirations that possessed him, no intermittent soprano noises emitted by fluttering feminine fashion, no calflike barytones from masculine adolescence to drive him to the woods, where it was always rather difficult for him to focus his attention on printed pages. The balm of heavenly silence pervaded the house, and in its beneficent atmosphere he worked in his undershirt, inhaling inspiration and the aroma of whale-oil, soap, and carbolic solutions.

Neither Kathleen nor his sister being present to limit his operations, the entire house was becoming a vast mess. Living-rooms, library, halls, billiard-room, were obstructed with "scientific" paraphernalia; hundreds of glass fruit jars, filled with earth containing the whitish, globular eggs of the Rose-beetle, encumbered mantel and furniture; glass aquariums half full of earth, sod, and youthful larvae of the same sinful beetle lent pleasing variety to the monotony of Scott's interior decorative effects. Microscopes, phials, shallow trays bristling with sprouting seeds, watering-cans, note-books, buckets of tepid water, jars brimming with chemical solutions, blockaded the legitimate and natural runways of chamber-maid, parlour-maid, and housekeeper; a loud scream now and then punctured the scientific silence, recording the Hibernian discovery of some large, green caterpillar travelling casually somewhere in the house.

"Mr. Seagrave, sir," stammered Lang, the second man, perspiring horror, "your bedroom is full of humming birds and bats, sir, and I can't stand it no more!"

But it was only a wholesale hatching of huge hawk-moths that came whizzing around Lang when he turned on the electric lights; and which, escaping, swarmed throughout the house, filling it with their loud, feathery humming, and the shrieks of Milesian domestics.

And it was into these lively household conditions that Kathleen and Geraldine unexpectedly arrived from the Berkshires, worn out with their round of fashionable visits, anxious for the quiet and comfort that is supposed to be found only under one's own roof-tree. This is what they found:

In Geraldine's bath-tub a colony of water-lilies were attempting to take root for the benefit of several species of water-beetles. The formidable larvae of dragon-flies occupied Kathleen's bath; turtles peered at them from vantage points under the modern plumbing; an enormous frog regarded Kathleen solemnly from the wet, tiled floor. "Oh, dear," she said as Scott greeted her rapturously, "have I got to move all these horrid creatures?"

"For Heaven's sake don't touch a thing," protested Scott, welcoming his sister with a perfunctory kiss; "I'll find places for them in a minute."

"How *could* you, Scott!" exclaimed Geraldine, backing hastily away from a branch of green leaves on which several gigantic horned caterpillars were feeding. "I don't feel like ever sleeping in this room again," she added, exasperated.

"Why, Sis," he explained mildly, "those are the caterpillars of the magnificent Regal moth! They're perfectly harmless, and it's jolly to watch them tuck away walnut leaves. You'll like to have them here in your room when you understand how to weigh them on these bully little scales I've just had sent up from Tiffany's."

But his sister was too annoyed and too tired to speak. She stood limply leaning against Kathleen while her brother disposed of his uncanny menagerie, talking away very cheerfully all the while absorbed in his grewsome pets.

But it was not to his sister, it was to Kathleen that his pride in his achievements was naively displayed; his running accompaniment of chatter was for Kathleen's benefit, his appeals were to her sympathy and understanding, not to his sister's.

Geraldine watched him in silence. Tired, not physically very well, this home-coming meant something to her. She had looked forward to it, and to her brother, unconsciously wistful for the protection of home and kin. For the day had been a hard one; she was able to affix the red-cross mark to her letter to Duane that morning, but it had been a bad day for her, very bad.

And now as she stood there, white, nerveless, fatigued, an ache grew in her breast, a dull desire for somebody of her own kin to lean on; and, following it, a slow realisation of how far apart from her brother she had drifted since the old days of cordial understanding in the schoolroom - the days of loyal sympathy through calm and stress, in predatory alliance or in the frank conflicts of the squared circle.

Suddenly her whole heart filled with a blind need of her brother's sympathy - a desire to return to the old intimacy as though in it there lay comfort, protection, sanctuary for herself from all that threatened her - herself!

Kathleen was assisting Scott to envelop the frog in a bath towel for the benevolent purpose of transplanting him presently to some other bath-tub; and Kathleen's golden head and Scott's brown one were very close together, and they were laughing in that intimate undertone characteristic of thorough understanding. Her brother's expression as he looked up at Kathleen Severn, was a revelation to his sister, and it pierced her with a pang of loneliness so keen that she started forward in sheer desperation, as though to force a path through something that was pushing her away from him.

"Let me take his frogship," she said with a nervous laugh. "I'll put him into a jolly big tub where you can grow all the water-weeds you like, Scott."

Her brother, surprised and gratified, handed her the bath-towel in the depths of which reposed the batrachian.

"He's really an interesting fellow, Sis," explained Scott; "he exudes a sticky, viscous fluid from his pores which is slightly toxic. I'm going to try it on a Rose-beetle."

Geraldine shuddered, but forced a smile, and, holding the imprisoned one with dainty caution, bore him to a palatial and porcelain-lined bath-tub, into which she shook him with determination and a suppressed shriek.

That night at dinner Scott looked up at his sister with something of the old-time interest and confidence.

"I was pretty sure you'd take an interest in all these things, sooner or later. I tell you, Geraldine, it will be half the fun if you'll go into it with us."

"I want to," said his sister, smiling, "but don't hurry my progress or you'll scare me half to death."

The tragic necessity for occupation, for interesting herself in something sufficient to take her out of herself, she now understood, and the deep longing for the love of all she had of kith and kin was steadily tightening its grip on her, increasing day by day. Nothing else could take its place; she began to understand that; not her intimacy with Kathleen, not even her love for Duane. Outside of these there existed a zone of loneliness in which she was doomed to wander, a zone peopled only by the phantoms of the parents she had never known long enough to remember - a dreaded zone of solitude and desolation and peril for her. The danger line marked its boundary; beyond lay folly and destruction.

Little by little Scott began to notice that his sister evidently found his company desirable, that she followed him about, watching his so-called scientific pursuits with a curiosity too constant to be assumed. And it pleased him immensely; and at times he held forth to her and instructed her with brotherly condescension.

He noticed, too, that her spirits did not appear to be particularly lively; there were often long intervals of silence when, together by the window in the library where he was fussing over his "Life History," she never spoke, never even moved from her characteristic attitude - seated deep in a leather chair, arms resting on the padded chair-arms, ankles crossed, and her head a trifle lowered, as though absorbed in studying the Herati design on a Persian rug.

Once, looking up suddenly, he surprised her brown eyes full of tears.

"Hello!" he said, amazed; "what's the row, Sis?"

But she only laughed and dried her eyes, denying that there was any explanation except that girls were sometimes that way for no reason at all.

One day he asked Kathleen privately about this, but she merely confirmed Geraldine's diagnosis of the phenomenon:

"Tears come into girls' eyes," she said, "and there isn't anybody on earth who can tell a man why, and he wouldn't comprehend it if anybody did tell him."

"I'll tell you one thing," he said sceptically; "if Rose-beetles shed tears, I'd never rest until I found out why. You bet there's always a reason that starts anything and always somebody to find it out and tell another fellow who can understand it!"

With which brilliant burst of higher philosophy they went out into the October woods together to hunt for cocoons.

Geraldine, rather flushed and nervous, met them at Hurryon Gate, carrying a rifle and wearing the shortest skirts her brother had ever beheld. The symmetry of her legs moved him to reproof:

"I thought people looked that way only in tailor's fashion plates," he said. "What are you after - chipmunks?"

"Not at all," said his sister. "Do you know what happened to me an hour ago? I was paddling your canoe into the Hurryon Inlet, and I suppose I made no noise in disembarking, and I came right on a baby wild boar in the junipers. It was a tiny thing, not eighteen inches long, Kathleen, and so cunning and furry and yellowish, with brown stripes on its back, that I tried to catch it - just to hug it."

"That was silly," said her brother.

"I know it was, now. Because I ran after it, and it ran; and, one by one, a whole herd of the cunning little things sprang out of the hemlock scrub and went off bucking and bucketing in all directions, and I, like a simpleton, hard after one of them -"

"Little idiot," said her brother solicitously. "Are you stark mad?"

"No, I'm just plain mad. Because, before I knew it, there came a crash in the underbrush and the biggest, furriest, and wickedest wild boar I ever saw halted in front of me, ears forward, every hair on end -"

"Lord save us, you jumped the sow!" groaned her brother. "She might have torn you to pieces, you ninny!"

"She meant to, I think. The next thing I knew she came headlong, mouth open, fairly screaming at me; and I turned and jumped clean into the Gray Water. Oh, Scott, it was humiliating to have to swim to the point with all my clothes on, scramble into the canoe, and shove off because a very angry wild creature drove me out of my own woods!"

"Well, dear, you won't ever interfere with a sow and pigs again, will you?" said Kathleen so earnestly that everybody laughed.

"What's the rifle for?" inquired Scott. "You don't intend to hunt for her, do you?"

"Of course not. I'm not vindictive or cruel. But old Miller said, when I came past the lodge, dripping wet, that the boar are increasing too fast and that you ought to keep them down either by shooting or by trapping them, and sending them to other people for stocking purposes. The Pink 'uns want some; why don't you?"

"I don't want to shoot or trap them," said Scott obstinately.

"Miller says they pulled down deer last winter and tore them to shreds. Everything in the forest is afraid of them; they drive the deer from the feeding-grounds, and I don't believe a lynx or even any of the bear that climb over the fence would dare attack them."

Kathleen said: "You really ought to ask some men up here to shoot, Scott. I don't wish to be chased about by a boar."

"They never bother people," he protested. "What are you going to do with that rifle, Geraldine?"

"My nerve has gone," she confessed, laughing; "I prefer to have it with me when I take walks. It's really safer," she added seriously to Kathleen. "Miller says that a buck deer can be ugly, too."

"Oh, Lord!" said her brother, laughing; "it's only because you're the prettiest thing ever, in that hunting dress! Don't tell me; and kindly be careful where you point that rifle."

"As if I needed instructions!" retorted his sister. "I wish I could see a boar - a big one with a particularly frightful temper and tusks to match."

"I'll bet you that you can't kill a boar," he said in good-humoured disdain.

"I don't see any to kill."

"Well, I bet you can't find one. And if you do, I bet you don't kill him."

"How long," asked Geraldine dangerously, "does that bet hold good?"

"All winter, if you like. It's the prettiest single jewel you can pick out against a new saddle-horse. I need a gay one; I'm getting out of condition. And all our horses are as interesting as chevaux de bois when the mechanism is freshly oiled and the organ plays the 'Ride of the Valkyries.'"

"I've half a mind to take that wager," said Geraldine, very pink and bright-eyed. "I think I will take it if -"

"Please don't, dear," said Kathleen anxiously. "The keepers say that a wounded boar is perfectly horrid sometimes."

"Dangerous?" Her eyes glimmered brighter still.

"Certainly, a wounded boar is dangerous. I heard Miller say -"

"Bosh!" said Scott. "They run away from you every time. Besides, Geraldine isn't going to have enough sporting blood in her to take that bet and make good."

Something in the quick flush and tilt of her head reminded Scott of the old days when their differences were settled with eight-ounce gloves. The same feeling possessed his sister, thrilled her like a sudden, unexpected glimpse of a happiness which apparently had long been ended for ever.

"Oh, Scott," she exclaimed, still thrilling, "it *is* like old times to hear you try to bully me. It's so long since I've had enough spirit to defy you. But I do now! - oh, yes, I do! Why, I believe that if we had the gloves here, I'd make you fight me or take back what you said about my not having any sporting spirit!"

He laughed: "I was thinking of that, too. You're a good sport, Sis. Don't bother to take that wager -"

"I *do* take it!" she cried; "it's like old times and I love it. Now, Scott, I'll show you a boar before we go to town or I'll buy you a horse. No backing out; what's said can't be unsaid, remember:

"King, king, double king,
Can't take back a given thing!
Queen, queen, queen of queens,
What she promises she means!"

That was a very solemn incantation in nursery days; she laughed a little in tender tribute to the past.

Scott was a trifle perturbed. He glanced uneasily at Kathleen, who told him very plainly that he had contrived to make her anxious and unhappy. Then she fell back into step with

Geraldine, letting Scott wander disconsolately forward:

"Dear," she said, passing one arm around the younger girl, "I didn't quite dare to object too strongly. You looked so - so interested, so deliciously defiant - so like your real self -"

"I feel like it to-day, Kathleen; let me turn back in my own footsteps - if I can. I've been trying so very hard to - to get back to where there was no - no terror in the world."

"I know. But, darling, you won't run into any danger, will you?"

"Do you call a hard-hit beast a danger? I've wounded a more terrible one than any boar that ever bristled. I'm trying to kill something more terrifying. And I shall if I live."

"You poor, brave little martyr!" whispered Kathleen, her violet eyes filled with sudden tears; "don't you suppose I know what you are doing? Don't you suppose I watch and pray -"

"Did *you* know I was really trying?" asked the girl, astonished - "I mean before I told you?"

"Know it! Angels above! Of course I know it. Don't you suppose I've been watching you slowly winning back to your old dear self - tired, weary-footed, desolate, almost hopeless, yet always surely finding your way back through the dreadful twilight to the dear, sweet, generous self that I know so well - the straightforward, innocent, brave little self that grew at my knee! - Geraldine - Geraldine, my own dear child!"

"Hush - I did not know you knew. I am trying. Once I failed. That was not very long ago, either. Oh, Kathleen, I am trying so hard, so hard! And to-day has been a dreadful day for me. That is why I went off by myself; I paddled until I was ready to drop into the lake; and the fright that the boar gave me almost ended me; but it could not end desire!... So I took a rifle - anything to interest me - keep me on my feet and moving somewhere - doing something - anything - anything, Kathleen - until I can crush it out of me - until there's a chance that I can sleep -"

"I know - I know! That is why I dared not remonstrate when I saw you drifting again toward your old affectionate relations with Scott. I'm afraid of animals - except what few Scott has persuaded me to tolerate - butterflies and frogs and things. But if anything on earth is going to interest you - take your mind off yourself - and bring you and Scott any nearer together, I shall not utter one word against it - even when it puts you in physical danger and frightens me. Do you understand?"

The girl nodded, turned and kissed her. They were following a path made by game; Scott was out of sight ahead somewhere; they could hear his boots crashing through the underbrush. After a while the sound died away in the forest.

"The main thing," said Geraldine, "is to keep up my interest in the world. I want to do things. To sit idle is pure destruction to me. I write to Duane every morning, I read, I do a dozen things that require my attention - little duties that everybody has. But I can't continue to write to Duane all day. I can't read all day; duties are soon ended. And, Kathleen, it's the idle intervals I dread so - the brooding, the memories, the waiting for events scheduled in domestic routine - like dinner - the - the terrible waiting for sleep! That is the worst. I tell you, physical fatigue must help to save me - must help my love for Duane, my love for you and Scott, my self-respect - what is left of it. This rifle" - she held it out - "would turn into a nuisance if I let it. But I won't; I can't; I've got to use everything to help me."

"You ride every day, don't you?" ventured the other woman timidly.

"Before breakfast. That helps. I wish I had a vicious horse to break. I wish there was rough water where canoes ought not to go!" she exclaimed fiercely. "I need something of that sort."

"You drove Scott's Blue Racer yesterday so fast that Felix came to me about it," said Kathleen gently.

Geraldine laughed. "It couldn't go fast enough, dear; that was the only trouble." Then, serious and wistful: "If I could only have Duane.... Don't be alarmed; I can't - yet. But if I only could have him now! You see, his life is already very full; his work is absorbing him. It would absorb me. I don't know anything about it technically, but it interests me. If I could only have him now; think about him every second of the day - to keep me from myself -"

She checked herself; suddenly her eyes filled, her lip quivered:

"I want him now!" she said desperately. "He could save me; I know it! I want him now - his love, his arms to keep me safe at night! I want him to love me - *love* me! Oh, Kathleen! if I could only have him!"

A delicate colour tinted Kathleen's face; her ears shrank from the girl's low-voiced cry, with its glimmer of a passion scarcely understood.

Long, long, the memory of his embrace had tormented her - the feeling of happy safety she had in his arms - the contact that thrilled almost past endurance, yet filled her with a glorious and splendid strength - that set wild pulses beating, wild blood leaping in her veins - that aroused her very soul to meet his lips and heed his words and be what his behest would have her.

And the memory of it now possessed her so that she stood straight and slim and tall, trembling in the forest path, and her dark eyes looked into Kathleen's with a strange, fiery glimmer of pride:

"I need him, but I love him too well to take him. Can I do more for him than that?"

"Oh, my darling, my darling," said Kathleen brokenly, "if you believe that he can save you - if you really feel that he can -"

"I am trying to save myself - I am trying." She turned and looked off through the forest, a straight, slender shape in the moving shadows of the leaves.

"But if he could really help you - if you truly believe it, dear, I - I don't know whether you might not venture - now -"

"No, dear." She slowly closed her eyes, remained motionless for a moment, drew a deep, long breath, and looked up through the sunlit branches overhead.

"I've got to be fair to him," she said aloud to herself; "I must give myself to him as I ought to be, or not at all.... That is settled."

She turned to Kathleen and took her hand:

"Come on, fellow-pilgrim," she said with an effort to smile. "My cowardice is over for the present."

A few steps forward they sighted Scott coming back. He was unusually red in the face and rather excited, and he flourished a stick.

"Of all the infernal impudence!" he said. "What do you think has happened to me? I saw a wild boar back there - not a very big one - and he came out into the trail ahead, and I kept straight on, thinking he'd hear me and run. And I'm blessed if the brute didn't whirl around and roughen up, and clatter his tusks until I actually had to come to a halt!"

"I don't want to walk in these woods any more," said Kathleen with sudden conviction. "Please come home, all of us."

"Nonsense," he said. "I won't stand for being hustled out of my own woods. Give me that rifle, Geraldine."

"I certainly will not," she said, smiling.

"What! Why not?"

"Because it rather looks as though I'm about to win my bet with you," observed Geraldine. "Please show me your boar, Scott." And she threw a cartridge into the magazine and started forward.

"Don't let her!" pleaded Kathleen. "Scott, it's ridiculous to let that child do such silly things -"

"Then stop her if you can," said Scott gloomily, following his sister. "I don't know anything about wild boar, but I suppose straight shooting will take care of them, and Sis can do that if she keeps her nerve."

Geraldine, hastening ahead, rifle poised, scanned the woods with the palpitating curiosity of an amateur. Eyes and ears alert, she kept mechanically reassuring herself that the thing to do was to shoot straight and keep cool, and to keep on shooting whichever way the boar might take it into his porcine head to run.

Scott hastened forward to her side:

"Here's the place," he said, looking about him. "He's concluded to make off, you see. They usually go off; they only stand when wounded or when they think they can't get away. He's harmless, I suppose - only it made me very tired to have him act that way. I hate to be backed out of my own property."

Geraldine, rather relieved, yet ashamed not to do all she could, began to walk toward a clump of low hemlocks. She had heard that wild boar take that sort of cover. She did not really expect to find anything there, so when a big black streak crashed out ahead of her she stood stock still in frozen astonishment, rifle clutched to her breast.

"Shoot!" shouted her brother.

"Oh, dear, oh, dear," she said helplessly, "he's gone out of sight! And I had such a splendid shot!" She stamped with vexation. "What a goose!" she repeated. "I had a perfectly splendid shot. And all I did was to jump like a scared cat and stare!"

"Anyway, you didn't run, and that's a point gained," observed her brother. "I had to. And that's one on me."

A moment later he said: "I believe those impudent boar do need a little thinning out. When is Duane coming?"

"In November," said Geraldine, still looking vaguely about for the departed pig.

"Early?"

"I think so, if his father is all right again. I've asked Naida, too. Rosalie wants to come -"

"Oh, for Heaven's sake, don't," he protested. "All I wanted was a shooting party to do a little scientific thinning out of these boar. I'll do some myself, too."

Geraldine laughed. "Rosalie is a dead shot at a target, dear. She wrote asking us to invite her to shoot. I don't see how I can very well refuse her. Do you?"

"That means her husband, too," grumbled Scott, "and that entire bunch."

"No; if it's a shooting party, I don't have to ask him."

Her brother said ungraciously: "Well, I don't care who you ask if they'll thin out these cheeky brutes. Fancy that two-year-old pig clattering his tusks at me, planted there in the path with his mane on end! - You know it mortifies me, Kathleen - it certainly does. One of these fine days some facetious pig will send me shinning up a tree!" He grew madder at the speculative indignity. "By ginger! I'm going to have a shooting party before the snow flies," he muttered, walking forward between Kathleen and his sister. "Keep your eyes out ahead; we may jump another at any time, as the wind is all right. And if we do, let him have it, Geraldine!"

It was a beautiful woodland through which they moved.

The late autumn foliage was unusually magnificent, lacking, this year, those garish and discordant hues which Americans think it necessary to admire. Oak brown and elm yellow, deep chrome bronze and sombre crimson the hard woods glowed against backgrounds of pine and hemlock. Larches were mossy cones of feathery gold; birches slim shafts of snowy gray, ochre-crowned; silver and green the balsams' spires pierced the canopy of splendid tapestry upborne by ash and oak and towering pine under a sky of blue so deep and intense that the lakes reflecting it seemed no less vivid.

Already in the brooks they passed painted trout hung low over every bed of gravel and white sand; the male trout wore his best scarlet fins, and his sides glowed in alternate patterns, jewelled with ruby and sapphire spots. Already the ruffed grouse thundered up by coveys, though they had not yet packed, for the broods still retained their autonomy.

But somewhere beyond the royal azure of the northern sky, very, very far away, there was cold in the world, for even last week, through the violet and primrose dusk, out of the north, shadowy winged things came speeding, batlike phantoms against the dying light - flight-woodcock coming through hill-cleft and valley to the land where summer lingered still.

And there in mid-forest, right in the tall timber, Scott, advancing, flushed a woodcock, which darted up, filling the forest with twittering music - the truest music of our eastern autumn, clear, bewildering, charming in its evanescent sweetness which leaves in its wake a startling silence.

Ahead, lining both sides of a gully deep with last year's leaves, was an oak grove in mid-forest. Here the brown earth was usually furrowed by the black snouts of wild boar, for mast lay thick here in autumn and tender roots invited investigation.

"Get down flat and crawl," whispered Scott; "there may be a boar or two on the grounds."

Kathleen, in her pretty white gown of lace and some sheer stuff, looked at him piteously; but when he and Geraldine dropped flat and wriggled forward into the wind, misgiving of what might prowl behind seized her, and she tucked up her skirts and gave herself to the brown earth with a tremor of indignation and despair.

Nearer and nearer they crept, making very little sound; but they made enough to rouse a young boar, who jerked his head into the air, where he stood among the acorns, big, furry ears high and wide, nose working nervously.

"He's only a yearling," breathed Scott in his sister's ear. "There are traces of stripes, if you look hard. Wait for a better one."

They lay silent, all three peering down at the yearling, who stood motionless, nosing for tainted air, listening, peering about with dull, near-sighted eyes.

And, after a long time, as they made no sound, the brute wheeled suddenly, made a complete circle at a nervous trout, uttered a series of short, staccato sounds that, when he became older, would become deeper, more of an ominous roar than a hoarse and irritated grunt.

Two deer, a doe and a fawn, came picking their way cautiously along the edge of the gully, sometimes flattening their ears, sometimes necks outstretched, ears forward, peering ahead at the young and bad-tempered pig.

The latter saw them, turned in fury and charged with swiftness incredible, and the deer stampeded headlong through the forest.

"What a fierce, little brute!" whispered Kathleen, appalled. "Scott, if he comes any nearer, I'm going to get into a tree."

"If he sees us or winds us he'll run. Don't move; there may be a good boar in presently. I've thought two or three times that I heard something on that hemlock ridge."

They listened, holding their breath. Crack! went a distant stick. Silence; nothing stirred except the yearling who had returned to the mast and was eagerly nosing among the acorns. They could hear him crunching the husks, see the gleam of long white teeth which one day would grow outside that furry muzzle and curve up and backward like ivory sabres.

Geraldine whispered: "There's a huge black thing moving in the hemlock scrub. I can see its feet against the sky-line, and sometimes part of its bulk -"

"Oh, heavens," breathed Kathleen, "what is that?"

Out of the scrub trotted a huge, shaggy, black thing, all head and shoulders, with body slanting back abruptly to a pair of weak hindquarters. Down the slope it ran in quick, noiseless, jerky steps; the yearling turned his head, still munching, ears cocked forward. And suddenly the monster rushed at him with a squeal, and the yearling shrieked and fled, chased clear up the slope.

"It's a sow; don't shoot," whispered Scott. "Look, Sis, you can't see a sign of tusks. Good heavens, what a huge creature she is!"

Fierce, formidable, the great beast halted; three striped, partly grown pigs came rushing and frisking down the gully to join her, filling the forest with their clumsy clatter and baby squealing. From the ridge the two deer, who had sneaked back, regarded the scene with terrified fascination.

Presently the yearling rushed them out again, then sidled down, venturing to the edge of the feeding-ground, where he began to crunch acorns again with a cautious eye on the sow and her noisy brood.

Here and there a brilliant blue-jay floated down, seized an acorn, and winged hastily to some near tree where presently he filled the woods with the noise he made in hammering the acorn into some cleft in the bark.

Gradually the sunlight on the leaves reddened; long, luminous shadows lengthened eastward. Kathleen, lying at full length, her pretty face between her hands, suddenly sneezed.

The next moment the feeding-ground was deserted; only a distant crashing betrayed the line of flight where the great fierce sow and her young were rushing upward toward the rocks of the Gilded Dome.

"I'm so sorry," faltered Kathleen, very pink and embarrassed.

Geraldine sat up and laughed, laying the uncocked rifle across her knees.

"Some of these days I'm going to win my wager," she said to her brother. "And it won't be with a striped yearling, either; it will be with the biggest, shaggiest, fiercest, tuskiest boar that ranges the Gilded Dome. And that," she added, looking at Kathleen, "will give me something to think of and keep me rather busy, I believe."

"Rather," observed her brother, getting up and helping Kathleen to her feet. He added, to torment her: "Probably you'll get Duane to win your bet for you, Sis."

"No," said the girl gravely; "whatever is to die I must slay all by myself, Scott - all alone, with no man's help."

He nodded: "Sure thing; it's the only sporting way. There's no stunt to it; only keep cool and keep shooting, and drop him before he comes to close quarters."

"Yes," she said, looking up at Kathleen.

Her brother drew her to her feet. She gave him a little hug.

"Believe in me, dear," she said. "I'll do it easier if you do."

"Of course I do. You're a better sport than I. You always were. And that's no idle jest; witness my nose and Duane's in days gone by."

The girl smiled. As they turned homeward she slung her rifle, passed her right arm through Kathleen's, and dropped her left on her brother's shoulder. She was very tired, and hopeful that she might sleep.

And tired, hopeful, thinking of her lover, she passed through the woods, leaning on those who were nearest and most dear.

Somehow - and just why was not clear to her - it seemed at that moment as though she had passed the danger mark - as though the very worst lay behind her - close, scarcely clear of her skirts yet, but all the same it lay behind her, not ahead.

She knew, and dreaded, and shrank from what still lay before her; she understood into what ruin treachery to self might precipitate her still at any moment. And yet, somehow, she felt vaguely that something had been gained that day which never before had been gained. And she thought of her lover as she passed through the forest, leaning on Scott and Kathleen, her little feet keeping step with theirs, her eyes steady in the red western glare that flooded the forest to an infernal beauty.

Behind her streamed her gigantic shadow; behind her lay

another shadow, cast by her soul and floating wide of it now. And it must never touch her soul again, God helping.

Suddenly her heart almost ceased its beating. Far away within, stirring in unsuspected depths, something moved furtively.

Her face whitened a little; her eyes closed, the lids fluttered, opened; she gazed straight in front of her, walked on, small head erect, lips firm, facing the hell that lay before her - lay surely, surely before her. For the breath of it glowed already in her veins and the voices of it were already busy in her ears, and the unseen stirring of it had begun once more within her body - that tired white, slender body of hers which had endured so bravely and so long.

If sleep would only aid her, come to her in her need, be her ally in the peril of her solitude - if it would only come, and help her to endure!

And wondering if it would, not knowing, hoping, she walked onward through the falling night.

CHAPTER XVII

THE DANGER MARK

Her letters to him still bore the red cross:

> "I understand perfectly why you cannot come," she wrote; "I would do exactly as you are doing if I had a father. It must be a very great happiness to have one. My need of you is not as great as his; I can hold my own alone, I think. You see I am doing it, and you must not worry. Only, dear, when you have the opportunity, come up if only for a day."

And again, in November:

> "You are the sweetest boy, and it is not difficult to understand why your father cannot endure to have you out of his sight. But is this not a very heavy strain on you? Of course your mother and Naida must not be left alone with him; you are the only son, and your place is there.
>
> "Dear, I know what you are going through is one of the most dreadful things that any man is called upon to bear - your father stricken, your mother and sister prostrate; the newspapers - for I have read them - cruel beyond belief! But whatever they say, whatever is true or untrue, Duane, remember that it cannot affect my regard for you and yours.

"If I had a father, whatever he might have done, or permitted others to do, would not, *could* not alter my affection for him.

"Men say that women have no sense of honour. I do not know what that sense may be if it falters when loyalty and compassion are needed, too.

"I have read the papers; I know only what I read and what you tell me. The rules that custom has framed to safeguard and govern financial operations, I do not understand; but, as far as I can comprehend, it seems to me that custom has hitherto sanctioned what disaster has now placed under a bann. It seems to me that the very men who now blame your father have all done successfully what he did so disastrously.

"One thing I know: no kinder, dearer man than your father ever lived; and I love him, and I love his family, and I will marry his son when I am fit to do it."

And again she wrote:

"I saw in the papers that the Algonquin Trust Company had closed its doors; I read the heartbreaking details of the crowds besieging it, the lines of frightened people standing there in the rain all night long. It is dreadful, terrible!

"Who are these Wall Street men who would not help the Algonquin when they could? Why is the Clearing House so bitter? I don't know what it all means; I read columns about poor Jack Dysart - words and figures and technical phrases and stock quotations - and it means nothing, and I understand nothing of it save that it is all a fierce outcry against him and against the men with whom he was financially involved.

"The papers are so gloomy, so eager in their search for

evil, so merciless, so exultant when scandal is unearthed, that I can scarcely bear to read them. Why do they drag in unhappy people who know nothing about these matters? The interview with your mother and Naida, which you say is false, was most dreadful. How cruel men are!

"Tell them I love them dearly; tell your father, too. And, dear, I don't know exactly how Scott and I are situated, but if we can be of any financial use to you, please, please let us! Our fortune, when it came to us, was, I believe, all in first mortgages and railroad securities. I believe that Scott made some changes in our investments under advice from your father. I don't know what they were.

"Don't bother your father with such details now; he has enough to think of lying there in his grief, bewildered, broken in mind and body. Duane, is it not more merciful that he is unable to understand what the papers are saying?

"Dear, heart and soul I am loyal to you and yours."

She wrote again:

"Yes, I had a talk with Scott. I did not know he had been receiving all those letters from your attorneys. Magnelius Grandcourt manages the investments. Scott's brokers are Stainer & Elting; our attorneys are, as you know, Landon, Brooks & Gayfield.

"Duane, I absolutely forbid you to worry. My brother is of age, sound in mind and body, responsible for whatever he does or has done. It is his affair if he solicits advice, his affair if he follows it. Your father has no responsibility whatever in the matter of the Cascade Development and Securities Company. Besides, Scott tells me that what he did was against the advice of Mr. Tappan.

"I remember last winter that he brought a Mr. Skelton to

luncheon, and a horrid man named Klawber.

"Poor Scott! He certainly knows nothing about business matters. I know he had no desire to increase his private fortune; he tells me that what interested him in the Cascade Development and Securities Company was the chance that cheap radium might stimulate scientific research the world over. Poor Scott!

"Dear, you are not to think for one instant that any trouble which may involve Scott is due to you or yours. And if it were, Duane, it could make no difference to him or to me. Money and what it buys is such a pitiful detail in what goes to make up happiness. Who but I should understand that!

"Loss of social prestige and position, is a serious matter, I suppose; I may show my ignorance and inexperience when I tell you how much more serious to me are other things - like the loss of faith in one's self or in others - or the loss of the gentler virtues, which means the loss of what one once was.

"The loss of honour is, as you say, a pitiful thing; yet, I think that when that happens, love and compassion were never more truly needed.

"Honour, as I understand it, is not to take advantage of others or of one's better self. This is a young girl's definition. I cannot see - if one has yielded once to temptation, and truly repents - why honour cannot be regained.

"The honour of men and nations that seems to require arrogance, aggression, violence for its defence, I do not understand. How can the misdeeds of others impair one's true honour? How can punishment for such misdeeds restore it? No; it lies within one, quite intangible save by one's self.

"Why should I not know, dear? - I who have lost my own and found it, have held it desperately for a while, then lost it, then regained it, holding it again as I do now - alas! - against no other enemy than I who write this record for your eyes!

"Dear, I know of nothing lost which may not be regained, except life. I know of nothing which cannot be rendered tolerable through loyalty.

"That material happiness which means so much to some, means now so very little to me, perhaps because I have never lacked it.

"Yet I know that, once mistress of myself, nothing else could matter unless your love failed."

Again she wrote him toward the end of November:

"Why will you not let me help you, dear? My fortune is practically intact so far, except that, of course, I met those obligations which Scott could not meet. Poor Scott!

"You know it's rather bewildering to me where millions go to. I don't quite comprehend how they can so utterly vanish in such a short time, even in such a frightful fiasco as the Cascade Development Company.

"So many people have been here - Mr. Landon and Mr. Gayfield, Mr. Stainer of Elting & Stainer, that dreadful creature Klawber, a very horrid man named Amos Flack - and dear, grim, pig-headed Mr. Tappan - old Remsen Tappan of all men!

"He practically kicked out Mr. Flack and the creature Klawber, who had been trying to frighten Scott and me and even our lawyers.

"And think, Duane! He never uttered one sarcasm, one

reproach for Scott's foolishness; he sat grim and rusty as the iron that he once dealt in, listening to what Scott had to tell him, never opening that cragged jaw, never unclosing that thin line of cleavage which is his mouth.

"We did not know what he had come for; but we know now. He is *so* good - so good, Duane! And I, who hated him as a child, as a girl - I am almost too ashamed to let him take command and untangle for us, with those knotted, steel-sinewed fingers of his, the wretched, tangled mess that has coiled around Scott and me.

"Surely, this man Klawber is a very great villain; and it seems that Mr. Skelton and the wretched Flack creature are little less. As for Jack Dysart, it is all too sorrowful to think about. How must he feel! Surely, surely he could not have known what he was doing. He must have been desperate to go to Delancy Grandcourt. It was wrong; nothing on earth could have propped up the Algonquin, and why did he let his best friend go down with it?

"But it was fine of Delancy to stand by him - fine, fine! His father is perfectly furious, but, Duane, it *was* fine!

"And now, dear, about Scott. It will amuse you, and perhaps horrify you, if I tell you that he has not turned a hair.

"Not that he doesn't care; not that he is not more or less mortified. But he blames nobody except himself; and he's laying plans quite cheerfully for a career on a small income that really does not require the austerity and frugality he imagines.

"One thing is certain; the town house is to be sold. My income is not sufficient to maintain it and Roya-Neh, and live as we do, and have anything left. I don't yet know how far my fortune is involved, but I have a very unpleasant premonition that there is going to be much less left than anybody believes, and that ultimately we ought to sell Roya-Neh.

"However, it is far too early to speculate; besides, this family has done enough speculating for one generation.

"Dear, you ask about myself. I am not one bit worried, sad, or apprehensive. I am *better*, Duane. Do you understand? All this has developed a set of steadier nerves in me than I have had since I was a child.

"A new and curiously keen enjoyment has been slowly growing in me - a happiness in physical and violent effort. I've a devilish horse to ride; and I love it! I've climbed all over the Gilded Dome and Lynx Peak after the biggest and shaggiest boar you ever saw. Oh, Duane! I came on him just at the edge of evening, and he winded me and went thundering down the Westgate ravine, and I fired too quickly.

"But I'm after him almost every day with old Miller, and my arms and legs are getting so strong, and my flesh so firm, and actually I'm becoming almost plump in the face! Don't you care for that kind of a girl?

"Dear, do you think I've passed the danger mark? Tell me honestly - not what you want to think, but what you do believe. I don't know whether I have passed it yet. I feel, somehow, whichever side of it I am on, that the danger mark is not very far away from me. I've got to get farther away. The house in town is open. Mrs. Farren, Hilda, and Nellie are there if we run into town.

"Kathleen is so happy for me. I've told her about the red cross. She is too sweet to Scott; she seems to think he really grieves deeply over the loss of his private fortune. What a dear she is! She is willing to marry him now; but Scott strikes attitudes and declares she shall have a man whose name stands for an achievement - meaning, of course, the Seagrave process for the extermination of the Rose-beetle.

"Duane, I am quite unaccountably happy to-day. Nothing seems to threaten. But don't stop loving me."

Followed three letters less confident, and another very pitiful – a frightened letter asking him to come if he could. But his father's condition forbade it and he dared not.

Then another letter came, desperate, almost incoherent, yet still bearing the red cross faintly traced. And on the heels of it a telegram:

"Could you stand by me until this is over? I am afraid of to-night. Am on my way to town with my maid, very ill. I know you cannot leave your father except at night. I will telephone you from the house.

"G.S."

On the train a dispatch was handed her:

"I will be at your house as soon as my father is asleep. Don't worry.

"DUANE."

Hour after hour she sat motionless beside the car-window, quiet, pale, dark eyes remote; trees, houses, trains, telegraph-poles streamed past in one gray, unending blur; rain which at first had only streaked the grimy window-glass with cinders, became sleet, then snow, clotting the dripping panes.

At last, far away under a heavy sky, the vast misshapen landmarks of New York loomed up gray through the falling snow; the train roared over the Harlem, halted at 125th Street, rolled on into the black tunnel, faster, faster, slower, then more slowly, and stopped. All sounds ceased at the same moment;

silence surrounded her, dreary as the ominous silence within.

Dunn met her with a brougham; Fifth Avenue was slippery with filthy, melting slush; yet, somehow, into her mind came the memory of her return from her first opera - the white avenue at midnight, the carriage, lamps lighted, speeding through the driving snow. Yesterday, the quiet, untainted whiteness of childhood; to-day, trouble and stress and stained snow melting into mud - so far behind her lay innocence and peace on the long road she had travelled! So far had she already journeyed - toward what?

She pressed her lips more tightly together and buried her chin in her sable muff. Beside her, her maid sat shivering and stifling yawn after yawn and thinking of dinner and creature comforts, and of Dunn, the footman, whom she did ardently admire.

The big red brick house among its naked trees seemed sad and deserted as the brougham flashed into the drive and stopped, the horses stamping and pawing the frozen gravel. Geraldine had never before been away from home so long, and now as she descended from the carriage and looked vaguely about her it seemed as though she had, somehow, become very, very young again - that it was her child-self that entered under the porte-cochere after the prescribed drive that always ended outdoor exercise in the early winter evenings; and she half expected to see old Howker in the hall, and Margaret trotting up to undo her furs and leggings - half expected to hear Kathleen's gay greeting, to see her on the stairs, so young, so sweetly radiant, her arms outstretched in welcome to her children who had been away scarcely a full hour.

“I'd like to have a fire in my bedroom and in the upper library,” she said to Hilda, who had smilingly opened the door for her. “I'll dine in the upper library, too. When Mr. Mallett arrives, you need not come up to announce him. Ask him to find me in the library.”

To Mrs. Farren she said: "Nobody need sit up. When Mr. Mallett leaves, I will put the chains on and bolt everything."

She was destined not to keep this promise.

* * * * *

Bathed, her hair brushed and dressed, she suffered her maid to hook her into a gown which she could put off again unassisted - one of those gowns that excite masculine admiration by reason of its apparent inexpensiveness and extreme simplicity. It was horribly expensive, of course - white, and cut out in a circle around her neck like a young girl's gown; and it suited Geraldine's slender, rounded throat and her dainty head with its heavy, loosely drawn masses of brown hair, just shadowing cheeks and brow.

When the last hook was looped she dismissed her maid for the night; Hilda served her at dinner, but she ate little, and the waitress bore away the last of the almost untouched food, leaving her young mistress seated before the fire and looking steadily into it.

The fire was a good one; the fuel oak and ash and beech. The flames made a silky, rustling sound; now and then a coal fell with a softly agreeable crash and a swarm of golden sparks whirled up the chimney, snapping, scintillating, like day fireworks.

Geraldine sat very still, her mouth resting on her white wrist, and when she lifted her head the marks of her teeth showed on the skin. Then the other hand, clutching the arm of her chair, fell to her side cramped and quivering; she stood up, looked at the fire, pressed both palms across her eyes, turned and began to pace the room.

To and fro she moved, slowly, quickly, as the craving for motion ebbed or increased. At times she made unconscious movements with her arms, now flinging them wide, now flexing the muscles, clenching the hands; but always the arms fell helpless, hopeless; the slim, desperate fingers relaxed; and she moved on again, to and fro, up and down, turning her gaze toward the clock each time she passed it.

In her eyes there seemed to be growing a dreadful sort of beauty; there was fire in them, the luminous brightness of the tortured. On both cheeks a splendid colour glowed and waned; the slightly drawn lips were vivid.

But this - all of it changed as the slow minutes dragged their course; into the brown eyes crept the first frosty glimmer of desperation; colour faded from the face, leaving it snowy white; the fulness of the lips vanished, the chin seemed to grow pointed, and under the eyes bluish shadows deepened. It promised to go hard with her that night; it was already going very badly. She knew it, and digging her nails into her delicate palms, set her teeth together and drew a deep, unsteady breath.

She had looked at the clock four times, and the hands seemed to have moved no more than a minute's space across the dial; and once more she turned to pace the floor.

Her lips had lost almost all their colour now; they moved, muttering tremulous incoherences; the outline of every feature grew finer, sharper, more spiritual, but dreadfully white.

Later she found herself on her knees beside the couch, face buried in the cushions, her small teeth marking her wrist again - heard herself crying out for somebody to help her - yet her lips had uttered no sound; it was only her soul in its agony, while the youthful, curved body and rigid limbs burnt steadily in hell's own flames.

Again she raised her head and lifted her white face toward the clock. Only a minute had crept by, and she turned, twisting her interlocked hands, dry-eyed, dry lips parted, and stared about her. Half stupefied with pain, stunned, dismayed by the million tiny voices of temptation assailing her, dinning in her senses, she reeled where she knelt, fell forward, laid her slender length across the hearth-rug, and set her teeth in her wrist again, choking back the cry of terror and desolation.

And there her senses tricked her - or she may have lost consciousness - for it seemed that the next moment she was on the stairs, moving stealthily - where? God and her tormented body seemed to know, for she caught herself halfway down the stairs, cried out on her Maker for strength, stood swaying, breathless, quivering in the agony of it - and dragged herself back and up the stairs once more, step by step, to the landing.

For a moment she stood there, shaking, ghastly, staring down into the regions below, where relief lay within her reach. And she dared not even stare too long; she turned blindly, arms outstretched, feeling her way back. Every sense within her seemed for the moment deadened; sounds scarcely penetrated, had no meaning; she heard the grille clash, steps on the stair; she was trying to get back to the library, paused to rest at the door, was caught in two strong arms, drawn into them:

"Duane," she whispered.

"Darling!" - and as he saw her face - "My God!"

"Mine, too, Duane. Don't be afraid; I'm holding firm, so far. But I am very, very ill. Could you help me a little?"

"Yes, child! - yes, little Geraldine - my little, little girl -"

"Can you stay near me?"

"Yes! Good God, yes!"

"How long?"

"As long as you want me."

"Then I can get through with this. I think to-night decides....

If you will remain with me - for a while -"

"Yes, dear."

He drew a chair to the fire; she sank into it; he seated himself beside her and she clung to his hand with both of hers.

His eyes fell upon her wrist where the marks of her teeth were imprinted; he felt her body trembling, saw the tragedy in her eyes, rose, lifted her as though she were a child, and seating himself, drew her close against his breast.

The night was a hard one; sometimes in an access of pain she struggled for freedom, and all his strength was needed to keep her where she lay. At times, too, her senses seemed clouded, and she talked incoherently; sometimes she begged for relief, shamelessly craved it; sometimes she used all her force, and, almost beside herself, defied him, threatened him, turned on him infuriated; but his strength held her locked in a vicelike embrace, and, toward morning, she suddenly relaxed - crumpled up like a white flower in his arms. For a while her tears fell hot and fast; then utter prostration left her limp, without movement, even without a tremor, a dead weight in his arms.

And, for the second time in his life, lifting her, he bore her to her room, laid her among the pillows, slipped off her shoes, and, bending above her, listened.

She slept profoundly - but it was not the stupor that had chained her limbs that other time when he had brought her here.

He went into the library and waited for an hour. Then, very quietly, he descended the stairs and let himself out into the bitter darkness of a November morning.

* * * * *

About noon next day the Seagraves' brougham drew up before the Mallett house and Geraldine, in furs, stepped out and crossed the sidewalk with that swift, lithe grace of hers. The servant opened the grille; she entered and stood by the great marble-topped hall-table until Duane came down. Then she gave him her gloved hands, looking him straight in the eyes.

She was still pale but self-possessed, and wonderfully pretty in her fur jacket and toque; and as she stood there, both hands dropped into his, that nameless and winning grace which had always fascinated him held him now - something about her that recalled the child in the garden with clustering hair and slim, straight limbs.

"You look about fifteen," he said, "you beautiful, slender thing! Did you come to see my father?"

"Yes - and your father's son."

"Me?"

"Is there another like you, Duane - in all the world?"

"Plenty -"

"Hush!... When did you go last night?"

"When you left me for the land of dreams, little lady."

"So you - carried me."

He smiled, and a bright flush covered her cheeks.

"That makes twice," she said steadily.

"Yes, dear."

"There will be no third time."

"Not unless I have a sleepy wife who nods before the fire like a drowsy child."

"Do you want that kind?"

"I want the kind that lay close in my arms before the fire last night."

"Do you? I think I should like the sort of husband who is strong enough to cradle that sort of a child.... Could your mother and Naida receive me? Could I see your father?"

"Yes. When are you going back to Roya-Neh?"

"To-night."

He said quietly: "Is it safe?"

"For me to go? Yes - yes, my darling" - her hands tightened over his - "yes, it is safe - because you made it so. If you knew - if you knew what is in my heart to - to give you! - what I will be to you some day, dearest of men -"

He said unsteadily: "Come upstairs.... My father is very feeble, but quite cheerful. Do you understand that - that his mind - his memory, rather, is a little impaired?"

She lifted his hands and laid her soft lips against them:

"Will you take me to him, Duane?"

Colonel Mallett lay in the pale November sunlight, very still, his hands folded on his breast. And at first she did not know him in this ghost of the tall, well-built, gray-haired man with ruddy colour and firm, clear skin.

As she bent over, he opened his eyes, smiled, pronounced her name, still smiling and keeping his sunken eyes on her. They were filmy and bluish, like the eyes of the very old; and the hand she lifted and held was the stricken hand of age - inert, lifeless, without weight.

She said that she was so happy to know he was recovering; she told him how proud everybody was of Duane, what exceptional talent he possessed, how wonderfully he had painted Miller's children. She spoke to him of Roya-Neh, and how interesting it had become to them all, told him about the wild boar and her own mishaps with the guileful pig.

He smiled, watching her at times; but his wistful gaze always reverted to his son, who sat at the foot of the couch, chin balanced between his long, lean hands.

"You won't go, will you?" he whispered.

"Where, father?"

"Away."

"No, of course not."

"I mean with - Geraldine," he said feebly.

"If I did, father, we'd take you with us," he laughed.

"It is too far, my son.... You and Geraldine are going too far for me to follow.... Wait a little while."

Geraldine, blushing, bent down swiftly, her lips brushing the sick man's wasted face:

"I would not care for him if I could take him from you."

"Your father and I were old friends. Your grandfather was a very fine gentleman.... I am glad.... I am a little tired - a little confused. Is your grandfather here with you? I would like to see him."

She said, after a moment, in a low voice: "He did not come with me to-day."

"Give him my regards and compliments. And say to him that it would be a pleasure to see him. I am not very well; has he heard of my indisposition?"

"I think he - has."

"Then he will come," said Colonel Mallett feebly. "Duane, you are not going, are you? I am a little tired. I think I could sleep if you would lower the shade and ask your mother to sit by me.... But you won't go until I am asleep, will you?"

"No," he said gently, as his mother and Naida entered and Geraldine rose to greet them, shocked at the change in Mrs. Mallett.

She and Naida went away together; later Duane joined them in the library, saying that his father was asleep, holding fast to his wife's hand.

Geraldine, her arm around Naida's waist, had been looking at one of Duane's pictures - the only one of his in the house - merely a stretch of silvery marsh and a gray, wet sky beyond.

"Father liked it," he said; "that's why it's here, Geraldine."

"You never made one brush-stroke that was commonplace in all your life," said Geraldine abruptly. "Even I can see that."

"Such praise from a lady!" he exclaimed, laughing. Geraldine smiled, too, and Naida's pallid face lightened for a moment. But grief had set its seal on the house of Mallett; that was plain everywhere; and when Geraldine kissed Naida good-bye and walked to the door beside her lover, a passion of tenderness for him and his overwhelmed her, and when he put her into her brougham she leaned from the lowered window, clinging to his hand, careless of who might see them.

"*Can* I help in any way?" she whispered. "I told you that my fortune is still my own - most of it -"

"Dear, wait!"

There was a strange look in his eyes; she said no more with her lips, but her eyes told him all. Then he stepped back, directing Dunn to drive his mistress to the Commonwealth Club, where she was to lunch with Sylvia Quest, whom she had met that morning in the blockade at Forty-second Street, and who had invited her from her motor across the crupper of a traffic-policeman's horse.

CHAPTER XVIII

BON CHIEN

The chronology of that last dark and bitter week in November might have been written "necrology."

On Monday Colonel Mallett died about sundown; on Wednesday the Hon. John D. Ellis, while examining an automatic revolver in his bath-room, met with one of those unfortunate and fatal accidents which sometimes happen in times of great financial depression.

Thursday Amos Flack carelessly disappeared, leaving no address; and on the last day of the week Emanuel Klawber politely excused himself to a group of very solemn gentlemen who had been assisting him in the well-known and popular game of "Hunt the Books"; and, stepping outside the door of the director's office, carefully destroyed what little life had not already been scared out of his three-hundred-pound person.

It had been raining all day; Dysart had not felt very well, and Klawber's unpleasant performance made him ill. He stood in the rain watching the ambulance arriving at a gallop, then, sickened, turned away through the dark and dripping crowds, crossed the street, and, lowering his head against the storm, drove both gloved hands deep into the pockets of his fashionably cut rain-coat, and started for home.

It mattered nothing to him that several hard-working

newspaper men might desire to secure his version of Mr. Klawber's taking off, or of his explanation for it or his sensations concerning it. It mattered nothing to him that the afternoon papers reported the arrest of James Skelton, or that Max Moebus had inadvertently, and no doubt in a moment of intense abstraction, taken a steamer for Europe and the books of the Shoshone Bank.

These matters, now seemed a great way off - too unreal to be of personal moment. He was feeling sick; that occupied his mind. Also the slush on the sidewalk had wet through his shoes, which probably was not good for his cough.

It was scarcely two in the afternoon, yet there remained so little daylight that the electricity burned in the shops along Fifth Avenue. Through a smutty, grayish gloom, rain drove densely; his hat and waterproof coat were heavy with it, the bottoms of his trousers soaked.

Passing the Patroons Club it occurred to him that hot whiskey might extinguish his cough. The liveried servants at the door, in the cloak-room - the page who took his order, the white-headed butler who had always personally served him, and who served him now, all hesitated and gazed curiously at him. He paid no attention at the time but remembered it afterward.

For an hour he sat alone in the vast empty room before a fire of English cannel coal, taking his hot whiskey and lemon in slow, absent-minded gulps. Patches of deep colour lay flat under his cheek-bones, his sunken abstracted eyes never left the coals.

The painted gaze of dead Presidents and Governors looked down at him from their old-time frames ranged in stately ranks along the oaken wainscot. Over the mantel the amazing, Hebraic countenance of a moose leered at him out of little sly, sardonic little eyes, almost bantering in their evil immobility.

He had presented the trophy to the club after a trip

somewhere, leaving the impression that he had shot it. He seldom looked at it, never at the silver-engraved inscription on the walnut shield.

Strangely enough, now as he sat there, he thought of the trophy and looked up at it; and for the first time in his life read the inscription.

It made no visible impression upon him except that for a brief moment the small and vivid patches of colour in his wasted cheeks faintly tinted the general pallor. But this died out as soon as it appeared; he drank deliberately, set the hot glass on a table at his elbow, long, bony fingers still retaining a grip upon it.

And into his unconcentrated thoughts, strangely enough, came the memories of little meannesses which he had committed - trivial things that he supposed he had forgotten long ago; and at first, annoyed, he let memory drift.

But, imperceptibly, from the shallows of these little long-forgotten meannesses, memory drifted uncontrolled into deeper currents; and, disdainful, he made no effort to control it; and later, could not. And for the first time in his life he took the trouble to understand the reason of his unpopularity among men. He had cared nothing for them.

He cared nothing for them now, unless that half tolerant, half disdainful companionship of years with Delancy Grandcourt could be called caring for a man. If their relations ever had been anything more than a habit he did not know; on what their friendship had ever been founded he could not tell. It had been his habit to take from Delancy, accept, or help himself. He had helped himself to Rosalie Dene; and not long ago he had accepted all that Delancy offered, almost convinced at the time that it would disappear in the debacle when the Algonquin crumbled into a rubbish heap of rotten securities.

A curious friendship - and the only friend he ever had had

among men - stupid, inertly at hand, as inevitably to be counted on as some battered toy of childhood which escaped the dust heap so long that custom tolerates its occupation of any closet space convenient: and habit, at intervals, picks it up to see what's left of it.

* * * * *

He had finished his whiskey; the fire seemed to have grown too hot, and he shoved back his chair. But the room, too, was becoming close, even stifling. Perspiration glistened on his forehead; he rose and began to wander from room to room, followed always by the stealthy glances of servants.

The sweat on his face had become unpleasantly cold; he came back to the fire, endured it for a few moments, then, burning and shivering at the same time, and preferring the latter sensation, he went out to his letter-box and unlocked it. There was only one envelope there, a letter from the governing board of the club requesting his resignation.

The possibility of such an event had never occurred to him; he read the letter again, folded and placed it in his pocket, went back to the fire with the idea of burning it, took it out, read it again, folded it absently, and replaced it in his pocket.

At that time, except for the dull surprise, the episode did not seem to affect him particularly. So many things had been accumulating, so many matters had been menacing him, that one cloud more among the dark, ominous masses gathering made no deeper impression than slight surprise.

For a while he stood motionless, hands in his trousers' pockets, head lowered; then, as somebody entered the farther door, he turned instinctively and stepped into a private card room, closing the polished mahogany door. The door opened a moment later and Delancy Grandcourt walked in.

"Hello," he said briefly. Dysart, by the window, looked around at him without any expression whatever.

"Have you heard about Klawber?" asked Delancy. "They're calling the extra."

Dysart looked out of the window. "That's fast work," he said.

Grandcourt stood for a while in silence, then seated himself, saying:

"He ought to have lived and tried to make good."

"He couldn't."

"He ought to have tried. What's the good of lying down that way?"

"I don't know. I guess he was tired."

"That doesn't relieve his creditors."

"No, but it relieves Klawber."

Grandcourt said: "You always view things from that side, don't you?"

"What side?"

"That of personal convenience."

"Yes. Why not?"

"I don't know. Where is it landing you?"

"I haven't gone into that very thoroughly." There was a trace of irritation in Dysart's voice; he passed one hand over his forehead; it was icy, and the hair on it damp. "What the devil do you want of me, anyway?" he asked.

"Nothing.... I have never wanted anything of you, have I?"

Dysart walked the width of the room, then the length of it, then came and stood by the table, resting on it with one thin hand, in which his damp handkerchief was crushed to a wad.

"*What* is it you've got to say, Delancy? Is it about that loan?"

"No. Have you heard a word out of me about it?"

"You've been devilish glum. Good God, I don't blame you; I ought not to have touched it; I must have been crazy to let you try to help me -"

"It was my affair. What I choose to do concerns myself," said Grandcourt, his heavy, troubled face turning redder. "And, Jack, I understand that my father is making things disagreeable for you. I've told him not to; and you mustn't let it worry you, because what I had was my own and what I did with it my own business."

"Anyway," observed Dysart, after a moment's reflection, "your family is wealthy."

A darker flush stained Grandcourt's face; and Dysart's misinterpretation of his philosophy almost stung him into fierce retort; but as his heavy lips unclosed in anger, his eyes fell on Dysart's ravaged face, and he sat silent, his personal feelings merged in an evergrowing anxiety.

"Why do you cough like that, Jack?" he demanded after a paroxysm had shaken the other into an armchair, where he lay sweating and panting:

"It's a cold," Dysart managed to say; "been hanging on for a month."

"Three months," said Grandcourt tersely. "Why don't you take care of it?"

There was a silence; nothing more was said about the cold; and presently Grandcourt drew a letter from his pocket and handed it silently to Dysart. It was in Rosalie's handwriting, dated two months before, and directed to Dysart at Baltimore. The post-office authorities had marked it, "No address," and had returned it a few days since to the sender.

These details Dysart noticed on the envelope and the heading of the first page; he glanced over a line or two, lowered the letter, and looked questioningly over it at Grandcourt:

"What's it about? - if you know," he asked wearily. "I'm not inclined just now to read anything that may be unpleasant."

Grandcourt said quietly:

"I have not read the letter, but your wife has told me something of what it contains. She wrote and mailed it to you weeks ago - before the crash - saying, I believe, that adversity was not the time for the settlement of domestic differences, and that if her private fortune could avert disaster, you were to write immediately to her attorneys."

Dysart gazed at him as though stunned; then his dull gaze fell once more on the envelope. He examined it, went all over it with lack-lustre eyes, laid it aside, and finally began to read his wife's letter - the letter that had never reached him because he had used another name on the hotel register in Baltimore.

Grandcourt watched him with painful interest as he sat, hunched up, coughing at intervals, and poring over his wife's long, angular chirography. There was much between the lines to read, but Dysart could never read it; much to understand, but he could never understand it.

> "Delancy tells me," she wrote, "that you are threatened with very serious difficulties. Once or twice you yourself have said as much to me; and my answer was that they no longer concerned me.

"The situation is this: I have, as you know, consulted counsel with a view to begin proceedings for a separation. This has been discontinued - temporarily, at any rate - because I have been led to believe by your friend, Delancy Grandcourt, that the present is no time to add to your perplexities.

"He has, I may add, induced me to believe other things which my better sense rejects; but no woman's logic - which is always half sentiment - could remain unshaken by the simple loyalty to you and to me of this friend of yours and of mine. And this letter would never have been written except, practically, at his dictation. Kindly refrain from showing it to him as my acknowledgment here of his influence in the matter would grieve him very deeply.

"Because he believes that it is still possible for you and me to return to civilised relations; he believes that I care for you, that, in your own leisurely and superficial fashion, you still really honour the vows that bound you - still in your heart care for me. Let him believe it; and if you will, for his sake, let us resume the surface semblance of a common life which, until he persuaded me, I was determined to abandon.

"It is an effort to write this; I do it for his sake, and, in that way, for yours. I don't think you care about me; I don't think you ever did or ever will. Yet you must know how it was with me until I could endure my isolation no longer. And I say to you perfectly frankly that now I care more for this friend of yours, Delancy Grandcourt, than I care for anybody in the world. Which is why I write you to offer what I have offered, and to say that if my private fortune can carry you through the disaster which is so plainly impending, please write to my attorneys at once as they have all power in the matter."

The postscript was dated ten days later, from Dysart's own house:

"Receiving no reply, I telephoned you, but Brandon says you are away from the city on business and have left no address, so I took the liberty of entering your house, selecting this letter from the mass of nine days' old mail awaiting you, and shall direct it to you at the hotel in Baltimore where Bunny Gray says that somebody has seen you several times with a Mr. Skelton."

As Dysart read, he wiped the chilly perspiration from his haggard face at intervals, never taking his eyes from the written pages. And at last he finished his wife's letter, sat very silent, save when the cough shook him, the sheets of the letter lying loosely in his nerveless hand.

It was becoming plain to him, in a confused sort of way, that something beside bad luck and his own miscalculations, was working against him - had been stealthily moving toward his undoing for a year, now; something occult, sinister, inexorable.

He thought of the register at the hotel in Baltimore, of the name he lived under there during that interval in his career for which he had accounted to nobody, and never would account - on earth. And into his memory rose the pale face of Sylvia Quest; and he looked down at the letter trembling in his hand and thought of her and of his wife and of the Algonquin Trust Company, and of the chances of salvation he had missed.

Grandcourt sat looking at him; there was something in his gaze almost doglike:

"Have you read it?" he asked.

Dysart glanced up abstractedly: "Yes."

"Is it what I told you?"

"Yes - substantially." He dried his damp face; "it comes rather late, you know."

"Not *too* late," said the other, mistaking him; "your wife is still ready to meet you half-way, Jack."

"Oh - that? I meant the Algonquin matter -" He checked himself, seeing for the first time in his life contempt distorting Grandcourt's heavy face.

"Man! Man!" he said thickly, "is there nothing in that letter for you except money offered?"

"What do you mean?"

"I say, is there nothing in that message to you that touches the manhood in you?"

"You don't know what is in it," said Dysart listlessly. Even Grandcourt's contempt no longer produced any sensation; he looked at the letter, tore it into long strips, crumpled them and stood up with a physical effort:

"I'm going to burn this. Have you anything else to say?"

"Yes. Good God, Jack, *don't* you care for your wife? *Can't* you?"

"No."

"Why?"

"I don't know." His tone became querulous. "How can a man tell why he becomes indifferent to a woman? I don't know. I never did know. I can't explain it. But he does."

Grandcourt stared at him. And suddenly the latent fear that had been torturing him for the last two weeks died out utterly: this man would never need watching to prevent any attempt at self-destruction; this man before him was not of that caste. His self-centred absorption was of a totally different nature.

He said, very red in the face, but with a voice well modulated and even:

"I think I've made a good deal of an ass of myself. I think I may safely be cast for that role in future. Most people, including yourself, think I'm fitted for it; and most people, and yourself, are right. And I'll admit it now by taking the liberty of asking you whom you were with in Baltimore."

"None of your damned business!" said Dysart, wheeling short on him.

"Perhaps not. I did not believe it at the time, but I do now.... And her brother is after you with a gun."

"What do you mean?"

"That you'd better get out of town unless you want an uglier scandal on your hands."

Dysart stood breathing fast and with such effort that his chest moved visibly as the lungs strained under the tension:

"Do you mean to say that drunken whelp suspects anything so - so wildly absurd -"

"Which drunken whelp? There are several in town?"

Dysart glared at him, careless of what he might now believe.

"I take it you mean that little cur, Quest."

"Yes, I happen to mean Quest."

Dysart gave an ugly laugh and turned short on his heel:

"The whole damn lot of you make me sick," he said. "So does this club."

A servant held his rain-coat and handed him his hat; he shook his bent shoulders, stifled a cough, and went out into the rain.

In his own home his little old father, carefully be-wigged, painted, cleaned and dressed, came trotting into the lamp-lit living-room fresh from the ministrations of his valet.

"There you are, Jack! - te-he! Oh, yes, there you are, you young dog! - all a-drip with rain for the love o' the ladies, eh, Jack? Te-he - one's been here to see you - a little white doll in chinchillas, and scared to death at my civilities - as though she knew the Dysarts - te-he! Oh, yes, the Dysarts, Jack. But it was monstrous imprudent, my son - and a good thing that your wife remains at Lenox so late this season - te-he! A lucky thing, you young dog! And what the devil do you mean by it - eh? What d'ye mean, I say!"

Leering, peering, his painted lips pursed up, the little old man seated himself, gazing with dim, restless eyes at the shadowy blur which represented to him his handsome son - a Dysart all through, elegant, debonair, resistless, and, married or single, fatal to feminine peace of mind. Generations ago Dysarts had been shot very conventionally at ten paces owing to this same debonair resistlessness; Dysarts had slipped into and out of all sorts of unsavoury messes on account of this fatal family failing; some had been neatly winged, some thrust through; some, in a more sordid age, permitted counsel of ability to explain to a jury how guiltless a careless gentleman could be under the most unfortunate and extenuating appearances.

The son stood in his wet clothes, haggard, lined, ghastly in contrast to the startling red of his lips, looking at his smirking father: then he leaned over and touched a bell.

"Who was it who called on Mrs. Dysart?" he asked, as a servant appeared.

"Miss Quest, sir," said the man, accepting the cue with stolid philosophy.

"Did Miss Quest leave any message?"

"Yes, sir: Miss Quest desired *Mrs.* Dysart to telephone her on *Mrs.* Dysart's return from - the country, sir - it being a matter of very great importance."

"Thank you."

"Thank *you*, sir."

The servant withdrew; the son stood gazing into the hallway. Behind him his father mumbled and muttered and chuckled to himself in his easy-chair by the fire!

"Te-he! They are all alike, the Dysarts - oh, yes, all alike! And now it's that young dog - Jack! - te-he! - yes, it's Jack, now! But he's a good son, my boy Jack; he's a good son to me and he's all Dysart, all Dysart; bon chien chasse de race! - te-he! Oui, ma fois! - bon chien chasse de race."

CHAPTER XIX

QUESTIONS AND ANSWERS

By the first of January it became plain that there was not very much left of Colonel Mallett's fortune, less of his business reputation, and even less of his wife's health. But she was now able to travel, and toward the middle of the month she sailed with Naida and one maid for Naples, leaving her son to gather up and straighten out what little of value still remained in the wreckage of the house of Mallett. What he cared most about was to straighten out his father's personal reputation; and this was possible only as far as it concerned Colonel Mallett's individual honesty. But the rehabilitation was accomplished at the expense of his father's reputation for business intelligence; and New York never really excuses such things.

Not much remained after the amounts due every creditor had been checked up and provided for; and it took practically all Duane had, almost all Naida had, and also the sacrifice of the town house and country villa to properly protect those who had suffered. Part of his mother's estate remained intact, enough to permit her and her daughter to live by practising those inconsequential economies, the necessity for which fills Europe with about the only sort of Americans cultivated foreigners can tolerate, and for which predatory Europeans have no use whatever.

As for Duane, matters were now in such shape that he found it possible to rent a studio with adjoining bath and bedroom - an installation which, at one time, was more than he expected to be able to afford.

The loss of that luxury, which custom had made a necessity, filled his daily life full of trifling annoyances and surprises which were often unpleasant and sometimes humorous; but the new and arid order of things kept him so busy that he had little time for the apathy, bitterness, or self-commiseration which, in linked sequence, usually follow sudden disaster.

Sooner or later it was inevitable that he must feel more keenly the death of a father who, until in the shadow of impending disaster, had never offered him a very close intimacy. Their relations had been merely warm and pleasant - an easy camaraderie between friends - neither questioned the other's rights to reticence and privacy. Their mutual silence concerning business pursuits was instinctive; neither father nor son understood the other's affairs, nor were they interested except in the success of a good comrade.

It was inevitable that, in years to come, the realisation of his loss would become keener and deeper; but now, in the reaction from shock, and in the anxiety and stress and dire necessity for activity, only the surface sorrow was understood - the pity of it, the distressing circumstances surrounding the death of a good father, a good friend, and a personally upright man.

The funeral was private; only the immediate family attended. Duane had written to Geraldine, Kathleen, and Scott not to come, and he had also asked if he might not go to them when the chance arrived.

And now the chance had come at last, in the dead of winter; but the prospect of escape to Geraldine brightened the whole world for him and gilded the snowy streets of the city with that magic radiance no flaming planet ever cast.

He had already shipped a crate of canvases to Roya-Neh; his trunk had gone, and now, checking with an amused shrug a natural impulse to hail a cab, he swung his suit-case and himself aboard a car, bound for the Patroons Club, where he meant to lunch before taking the train for Roya-Neh.

He had not been to the club since the catastrophe and his father's death, and he was very serious and sombre and slightly embarrassed when he entered.

A servant took his coat and suit-case with marked but subdued respect. Men whom he knew and some men whom he scarcely knew at all made it a point to speak to him or bow to him with a cordiality too pointed not to affect him, because in it he recognised the acceptance of what he had fought for - the verdict that publicly exonerated his father from anything worse than a bad but honest mistake.

For a second or two he stood in the great marble rotunda looking around him. In that club familiar figures were lacking - men whose social and financial position only a few months before seemed impregnable, men who had gone down in ruin, one or two who had perished by their own hand, several whose physical and financial stamina had been shattered at the same terrible moment. Some were ill, some dead, some had resigned, others had been forced to write their resignations - such men as Dysart for example, and James Skelton, now in prison, unable to furnish bail.

But the Patroons was a club of men above the average; a number among them even belonged to the Pyramid; and the financial disasters of that summer and winter had spared no club in the five boroughs and no membership list had been immune from the sinister consequences of a crash that had resounded from ocean to ocean and had set humble and great scurrying to cover in every Bourse of the civilised world.

* * * * *

As he entered the dining-room and passed to his usual table, he caught sight of Delancy Grandcourt lunching alone at the table directly behind him.

"Hello, Delancy," he said; "shall we join forces?"

"I'd be glad to; it's very kind of you, Duane," replied Grandcourt, showing his pleasure at the proposal in the direct honesty of his response. Few men considered it worth while to cultivate Grandcourt. To lunch with him was a bore; a tete-a-tete with him assumed the proportions of a visitation; his slowness and stupidity had become proverbial in that club; and yet almost the only foundation for it had been Dysart's attitude toward him; and men's estimate of him was the more illogical because few men really cared for Dysart's opinions. But Dysart had introduced him, elected him, and somehow had contrived to make the public accept his half-sneering measure of Grandcourt as Grandcourt's true stature. And the man, being shy, reticent, slow to anger, slower still to take his own part, was tolerated and good-humouredly avoided when decently possible. So much for the average man's judgment of an average man.

Seated opposite to Duane, Grandcourt expressed his pleasure at seeing him with a simplicity that touched the other. Then, in perfectly good taste, but with great diffidence, he spoke of Duane's bereavement.

For a little while they asked and answered those amiably formal questions convention requires under similar circumstances; then Duane spoke of Dysart gravely, because new rumours were rife concerning him, even a veiled hint of possible indictment and arrest.

"I hope not," said Grandcourt, his heavy features becoming troubled; "he is a broken man, and no court and jury can punish him more severely than he has been punished. Nor do I know what they could get out of him. He has nothing left; everything he possessed has been turned over. He sits all day in a house that is no longer his, doing nothing, hoping nothing, hearing nothing, except the childish babble of his old father or the voices from the hall below, where his servants are fighting off reporters and cranks and people with grievances. Oh, I tell you, Duane, it's pitiable, all right!"

"There was a rumour yesterday of his suicide," said Duane in a low voice. "I did not credit it."

Grandcourt shook his head: "He never would do that. He totally lacks whatever you call it - cowardice or courage - to do that. It is not like Dysart; it is not in him to do it. He never will, never could. I know him, Duane."

Duane nodded.

Grandcourt spoke again: "He cares for few things; life is one of them. His father, his social position, his harmless - success with women -" Grandcourt hesitated, caught Duane's eye. Both men's features became expressionless.

Duane said: "I had an exceedingly nice note from Rosalie the other day. She has bought one of those double-deck apartments - but I fancy you know about it."

"Yes," said Grandcourt, turning red. "She was good enough to ask my opinion." He added with a laugh: "I shouldn't think anybody would want my opinion after the way I've smashed my own affairs."

Duane smiled, too. "I've heard," he said, "that yours was the decentest smash of the season. What is that scriptural business about - about a man who lays down his fortune for a friend?"

"His *life*," corrected Grandcourt, very red, "but please don't confound what I did with anything of importance to anybody." He lighted a cigar from the burning match offered by Duane, very much embarrassed for a moment, then suddenly brightened up:

"I'm in business now," he observed, with a glance at the other, partly timid, partly of pride. "My father was thoroughly disgusted with me - and nobody blames him - so he bought me a seat and, Duane, do you know that I am doing rather well, considering that nobody is doing anything at all."

Duane laughed heartily, but his mirth did not hurt Grandcourt, who sat smiling and enjoying his cigar, and looking with confidence into a face that was so frankly and unusually friendly.

"You know I always admired you, Duane - even in the days when you never bothered your head about me," he added naively. "Do you remember at school the caricature you drew of me - all hands and feet and face, and absolutely no body? I've got that yet; and I'm very proud to have it when I hear people speak of your artistic success. Some day, if I ever have any money again, I'll ask you to paint a better portrait of me, if you have time."

They laughed again over this mild pleasantry; a cordial understanding was developing between them, which meant much to Grandcourt, for he was a lonely man and his shyness had always deprived him of what he most cared for - what really might have been his only resource - the friendship of other men.

For some time, while they were talking, Duane had noticed out of the corner of his eye another man at a neighbouring table - a thin, pop-eyed, hollow-chested, unhealthy young fellow, who, at intervals, stared insolently at Grandcourt, and once or twice contrived to knock over his glass of whiskey while reaching unsteadily for a fresh cigarette.

The man was Stuyvesant Quest, drunk as usual, and evidently in an unpleasant mood.

Grandcourt's back was toward him; Duane paid him no particular attention, though at moments he noticed him scowling in their direction and seemed to hear him fussing and muttering over his whiskey and soda, which, with cigarettes, comprised his luncheon.

"I wish I were going up to Roya-Neh with you," repeated Grandcourt. "I had a bully time up there - everybody was unusually nice to me, and I had a fine time."

"I know they'll ask you up whenever you can get away," said Duane. "Geraldine Seagrave likes you immensely."

"Does she?" exclaimed Grandcourt, blushing. "I'd rather believe that than almost anything! She was very, very kind to me, I can tell you; and Lord knows why, because I've nothing intellectual to offer anybody, and I certainly am not pretty!"

Duane, very much amused, looked at his watch.

"When does your train leave?" asked Grandcourt.

"I've an hour yet."

"Come up to my room and smoke. I've better whiskey than we dispense down here. I'm living at the club, you know. They haven't yet got over my fiasco at home and I can't stand their joshing."

Neither of the men noticed that a third man followed them, stumbling up the stairs as they took the elevator. Duane was seated in an easy chair by the fire, Grandcourt in another, the decanter stood on a low table between them, when, without formality, the door opened and young Quest appeared on the threshold, white, self-assertive, and aggressively at his ease:

"If you fellows don't mind, I'll butt in a moment," he said. "How are you, Mallett? How are you?" giving Grandcourt an impertinent look; and added: "Do you, by any chance, expect your friend Dysart in here this afternoon?"

"Dysart is no longer a member of this club," said Grandcourt quietly. "I've told you that a dozen times."

"All right, I'll ask you two dozen times more, if I choose," retorted Quest. "Why not?" And he gave him an ugly stare.

The man was just drunk enough to be quarrelsome. Duane paid him no further attention; Grandcourt asked him very civilly if he could do anything for him.

"Sure," sneered Quest. "You can tell Dysart that if I ever come across him I'll shoot him on sight! Tell him that and be damned!"

"I've already told him that," said Grandcourt with a shrug of contempt.

The weak, vicious face of the other reddened:

"What do you mean by taking that tone with me?" he demanded loudly. "Do you think I won't make good?" He fumbled around in his clothing for a moment and presently jerked a pistol free - one of the automatic kind with rubber butt and blued barrel.

"Unless you are drunker than I've ever seen you," said Grandcourt, "you'll put up that pistol before I do."

Quest cursed him steadily for a minute: "Do you think I haven't got the nerve to use it when m' honour's 'volved? I tell you," he said thickly, "when m' honour's 'volved -"

"You get drunk, don't you?" observed Duane. "What a pitiful pup you are, anyway. Go to bed."

Quest stood swaying slightly on his heels and considering Duane with the inquiring solemnity of one who is in process of grasping and digesting an abstruse proposition.

"B-bed?" he repeated; "me?"

"Certainly. A member of this club disgracefully drunk in the afternoon will certainly hear from the governing board unless he keeps out of sight until he's sane again."

"Thank you," said Quest with owlish condescension; "I'm indebted to you for calling 'tention to m-matters which 'volve honour of m' own club and -"

His voice rambled off into a mutter; he sat or rather fell into an armchair and lay there twitching and mumbling to himself and inspecting his automatic pistol with prominent watery eyes.

"You'd better leave that squirt-gun with me," said Grandcourt.

Quest refused with an oath, and, leaning forward and hammering the padded chair-arm with his unhealthy looking fist, he broke out into a violent arraignment of Dysart:

"Damn him!" he yelled, "I've written him, I've asked for an explanation, I've 'm-manded t' know why his name's coupled with my sister's -"

Duane leaned over, slammed the door, and turned short on Quest:

"Shut up!" he said sharply. "Do you hear! Shut up!"

"No, I won't shut up! I'll say what I damn please -"

"Haven't you any decency at all -"

"I've enough to fix Dysart good and plenty, and I'll do it! I'll - let go of me, Mallett! - let go, I tell you or -"

Duane jerked the pistol from his shaky fingers, and when Quest struggled to his feet with a baffled howl, jammed him back into the chair again and handed the pistol to Grandcourt, who locked it in a bureau drawer and pocketed the key.

"You belong in Matteawan," said the latter, flinging Quest back into the chair again as the infuriated man still struggled to rise. "You miserable drunken kid - do you think you would be enhancing your sister's reputation by dragging her name into a murder trial? What are you, anyway? By God, if I didn't know your sister as a thoroughbred, I'd have you posted here for a mongrel and sent packing. The pound is your proper place, not a club-house"; which was an astonishing speech for Delancy Grandcourt.

Again, half contemptuously, but with something almost vicious in his violence, Grandcourt slammed young Quest back into the chair from which he had attempted to hurl himself: "Keep quiet," he said; "you're a particularly vile little wretch, particularly pitiable; but your sister is a girl of gentle breeding - a sweet, charming, sincere young girl whom everybody admires and respects. If you are anything but a gutter-mut, you'll respect her, too, and the only way you can do it is by shutting that unsanitary whiskey-trap of yours - and keeping it shut - and by remaining as far away from her as you can, permanently."

There were one or two more encounters, brief ones; then Quest collapsed and began to cry. He was shaking, too, all over, apparently on the verge of some alcoholic crisis.

Grandcourt went over to Duane:

"The man is sick, helplessly sick in mind and body. If you'll telephone Bailey at the Knickerbocker Hospital, he'll send an ambulance and I'll go up there with this fool boy. He's been like this before. Bailey knows what to do. Telephone from the station; I don't want the club servants to gossip any more than is necessary. Do you mind doing it?"

"Of course not," said Duane. He glanced at the miserable, snivelling, twitching creature by the fire: "Do you think he'll get over this, or will he buy another pistol the next time he gets the jumps?"

Grandcourt looked troubled:

"I don't know what this breed is likely to do. He's absolutely no good. He's the only person in the world that is left of the family - except his sister. He's all she has had to look out for her - a fine legacy, a fine prop for her to lean on. That's the sort of protection she has had all her life; that's the example set her in her own home. I don't know what she's done; it's none of my business; but, Duane, I'm for her!"

"So am I."

They stood together in silence for a moment; maudlin sniffles of self-pity arose from the corner by the fire, alternating with more hysterical and more ominous sounds presaging some spasmodic crisis.

Grandcourt said: "Bunny Gray has helped me kennel this pup once or twice. He's in the club; I think I'll send for him."

"You'll need help," nodded Duane. "I'll call up the hospital on my way to the station. Good-bye, Delancy."

They shook hands and parted.

At the station Duane telephoned to the hospital, got Dr. Bailey, arranged for a room in a private ward, and had barely time to catch his train - in fact, he was in such a hurry that he passed by without seeing the sister of the very man for whom he had been making such significant arrangements.

She wore, as usual, her pretty chinchilla furs, but was so closely veiled that he might not have recognised her under any circumstances. She, however, forgetting that she was veiled, remained uncertain as to whether his failure to speak to her had been intentional or otherwise. She had halted, expecting him to speak; now she passed on, cheeks burning, a faint sinking sensation in her heart.

For she cared a great deal about Duane's friendship; and she was very unhappy, and morbid and more easily wounded than ever, because somehow it had come to her ears that rumour was busily hinting things unthinkable concerning her - nothing definite; yet the very vagueness of it added to her distress and horror.

Around her silly head trouble was accumulating very fast since Jack Dysart had come sauntering into her youthful isolation; and in the beginning it had been what it usually is to lonely hearts - shy and grateful recognition of a friendship that flattered; fascination, an infatuation, innocent enough, until the man in the combination awoke her to the terrors of stranger emotions involving her deeper and deeper until she lost her head, and he, for the first time in all his career, lost his coolly selfish caution.

How any rumours concerning herself and him had arisen nobody could explain. There never is any explanation. But they always arise.

In their small but pretty house, terrible scenes had already occurred between her and her brother - consternation, anger, and passionate denial on her part; on his, fury, threats, maudlin paroxysms of self-pity, and every attitude that drink and utter demoralisation can distort into a parody on what a brother might say and do.

To escape it she had gone to Tuxedo for a week; now, fear and foreboding had brought her back - fear intensified at the very threshold of the city when Duane seemed to look straight at her and pass her by without recognition. Men don't do that, but she was too inexperienced to know it; and she hastened on with a heavy heart, found a taxi-cab to take her to the only home she had ever known, descended, and rang for admittance.

In these miserable days she had come to look for hidden meaning even in the expressionless faces of her trained servants, and now she misconstrued the respectful smile of welcome, brushed hastily past the maid who admitted her, and ran upstairs.

Except for the servants she was alone. She rang for information concerning her brother; nobody had any. He had not been home in a week.

Her toilet, after the journey, took her two hours or more to accomplish; it was dark at five o'clock and snowing heavily when tea was served. She tasted it, then, unable to subdue her restlessness, went to the telephone; and after a long delay, heard the voice she tremblingly expected:

“Is that you, Jack?” she asked.

“Yes.”

“H-how are you?”

“Not very well.”

“Have you heard anything new about certain proceedings?” she inquired tremulously.

“Yes; she's begun them.”

“On - on w-what grounds?”

“Not on any grounds to scare you. It will be a Western matter.”

Her frightened sigh of relief turned her voice to a whisper:

“Has Stuyve - has a certain relative - annoyed you since I've been away?”

“Yes, over the telephone, drunk, as usual.”

"Did he make - make any more threats, Jack?"

"The usual string. Where is he?"

"I don't know," she said; "he hasn't been home in a week, they tell me. Jack, do you think it safe for you to drop in here for a few moments before dinner?"

"Just as you say. If he comes in, there may be trouble. Which isn't a good idea, on your account."

No woman in such circumstances is moved very much by an appeal to her caution.

"But I want to see you, Jack," she said miserably.

"That seems to be the only instinct that governs you," he retorted, slightly impatient. "Can't you ever learn the elements of prudence? It seems to me about time that you substituted common sense for immature impulse in dealing with present problems."

His voice was cold, emotionless, unpleasant. She stood with the receiver at her ears, flushing to the tips of them under his rebuke. She always did; she had known many, recently, but the quick pang of pain was never any less keen. On the contrary.

"Don't you want to see me? I have been away for ten days."

"Yes, I want to see you, of course, but I'm not anxious to spring a mine under myself - under us both by going into your house at this time."

"My brother has not been here in a week."

"Does that accidental fact bar his possible appearance ten minutes from now?"

She wondered, vaguely, whether he was afraid of anything

except possible damage to her reputation. She had, lately, considered this question on several occasions. Being no coward, as far as mere fear for her life was concerned, she found it difficult to attribute such fear to him. Indeed, one of the traits in her which he found inexplicable and which he disliked was a curious fearlessness of death - not uncommon among women who, all their lives, have had little to live for.

She said: "If I am not worth a little risk, what is my value to you?"

"You talk like a baby," he retorted. "Is an interview worth risking a scandal that will spatter the whole town?"

"I never count such risks," she said wearily. "Do as you please."

His voice became angry: "Haven't I enough to face already without hunting more trouble at present? I supposed I could look to you for sympathy and aid and common sense, and every day you call me up and demand that I shall drop everything and fling caution to the winds, and meet you somewhere! Every day of the year you do it -"

"I have been away ten days -" she faltered, turning sick and white at the words he was shouting through the telephone.

"Well, it was understood you'd stay for a month, wasn't it? Can't you give me time to turn around? Can't you give me half a chance? Do you realise what I'm facing? *Do* you?"

"Yes. I'm sorry I called you; I was so miserable and lonely -"

"Well, try to think of somebody besides yourself. You're not the only miserable person in this city. I've all the misery I can carry at present; and if you wish to help me, don't make any demands on me until I'm clear of the tangle that's choking me."

"Dear, I only wanted to help you -" she stammered, appalled

at his tone and words.

"All right, then, let me alone!" he snarled, losing all self-command. "I've stood about all of this I'm going to, from you and your brother both! Is that plain? I want to be let alone. That is plainer still, isn't it?"

"Yes," she said. Her face had become deathly white; she stood frozen, motionless, clutching the receiver in her small hand.

His voice altered as he spoke again:

"Don't feel hurt; I lost my temper and I ask your pardon. But I'm half crazy with worry - you've seen to-day's papers, I suppose - so you can understand a man's losing his temper. Please forgive me; I'll try to see you when I can - when it's advisable. Does that satisfy you?"

"Yes," she said in a dull voice.

She put away the receiver and, turning, dropped onto her bed. At eight o'clock the maid who had come to announce dinner found her young mistress lying there, clenched hands over her eyes, lying slim and rigid on her back in the darkness.

When the electric lamps were lighted she rose, went to the mirror and looked steadily at herself for a long, long time.

* * * * *

She tasted what was offered, seeing nothing, hearing nothing; later, in her room, a servant came saying that Mr. Gray begged a moment's interview on a matter of importance connected with her brother.

It was the only thing that could have moved her to see him. She had denied herself to him all that winter; she had been obliged to make it plainer after a letter from him - a nice, stupid, boyish letter, asking her to marry him. And her reply terminated the attempts of Bunbury Gray to secure a hearing from the girl who had apparently taken so sudden and so strange an aversion to a man who had been nice to her all her life.

They had, at one time, been virtually engaged, after Geraldine Seagrave had cut him loose, and before Dysart took the trouble to seriously notice her. But Bunny was youthful and frisky and his tastes were catholic, and it did not seem to make much difference that Dysart again stepped casually between them in his graceful way. Yet, curiously enough, each preserved for the other a shy sort of admiration which, until last autumn, had made their somewhat infrequent encounters exceedingly interesting. Autumn had altered their attitudes; Bunny became serious in proportion to the distance she put between them - which is of course the usual incentive to masculine importunity. They had had one or two little scenes at Roya-Neh; the girl even hesitated, unquietly curious, perplexed at her own attitude, yet diffidently interested in the man.

A straw was all that her balance required to incline it; Dysart dropped it, casually. And there were no more pretty scenes between Bunny Gray and his lady-love that autumn, only sulks from the youth, and, after many attempts to secure a hearing, a very direct and honest letter that winter, which had resulted in his dismissal.

* * * * *

She came down to the drawing-room, looking the spectre of herself, but her stillness and self-possession kept Bunny at his distance, staring, restless, amazed - all of which very evident symptoms and emotions she ignored.

“I have your message,” she said. “Has anything happened to my brother?”

He began: “You mustn't be alarmed, but he is not very well -”

"I am alarmed. Where is he?"

"In the Knickerbocker Hospital."

"Seriously ill?"

"No. He is in a private ward -"

"The - alcoholic?" she asked quietly.

"Yes," he said, flushing with the shame that had not burnt her white face.

"May I go to him?" she asked.

"No!" he exclaimed, horrified.

She seated herself, hands folded loosely on her lap:

"What am I to do, Bunny?"

"Nothing.... I only came to tell you so that you'd know. To-morrow if you care to telephone Bailey -"

"Yes; thank you." She closed her eyes; opened them with an effort.

"If you'll let me, Sylvia, I'll keep you informed," he ventured.

"Would you? I'd be very glad."

"Sure thing!" he said with great animation; "I'll go to the hospital as many times a day as I am allowed, and I'll bring you back a full account of Stuyve's progress after every visit.... May I, Sylvie?"

She said nothing. He sat looking at her. He had no great amount ofintellect, but he possessed an undue proportion of heart under the somewhat striking waistcoats which at all times characterised his attire.

"I'm terribly sorry for you," he said, his eyes very wide and round.

She gazed into space, past him.

"Do you - would you prefer to have me go?" he stammered.

There was no reply.

"Because," he said miserably, "I take it that you haven't much use for me."

No word from her.

"Sylvie?"

Silence; but she looked up at him. "I haven't changed," he said, and the healthy colour turned him pink. "I - just - wanted you to know. I thought perhaps you might like to know -"

"Why?" Her voice was utterly unlike her own.

"Why?" he repeated, getting redder. "I don't know - I only thought you might - it might - amuse you - to know that I haven't changed -"

"As others have? Is that what you mean, Bunny?"

"No, no, I didn't think - I didn't mean -"

"Yes, you did. Why not say it to me? You mean that you, and others, have heard rumours. You mean that you, unlike others, are trying to make me understand that you are still loyal to me. Is that it?"

"Y-yes. Good Lord! Loyal! Why, of course I am. Why, you

didn't suppose I'd be anything else, did you?"

She opened her pallid lips to speak and could not.

"Loyal!" he repeated indignantly. "There's no merit in that when a man's been in love with a girl all his life and didn't know it until she'd got good and tired of him! You know I'm for you every time, Sylvia; what's the game in pretending you didn't know it?"

"No game.... I didn't - know it."

"Well, you do now, don't you?"

Her face was colourless as marble. She said, looking at him: "Suppose the rumour is true?"

His face flamed: "You don't know what you are saying!" he retorted, horrified.

"Suppose it is true?"

"Sylvia - for Heaven's sake -"

"Suppose it *is* true," she repeated in a dead, even voice; "how loyal would you remain to me then?"

"As loyal as I am now!" he answered angrily, "if you insist on my answering such a silly question -"

"Is that your answer?"

"Certainly. But -"

"Are you *sure*?"

He glared at her; something struck coldly through him, checking breath and pulse, then releasing both till the heavy beating of his heart made speech impossible.

"I thought you were not sure," she said.

"I *am* sure!" he broke out. "Good God, Sylvia, what are you doing to me?"

"Destroying your faith in me."

"You can't! I love you!"

She gave a little gasp:

"The rumour *is* true," she said.

He reeled to his feet; she sat looking up at him, white, silent hands twisted on her lap.

"Now you know," she managed to say. "Why don't you go? If you've any self-respect, you'll go. I've told you what I am; do you want me to speak more plainly?"

"Yes," he said between his teeth.

"Very well; what do you wish to know?"

"Only one thing.... Do you - care for him?"

She sat, minute after minute, head bent, thinking, thinking. He never moved a muscle; and at last she lifted her head.

"No," she said.

"Could you care for - me?"

She made a gesture as though to check him, half rose, fell back, sat swaying a moment, and suddenly tumbled over sideways, lying a white heap on the rug at his feet.

CHAPTER XX

IN SEARCH OF HERSELF

As his train slowed down through the darkness and stopped at the snow-choked station, Duane, carrying suit-case, satchel, and fur coat, swung himself off the icy steps of the smoker and stood for a moment on the platform in the yellow glare of the railway lanterns, looking about him.

Sleigh-bells sounded near - chiming through the still, cold air; he caught sight of two shadowy restive horses, a gaily plumed sleigh, and, at the same moment, the driver leaned sideways from her buffalo-robed seat, calling out to him by name.

"Why, Kathleen!" he exclaimed, hastening forward. "Did you really drive down here all alone to meet me?"

She bent over and saluted him, demure, amused, bewitchingly pretty in her Isabella bear furs:

"I really did, Duane, without even a groom, so we could talk about everything and anything all the way home. Give your checks to the station agent - there he is! - Oh, Mr. Whitley, would you mind sending up Mr. Mallett's trunks to-night? Thank you *so* much. Now, Duane, dear -"

He tossed suit-case and satchel into the sleigh, put on his fur coat, and climbing up beside Kathleen, burrowed into the robes.

"I tell you what," he said seriously, "you're getting to be a howling beauty; not just an ordinary beauty, but a miracle. Do you mind if I kiss you again?"

"Not after that," she said, presenting him a fresh-curved cheek tinted with rose, and snowy cold. Then, laughing, she swung the impatient horses to the left; a jingling shower of golden bell-notes followed; and they were off through the starlight, tearing northward across the snow.

"Duane!" she said, pulling the young horses down into a swift, swinging trot, "*what* do you think! Geraldine doesn't know you're coming!"

"Why not?" he asked, surprised. "I telegraphed."

"Yes, but she's been on the mountain with old Miller for three days. Three of your letters are waiting for her; and then came your telegram, and of course Scott and I thought we ought to open it."

"Of course. But what on earth sent Geraldine up the Golden Dome in the dead of winter?"

Kathleen shook her pretty head:

"She's turned into the most uncontrollable sporting proposition you ever heard of! She's up there at Lynx Peak camp, with her rifle, and old Miller. They're after that big boar - the biggest, horridest thing in the whole forest. I saw him once. He's disgusting. Scott objected, and so did I, but, somehow, I'm becoming reconciled to these break-neck enterprises she goes in for so hard - so terribly hard, Duane! and all I do is to fuss a little and make a few tearful objections, and she laughs and does what she pleases."

He said: "It is better, is it not, to let her?"

"Yes," returned Kathleen quietly, "it is better. That is why I say very little."

There was a moment's silence, but the constraint did not last.

"It's twenty below zero, my poor friend," observed Kathleen. "Luckily, there is no wind to-night, but, all the same, you ought to keep in touch with your nose and ears."

Duane investigated cautiously.

"My features are still sticking to my face," he announced; "is it really twenty below? It doesn't seem so."

"It is. Yesterday the thermometers registered thirty below, but nobody here minds it when the wind doesn't blow; and Geraldine has acquired the most exquisite colour! - and she's so maddeningly pretty, Duane, and actually plump, in that long slim way of hers.... And there's another thing; she is *happier* than she has been for a long, long while."

"Has that fact any particular significance to you?" he asked slowly.

"Vital!... Do you understand me, Duane, dear?"

"Yes."

A moment later she called in her clear voice: "Gate, please!" A lantern flashed; a door opened in the lodge; there came a crunch of snow, a creak, and the gates of Roya-Neh swung wide in the starlight.

Kathleen nodded her thanks to the keeper, let the whip whistle, and spent several minutes in consequence recovering control of the fiery young horses who were racing like scared deer. The road was wide, crossed here and there by snowy "rides," and bordered by the splendid Roya-Neh forests; wide enough to admit a white glow from myriads of stars. Never had Duane seen so many stars swarming in the heavens; the winter constellations were magnificent, their diamond-like lustre silvered the world.

“I suppose you want to hear all the news, all the gossip, from three snow-bound rustics, don't you?” she asked. “Well, then, let me immediately report a most overwhelming tragedy. Scott has just discovered that several inconsiderate entomologists, who died before he was born, all wrote elaborate life histories of the Rose-beetle. Isn't it pathetic? And he's worked *so* hard, and he's been like a father to the horrid young grubs, feeding them nice juicy roots, taking their weights and measures, photographing them, counting their degraded internal organs - oh, it is too vexing! Because, if you should ask me, I may say that I've been a mother to them, too, and it enrages me to find out that all those wretched, squirming, thankless creatures have been petted and studied and have had their legs counted and their Bertillon measurements taken years before either Scott or I came into this old fraud of a scientific world!”

Duane's unrestrained laughter excited her merriment; the star-lit woodlands rang with it and the treble chiming of the sleigh-bells.

“What on earth will he find to do now?” asked Duane.

“He's going to see it through, he says. Isn't it fine of him? There is just a bare chance that he may discover something that those prying entomological people overlooked. Anyway, we are going to devote next summer to studying the parasites of the Rose-beetle, and try to find out what sort of creatures prey upon them. And I want to tell you something exciting, Duane. Promise you won't breathe one word!”

“Not a word!”

“Well, then - Scott was going to tell you, anyway! - we *think* but, of course, we are not sure by any means! - but we venture to think that we have discovered a disease which kills Rose-beetles. We don't know exactly what it is yet, or how they get it, but we are practically convinced that it is a sort of fungus."

She was very serious, very earnest, charming in her conscientious imitation of that scientific caution which abhors speculation and never dares assert anything except dry and proven facts.

"What are you and Scott aiming at? Are you going to try to start an epidemic among the Rose-beetles?" he inquired.

"Oh, it's far too early to even outline our ideas -"

"That's right; don't tell anything Scott wants to keep quiet about! I'll never say a word, Kathleen, only if you'll take my advice, feed 'em fungus! Stuff 'em with it three times a day - give it to them boiled, fried, au gratin, a la Newburg! That'll fetch 'em!... How is old Scott, anyway?"

"Perfectly well," she said demurely. "He informs us daily that he weighs one hundred and ninety pounds, and stands six feet two in his snow-shoes. He always mentions it when he tells us that he is going to scrub your face in a snow-drift, and Geraldine invariably insists that he isn't man enough. You know, as a matter of fact, we're all behaving like very silly children up here. Goodness knows what the servants think." Her smiling face became graver.

"I am so glad that matters are settled and that there's enough of your estate left to keep your mother and Naida in comfort."

He nodded. "How is Scott coming out?"

"Why - he'll tell you. I don't believe he has very much left. Geraldine's part is sufficient to run Roya-Neh, and the house in town, if she and Scott conclude to keep it. Old Mr. Tappan has been quite wonderful. Why, Duane, he's a perfect old dear; and we all are so terribly contrite and so anxious to make amends for our horrid attitude toward him when he ruled us with an iron rod."

"He's a funny old duck," mused Duane. "That son of his, Peter, has had the 'indiwidool cultiwated' clean out of him. He's only a type, like Gibson's drawings of Tag's son. Old Tappan may be as honest as a block of granite, but it's an awful thing that he should ever have presided over the destinies of children."

Kathleen sighed. "According to his light he was faithful. I know that his system was almost impossible; I had to live and see my children driven into themselves until they were becoming too self-centred to care for anything else - to realise that there was anything else or anybody else except their wishes and themselves to consider.... But, Duane, you see the right quality was latent in them. They are coming out - they have emerged splendidly. It has altered their lives fundamentally, of course, but, sometimes, I wonder whether, in their particular cases, it was not better to cripple the easy, irresponsible, and delightfully casual social instincts of the House of Seagrave. Educated according to my own ideas, they must inevitably have become, in a measure, types of the set with which they are identified.... And the only serious flaw in the Seagraves was - weakness."

Duane nodded, looking ahead into the star-illumined night.

"I don't know. Tappan's poison may have been the antidote for them in this case. Tell me, Kathleen, has Geraldine - suffered?"

"Yes."

"Very - much?"

"Very much, Duane. Has she said nothing about it to you in her letters?"

"Nothing since she went to town that time. Every letter flies the red cross. Does she still suffer?"

"I don't think so. She seems so wonderfully happy - so vigorous, in such superb physical condition. For a month I have not seen that pitiful, haunted expression come into her eyes. And it is not mere restlessness that drives her into perpetual motion now; it's a new delight in living hard and with all her might every moment of the day!... She overdoes it; you will turn her energy into other channels. She's ready for you, I think."

They drove on in silence for a few minutes, then swung into a broader avenue of pines. Straight ahead glimmered the lights of Roya-Neh.

Duane said naively: "I don't suppose I could get up to Lynx Peak camp to-night, could I?"

Kathleen threw back her head, making no effort to control her laughter.

"It isn't necessary," she managed to explain; "I sent a messenger up the mountain with a note to her saying that matters of importance required her immediate return. She'll come down to-night by sleigh from The Green Pass and Westgate Centre."

"Won't she be furious?" he inquired, with a hypocritical side glance at Kathleen, who laughed derisively and drew in the horses under the porte-cochere. A groom took their heads; Duane swung Kathleen clear to the steps just as Scott Seagrave, hearing sleigh-bells, came out, bareheaded, his dinner-jacket wide open, as though he luxuriated in the bitter air.

"Good work!" he said. "How are you, Duane? Geraldine arrived from The Green Pass about five minutes ago. She thinks you're sleighing, Kathleen, and she's tremendously curious to know why you want her."

"She probably suspects," said Kathleen, disappointed.

"No, she doesn't. I began to talk business immediately, and I know she thinks that some of Mr. Tappan's lawyers are coming. So they are - next month," he added with a grin, and, turning on Duane:

"I think I'll begin festivities by washing your face in the snow."

"You're not man enough," remarked the other; and the next moment they had clinched and were swaying and struggling all over the terrace, to the scandal of the servants peering from the door.

"He's tired and half frozen!" exclaimed Kathleen; "what a brute you are to bully him, Scott!"

"I'll include you in a moment," he panted, loosing Duane and snatching a handful of snow. Whereupon she caught up sufficient snow to fill the hollow of her driving glove, powdered his face thoroughly with the feathery flakes, picked up her skirt and ran for it, knowing full well she could expect no mercy.

Duane watched their reckless flight through the hall and upstairs, then walked in, dropped his coat, and advanced across the heavy rugs toward the fireplace.

On the landing above he heard Geraldine's laughter, then silence, then her clear, careless singing as she descended the stairs:

> "Lisetto quittee la plaine,
> Moi perdi bonheur a moi -
> Yeux a moi semblent fontaine
> Depuis moi pas mire toi!"

At the doorway she halted, seeing a man's figure silhouetted against the firelight. Then she moved forward inquiringly, the ruddy glow full in her brown eyes; and a little shock passed straight through her.

"Duane!" she whispered.

He caught her in his arms, kissed her, locked her closer; her arms sought his head, clung, quivered, fell away; and with a nervous movement she twisted clear of him and stood breathing fast, the clamour of her heart almost suffocating her. And when again he would have drawn her to him she eluded him, wide-eyed, flushed, lips parted in the struggle for speech which came at last, brokenly:

"Dear, you must not take me - that way - yet. I am not ready, Duane. You must give me time!"

"Time! Is anything - has anything gone wrong?"

"No - oh, no, no, no! Don't you understand I must take my own time? I've won the right to it; I'm winning out, Duane - winning back myself. I must have my little year of self-respect. Oh, *can't* you understand that you mustn't sweep me off my feet this way? - that I'm too proud to go to you - have you take me while there remains the faintest shadow of risk?"

"But I don't care! I want you!" he cried.

"I love you for it; I want you, Duane. But be fair to me; don't take me until I am as clean and straight and untainted as the girl I was - as I am becoming - as I will be - surely, surely - my darling!"

She caught his hands in hers and, close to him, looked into his eyes smilingly, tearfully, and a little proudly. The sensitive under-lip quivered; but she held her head high.

"Don't ask me to give you what is less perfect than I can make it. Don't let me remember my gift and be ashamed, dear. There must be no memory of your mistaken generosity to trouble me in the years to come - the long, splendid years with you. Let me always remember that I gave you myself as I really can be; let me always know that neither your love nor compassion were needed to overlook any flaw in what I give."

She bent her proud little head and laid her lips on his hands, which she held close between her own.

"You can so easily carry me by storm, Duane; and in your arms I might be weak enough to waver and forget and promise to give you now what there is of me if you demanded it. Don't ask it; don't carry me out of my depth. There is more to me than I can give you yet. Let me wait to give it lest I remember your unfairness and my humiliation through the years to come."

She lifted her lips to his, offering them; he kissed her; then, with a little laugh, she abandoned his hands and stepped back, mocking, tormenting, enjoying his discomfiture.

"It's cruel, isn't it, you poor lamb! But do you know the year is already flying very, very fast? Do you think I'm not counting the days?" - and, suddenly yielding - "if you wish - if you truly do wish it, dear, I will marry you on the very day that the year - my year - ends. Come over here" - she seated herself and made a place for him - "and you won't caress me too much - will you? You wouldn't make me unhappy, would you?... Why, yes, I suppose that I might let you touch me occasionally.... And kiss me - at rare intervals.... But not - as we have.... You won't, will you? Then you may sit here - a little nearer if you think it wise - and I'm ready to listen to your views concerning anything on earth, Duane, even including love and wedlock."

It was very hard for them to judge just what they might or might not permit each other - how near it was perfectly safe to sit, how long they might, with impunity, look into each other's eyes in that odd and rather silly fashion which never seems to be out of date.

What worried him was the notion that if she would only marry him at once her safety was secured beyond question; but she explained very sweetly that her safety was almost secured already; that, if let alone, she was at present in absolute command of her fate, mistress of her desires, in full tide of self-control. Now all she required was an interval to develop character and self-mastery, so that they could meet on even ground and equal terms when the day arrived for her to surrender to him the soul and body she had regained.

"I suppose it's all right," he said with a sigh, but utterly unconvinced. "You always were fair about things, and if it's your idea of justice to me and to yourself, that settles it."

"You dear old stupid!" she said, tenderly amused; "it is the best thing for our future. The 'sphere of influence' and the 'balance of power' are as delicate matters to adjust in marriage as they are in world-politics. You're going to be too famous a painter for your wife to be anything less than a thorough woman."

She drew a little away from him, bent her head and clasped both hands around her knee.

"There is another reason why I should be in autocratic command over myself when we marry.... It is difficult for me to explain to you.... Do you remember that I wrote you once that I was - afraid to marry you - *not* for our own sakes?"

Her young face was grave and serious; she bent her gaze on her ringlessfingers.

"That," she said, "is the most vital and - sacred reason of all."

"Yes, dear." He did not dare to touch her, scarcely dared look at the pure, thoughtful profile until she lifted her head and her fearless eyes sought his.

And they smiled, unembarrassed, unafraid.

* * * * *

"Those people are deliberately leaving us here to spoon," she declared indignantly. "I know perfectly well that dinner was announced ages ago!" And, raising her voice: "Scott, you silly ninny! Where in the world are you?"

Scott appeared with alacrity from the library, evidently detained there in hunger and impatience by Kathleen, who came in a moment later, pretty eyes innocently perplexed.

"I declare," she said, "it is nine o'clock and dinner is supposed to be served at eight!" And she seemed more surprised than ever when old Howker, who evidently had been listening off stage, entered with reproachful dignity and announced that ceremony.

And it was the gayest kind of a ceremony, for they ate and chattered and laughed there together as inconsequentially as four children, and when Howker, with pomp and circumstance, brought in a roast boar's head garnished with holly-like crimson elder, they all stood up and cheered as though they really liked the idea of eating it. However, there was, from the same animal, a saddle to follow the jowl, which everybody tasted and only Scott really liked; and, to Duane's uneasy surprise, great silver tankards of delicious home-brewed ale were set at every cover except Geraldine's.

Catching his eye she shrugged slightly and smiled; and her engaging glance returned to him at intervals, reassuring, humorously disdainful; and her serenely amused smile seemed to say:

"My dear fellow, please enjoy your ale. There is not the slightest desire on my part to join you."

"That isn't a very big wild boar," observed Scott, critically eyeing the saddle.

"It's a two-year-old," admitted Geraldine. "I only shot him because Lacy said we were out of meat."

"*you* killed him!" exclaimed Duane.

She gave him a condescending glance; and Scott laughed.

"She and Miller save this establishment from daily famine," he said. "You have no idea how many deer and boar it takes to keep the game within limits and ourselves and domestics decently fed. Just look at the heads up there on the walls." He waved his arm around the oak wainscoting, where, at intervals, the great furry heads of wild boar loomed in the candlelight, ears and mane on end, eyes and white sabre-like tusks gleaming. "Those are Geraldine's," he said with brotherly pride.

"I want to shoot one, too!" said Duane firmly. "Do you think I'm going to let my affianced put it all over me like that?"

"*Isn't* it like a man?" said Geraldine, appealing to Kathleen. "They simply can't endure it if a girl ventures competition -"

"You talk like a suffragette," observed her brother. "Duane doesn't care how many piglings you shoot; he wants to go out alone and get that old grandfather of all boars, the one which kept you on the mountain for the last three days -"

"*My* boar!" she cried indignantly. "I won't have it! I won't let him. Oh, Duane, *am* I a pig to want to manage this affair when I've been after him all winter? - and he's the biggest, grayest, wiliest thing you ever saw - a perfectly enormous silvery fellow with two pairs of Japanese sabre-sheaths for tusks and a mane like a lion, and a double bend in his nose and -"

Shouts of laughter checked her flushed animation.

"Of course I'm not going to sneak out all alone and pot your old pig," said Duane; "I'll find one for myself on some other mountain -"

"But I want you to shoot with me!" she exclaimed in dismay. "I wanted you to see me stalk this boar and mark him down, and have you kill him. Oh, Duane, that was the fun. I've been saving him, I really have. Miller knows that I had a shot once - a pretty good one - and wouldn't take it. I killed a four-year near Hurryon instead, just to save that one -"

"You're the finest little sport in the land!" said Duane, "and we are just tormenting you. Of course I'll go with you, but I'm blessed if I pull trigger on that gentleman pig -"

"You *must*! I've saved him. Scott, make him say he will! Kathleen, this is really too annoying! A girl plans and plans and pictures to herself the happiness and surprise she's going to give a man, and he's too stupid to comprehend -"

"Meaning me!" observed Duane. "But I leave it to you, Scott; a man can't do such a thing decently -"

"Oh, you silly people," laughed Kathleen; "you may never again see that boar. Denman, keeper at Northgate when Mr. Atwood owned the estate, told me that everybody had been after that boar and nobody ever got a shot at him. Which," she added, "does not surprise me, as there are some hundred square miles of mountain and forest on this estate, and Scott is lazy and aging very fast."

"By the way, Sis, you say you got a four-year near The Green Pass?"

She nodded, busy with her bon-bon.

"Was it exciting?" asked Duane, secretly eaten up with pride over her achievements and sportsmanship.

"No, not very." She went on with her bon-bon, then glanced up at her brother, askance, like a bad child afraid of being reported.

"Old Miller is so fussy," she said - "the old, spoilt tyrant! He is really very absurd sometimes."

"Oho!" said Scott suspiciously, "so Miller is coming to me again!"

"He - I'm afraid he is. Did you," appealing to Kathleen, "ever know a more obstinate, unreasoning old man -"

"Geraldine! What did you do!" she exclaimed.

"Yes," said Scott, annoyed, "what the deuce have you been up to now? Miller is perfectly right; he's an old hunter and knows his business, and when he comes to me and complains that you take fool risks, he's doing his duty!"

He turned to Duane:

"That idiot girl," he said, nodding toward his abashed sister, "knocked over a boar last month, ran up to look at his tusks, and was hurled into a snowdrift by the beast, who was only creased. He went for Miller, too, and how he and my sister ever escaped without a terrible slashing before Geraldine shot the brute, nobody knows.... There's his head up there - the wicked-looking one over the fireplace."

"That's not good sportsmanship," said Duane gravely.

Geraldine hung her head, colouring.

"I know it; I mean to keep cool; truly, I do. But things happen so quickly -"

"Why are you afraid Miller is going to complain?" interrupted her brother.

"Scott - it wasn't anything very much - that is, I didn't think so. You'd have done it - you know it's a point of honour to track down wounded game."

She turned to Duane:

"The Green Pass feeding-ground was about a thousand yards ahead in the alders, and I made Miller wait while I crept up. There was a fine boar feeding about two hundred yards off, and I fired and he went over like a cat in a fit, and then up and off, and I after him, and Miller after me, telling me to look out."

She laughed excitedly, and made a little gesture. "That's just why I ran - to look out! - and the trail was deep and strong and not much blood-dust. I was so vexed, so distressed, because it was almost sunset and the boar seemed to be going strongly and faster than a grayhound. And suddenly Miller shouted something about 'scrub hemlock' - I didn't know he meant for me to halt! - So I - I" - she looked anxiously at her brother - "I jumped into the scrub and kicked him up before I knew it - and he - he tore my kilts - just one or two tears, but it didn't wound me, Scott, it only just made my leg black and blue - and, anyway, I got him -"

"Oh, Lord," groaned her brother, "don't you know enough to reconnoitre a wounded boar in the scrub? *I* don't know why he didn't rip you. Do you want to be killed by a *pig*? What's the use of being all cut and bitten to pieces, anyway?"

"No use, dear," she admitted so meekly that Duane scarcely managed to retain his gravity.

She came over and humbly slipped her arm through his as they all rose from the table.

"Don't think I'm a perfect idiot," she said under her breath; "it's only inexperience under excitement. You'll see that I've learned a lot when we go out together. Miller will admit that I'm usually prudent, because, two weeks ago, I hit a boar and he charged me, and my rifle jammed, and I went up a tree! Wasn't that prudent?"

"Perfectly," he said gravely; "only I'd feel safer if you went up a tree in the first place and remained there. What a child you are, anyway!"

"Do you know," she confided in him, "I am a regular baby sometimes. I do the silliest things in the woods. Once I gave Miller the slip and went off and built a doll's house out of snow and made three snow dolls and played with them! Isn't that the silliest thing? And another time a boar came out by the Westgate Oaks, and he was a black, hairy fellow, and so funny with his chin-whiskers all dotted with icicles that I began to say aloud:

'I swear by the beard
On my chinny-chin-chin - '

And of course he was off before I could pull trigger for laughing. Isn't that foolish?"

"Adorably," he whispered. "You are finding the little girl in the garden, Geraldine."

She looked up at him, serious, wistful.

"It's the boy who found her; I only helped. But I want to bring her home all alone."

CHAPTER XXI

THE GOLDEN HOURS

The weather was unsuitable for hunting. It snowed for a week, thawed over night, then froze, then snowed again, but the moon that night promised a perfect day.

Young Mallett supposed that he was afoot and afield before anybody else in house could be stirring, but as he pitched his sketching easel on the edges of the frozen pasture brook, and opened his field-box, a far hail from the white hill-top arrested him.

High poised on the snowy crest above him, clothed in white wool from collar to knee-kilts, and her thick clustering hair flying, she came flashing down the hill on her skis, soared high into the sunlight, landed, and shot downward, pole balanced.

Like a silvery meteor she came flashing toward him, then her hair-raising speed slackened, and swinging in a widely gracious curve she came gliding across the glittering field of snow and quietly stopped in front of him.

"Since when, angel, have you acquired this miraculous accomplishment?" he demanded.

"Do I do it well, Duane?"

"A swallow from paradise isn't in your class, dear," he

admitted, fascinated. "Is it easy - this new stunt of yours?"

"Try it," she said so sweetly that he missed the wickedness in her smile.

So, balancing, one hand on his shoulder, she disengaged her moccasins from the toe-clips, and he shoved his felt timber-jack boots into the leather loops, and leaning on the pointed pole which she handed him, gazed with sudden misgiving down the gentle acclivity below. She encouraged him; he listened, nodding his comprehension of her instructions, but still gazing down the hill, a trifle ill at ease.

However, as skates and snow-shoes were no mystery to him, he glanced at the long, narrow runners curved upward at the extremities, with more assurance, and his masculine confidence in all things masculine returned. Then he started, waved his hand, smiling his condescension; then he realised that he was going faster than he desired to; then his legs began to do disrespectful things to him. The treachery of his own private legs was most disheartening, for they wavered and wobbled deplorably, now threatening to cross each other, now veering alarmingly wide of his body. He made a feebly desperate attempt to use his trail-pole; and the next second all that Geraldine could see of the episode was mercifully enveloped in a spouting pinwheel of snow.

Like all masculine neophytes, he picked himself up and came back, savagely confident in his humiliation. She tried to guide his first toddling ski-steps, but he was mad all through and would have his own way. With a set and mirthless smile, again and again he gave himself to the slope and the mercy of his insurgent legs, and at length, bearing heavily on his trail-pole, managed to reach the level below without capsizing.

She praised him warmly, rescued his wool gloves and cap from snowy furrows into which their owner had angrily but helplessly dived; and then she stepped into her skis and ascended the hill beside him with that long-limbed, graceful, swinging stride which he had ventured to believe might become him also.

He said hopelessly: “If you expect me to hunt wild boar with you on skis, there'll be some wild and widely distributed shooting in this county. How can I hit a boar while describing unwilling ellipses in mid-air or how can I run away from one while I'm sticking nose down in a snow-drift?”

Too faint with laughter to reply, she stood leaning on her trailing-pole and looking over his shoulder as he repitched his sketching easel, squeezed the colours from the leaden tubes, and set his palette.

“I'm horribly hungry,” he grumbled; “too hungry to make a decent sketch. How cold is it, anyway? I believe that this paint is trying to freeze on my palette!”

“What are you going to paint?” she asked, her rounded chin resting on his shoulder.

“That frozen brook.” He looked around at her, hesitating; and she laughed and nodded her comprehension.

“You want to make a sketch of me, dear. Why don't you ask me? Do you think I'd refuse?”

“It's so beastly cold to ask you to stand still -”

“Cold! Why, it's much warmer; it's ten above zero. I'll stand wherever you wish. Where do you want me; here above you, against the snow and sky?”

The transcendent loveliness of the picture she made set that excited thrill quivering through every vein; but he took a matter-of-fact grip on his emotions because good work is done in cold blood, even if it sometimes may be conceived in exaltation.

"Don't move," he said serenely; "you are exactly right as you stand. Tell me the very moment you feel cold. Promise?"

"Yes, dear."

His freezing colours bothered him, and at times he used them almost like pastels. He worked rapidly, calmly, and with that impersonal precision that made every brush stroke an integral factor in the ensemble.

At almost any stage of the study the accidental brilliancy of his progress might have been terminated abruptly, leaving a sketch rarely beautiful in its indicated and unfinished promise.

But the pitfalls of the accidental had no allurements for him. She rested, changed position, stretched her limbs, took a long circle or two, skimming the hillside when she needed the reaction. But always she came swinging back again to stand and watch her lover with a half-smiling, half-tender gaze that tried his sangfroid terribly when he strove to catch it and record it in the calm and scientific technique which might excite anybody except the workman.

"Am I pretty, Duane?"

"Annoyingly divine. I'm trying not to think of it, dear, until my hand and heart may wobble with impunity. Are you cold?"

"No.... Do you think you'll make a full-fledged picture from this motive?"

"How did you guess?"

"I don't know. I've a premonition that your reputation is going to soar up like a blazing star from this waste of snow around us.... I wish - I wish that it might be from me, through me - my humble aid - that your glory breaks out -"

"If it ever does, it will do it through you. I told you that long ago."

"Yes."

"I've known it a long, long time, Geraldine. Without you there's nothing to me except surface. You are the depths of me."

"And you of me, Duane." Sweet eyes remote, she stood looking into space; at peace with her soul, dreaming, content. And it was then that he caught and imprisoned in colour the nameless beauty which was the foundation for his first famous picture, whose snowy splendour silenced all except those little critics who chirp automatically, eternally, on the ruddy hearthstone of the gods.

* * * * *

From the distant hill-top a voice bellowed at them through a megaphone; and, looking aloft, they beheld Scott gesticulating.

"If you two mental irresponsibles want any breakfast," he shouted, "you'd better hustle! Miller telephones that the big boar fed below Cloudy Mountain at sunrise!"

Geraldine looked at her lover, cheeks pink with excitement. He was immensely interested, too, and as soon as he could fold his easel, lock up brushes and palette, protect his canvas with a fresh one faced with cork buffers, they started for the house, discussing the chances for a shot that afternoon.

Like the most desirable and wary of most species of game, furry or finny, the huge, heavily tusked veterans of the wild-boar family often feed after dark, being too cunning to banquet by daylight and carouse with the gayer blades and the big, fierce sows of the neighbourhood.

Sometimes in the white gloom of snow-storms there is a

chance for a shot; sometimes in a remoter fastness a big boar may deem himself secure enough to venture out where there are no witnesses to his solitary gastronomic revels save an Arctic owl or two huddled high in the hemlocks.

And it was in the rocky oak-ridges of the wild country under Cloudy Mountain that Miller had marked down the monarch of all wild pigs - the great, shaggy, silver-tipped boar, hock-deep in snow, crunching frozen acorns and glaring off over the gully where mile after mile of white valley and mountain ranges stretched away, clotted and streaked with pine.

"Why don't we all go?" asked Geraldine, seating herself behind the coffee-urn and looking cordially around at the others.

"Because, dear," said Kathleen, "I haven't the slightest desire to run after a wild boar or permit him to amble after me; and all that reconciles me to your doing it is that Duane is going with you."

"I personally don't like to kill things," observed Scott briefly. "My sister is the primitive of this outfit. She's the slayer, the head hunter, the lady-boss of this kraal."

"Is it very horrid of me, Duane?" she asked anxiously, "to find excitement in this sort of thing? Besides, we do need meat, and the game must be kept thinned down by somebody. And Scott won't."

"Whatever you do is all right," said Duane, laughing, "even when you jeer at my gymnastics on skis. Oh, Lord! but I'm hungry. Scott, are you going to take all those sausages and muffins, you bespectacled ruffian! Kathleen, heave a plate at him!"

Kathleen was too scandalised to reply; Scott surrendered the desired muffins, and sorted the morning mail, which had just been brought in.

"Nothing for you, Sis, except bills; one letter for Duane, two for Kathleen, and the rest for me" - he examined the envelopes - "all from brother correspondents and eager aspirants for entomological honours.... Here's your letter, Duane!" scaling it across the table in spite of Kathleen's protest.

They had the grace to ask each other's permission to read.

"Oh, listen to this!" exclaimed Scott gleefully:

> "DEAR SIR: Your name has been presented to the Grand Council which has decided that you are eligible for membership in the International Entomological Society of East Orange, N.J., and you have, therefore, been unanimously elected.
>
> "Have the kindness to inform me of your acceptance and inclose your check for $25, which includes your dues for five years and a free subscription to the society's monthly magazine, *The Fly-Paper* -"

"Scott, don't do it. You get one of those kind of things every day!" exclaimed Geraldine. "They only want your $25, anyway."

"It's an innocent recreation," grinned Duane. "Why not let Scott append to his signature - 'M.I.E.S.E.O.N.J.' - Member International Entomological Society, East Orange, New Jersey. It only costs $25 to do it -"

"That's all right," said Scott, reddening, "but possibly they may have read my paper on the Prionians in the last Yonkers *Magazine of Science*. It wasn't a perfectly rotten paper, was it, Kathleen?"

"It was mighty clever!" she said warmly. "Don't mind those two scoffers, Scott. If you take my advice you will join this East Orange Society. That would make six scientific societies he has joined since Christmas," she continued, turning on

Duane with severe pride; adding, "and there's a different coloured ribbon decoration for his buttonhole from each society."

But Duane and Geraldine were very disrespectful; they politely offered each other memberships in all sorts of societies, including one yard of ribbon decoration, one sleigh-bell, and five green trading stamps, until Scott hurled an orange at Duane, who caught it and blew a kiss at him as recompense.

Then they went outside, on Scott's curt invitation, and wrestled and scuffled and scrubbed each other's faces with snow like schoolboys, until, declaring they were hungry again, they came back to the breakfast-room and demanded more muffins and sausages and coffee.

Kathleen rang and, leaning over, handed Geraldine a brief letter from Rosalie Dysart:

> "Do you think Geraldine would ask me up for a few days?" it began. "I'm horribly lonesome and unhappy and I'm being talked about, and I'd rather be with you wholesome people than with anybody I know, if you don't mind my making a refuge of your generosity. I'm a real victim of that dreadful sheet in town, which we all have a contempt for and never subscribe to, and which some of us borrow from our maids or read at our modistes - the sheet that some of us are genuinely afraid of - and part of our fear is that it may neglect us! You know, don't you, what really vile things it is saying about me? If you don't, your servants do.
>
> "So if you'd rather not have me, I won't be offended, and, anyway, you are dear and decent people and I love you.
>
> "ROSALIE DENE."

"How funny," mused Geraldine. "She's dropped Jack Dysart's name already in private correspondence.... Poor child!"

Looking up at Kathleen, "We must ask her, mustn't we, dear?"

There was more of virginal severity in Kathleen. She did not see why Rosalie, under the circumstances, should make a convenience of Geraldine, but she did not say so; and, perhaps, glancing at the wistful young girl before her, she understood this new toleration for those in dubious circumstances - comprehended the unusual gentleness of judgment which often softens the verdict of those who themselves have drifted too near the danger mark ever to forget it or to condemn those still adrift.

"Yes," she said, "ask her."

Duane looked up from the perusal of his own letter as Kathleen and Scott strolled off toward the greenhouses where the latter's daily entomological researches continued under glass and the stimulous artificial heat and Kathleen Severn.

"Geraldine," he said, "here's a letter from Bunny Gray. He and Sylvia Quest were married yesterday very quietly, and they sailed for Cape Town this morning!"

"What!"

"That's what he writes. Did you ever hear of anything quicker?"

"How funny," she said. "Bunny and Sylvia? I knew he was attentive to her but -"

"You mean Dysart?" he said carelessly. "Oh, he's only a confirmed debutante chaser; a sort of social measles. They all recover rapidly."

"I had the - social measles," said Geraldine, smiling.

Duane repressed a shiver. "It's inevitable," he said gaily.... "That Bunny is a decent fellow."

"Will you show me his letter?" she asked, extending her hand as a matter of course.

"No, dear."

She looked up surprised.

"Why not? Oh - I beg your pardon, dear -"

Duane bent over, kissed her hand, and tossed the letter into the fire. It was her first experience in shadows cast before, and it came to her with a little shock that no two are ever one in the prosier sense of the theory.

The letter that Duane had read was this:

> "Sylvia and I were married quietly yesterday and she has told me that you will know why. There is little further for me to say, Duane. My wife is ill. We're going to Cape Town to live for a while. We're going to be happy. I am now. She will be.
>
> "My wife asked me to write you. Her regard for you is very high. She wishes me to tell you that I know everything I ought to have known when we were married. You were very kind to her. You're a good deal of a man, Duane.
>
> "I want to add something: her brother, Stuyve, is out of the hospital and loose again. He's got all the virtues of a Pomeranian pup - that is, none; and he'll make a rotten bad fist of it. I'll tell you now that, during the past winter, twice, when drunk, he shot at his sister. She did not tell me this; he did, when in a snivelling condition at the hospital.
>
> "So God knows what he may do in this matter. It seems that the blackguard in question has been warned to steer clear of Stuyvesant. It's up to them. I shall be glad to have

Sylvia at Cape Town for a while.

"Delancy Grandcourt was witness for me, Rosalie for Sylvia. Delancy is a brick. Won't you ask him up to Roya-Neh? He's dying to go.

"And this is all. It's a queer life, isn't it, old fellow? But a good sporting proposition, anyway. It suits me.

"Our love to you, to the little chatelaine of Roya-Neh, to her brother, to Kathleen.

"Tell them we are married and off for Cape Town, but tell them no more.

"B. Gray."

"It isn't necessary to say burn this scrawl."

Geraldine, watching him in calm speculation, said:

"I don't see why they were married so quietly. Nobody's in mourning -"

"Dear?"

"What, dear?"

"Do something for me."

"I promise."

"Then ask Delancy up here to shoot. Do you mind?"

"I'd love to. Can he come?"

"I think so."

"I'll write now. Won't it be jolly," she said innocently, " to have him and Rosalie here together -"

The blank change on his face checked her. "Isn't it all right?" she asked, astonished.

He had made his blunder. There was only one thing for him to say and he said it cordially, mentally damning himself for forgetting that Rosalie was to be invited.

"I'll write to them both this morning," concluded Geraldine. "Of course poor Jack Dysart is out of the question."

"A little," he said mildly. And, furious with himself, he rose as she stood up, and followed her into the armory, her cool little hand trailing and just touching his.

For half an hour they prowled about, examining Winchesters, Stevens, Maenlichers - every make and pattern of rifle and fowling-piece was represented in Scott's collection.

"Odd, isn't it, that he never shoots," mused Duane, lifting out a superb weapon from the rack behind the glass doors. "This seems to be one of those murderous, low trajectory pieces that fires a sort of brassy shot which is still rising when it's a mile beyond the bunker. Now, sweetheart, if you've a heavy suit of ancient armour which I can crawl into, I'll defy any boar that roots for mast on Cloudy Mountain."

It was great fun for Geraldine to lay out their equipment in two neat piles; a rifle apiece with cases and bandoliers; cartridges, two hunting-knives with leather sheaths, shooting hoods and coats; and timberjack's boots for her lover, moccasins for her; a pair of heavy sweaters for each, and woollen mitts, fashioned to leave the trigger finger free.

Beside these she laid two fur-lined overcoats, and backed away in naïve admiration at her industry.

"Wonderful, wonderful," he said. "We'll only require

saucepans and boiler lids to look exactly like Tweedle-dum and Tweedle-dee arrayed for battle. I say, Geraldine, how am I going to flee up a tree with all that on - and snow-shoes to boot-s," he added shamelessly, grinning over his degraded wit.

She ignored it, advised him with motherly directness concerning the proper underwear he must don, looked at her rifle, examined his and, bidding him assume it, led him out to the range in the orchard and made him target his weapon at a hundred yards.

There was a terrific fusillade for half an hour or so; his work was respectable, and, satisfied, she led him proudly back to the house and, curling up on the leather divan in the library, invited him to sit beside her.

"Do you love me?" she inquired with such impersonal curiosity that he revenged himself fully then and there; and she rose and, instinctively repairing the disorder of her hair, seated herself reproachfully at a distance.

"Can't a girl ask a simple question?" she said, aggrieved.

"Sure. Ask it again, dearest."

She disdained to reply, and sat coaxing the tendrils of her dark hair to obey the dainty discipline of her slender fingers.

"I thought you weren't going to," she observed irrelevantly. But he seemed to know what she meant.

"Don't you want me to even touch you for a year?"

"It isn't a year. Months of it are over."

"But in the months before us -"

"No."

She picked up a book. When he reached for a magazine she looked over the top of her book at him, then read a little, glanced up, read a little more, and looked at him again.

"Duane?"

"What?"

"This is a fool of a book. Do you want to read it?"

"No, thanks."

"Over my shoulder, I mean?"

He got up, seated himself on the arm of her chair, and looked at the printed page over her shoulder.

For a full minute neither moved; then she turned her head, very slowly, and, looking into his eyes, she rested her lips on his.

"My darling," she said; "my darling."

Which is one of the countless variations of the malady which makes the world spin round in one continual and perpetual fit.

CHAPTER XXII

CLOUDY MOUNTAIN

Five days running, Geraldine, Duane, and old Miller watched for the big gray boar among the rocky oak ridges under Cloudy Mountain; and though once they saw his huge tracks, they did not see him.

Every night, on their return, Scott jeered them and taunted them until a personal encounter with Duane was absolutely necessary, and they always adjourned to the snowy field of honour to wipe off the score and each other's faces with the unblemished snow.

Rosalie and a Chow-dog arrived by the middle of the week; Delancy toward the end of it, unencumbered. Duane made a mental note of his own assininity, and let it go at that. He was as glad to see Rosalie as anybody, and just as glad to see Delancy, but he'd have preferred to enjoy the pleasures separately, though it really didn't matter, after all.

“Sooner or later,” he admitted to himself, “that Delancy man is going to marry her; and it seems to me she's entitled to another chance in the world. Even our earthly courts are lenient toward first offenders. As for the ethics - puzzle it out, you!” He made a gesture including the world in general, lighted a cigarette, and went out to the gun-room to join Geraldine.

"Rosalie and Delancy want to go shooting with us," he explained with a shrug.

"Oh, Duane! - and our solitary and very heavenly trips alone together!"

"I know it. I have just telephoned Miller to get Kemp from Westgate for them. Is that all right?"

"Yes" - she hesitated - "I think so."

"Let Kemp guide them," he insisted. "They'll never hold out as far as Cloudy Mountain. All they want is to shoot a boar, no matter how big it is. Miller says the boar are feeding again near the Green Pass. It's easy enough to send them there."

"Do you think that is perfectly hospitable? Rosalie and Delancy may find it rather stupid going off alone together with only Kemp to amuse them. I am fond of him," she added, "but you know what a woman like Rosalie is prone to think of Delancy."

He glanced at her keenly; she had, evidently, not the slightest notion of the *status quo.*

"Oh, they'll get along together, all right," he said carelessly. "If they choose to remain with us, of course we all can keep on to Cloudy Mountain; but you'll see them accept Kemp and the Green Pass with grateful alacrity after two miles of snow-shoeing through the brush; and we'll have the mountain all to ourselves."

"You're a shameless deviser of schemes, aren't you, dear?" she asked, considering him with that faint, intimate smile, which, however, had always in it something of curiosity. "You know perfectly well we could drive those poor people the whole way to Cloudy Mountain."

"Why, that *is* so!" he exclaimed, pretending surprise; "but, after all, dear, it's better sport to beat up the alders below Green Pass and try to jump a pig for them. That's true hospitality -"

She laughed, shaking her head. "Oh, Duane, Duane!" she murmured, suffering him to capture both her hands and lay them against his face to cover the glee that twitched it at his own unholy perfidy.

And so it came about that, after an early luncheon, a big double sleigh jingled up, received its jolly cargo, and sped away again into the white woodlands, Kathleen waving adieu and Scott deriding them with scoffing and snowballs.

The drive was very beautiful, particularly through the pine and hemlock belt where the great trees, clothed heavily with snow, bent branch and crest under the pale winter sunshine. Tall fir-balsams pricked the sky, perfect cones of white; spruces were snowy mounds; far into the forest twilight glimmered the unsullied snow.

As they sped along, Geraldine pointed out imprints of fox and rabbit, faint trails where a field-mouse had passed, the string of henlike footprints recording the deliberate progress of some ruffed grouse picking its leisurely way across the snow; the sharp, indented marks of squirrels.

Rosalie was enchanted, Delancy mildly so, but when a deeper trail ploughed the snow, running parallel to their progress, he regarded it with more animation.

"Pig," said Geraldine briefly.

"Wild?" he inquired.

"Of course," she smiled; "and probably a good big boar."

Rosalie thrilled and unconsciously rested her fur-gloved hand on Delancy's sleeve.

"You know," she said, "you must shoot a little straighter than you did at target practice this morning. Because I can't run very fast," she added with another delightful shudder.

Delancy, at her anxious request, modestly assured her that he would "plug" the first boar that showed his tusks; and Geraldine laughed and made Rosalie promise to do the same.

"You're both likely to have a shot," she said as the sleigh drew up on a stone bridge and Miller and Kemp came over and saluted - big, raw-boned men on snow-shoes, wearing no outer coats over their thin woollen shirts, although every thermometer at Roya-Neh recorded zero.

Gun-cases were handed out, rifles withdrawn, and the cases stowed away in the sleigh again. Fur coats were rolled in pairs, strapped, and slung behind the broad shoulders of the guides. Then snow-shoes were adjusted - skis for Geraldine; Miller walked westward and took post; Kemp's huge bulk closed the eastern extremity of the line, and between them, two and two at thirty paces apart, stood the hunters, Duane with Rosalie, Geraldine with Delancy, loading their magazines.

Ahead was an open wood of second growth, birch, beech, and maple; sunlight lay in white splashes here and there; nothing except these blinding pools of light and the soft impression of a fallen twig varied the immaculate snow surface as far as the eye could see.

"Forward and silence," called out Geraldine; the mellow swish of snow-shoes answered her, and she glided forward on her skis, instructing Delancy under her breath.

"The wind is right," she said. "They can't scent us here, though deeper in the mountains the wind cuts up and you never can be sure what it may do. There's just a chance of jumping a pig here, but there's a better chance when we strike the alder country. Try not to shoot a sow."

"How am I to tell?"

"Sows have no tusks that show. Be careful not to mistake the white patches of snow on a sow's jowl for tusks. They get them by rooting and it's not always easy to tell."

Delancy said very honestly: "You'll have to control me; I'm likely to let drive at anything."

"You're more likely to forget to shoot until the pig is out of sight," she whispered, laughing. "Look! Three trails! They were made last night."

"Boar?"

"Yes," she nodded, glancing at the deep cloven imprints. She leaned forward and glanced across the line at Miller, who caught her eye and signalled significantly with one hand.

"Be ready, Delancy," she whispered. "There's a boar somewhere ahead."

"How can you tell?"

"I can scent him. It's strong enough in the wind," she added, wrinkling her delicate nose with a smile.

Grandcourt sniffed and sniffed, and finally detected a slight acrid odour in the light, clear breeze. He looked wisely around him; Geraldine was skirting a fallen tree on her skis; he started on and was just rounding a clump of brush when there came a light, crashing noise directly ahead of him; a big, dark, shaggy creature went bounding and bucking across his line of vision - a most extraordinary animal, all head and shoulders and big, furry ears.

The snapping crack of a rifle echoed by the sharp racket of another shot aroused him to action too late, for Miller, knife drawn, was hastening across the snow to a distant dark, motionless heap; and Geraldine stood jerking back the ejector of her weapon and throwing a fresh cartridge into the breach.

"My goodness!" he faltered, "somebody got him! Who fired, Geraldine?"

She said: "I waited as long as I dared, Delancy. They go like lightning, you know. I'm terribly sorry you didn't fire."

"Good girl!" said Duane in a low voice as she sped by him on her skis, rifle ready for emergencies as old Miller cautiously approached the shaggy brown heap, knife glittering.

But there was no emergency; Miller's knife sank to the hilt; Geraldine uncocked her rifle and bent curiously over the dead boar.

"Nice tusks. Miss Seagrave," commented the old man. "He's fat as butter, too. I cal'late he'll tip the beam at a hundred and forty paound!"

The hunters clustered around with exclamations of admiration; Rosalie, distractingly pretty in her white wool kilts and cap, knelt down and touched the fierce, long-nosed head and stroked the furry jowl.

"Oh, Delancy!" she wailed, "why *didn't* you 'plug' him as you promised? *I* simply *couldn't* shoot; Duane tried to make me, but I was so excited and so surprised to see the creature run so fast that all my ideas went out of my head and I never thought of pulling that wretched trigger!"

"That," said Delancy, very red, "is precisely what happened to me." And, turning to Geraldine, who looked dreadfully repentant: "I heard you tell me to shoot, and I merely gawked at the beast like a rubbering jay at a ten-cent show."

"Everybody does that at first," said Duane cheerfully; "I'll bet anything that you and Rosalie empty your magazines at the next one."

"We really must, Delancy," insisted Rosalie as she and Geraldine turned away when Miller and Kemp tucked up their sleeves and unsheathed their knives in preparation for unpleasant but necessary details.

But they worked like lightning; and in exactly seven minutes the heavy beast was drawn, washed out with snow, roped, and hung to a tree well out of reach of any four-footed forest marauders that might prowl that way before night.

Geraldine, smiling her deprecation of their praise, waited with the others until the two guides were ready. Then, in the same order as before, they moved forward, descended the slope, and came into a strange wilderness of stark gray alders that stretched away in every direction. And threading, circling, crossing each other everywhere among the alders ran the trails of deer and wild boar, deep and fresh in the powdery snow.

At intervals, as they advanced, hard-wood ridges crossed the bewildering alder labyrinths. Twice, while ascending these ridges, Rosalie's heart jumped as a grouse thundered up. Once three steel-gray deer started out of the scrub and went bounding off, displaying enormous white flags; once a young buck, hunting for trouble, winded it, whistled, and came leaping past Rosalie so close that she shrank aside with a half-stifled cry of apprehension and delight.

Half a mile farther on Delancy, labouring along on his snow-shoes, suddenly halted, detaining Geraldine with a quick touch on the shoulder.

"There's something in that clearing," he whispered.

Miller had seen it, too; Duane motioned Rosalie forward to join Delancy, and, side by side, they crept ahead, keeping a clump of scrub hemlock between them and the edge of the clearing. It was the Green Pass feed-ground, a rocky strip of pasture climbing upward toward Lynx Peak; and there, clean cut against the snowy background, three dark objects were moving, trotting nervously here and there, nosing, nuzzling, tunnelling the snow with long, sharp muzzles.

Duane and Geraldine silently unslung their field-glasses.

"They're boar," he said.

"Two-year-olds," she nodded. "I do hope they will get one each. Duane, ought I to have shot that other one?"

"Of course, you generous child! Otherwise he'd have gone clear away. That was a cracking shot, too - clean through the backbone at the base of the skull.... Look at Rosalie! She's unstrapped her snow-shoes and she and Delancy are crawling on all-fours!"

Kemp had now joined the stalkers; he was a wise old hunter, and Duane and Geraldine, keeping very still, watched the operations side by side.

For half an hour Rosalie lay motionless in the snow on the forest's edge, and Geraldine was beginning to fret at the prospect of her being too benumbed by the cold to use her rifle, when Duane touched her on the arm and drew her attention to a fourth boar.

The animal came on from behind Rosalie and to Delancy's right - a good-sized, very black fellow, evidently suspicious yet tempted to reconnoitre the feeding-ground.

"Oh, dear, oh, dear!" she whispered; "what a shot Delancy has! Why *doesn't* he see him! What on earth is Kemp about? Why, the boar is within ten feet of Delancy's legs and doesn't see or wind him!"

"Look!"

Kemp had caught sight of the fourth boar. Geraldine and Duane saw his dilemma, saw him silently give Rosalie the signal to fire at the nearest boar in the open, then saw him turn like a flash and almost drag Delancy to his feet.

"Kill that pig, *now*!" he thundered - "unless you want him hackin' your shins!"

The boar stood in his tracks, bristling, furious, probably astounded to find himself so close to the only thing in all the forest that he feared and would have preferred to flee from.

Under such conditions boars lose their heads; there was a sudden clatter of tusks, a muffled, indescribable sound, half squeal, half roar; a fountain of feathery snow, and two shots close together. Then a third shot.

Rosalie, rather pale, threw another cartridge in as Delancy picked himself out of a snow-bank and looked around him in astonishment.

"Well done, young lady!" cried Kemp, running a fistful of snow over the blade of his hunting-knife and nodding his admiration. "I guess it's just as well you disobeyed orders and let this funny pig have what was coming to him. Y' ain't hurt, are ye, Mr. Grandcourt?"

"No; he didn't hit me; I tripped on that root. Did I miss him?"

"Not at all," said Duane, kneeling down while Miller lifted the great fierce head. "You hit him all right, but it didn't stop him; it only turned him. Here's your second bullet, too; and Rosalie, yours did the business for him. Good for you! It's fine, isn't it, Geraldine?"

Grandcourt, flushing heavily, turned to Rosalie and held out his hand. "Thank you," he said; "the brute was right on top of me."

"Oh, no," she said honestly, "he'd missed you and was going straight on. I don't know how on earth I ever hit him, but I was so frightened to see you go over backward and I thought that he'd knocked you down, and I was perfectly furious -"

She gave a little sob of excitement, laughed unsteadily, and sat down on a fallen log, burying her face in her hands.

They knew enough to let her alone and pretend not to notice her. Geraldine chattered away cheerfully to the two men while the keepers drew the game. Delancy tried to listen to her, but his anxious eyes kept turning toward Rosalie, and at length, unable to endure it, he went over and sat down beside her, careless of what others might infer.

"How funny," whispered Geraldine to Duane. "I had no idea that Delancy was so fond of her. Had you?"

He started slightly. "I? Oh, no," he said hastily - too hastily. He was a very poor actor.

Gravely, head bent, she walked forward beside him after Grandcourt had announced that he and Rosalie had had enough and that they wished Kemp to take them and their game to the sleigh.

Once, looking back, she saw the procession moving in the opposite direction through the woods, Kemp leading, rope over his shoulder, dragging the dead boar across the snow; Grandcourt, both rifles slung across his back, big arm supporting Rosalie, who walked as though very tired, her bright head drooping, her arm resting on his shoulder.

Geraldine looked up at Duane thoughtfully, and he supposed that she was about to speak, but her gaze became remote; she shifted her rifle, and walked on.

Before they came to the wild, shaggy country below Cloudy Mountain she said:

"I've been thinking it over, Duane. I can see in it nothing that can concern anybody except themselves. Can you?"

"Not a thing, dear.... I'm sorry I suggested his coming. I knew about this, but I clean forgot it when I asked you to invite him."

"I remember, now, your consternation when you realised it," she said, smiling. "After all, Duane, if it is bound to happen, I don't mind it happening here.... Poor, lonely little Rosalie!... I'm depraved enough to be glad for her - if it is really to be so."

"I'm glad, too.... Only she ought to begin her action, I think. It's more prudent and better taste."

"You said once that you had a contempt for divorce."

"I never entertain the same opinion of anything two days in succession," he said, smiling. "When there is any one moral law that can justly cover every case which it is framed to govern, I'll be glad to remain more constant in my beliefs."

"Then you *do* believe in divorce?"

"To-day I happen to."

"Duane, is that your attitude toward everything?"

"Everything except you," he said cheerfully. "That is literally true. Even in my painting and in my liking for the work of others, I veer about like a weather-vane, never holding very long to one point of view."

"You're very frank about it."

"Why not?"

"Isn't it a - a weakness?"

"I don't think so," he said so simply that she tucked her arm under his with a soft, confidential laugh.

"You goose; do you suppose I think there is a weak fibre in you? I've always adored the strength in you - even when it was rough enough to bruise me. Listen, dear; there's only one thing you might possibly weaken on. Promise you won't."

"I promise."

"Then," she said triumphantly, "you'll take first shot at the big boar! Are you angry because I made you promise? If you only knew, dear, how happy I have been, saving the best I had to offer, in this forest, for you! You will make me happy, won't you?"

"Of course I will, you little trump!" he said, encircling her waist, forgetful of old Miller, plodding along behind them.

But it was no secret to old Miller, nor to any native in the country-side for a radius of forty miles. No modern invention can equal the wireless celerity that distributes information concerning other people's business throughout the rural wastes of this great and gossipping nation.

She made him release her, blushing hotly as she remembered that Miller was behind them, and she scolded her lover roundly, until later, in a moment of thoughtlessness, she leaned close to his shoulder and told him she adored him with every breath she drew, which was no sillier than his reply.

The long blue shadows on the snow and the pink bars of late sunlight had died out together. It had grown warmer and grayer in the forest; and after a little one or two snow-flakes came sifting down through the trees.

They had not jumped the big silver boar, nor had they found a trace of him among the trails that crossed and recrossed the silent reaches of the forest. Light was fading to the colourless, opaque gray which heralded a snow-storm as they reached the feeding-ground, spread out their fur coats, and dropped, belly down, to reconnoitre.

Nothing moved among the oaks. They lay listening minute after minute; no significant sound broke the silence, no dead branch cracked in the hemlocks.

She lay close to him for warmth, chin resting on his shoulder, her cheek against his. Their snow-shoes were stuck upright in a drift behind them; beside these squatted old Miller, listening, peering, nostrils working in the wind like an old dog's.

They waited and watched through a fine veil of snow descending; in the white silence there was not a sound save the silken flutter of a lonely chickadee, friendly, inquiring, dropping from twig to twig until its tiny bright eyes peered level with Geraldine's.

Evidently the great boar was not feeding before night. Duane turned his head restlessly; old Miller, too, had become impatient and they saw him prowling noiselessly down among the rocks, scrutinising snow and thickets, casting wise glances among the trees, shaking his white head as though communing with himself.

"Well, little girl," breathed Duane, "it looks doubtful, doesn't it?"

She turned on her side toward him, looking him in the eyes:

"Does it matter?"

"No," he said, smiling.

She reached out her arms; they settled close around his neck, clung for a second's passionate silence, released him and covered her flushed face, all but the mouth. Under them his lips met hers.

The next instant she was on her knees, pink-cheeked, alert, ears straining in the wind.

"Miller is coming back very fast!" she whispered to her lover. "I believe he has good news!"

Miller was coming fast, holding out in one hand something red and gray - something that dangled and flapped as he strode - something that looked horrible and raw.

"Damn him!" said the old man fiercely, "no wonder he ain't a-feedin'! Look at this, Miss Seagrave. There's more of it below - a hull mess of it in the snow."

"It's a big strip of deer-hide - all raw and bleeding!" faltered the girl. "What in the world has happened?"

"*His* work," said Miller grimly.

"The - the big boar?"

"Yes'm. The deer yard over there. He sneaked in on 'em last night and this doe must have got stuck in a drift. And that devil caught her and pulled her down and tore her into bits. Why, the woods is all scattered with shreds o' hide like this! I wish to God you or Mr. Mallett could get one crack at him! I do, by thunder! Yes'm!"

But it was already too dusky among the trees to sight a rifle. In silence they strapped up the coats, fastened on snow-shoes, and moved out along the bare spur of the mountain, where there was still daylight in the open, although the thickening snow made everything gray and vague.

Here and there a spectral tree loomed up among the rocks; a white hare's track, paralleled by the big round imprints of a lynx, ran along the unseen path they followed as Miller guided them toward Westgate.

Later, outlined in the white waste, ancient apple-trees appeared, gnarled relics of some long-abandoned clearing; and, as they passed, Duane chanced to glance across the rocks to the left.

At first he thought he saw something move, but began to make up his mind that he was deceived.

Noticing that he had halted, Geraldine came back, and then Miller returned to where he stood, squinting through the falling flakes in the vague landscape beyond.

"It moved; I seen it," whispered Miller hoarsely.

"It's a deer," motioned Geraldine; "it's too big for anything else."

For five minutes in perfect silence they watched the gray, flat forms of scrub and rock; and Duane was beginning to lose faith in everybody's eyes when, without warning, a huge, colourless shape detached itself from the flat silhouettes and moved leisurely out into the open.

There was no need to speak; trembling slightly, he cleared his rifle sight of snow, steadied his nerves, raised the weapon, and fired.

A horrid sort of scream answered the shot; the boar lurched off among the rocks, and after him at top speed ran Duane and Miller, while Geraldine, on swift skis, sped eastward like the wind to block retreat to the mountain. She heard Duane's rifle crack again, then again; heard a heavy rush in the thicket in front of her, lifted her rifle, fired, was hurled sideways on the rocks, and knew no more until she unclosed her bewildered eyes in her lover's arms.

A sharp pain shot through her; she gasped, turned very white, and lay with wide eyes and parted lips staring at Duane.

Suddenly a penetrating aroma filled her lungs; with all her strength she pushed away the flask at her lips.

"No! No! Not that! I *will* not, Duane!"

"Dear," he said unsteadily, "you are very badly hurt. We are trying to carry you back. You must let me give you this -"

"No," she sobbed, "I will not! Duane - I -" Pain made her faint; her grasp on his arm tightened convulsively; with a supreme effort she struck the flask out of his hand and dropped back unconscious.

CHAPTER XXIII

SINE DIE

The message ran:

> "My sister badly hurt in an accident; concussion, intermittent consciousness. We fear spinal and internal injury. What train can you catch?
>
> SCOTT SEAGRAVE."

Which telegram to Josiah Bailey, M.D., started that eminent general practitioner toward Roya-Neh in company with young Dr. Goss, a surgeon whose brilliancy and skill did not interfere with his self-restraint when there were two ways of doing things.

They were to meet in an hour at the 5.07 train; but before Dr. Bailey set out for the rendezvous, and while his man was still packing his suit-case, the physician returned to his office, where a patient waited, head hanging, picking nervously at his fingers, his prominent, watery eyes fixed on vacancy.

The young man neither looked up nor stirred when the doctor entered and reseated himself, picking up a pencil and pad. He thought a moment, squinted through his glasses, and continued writing the prescription which the receipt of the telegram from Roya-Neh had interrupted.

When he had finished he glanced over the slip of paper, removed his gold-rimmed reading spectacles, folded them, balanced them thoughtfully in the palm of his large and healthy hand, considering the young fellow before him with grave, far-sighted eyes:

"Stuyvesant," he said, "this prescription is not going to cure you. No medicine that I can give you is going to perform any such miracle unless you help yourself. Nothing on earth that man has invented, or is likely to invent, can cure your disease unless by God's grace the patient pitches in and helps himself. Is that plain talk?"

Quest nodded and reached shakily for the prescription; but the doctor withheld it.

"You asked for plain talk; are you listening to what I'm saying?"

"Oh, hell, yes," burst out Quest; "I'm going to pull myself together. Didn't I tell you I would? But I've got to get a starter first, haven't I? I've got to have something to key me up first. I've explained to you that it's this crawling, squirming movement on the backs of my hands that I can't stand for. I want it stopped; I'll take anything you dope out; I'll do any turn you call for -"

"Very well. I've told you to go to Mulqueen's. Go *now*!"

"All right, doctor. Only they're too damn rough with a man. All right; I'll go. I *did* go last winter, and look where I am now!" he snarled suddenly. "Have I got to get up against all that business again?"

"You came out in perfectly good shape. It was up to you," said the doctor, coldly using the vernacular.

"How was it up to me? You all say that! How was it? I understood that if I cut it out and went up there and let that iron-fisted Irishman slam me around, that I'd come out all right. And the first little baby-drink I hit began the whole thing again!"

"Why did you take it? You didn't have to."

"I wanted it," retorted Quest angrily.

"Not badly enough to make self-control impossible. That's what you went up there for, to get back self-control. You got it but didn't use it. Do you think there is any sort of magic serum Mulqueen or I or anybody under Heaven can pump into you that will render you immune from the consequences of making an alcohol sewer of yourself?"

"I certainly supposed I could come out and drink like a gentleman," said the young man sullenly.

"Drink like a - *what*? A gentleman? What's that? What's drinking like a gentleman? I don't know what it is. You either drink alcohol or you don't; you either swill it or you don't. Anybody can do either. I'm not aware that either is peculiar to a gentleman. But I know that both are peculiar to fools."

Quest muttered, picking his fingers, and cast an ugly side look at the physician.

"I don't know what you just said," snapped Dr. Bailey, "but I'll tell you this: alcohol is poison and it has not - and never had - in any guise whatever, the slightest compensating value for internal use. It isn't a food; it's a poison; it isn't a beneficial stimulant; it's a poison; it isn't an aid to digestion; it's a poison; it isn't a life saver; it's a life taker. It's a parasite, forger, thief, pander, liar, brutalizer, murderer!

"Those are the plain facts. There isn't, and there never has been, one word to say for it or any excuse, except morbid predisposition or self-inculcated inclination, to offer for swallowing it. Now go to your brewers, your wine merchants, your champagne touts, your fool undergraduates, your clubmen, your guzzling viveurs - and they'll all tell you the contrary. So will some physicians. And you can take your choice. Any ass can. That is all, my boy."

The young man glowered sulkily at the prescription.

"Do I understand that this will stop the jumps?"

"If you really believe that, you have never heard me say so," snapped Dr. Bailey.

"Well, what the devil will it do?"

"The directions are there. You have my memorandum of the regime you are to follow. It will quiet you till you get to Mulqueen's. Those two bits of paper, however, are useless unless you help yourself. If you want to become convalescent you can - even yet. It won't be easy; it will hurt; but you can do it, as I say, even yet. But it is *you* who must do it, not I or that bit of paper or Mulqueen!

"Just now you happen to want to get well because the effect of alcohol poison disturbs you. Things crawl, as you say, on the back of your hand. Naturally, you don't care for such phenomena.

"Well, I've given you the key to mental and physical regeneration. Yours is not an inherited appetite; yours is not one of those almost foredoomed and pitiable cases. It's a stupid case; and a case of gross self-indulgence in stupidity that began in idleness. And that, my son, is the truth."

"Is that so?" sneered Quest, rising and pocketing the prescription.

"Yes, it is so. I've known your family for forty years, Stuyvesant. I knew your parents; I exonerate them absolutely. Sheer laziness and wilful depravity is what has brought you here to me on this errand. You deliberately acquired a taste for intoxicants; you haven't one excuse, one mitigating plea to offer for what you've done to yourself.

"You stood high in school and in college; you were Phi Beta Kappa, a convincing debater, a plausible speaker, an excellent writer of good English - by instinct a good newspaper man. Also you were a man adapted by nature to live regularly and beyond the coarser temptations. But you were lazy!"

Dr. Bailey struck his desk in emphasis.

"The germ of your self-indulgence lay in gross selfishness. You did what pleased you; and it suited you to do nothing. I'm telling you how you've betrayed yourself - how far you'll have to climb to win back. Some men need a jab with a knife to start their pride; some require a friend's strong helping arm around them. You need the jab. I'm trying to administer it without anaesthetics, by telling you what some men think of you - that it is your monstrous selfishness that has distorted your normal common sense and landed you where you are.

"Selfishness alone has resulted in a most cruel and unnatural neglect of your sister - your only living relative - in a deliberate relapse into slothful and vicious habits; in neglect of a most promising career which was already yours; in a contemptible willingness to live on your sister's income after gambling away your own fortune.

"I know you; I carried you through teething and measles, my son: and I've carried you through the horrors of alcoholic delirium. And I say to you now that, with the mental degeneration already apparent, and your naturally quick temper, if you break down a few more cells in that martyred brain of yours, you'll end in an asylum - possibly one reserved for the *criminal* insane."

A dull colour stained the pasty whiteness of Quest's face. For several minutes he stood there, his fingers working and picking at each other, his pale, prominent eyes glaring.

"That's a big indictment, doctor," he said at last.

"Thank God you think it so," returned the doctor. "If you will stand by your better self for one week - for only one week - after leaving Mulqueen's, I'll stand by you for life, my boy. Come! You were a good sport once. And that little sister of yours is worth it. Come, Stuyvesant; is it a bargain?"

He stepped forward and held out his large, firm, reassuring hand. The young fellow took it limply.

"Done with you, doctor," he said without conviction; "it's hell for mine, I suppose, if I don't make my face behave. You're right; I'm the goat; and if I don't quit butting I'll sure end by slapping some sissy citizen with an axe."

He gave the doctor's hand a perfunctory shake with his thin, damp fingers; dropped it, turned to go, halted, retraced his steps.

"Will it give me the willies if I kiss a cocktail good-bye before I start for that fresh guy, Mulqueen?"

"Start *now*, I tell you! Haven't I your word?"

"Yes - but on the way to buy transportation can't I offer myself one last -"

"*Can't* you be a good sport, Stuyve?"

The youth hesitated, scowled.

"Oh, very well," he said carelessly, turned and went out.

As he walked along in the slush he said to himself: "I guess it's up the river for mine.... By God, it's a shame, for I'm feeling pretty good, too, and that's no idle quip!... Old Squills handed out a line of talk all right-o!... He landed it, too.... I ought to find something to do."

As he walked, a faint glow stimulated his enervated intelligence; ideas, projects long abandoned, desires forgotten, even a far echo from the old ambition stirring in its slumber, quickened his slow pulses. The ghost of what he might have been, nay, what he *could* have made himself, rose wavering in his path. Other ghosts, long laid, floated beside him, accompanying him - the ghosts of dead opportunities, dead ideals, lofty inspirations long, long strangled.

"A job," he muttered; "that's the wholesome dope for Willy. There isn't a newspaper or magazine in town where I can't get next if I speak easy. I can deliver the goods, too; it's like wiping swipes off a bar -"

In his abstraction he had walked into the Holland House, and he suddenly became conscious that he was confronting a familiarly respectful bartender.

"Oh, hell," he said, greatly disconcerted, "I want some French vichy, Gus!" He made a wry face, and added: "Put a dash of tabasco in it, and salt it."

A thick-lipped, ruddy-cheeked young fellow, celebrated for his knowledge of horses, also notorious for other and less desirable characteristics, stood leaning against the bar, watching him.

They nodded civilly to one another. Quest swallowed his peppered vichy, pulled a long face and said:

"We're a pair of 'em, all right."

"Pair of what?" inquired the thick-lipped young man, face becoming rosier and looking more than ever like somebody's groom.

"Pair of bum whips. We've laid on the lash too hard. I'm going to stable my five nags - my five wits!" - he explained with a sneer as the other regarded him with all the bovine intelligence of one of his own stable-boys - "because they're foundered; and that's the why, young four-in-hand!"

He left the bar, adding as he passed:

"I'm a rotting citizen, but you" - he laughed insolently - "you have become phosphorescent!"

The street outside was all fog and melting snow; the cold vichy he had gulped made him internally uncomfortable.

"A gay day to go to Mulqueen's," he muttered sourly, gazing about for a taxicab.

There was none for hire at that moment; he walked on for a while, feeling the freezing slush penetrate his boot-soles; and by degrees a sullen temper rose within him, revolting - not at what he had done to himself - but at the consequences which were becoming more unpleasant every moment.

As he trudged along, slipping, sliding, his overcoat turned up around his pasty face, his cheeks wet with the icy fog, he continued swearing to himself, at himself, at the slush, the cold vichy in his belly, the appetite already awakened which must be denied.

Denied?... Was he never to have one more decent drink? Was this to be the absolute and final end? Certainly. Yet his imagination could not really comprehend, compass, picture to himself life made a nuisance by self-denial - life in any other guise except as a background for inertia and indulgence.

He swore again, profanely asking something occult why he should be singled out to be made miserable on a day like this? Why, among all the men he knew, he must go skulking about, lapping up cold mineral water and cocking one ear to the sounds of human revelry within the Tavern.

As for his work - yes, he ought to do it.... Interest in it was already colder; the flare-up was dying down; habitual apathy chilled it to its embers. Indifference, ill-temper, self-pity, resentment, these were the steps he was slowly taking backward. He took them, in their natural sequence, one by one.

Old Squills meant well, no doubt, but he had been damned impertinent.... And why had Old Squills dragged in his sister, Sylvia?... He had paid as much attention to her as any brother does to any sister.... And how had she repaid him?

Head lowered doggedly against the sleet which was now falling thickly, he shouldered his way forward, brooding on his "honour," on his sister, on Dysart.

He had not been home in weeks; he did not know of his sister's departure with Bunny Gray. She had left a letter at home for him, because she knew no other addresses except his clubs; and inquiry over the telephone elicited the information that he had not been to any of them.

But he was going to one of them now. He needed something to kill that vichy; he'd have one more honest drink in spite of all the Old Squills and Mulqueens in North America!

At the Cataract Club there were three fashion-haunting young men drinking hot Scotches: Dumont, his empurpled skin distended with whiskey and late suppers, and all his former brilliancy and wit cankered and rotten with it, and his slim figure and clean-cut face fattened and flabby with it; Myron Kelter, thin, elegant, exaggerated, talking eternally about women and his successes with the frailer ones - Myron Kelter, son of a gentleman, eking out his meagre income by fetching, carrying, pandering to the rich, who were too fastidious to do what they paid him for doing in their behalf; and the third, Forbes Winton, literary dilettante, large in every feature and in waistcoat and in gesture - large, hard, smooth - very smooth, and worth too many millions to be contradicted when misstating facts to suit the colour of his too luxuriant imagination.

These greeted Quest in their several and fashionably wearied manners, inviting his soul to loaf.

Later he had a slight dispute with Winton, who surveyed him coldly, and insolently repeated his former misstatement of a notorious fact.

"What rot!" said Quest; "I leave it to you, Kelter; am I right or not?"

Kelter began a soft and soothing discourse which led nowhere at first but ended finally in a re-order for four hot Scotches.

Then Dumont's witty French blood - or the muddied dregs which were left of it - began to be perversely amusing at Quest's expense. Epigrams slightly frayed, a jest or two a trifle stale, humorous inversions of well-known maxims, a biting retort, the originality of which was not entirely free from suspicion, were his contributions to the festivities.

Later Kelter's nicely modulated voice and almost affectionate manner restrained Quest from hurling his glass at the inflamed countenance of Mr. Dumont. But it did not prevent him from leaving the room in a vicious temper, and, ultimately, the Cataract Club.

The early winter night had turned cold and clear; sidewalks glittered, sheeted with ice. He inhaled a deep breath and expelled a reeking one, hailed a cab, and drove to the railroad station.

Here he bought his tickets, choosing a midnight train; for the journey to Mulqueen's was not a very long one; he could sleep till seven in the car; and, besides, he had his luggage to collect from the hotel he had been casually inhabiting. Also he had not yet dined.

Bodily he felt better, now that the vichy had been "killed"; mentally his temper became more vicious than ever as he thought of Dumont's blunted wit at his expense - a wit with edge enough left to make a ragged, nasty wound.

"He'll get what's coming to him some day," snarled Quest, returning to his cab; and he bade the driver take him to the Amphitheatre, a restaurant resort, wonderful in terra-cotta rocks, papier-mache grottos, and Croton waterfalls - haunted of certain semi-distinguished pushers of polite professions, among whom he had been known for years.

The place was one vast eruption of tiny electric lights, and the lights of "the profession," and the demi-monde. Virtue and its antithesis disguised alike in silk attire and pearl collars, rubbed elbows unconcernedly among the papier-mache grottos; the cascades foamed with municipal water, waiters sweated and scurried, lights winked and glimmered, and the music and electric fans annoyed nobody.

In its usual grotto Quest found the usual group, was welcomed automatically, sat down at one of the tables, and gave his order.

Artists, newspaper men, critics, and writers predominated. There was also a "journalist" doing "brilliant" space work on the *Sun*. He had been doing it nearly a month and he was only twenty-one. It was his first job. Ambition tickled his ribs; Fame leaned familiarly over his shoulder; Destiny made eyes at him. His name was Bunn.

There was also a smooth-shaven, tired-eyed, little man who had written a volume on Welsh-rarebits and now drew cartoons. His function was to torment Bunn; and Bunn never knew it.

A critic rose from the busy company and departed, to add lustre to his paper and a nail in the coffin of the only really clever play in town.

"Kismet," observed little Dill, who did the daily cartoon for the *Post*, "no critic would be a critic if he could be a fifth-rate anybody else - or," he added, looking at Bunn, "even a journalist."

"Is that supposed to be funny?" asked Bunn complacently. "*I* intend to do art criticism for the *Herald*."

"What's the objection to my getting a job on it, too?" inquired Quest, setting his empty glass aside and signalling the waiter for a re-order. He expected surprise and congratulation.

Somebody said, "*you* take a job!" so impudently that Quest reddened and turned, showing his narrow, defective teeth.

"It's my choice that I haven't taken one," he snarled. "Did you think otherwise?"

"Don't get huffy, Stuyve," said a large, placid, fat novelist, whose financial success with mediocre fiction had made him no warmer favourite among his brothers.

A row of artists glanced up and coldly continued their salad, their Vandyck beards all wagging in unison.

"I want you to understand," said Quest, leaning both elbows offensively on Dill's table, "that the job I ask for I expect to get."

"You might have expected that once," said the cool young man who had spoken before.

"And I do now!" retorted Quest, raising his voice. "Why not?"

Somebody said: "You can furnish good copy, all right, Quest; you do it every day that you're not working."

Quest, astonished and taken aback at such a universal revelation of the contempt in which he seemed to be held, found no reply ready - nothing at hand except another glass of whiskey and soda.

Minute after minute he sat there among them, sullen, silent, wincing, nursing his chagrin in deepening wrath and bitterness; and his clouding mind perceived in the rebuke nothing that he had ever done to deserve it.

Who the devil were these rag-tags and bob-tails of the world who presumed to snub him - these restaurant-haunting outsiders, among whom he condescended to sit, feeling always the subtle flattery they ought to accord him by virtue of a social position hopeless of attainment by any of them?

Who were they to turn on him like this when he had every reason to suppose they were not only aware of the great talent he had carelessly neglected to cultivate through all these years, but must, in the secret recesses of their grubby souls, reluctantly admire his disdain of the only distinctions they scrambled for and could ever hope for?

His black looks seemed to disturb nobody; Bunn, self-centred, cropped his salad complacently; the Vandyck beards wagged; another critic or two left, stern slaves to duty and paid ads.

* * * * *

The lights bothered him; tremors crawled over and over his skin; within him a dull rage was burning - a rage directed at no one thing, but which could at any moment be focussed.

Men rose and left the table singly, by twos, in groups. He sat, glowering, head partly averted, scowlingly aware of their going, aware of their human interest in one another but not in him, aware at last that he counted for nothing whatever among them.

Some spoke to him as they passed out; he made them no answer. And at last he was alone.

Reaching for his empty glass, he miscalculated the distance between it and his quivering fingers; it fell and broke to pieces. When the waiter came he cursed him, flung a bill at him, got up, demanded his coat and hat, swore at the pallid, little, button-covered page who brought it, and lurched out into the street.

A cab stood there; he entered it, fell heavily into a corner of the seat, bade the driver, "Keep going, damn you!" and sat swaying, muttering, brooding on the wrongs that the world had done him.

Wrongs! Yes, by God! Every hand was against him, every tongue slandered him. Who was he that he should endure it any longer in patience! Had he not been patient? Had he not submitted to the insults of a fool of a doctor? - had he not stayed his hand from punishing Dumont's red and distended face? - had he not silently accepted the insolent retorts of these Grub Street literati who turned on him and flouted the talent that lay dormant in him - dead, perhaps - but dead or dormant, it still matched theirs! And they knew it, damn them!

Had he not stood enough from the rotten world? - from his own sister, who had flung his honour into his face with impunity! - from Dysart, whose maddening and continual ignoring of his letters demanding an explanation -

There seemed to come a sudden flash in his brain; he leaned from the window and shouted an address to the cabman. His hat had fallen beside him, but he did not notice its absence on his fevered head.

"I'll begin with *him*!" he repeated with a thick laugh; "I'll settle with him first. Now we're going to see! Now we'll find out about several matters - or I'll break his neck off! - or I'll twist it off - wring it off!"

And he beat on his knees with his fists, railing, raging, talking incoherently, laughing sometimes, sometimes listening, as though, suddenly, near him, a voice was mocking him.

He had a pocket full of bills, crushed up; some he gave to the cabman, some he dropped as he stuffed the others into his pockets, stumbled toward a bronze-and-glass grille, and rang. The cabman brought him his hat, put it on him, gathered up the dropped money, and drove off with his tongue in his cheek.

Quest rang again; the door opened; he gave his card to the servant, and stealthily followed him upstairs over the velvet carpet.

Dysart, in a velvet dressing-gown knotted in close about his waist, looked over the servant's shoulders and saw Quest standing there in the hall, leering at him.

For a moment nobody spoke; Dysart took the offered card mechanically, glanced at it, looked at Quest, and nodded dismissal to the servant.

When he and the other man stood alone, he said in a low, uncertain voice:

"Get out of here!"

But Quest pushed past him into the lighted room beyond, and Dysart followed, very pale.

"What are you doing here?" he demanded.

"I've asked you questions, too," retorted Quest. "Answer mine first."

"Will you get out of here?"

"Not until I take my answer with me."

"You're drunk!"

"I know it. Look out!"

Dysart moistened his bloodless lips.

"What do you want to know?" And, as Quest shouted a question at him: "Keep quiet! Speak lower, I tell you. My father is in the next room."

"What in hell do I care for your father? Answer me or I'll choke it out of you! Answer me now, you dancing blackguard! I've got you; I want my answer, and you've got to give it to me!"

"If you don't lower your voice," said Dysart between his teeth, "I'll throw you out of that window!"

"Lower my voice? Why? Because the old fox might hear the young one yap! What do I care for you or your doddering family -"

He went down with a sharp crash; Dysart struck him again as he rose; then, beside himself, rained blows on him, drove him from corner to corner, out of the room, into the hall, striking him in the face till the young fellow reeled and fell against the bath-room door. It gave; he stumbled into darkness; and after him sprang Dysart, teeth set - sprang into the darkness which split before him with a roar into a million splinters of fire.

He stood for a second swaying, reaching out to grasp at nothing in a patient, persistent, meaningless way; then he fell backward, striking a terrified servant, who shrank away and screamed as the light fell on her apron and cuffs all streaked with blood.

She screamed again as a young man's white and battered face appeared in the dark doorway before her.

"Is he hurt?" he asked. His dilated eyes were fixed upon the thing on the floor. "What are you howling for? Is he - dead?"

whispered Quest. Suddenly terror overwhelmed him.

“Get out of my way!” he yelled, hurling the shrieking maid aside, striking the frightened butler who tried to seize him on the stairs. There was another manservant at the door, who stood his ground swinging a bronze statuette. Quest darted into the drawing-room, ran through the music-room and dining-room beyond, and slammed the door of the butler's pantry.

He stood there panting, glaring, his shoulder set against the door; then he saw a bolt, and shot it, and backed away, pistol swinging in his bleeding fist.

Servants were screaming somewhere in the house; doors slammed, a man was shouting through a telephone amid a confusion of voices that swelled continually until the four walls rang with the uproar. A little later a policeman ran through the basement into the yard beyond; another pushed his way to the pantry door and struck it heavily with his night-stick, demanding admittance.

For a second he waited; then the reply came, abrupt, deafening; and he hurled himself at the bolted door, and it flew wide open.

But Quest remained uninterested. Nothing concerned him now, lying there on his back, his bruised young face toward the ceiling, and every earthly question answered for him as long as time shall last.

* * * * *

Up-stairs a very old and shrunken man sat shivering in bed, staring vacantly at some policemen and making feeble efforts to reach a wig hanging from a chair beside him - a very glossy, expensive wig, nicely curled where it was intended to fall above the ears.

"I don't know," he quavered, smirking at everybody with crackled, painted lips, "I know nothing whatever about this affair. You must ask my son Jack, gentlemen - my son Jack - te-he! - oh, yes, he knows; he can tell you a thing or two, I warrant you! Yes, gentlemen, he's like all the Dysarts - fit for a fight or a frolic! - te-he! - he's all Dysart, gentlemen - my son Jack. But he is a good son to me - yes, yes! - a good son, a good son! Tell him I said so - and - good-night."

"Nutty," whispered a policeman. "Come on out o' this boodwar and lave th' ould wan be."

And they left him smirking, smiling, twitching his faded lips, and making vague sounds, lying there asleep in his dotage.

And all night long he lay mumbling his gums and smiling, his sleep undisturbed by the stir and lights and tramp of feet around him.

And all night long in the next room lay his son, white as marble and very still.

Toward morning he spoke, asking for his father. But they had decided to probe for the bullet, and he closed his eyes wearily and spoke no more.

They found it. What Dysart found as the winter sun rose over Manhattan town, his Maker only knows, for his sunken eyes opened unterrified yet infinitely sad. But there was a vague smile on his lips after he lay there dead.

Nor did his slayer lie less serenely where bars of sunlight moved behind the lowered curtains, calm as a schoolboy sleeping peacefully after the eternity of a summer day where he had played too long and fiercely with a world too rough for him.

And so, at last, the indictments were dismissed against them both and their cases adjourned *sine die*.

CHAPTER XXIV

THE PROLOGUE ENDS

"Your sister," observed Dr. Bailey to Scott Seagrave, "must be constructed of India-rubber. There's nothing whatever the matter with her spine or with her interior. The slight trace of concussion is disappearing; there's no injury to the skull; nothing serious to apprehend. Her body will probably be black and blue for a week or two; she'll doubtless prefer to remain in bed to-morrow and next day. And that is the worst news I have to tell you."

He smiled at Kathleen and Duane, who stood together, listening.

"I told you so," said Scott, intensely relieved. "Duane got scared and made me send that telegram. I fell out of a tree once, and my sister's symptoms were exactly like mine."

Kathleen stole silently from the room; Duane passed his arm through the doctor's and walked with him to the big, double sleigh which was waiting. Scott followed with Dr. Goss.

"About this other matter," said Dr. Bailey; "I can't make it out, Duane. I saw Jack Dysart two days ago. He was very nervous, but physically sound. I can't believe it was suicide."

He unfolded the telegram which had come that morning directed to Duane.

"Mrs. Jack Dysart's husband died this morning. Am trying to communicate with her. Wire if you know her whereabouts."

It was signed with old Mr. Dysart's name, but Dr. Bailey knew he could never have written the telegram or even have comprehended it.

The men stood grouped in the snow near the sleigh, waiting; and presently Rosalie came out on the terrace with Kathleen and Delancy Grandcourt. Her colour was very bad and there were heavy circles under her eyes, but she spoke with perfect self-possession, made her adieux quietly, kissed Kathleen twice, and suffered Grandcourt to help her into the sleigh.

Then Grandcourt got in beside her, the two doctors swung aboard in front, bells jingled, and they whirled away over the snow.

Kathleen, with Scott and Duane on either side of her, walked back to the house.

"Well," said Scott, his voice betraying nervous reaction, "we'll resume life where we left off when Geraldine did. Don't tell her anything about Dysart yet. Suppose we go and cheer her up!"

Geraldine lay on the pillows, rather pallid under the dark masses of hair clustering around and framing her face. She unclosed her eyes when Kathleen opened the door for a preliminary survey, and the others filed solemnly in.

"Hello," she said faintly, and smiled at Duane.

"How goes it, Sis?" asked her brother affectionately, shouldering Duane aside.

"A little sleepy, but all right. Why on earth did you send for Dr. Bailey? It was horribly expensive."

"Duane did," said her brother briefly. "He was scared blue."

Her eyes rested on her lover, indulgent, dreamily humorous.

"Such expensive habits," she murmured, "when everybody is economising. Kathleen, dear, he needs schooling. You and Mr. Tappan ought to take him in hand and cultiwate him good and hard!"

Scott, who had been wandering around his sister's room with innate masculine curiosity concerning the mysteries of intimate femininity, came upon a sketch of Duane's - the colour not entirely dry yet.

"It's Sis!" he exclaimed in unfeigned approval. "Lord, but you've made her a good-looker, Duane. Does she really appear like that to you?"

"And then some," said Duane. "Keep your fingers off it."

Scott admired in silence for a while, then: "You certainly are a shark at it, Duane.... You've struck your gait all right.... I wish I had.... This Rose-beetle business doesn't promise very well."

"You write most interestingly about it," said Kathleen warmly.

"Yes, I can write.... I believe journalism would suit me."

"The funny column?" suggested Geraldine.

"Yes, or the birth, marriage, and death column. I could head it, 'Hatched, Matched, and Snatched' -"

"That is perfectly horrid, Scott," protested his sister; "why do you let him say such rowdy things, Kathleen?"

"I can't help it," sighed Kathleen; "I haven't the slightest influence with him. Look at him now!" - as he laughingly passed his arm around her and made her two-step around the room, protesting, rosy, deliciously helpless in the arms of this tall young fellow who held her inflexibly but with a tenderness surprising.

Duane smiled and seated himself on the edge of the bed.

"You plucky little thing," he said, "were you perfectly mad to try to block that boar in the scrub? You won't ever try such a thing again, will you, dear?"

"I was so excited, Duane; I never thought there was any danger -"

"You didn't think whether there was or not. You didn't care."

She laughed, wincing under his accusing gaze.

"You *must* care, dear."

"I do," she said, serious when he became so grave. "Tell me again exactly what happened."

He said: "I don't think the brute saw you; he was hard hit and was going blind, and he side-swiped you and sent you flying into the air among those icy rocks." He drew a long breath, managed to smile in response to her light touch on his hand. "And that's how it was, dear. He crashed headlong into a tree; your last shot did it. But Miller and I thought he'd got you. We carried you in -"

"*you* did?" she whispered.

"Yes. I never was so thoroughly scared in all my life."

"You poor boy. Are the rifles safe? And did Miller save the head?"

"He did," said Duane grimly, "and your precious rifles are intact."

"Lean down, close," she said; "closer. There's more than the rifles intact, dear."

"Not your poor bruised body!"

"My self-respect," she whispered, the pink colour stealing into her cheeks. "I've won it back. Do you understand? I've gone after my other self and got her back. I'm mistress of myself, Duane; I'm in full control, first in command. Do you know what that means?"

"Does it mean - me?"

"Yes."

"When?"

"When you will."

He leaned above her, looking down into her eyes. Their fearless sweetness set him trembling.

On the floor below Kathleen, at the piano, was playing the Menuet d'Exaudet. When she ended, Scott, cheerily busy with his infant Rose-beetles, went about his affairs whistling the air.

"Our betrothal dance; do you remember?" murmured Geraldine. "Do you love me, Duane? Tell me so; I need it."

"I love you," he said.

She lay looking at him a moment, her head cradled in her dark hair. Then, moving slowly, and smiling at the pain it gave her, she put both bare arms around his neck, and lifted her lips to his.

It was the end of the prologue; the curtain trembled on the rise; the story of Fate was beginning. But they had no eyes except for each other, paid no heed save to each other.

And, unobserved by them, the vast curtain rose in silence, beginning the strange drama which neither time nor death, perhaps, has power to end.

George Eliot
George Gissing
George MacDonald
George Meredith
George Orwell
George Sylvester Viereck
George Tucker
George W. Cable
George Wharton James
Gertrude Atherton
Gordon Casserly
Grace E. King
Grace Gallatin
Grace Greenwood
Grant Allen
Guillermo A. Sherwell
Gulielma Zollinger
Gustav Flaubert
H. A. Cody
H. B. Irving
H.C. Bailey
H. G. Wells
H. H. Munro
H. Irving Hancock
H. Rider Haggard
H. W. C. Davis
Haldeman Julius
Hall Caine
Hamilton Wright Mabie
Hans Christian Andersen
Harold Avery
Harold McGrath
Harriet Beecher Stowe
Harry Castlemon
Harry Coghill
Harry Houidini
Hayden Carruth
Helent Hunt Jackson
Helen Nicolay
Hendrik Conscience
Hendy David Thoreau
Henri Barbusse
Henrik Ibsen
Henry Adams
Henry Ford
Henry Frost
Henry James
Henry Jones Ford
Henry Seton Merriman
Henry W Longfellow
Herbert A. Giles
Herbert Carter
Herbert N. Casson
Herman Hesse
Hildegard G. Frey
Homer
Honore De Balzac
Horace B. Day
Horace Walpole
Horatio Alger Jr.
Howard Pyle
Howard R. Garis
Hugh Lofting
Hugh Walpole
Humphry Ward
Ian Maclaren
Inez Haynes Gillmore
Irving Bacheller
Isabel Hornibrook
Israel Abrahams
Ivan Turgenev
J.G.Austin
J. Henri Fabre
J. M. Barrie
J. Macdonald Oxley
J. S. Fletcher
J. S. Knowles
J. Storer Clouston
Jack London
Jacob Abbott
James Allen
James Andrews
James Baldwin
James Branch Cabell
James DeMille
James Joyce
James Lane Allen
James Lane Allen
James Oliver Curwood
James Oppenheim
James Otis
James R. Driscoll
Jane Austen
Jane L. Stewart
Janet Aldridge
Jens Peter Jacobsen
Jerome K. Jerome
John Burroughs
John Cournos
John F. Kennedy
John Gay
John Glasworthy
John Habberton
John Joy Bell
John Kendrick Bangs
John Milton
John Philip Sousa
Jonas Lauritz Idemil Lie
Jonathan Swift
Joseph A. Altsheler
Joseph Carey
Joseph Conrad
Joseph E. Badger Jr
Joseph Hergesheimer
Joseph Jacobs
Jules Vernes
Julian Hawthrone
Julie A Lippmann
Justin Huntly McCarthy
Kakuzo Okakura
Kenneth Grahame
Kenneth McGaffey
Kate Langley Bosher
Kate Langley Bosher
Katherine Cecil Thurston
Katherine Stokes
L. A. Abbot
L. T. Meade
L. Frank Baum
Latta Griswold
Laura Dent Crane
Laura Lee Hope
Laurence Housman
Lawrence Beasley
Leo Tolstoy
Leonid Andreyev
Lewis Carroll
Lewis Sperry Chafer
Lilian Bell
Lloyd Osbourne
Louis Hughes
Louis Tracy
Louisa May Alcott
Lucy Fitch Perkins
Lucy Maud Montgomery
Luther Benson
Lydia Miller Middleton
Lyndon Orr
M. Corvus
M. H. Adams
Margaret E. Sangster
Margret Howth
Margaret Vandercook

Margret Penrose
Maria Edgeworth
Maria Thompson Daviess
Mariano Azuela
Marion Polk Angellotti
Mark Overton
Mark Twain
Mary Austin
Mary Catherine Crowley
Mary Cole
Mary Hastings Bradley
Mary Roberts Rinehart
Mary Rowlandson
M. Wollstonecraft Shelley
Maud Lindsay
Max Beerbohm
Myra Kelly
Nathaniel Hawthrone
Nicolo Machiavelli
O. F. Walton
Oscar Wilde
Owen Johnson
P.G. Wodehouse
Paul and Mabel Thorne
Paul G. Tomlinson
Paul Severing
Percy Brebner
Peter B. Kyne
Plato
R. Derby Holmes
R. L. Stevenson
R. S. Ball
Rabindranath Tagore
Rahul Alvares
Ralph Bonehill
Ralph Henry Barbour
Ralph Victor
Ralph Waldo Emmerson
Rene Descartes
Rex Beach
Rex E. Beach
Richard Harding Davis
Richard Jefferies
Richard Le Gallienne
Robert Barr
Robert Frost
Robert Gordon Anderson
Robert L. Drake
Robert Lansing
Robert Lynd
Robert Michael Ballantyne
Robert W. Chambers
Rosa Nouchette Carey
Rudyard Kipling
Samuel B. Allison
Samuel Hopkins Adams
Sarah Bernhardt
Sarah C. Hallowell
Selma Lagerlof
Sherwood Anderson
Sigmund Freud
Standish O'Grady
Stanley Weyman
Stella Benson
Stella M. Francis
Stephen Crane
Stewart Edward White
Stijn Streuvels
Swami Abhedananda
Swami Parmananda
T. S. Ackland
T. S. Arthur
The Princess Der Ling
Thomas A. Janvier
Thomas A Kempis
Thomas Anderton
Thomas Bailey Aldrich
Thomas Bulfinch
Thomas De Quincey
Thomas Dixon
Thomas H. Huxley
Thomas Hardy
Thomas More
Thornton W. Burgess
U. S. Grant
Valentine Williams
Various Authors
Vaughan Kester
Victor Appleton
Victoria Cross
Virginia Woolf
Wadsworth Camp
Walter Camp
Walter Scott
Washington Irving
Wilbur Lawton
Wilkie Collins
Willa Cather
Willard F. Baker
William Dean Howells
William le Queux
W. Makepeace Thackeray
William W. Walter
William Shakespeare
Winston Churchill
Yei Theodora Ozaki
Yogi Ramacharaka
Young E. Allison
Zane Grey

www.ingramcontent.com/pod-product-compliance
Lightning Source LLC
LaVergne TN
LVHW091639100826
845152LV00006B/93/J
* 9 7 8 1 4 2 1 8 2 4 0 4 8 *